Noodle 365

(Noodle - Volume 1)

Enjoy 365 Days with Amazing Noodle Recipes in Your Own Noodle Cookbook!

Jack Lemmon

Copyright: Published in the United States by Jack Lemmon / © JACK LEMMON

Published on November 18, 2018

All rights reserved. No part of this publication may be reproduced, stored in retrieval system, copied in any form or by any means, electronic, mechanical, photocopying, recording or otherwise transmitted without written permission from the publisher. Please do not participate in or encourage piracy of this material in any way. You must not circulate this book in any format. JACK LEMMON does not control or direct users' actions and is not responsible for the information or content shared, harm and/or actions of the book readers.

In accordance with the U.S. Copyright Act of 1976, the scanning, uploading and electronic sharing of any part of this book without the permission of the publisher constitute unlawful piracy and theft of the author's intellectual property. If you would like to use material from the book (other than just simply for reviewing the book), prior permission must be obtained by contacting the author at *chefjacklemmon@gmail.com*

Thank you for your support of the author's rights.

Contents

- **CONTENTS** 3
- **INTRODUCTION** 9
- **CHAPTER 1: CHOW MEIN NOODLES** ... 10
  1. Asian Bok Choy Salad 10
  2. Asian Chicken and Wild Rice Salad 11
  3. Asian Chicken Salad in a Jar 11
  4. Birds Nests II 12
  5. Birds Nests III 12
  6. Bok Choy Salad with Chow Mein 13
  7. Butterscotch Crunch 13
  8. Cantonese Chicken Chow Mein 14
  9. Cao Lau Vietnamese Noodle Bowl 14
  10. Caramel Crispy Treats I 15
  11. Carols Chow Mein Noodle Casserole .. 16
  12. Chicken and Chinese Noodles Casserole 16
  13. Chinese Chicken Casserole Surprise 17
  14. Chinese Chicken Salad II 17
  15. Chinese New Year Chocolate Candy 18
  16. Chocolate Clusters 18
  17. Chocolate Spiders 18
  18. Chocolaty Peanut Butter Haystacks 19
  19. Chow Clusters 19
  20. Chow Mein Clusters 20
  21. Chow Mein Noodle Bars 20
  22. Chow Mein Noodle Casserole 20
  23. Chow Mein Noodle Cookie 21
  24. Chow Mein with Chicken and Vegetables 21
  25. Coleslaw Gado Gado 22
  26. Crunchy Fun Drops 22
  27. Crunchy Lettuce 23
  28. Easter Birds Nests 23
  29. Edible Spiders 24
  30. Five Can Casserole 24
  31. Fresh Vegetable StirFry with Peppery Orange Beef 25
  32. Grilled Salmon Snap Peas and Spring Mix Salad with Chow Mein Noodles 26
  33. Happy Mountain 26
  34. Hawaiian Haystacks 27
  35. Haystacks II 27
  36. Haystacks IV 28
  37. Imperial Vegetables and Noodles 28
  38. Jelly Bean Nests 29
  39. Orange Chicken Stir Fry 29
  40. Peanut Butter Haystacks 30
  41. Quick Hawaiian Haystacks 30
  42. Rocky Road Drops 30
  43. Sashimi Tuna Salad With Mint Lime Cilantro Dressing 31
  44. Shrimp Chinese Chow Mein 32
  45. Snow on the Mountain II 32
  46. Spicy Beef and Broccoli Chow Mein 33
  47. StirFried Shanghai Noodles 33
  48. Thai Peanut Chicken Lo Mein 34
  49. Tuna Cashew Casserole 35
  50. Twig Salad 35
  51. Vegetable Lo Mein Delight 36
  52. Yummy Bok Choy Salad 36

- **CHAPTER 2: EGG NOODLES** 37
  53. A1 Chicken Soup 37
  54. Amish Casserole 38
  55. Annas Amazing Easy Pleasy Meatballs over Buttered Noodles 38
  56. Applesauce Noodle Kugel 39
  57. Apricot Noodle Kugel 39
  58. Artichoke Piccata 40
  59. AsianInspired Vegetable Noodle Bowl 40
  60. Asparagus and Ham Mac and Cheese ... 41
  61. Awesome Chicken Noodle Soup 41
  62. Beef and Mushroom Stroganoff Aussie Style 42
  63. Beef and Noodle Casserole 43
  64. Beef and Noodles 43
  65. Beef Florentine 44
  66. Beef Stroganoff in an Instant 44
  67. Best Beef Chow Mein 45
  68. Best Beef Stroganoff 46

69. Best Tuna Casserole 47
70. Broccoli Noodles and Cheese Casserole 47
71. Buffalo Ranch Pasta 47
72. Burgundy Stroganoff 48
73. Busy Mom Lasagna 49
74. Butter Garlic Cabbage and Kluski Noodles 49
75. Cabbage and Noodles 50
76. Cabbage Balushka or Cabbage and Noodles 50
77. Campbells Kitchen Beef Stroganoff 51
78. Cheesy Goulash 51
79. Chef Johns Turkey Noodle Casserole .. 52
80. Chicken and Cold Noodles with Spicy Sauce 52
81. Chicken and Noodle Casserole 53
82. Chicken Chow Mein West Indian Style 54
83. Chicken I Hate You 54
84. Chicken Livers Stroganoff 55
85. Chicken Noodle Casserole I 55
86. Chicken Noodle Casserole II 56
87. Chicken Noodle Soup 56
88. Chicken Noodle Soup III 57
89. Chicken Tetrazzini II 57
90. Chili Casserole 58
91. Chili Casserole with Egg Noodles 59
92. Classic Beef Stroganoff 59
93. Classic Beef Stroganoff in a Slow Cooker 60
94. Classic Lukshen Noodle Kugel 61
95. Company Casserole 61
96. Corned Beef Noodle Casserole 62
97. Cowgirl Beef Stroganoff 62
98. Cream of Broccoli Cheese Soup I 63
99. Creamy Beef Stroganoff 63
100. Creamy Buffalo Chicken Noodle Soup 64
101. Creamy Cabbage with Noodles 64
102. Creamy Chicken Cordon Bleu Casserole 65
103. Creamy Chicken Egg Noodle Soup 66
104. Creamy Scallion and White Bean Pasta 66
105. Creamy Shrimp Casserole 67
106. Creamy Swiss Chicken Casserole 67
107. Dianes Beef Stroganoff 68
108. Easy and Quick Beef Stroganoff 69
109. Easy and Quick Halushki 69
110. Easy Beef Stroganoff 70
111. Easy Beef Strogonoff 70
112. Easy Cheesy Tuna Noodle Casserole 71
113. Easy Ham and Noodles 71
114. Easy Noodle Kugel 72
115. Easy Polish Noodles 72
116. Easy Slow Cooker Stroganoff 73
117. Easy Turkey Tetrazzini 73
118. Easy Weeknight Beef Stroganoff 74
119. Egg Noodles 74
120. Egg Noodles with Spinach 75
121. Emilys Super Eggplant Sauce 75
122. Fairy Godmother Rice 76
123. Firehouse Haluski 76
124. Fruit Kugel 77
125. Funfetti Spaghetti 77
126. Garlic Chive Chicken 78
127. Goulash I 78
128. Grandma Earharts Pepper Pot Casserole 79
129. Grandmas Dried Beef Casserole 80
130. Grandmas Ground Beef Casserole 80
131. Grandmas Hamburger Hot Dish 81
132. Grandmas Noodle Pudding Kugel 81
133. Grandmas Noodles I 82
134. Grandmas Noodles II 82
135. Grilled Chicken Noodle Soup 83
136. Ground Beef Mexican Style 83
137. Ground Turkey Noodle Bake 84
138. Gunk on Noodles 84
139. Ham and Swiss Casserole 85
140. Hamburger Casserole 85
141. Hamburger Noodle Casserole 86
142. Haviland Glop 86
143. Hearty Chicken and Noodle Casserole . 87
144. Hearty Chicken Vegetable Soup I 87
145. Hearty Sausage Soup II 88
146. Hearty Tuna Casserole 88
147. Hillbilly Casserole 89
148. Holiday Apricot Kugel 89
149. Home Made Chicken Noodle Soup 90
150. Homemade Noodles 91
151. Hong KongStyle Chicken Chow Mein . 91
152. Hot Dog Noodle Casserole 92
153. Hungarian Goulash III 92
154. Italian Casserole 93
155. Italian Style Pot Roast 93

156.	ItalianStyle Pot Roast with Carrots and Fennel 94
157.	Jaeger Schnitzel 95
158.	JayBeez Beef Stroganoff 95
159.	Johnny Marzetti III 96
160.	Johnny Marzetti IV 96
161.	Kohlrabi and Egg Noodles..................... 97
162.	Kugel 97
163.	Lazygirls Ground Turkey Stroganoff ... 98
164.	Lemon Chicken and Veggie Pasta......... 98
165.	Lloyds Healthy Chicken Zoopa 99
166.	Lokshin Kugel Noodle Pudding.......... 100
167.	Louisiana Crawfish YaYa Pasta 100
168.	Lynns Easy Noodle Pudding 101
169.	Mama Longs Goulash Soup................. 102
170.	Marchetti.. 102
171.	Marcias Company Casserole 103
172.	Marks Cabbage and Hamburger Delight 103
173.	Meatballs in Sour Cream Gravy........... 104
174.	Modern Jewish Low Fat Kugel........... 104
175.	Mom Sykes Hungarian Goulash.......... 105
176.	Moms Casserole 106
177.	Mrs Strongs Casserole 106
178.	Mums DairyFree Stroganoff 107
179.	Mushroom Tuna Noodle Casserole.... 107
180.	NeverFail Chicken Noodle Soup 108
181.	NO YOLKS Beef Noodle Casserole .108
182.	NO YOLKS Lamb Stew 109
183.	NO YOLKS Luscious Kugel................ 109
184.	NO YOLKS Noodles Romanoff........ 110
185.	NO YOLKS Tuna Noodle Casserole 110
186.	NoFuss Turkey Noodle Soup 111
187.	Noodle Kugel Dairy 112
188.	Noodle Pudding 112
189.	Noodles..113
190.	Noodles Marmaduke 113
191.	Noodles Mexicana..................................... 114
192.	Noodles Napoli 114
193.	Noodles Riviera 115
194.	Noodles Romanoff 116
195.	One Dish Chicken Noodles 116
196.	One Skillet Cheesy Hamburger and Egg Noodle 117
197.	OnePot Ground Beef Stroganoff........ 117
198.	Pappardelle Pasta with California Walnut Pesto 118
199.	Pasta With Spinach Sauce 118
200.	Pasta With Veggies In a Tahini and Yogurt Sauce.. 119
201.	Pastira Macaroni Cake 119
202.	Pecan Noodle Kugel 120
203.	Pepperoni Pizza Casserole 120
204.	Pineapple Kugel 121
205.	Plantation 121
206.	Polish Cabbage Noodles 122
207.	Polish Chop Suey..................................... 122
208.	Polish Noodles... 123
209.	Polish Noodles Cottage Cheese and Noodles 123
210.	Poor Mans Stroganoff 124
211.	Porkolt Hungarian Stew Made With Pork 124
212.	Quick and Easy Chicken and Stuffing Casserole... 125
213.	Quick and Easy Chicken Noodle Soup 126
214.	Quick and Easy Goulash...................... 126
215.	Quick and Zesty Vegetable Soup 127
216.	Quick Chicken and Noodles 127
217.	Quick Meatball Stroganoff.................. 128
218.	Regular Chicken Soup 128
219.	Reuben Casserole with Egg Noodles. 129
220.	Reuben Hot Dish 129
221.	Reuben Mac and Cheese 130
222.	Reuben Noodle Bake............................. 131
223.	Rushin Casserole..................................... 131
224.	Sarahs Tofu Noodle Soup.................... 132
225.	Sauerbraten Beef in Gingersnap Gravy 132
226.	Sausage Apples and Noodles............... 133
227.	Scarletts Chicken Cacciatore................ 133
228.	Sensational Chicken Noodle Soup 134
229.	Sensational Turkey Noodle Soup 134
230.	ShowOff Stroganoff 135
231.	Shrimp and Asparagus.......................... 135
232.	Silvers Savory Chicken and Broccoli Casserole... 136
233.	Simple Beef Stroganoff......................... 137
234.	Simple Beef Tips and Noodles........... 137
235.	Simple Hamburger Stroganoff 138
236.	Slow Cooker Beef Stew II................... 138
237.	Slow Cooker Beef Stroganoff II 139
238.	Slow Cooker Chicken and Noodles ... 139

239. Smoked Paprika Goulash for the Slow Cooker 140
240. Spicy and Creamy Chicken Pasta 140
241. Spicy Noodles Malay Style....................141
242. Spinach Cheese Pasta 142
243. Spinach Kugel......................................142
244. Spring Vegetable Soup 143
245. Steves Chicken Noodle Soup...............143
246. Stroganoff Soup...................................144
247. Sues Minestrone 144
248. Super Easy Ground Beef Stroganoff..145
249. Susans Beef Stroganoff 145
250. Swiss Cheese Noodle Bake..................146
251. Swiss Steak Italian Style.......................146
252. Swiss Steak Quick and Easy 147
253. Tallerine 147
254. Tasty Turkey Tetrazzini 148
255. Tex Mex Shark and Shrimp.................148
256. The Best Ever Classic Jewish Noodle Kugel 149
257. Three Cheese Noodle Bake.................149
258. Throw Together Mexican Casserole...150
259. Thyme Salmon with Sage Pasta 150
260. Tofu Noodle Soup................................151
261. Traditional Apple Noodle Kugel..........152
262. Tuna Cheese Mac................................152
263. Tuna Delicious.....................................153
264. Tuna Noodle Asparagus Casserole 153
265. Tuna Noodle Casserole from Scratch 154
266. Tuna Noodle Casserole I 154
267. Tuna Noodle Casserole II 155
268. Turkey Noodle Soup Mix 155
269. Turos Csusza Pasta with Cottage Cheese 156
270. UberBraten Kielbasa and Sauerkraut Casserole 156
271. Ultimate Pasta.....................................157
272. Venison Stroganoff..............................157
273. Yummy Pork Noodle Casserole..........158

CHAPTER 3: RAMEN NOODLES 159

274. Asian Chicken Noodle Salad...............159
275. Asian Coleslaw Light 160
276. Asian Salad 160
277. Broccoli Slaw and Ramen Salad.........161
278. Cheesy Ramen Noodles 161
279. Chicken in Lemongrass Coconut Broth 161
280. Chinese Broccoli Slaw 162
281. Chinese Cabbage Salad I 163
282. Chinese Cabbage Salad II....................163
283. Chinese Chicken Soup.........................164
284. Chinese Fried Noodles 164
285. Chinese Noodle Salad.........................165
286. Chinese Pasta Salad 165
287. Cinnamon Snack Mix..........................166
288. Cloggers Delight Salad........................166
289. Crunchy Ramen Coleslaw 166
290. Crunchy Romaine Salad 167
291. Crunchy Romaine Toss 167
292. Donna Leighs Creamy Broccoli Slaw 168
293. Dorm Room Cheesy Tuna and Noodles 168
294. Easy Broccoli Slaw Salad.....................169
295. Easy Chicken Skillet 169
296. Easy Chinese Chicken Salad 170
297. Easy Kine Saimin Hawaiian Ramen ... 170
298. Fast and Easy Tofu LoMein 171
299. Fugi Salad 171
300. Italian Bean Ramen 172
301. LowCholesterol Egg Drop Noodle Soup 172
302. Mad Hatter Salad 173
303. Mie Goreng Indonesian Fried Noodles 173
304. Million Dollar Chinese Cabbage Salad174
305. Napa Cabbage Noodle Salad............... 174
306. Napa Cabbage Salad...........................175
307. Oceans of Fun Bento...........................176
308. Quick and Easy Ramen Soup 176
309. Quick Asian Beef Noodle Soup..........177
310. Ramen Chicken Noodle Soup............. 177
311. Ramen Noodle Frittata.......................178
312. Ramen Noodle Soup...........................178
313. Ramen Scrambled Eggs.......................178
314. Ramen Spinach Pasta Salad Supreme 179
315. Rubys Spicy Red Salad........................179
316. SixMinute SingleServing Spaghetti 180
317. Slightly Healthier College Ramen Soup 180
318. Slow Cooker Chicken Thai Ramen Noodles 181
319. South Sea Salad 181
320. Spicy Japanese Crab Noodle Salad 182

321. Spicy Korean Chicken and Ramen Noodle Packets 183
322. Spicy Thai Steak and Vegetable Stir Fry 183
323. StirFried Beef and Broccoli with Crisp Ramen Noodle Cake 184
324. TaiwaneseStyle Beef Noodles 185
325. The Mighty Chicken Stuff 185
326. Turkey Sausage Noodles 186

CHAPTER 4: RICE NOODLES 187

327. A Pad Thai Worth Making 187
328. Asian Noodle Bowl 188
329. Asian Vegan Tofu Noodles 188
330. Authentic Pad Thai 189
331. Authentic Pad Thai Noodles 190
332. Authentic Pho 191
333. Authentic Vietnamese Spring Rolls Nem Ran Hay Cha Gio 191
334. Carries Pad Thai Salad 192
335. Chinese Chicken Salad 193
336. Classic Pad Thai 193
337. Creole Crab Noodles 194
338. Dads Pad Thai 194
339. Fried Seafood Laksa Noodles 195
340. Grilled Shrimp and Rice Noodle Salad 196
341. Guay Diaw Lawd Pork Belly Chicken Wing and Noodle Stew 196
342. Joes Fusion Chicken Pad Thai 197
343. Korean Egg Roll Triangles 198
344. Nicolas Pad Thai 199
345. One Pot ThaiStyle Rice Noodles 199
346. Pasta with Vietnamese Pesto 200
347. Pho Ga Soup 201
348. Pork and Shrimp Pancit 201
349. Quick ChineseStyle Vermicelli Rice Noodles 202
350. Saigon Noodle Salad 202
351. Shrimp Pad Thai 203
352. Singapore Noodle Curry Shrimp 203
353. Spicy Peanut Shrimp Rice Noodles 204
354. Spicy Shrimp Pad Thai 204
355. Spicy Thai Shrimp Pasta 205
356. Spring Rolls with Coconut Peanut Sauce 206
357. Thai Curry Soup 206
358. Thai Rice Noodle Salad 207
359. Turkey Lettuce Wraps with Shiitake Mushrooms 208
360. Vietnamese Beef Noodle Soup 208
361. Vietnamese Beef Pho 209
362. Vietnamese Salad Rolls 209
363. Vietnamese Spring Rolls 210
364. Vietnamese Spring Rolls With Dipping Sauce 211
365. VietnameseStyle Shrimp Soup 211

INDEX 213
CONCLUSION 223
JACK LEMMON 223

Introduction

***

I'm neither a connoisseur of noodle nor an expert judge of its quality. Each time I pass by the aisles of noodles in any Chinese shop, the choices make me giddy as much as everybody else. But I can confidently say that I'm the right person for the job if you need someone to teach you how to cook excellent noodles and even give you some fun facts about noodles.

Yes, I'm a noodle enthusiast. A passionate cook and eater at that. I was raised by parents who are natives of Myanmar, where making and eating noodles are a way of life. The Burmese national dish is Mohinga, which is a wonderful fish chowder that combines smooth rice noodles, crisp white cabbage, fresh coriander, and crunchy pea fritters.

Khao swè is the Burmese word for noodles. It literally means to fold and pull, referring to the traditional way of making these noodles: constantly folding and pulling dough until it forms strands of noodles. Thus, "Noodle 365 Volume 1" has recipes that take you back to that age-old tradition, helping you learn how to create your own noodles from scratch. Don't be surprised, though, with some of the recipes here that include instant noodle. In this book, I believe there's no such thing as an awful noodle. If you're missing a traditional pasta favorite, I wish you'd find a new noodle to love.

With most noodle dishes coming from Asia, China is really worth noting here. It's where the noodle was born. Did you know that a bowl of millet-based noodles that existed as early as 4,000 years ago was dug up in Lajia, China in 2002 (Here I go again with my noodle trivia!)? As noodle dishes spread out from China to various parts of the world, they evolved and gave birth to multiple adaptations using local ingredients and flavors as time went by. You might observe that several noodle recipes here are distant relatives. Though I admit they must be recorded as wonderful dishes on their own.

A few recipes here may be quite challenging to make. But believe me, they're worth the time and effort you put in. The rest, though, can be prepared in a matter of minutes with just a few ingredients, yet they turn out to be great-tasting.

Noodles, being a practically neutral ingredient, can absorb any kind of flavors or act like a foil to rich, light, spicy, or comforting dishes. Their textures also vary, from crunchy to smooth.

The key takeaway here is the versatility of noodles. You won't be hard-pressed to find the right noodle dish for your needs—whether you're preparing for a sumptuous feast, a summer picnic, a quick lunch meal, a simple weeknight dinner, or a special treat for the weekend.

You also see more different types of noodle recipes such as:

- ✓ Ramen
- ✓ Rice Noodle
- ✓ Noodle Casserole
- ✓ Noodle Soup
- ✓ Ramen
- ✓ ...

Thank you for choosing "Noodle 365 Volume 1". I really hope that each book in the series will be always your best friend in your little kitchen.

Let's live happily and eat noodle every day!

Enjoy the book,

Chapter 1: Chow Mein Noodles

***

1. Asian Bok Choy Salad

"This wonderful vegan salad with an Asian flair is quick and simple, and is great for parties!"

Serving: 8 | Prep: 20 m | Ready in: 20 m

Ingredients

- 1/2 cup water
- 1/4 cup white sugar
- 1 lemon, juiced
- 3 tablespoons soy sauce
- 1/3 cup olive oil
- 2 medium heads bok choy
- 4 green onions, chopped
- 1 cup pine nuts
- 1 (5 ounce) can chow mein noodles

Direction

- Mix water and sugar in a medium saucepan, and bring to a boil. Cook 5 minutes, stirring occasionally, until a light syrup has formed. Remove from heat, and mix in lemon juice, soy sauce, and olive oil. Refrigerate until serving.
- In a medium bowl, toss together bok choy and green onions. Top with pine nuts and dried rice noodles. Sprinkle with the dressing to taste.

Nutrition Information

- Calories: 328 calories
- Total Fat: 23.5 g
- Cholesterol: 0 mg
- Sodium: 554 mg
- Total Carbohydrate: 25.8 g
- Protein: 9.4 g

2. Asian Chicken and Wild Rice Salad

"A healthier take on lettuce wraps. These are delicious!"

Serving: 8 | Prep: 20 m | Cook: 35 m | Ready in: 1 h 10 m

Ingredients

- 2 tablespoons soy sauce
- 2 tablespoons sesame oil
- 4 boneless, skinless chicken breasts
- 1 teaspoon salt
- 1/2 teaspoon ground black pepper
- 5 cups water
- 2 (6 ounce) packages long grain and wild rice mix
- 1 tablespoon butter (optional)
- 1 (15 ounce) can mandarin oranges, drained
- 1 (8 ounce) can sliced water chestnuts, drained
- 1 cup chopped green onion
- 1 cup chopped celery
- 1 cup chopped almonds
- 6 lettuce leaves, or as needed
- 1 (5 ounce) can chow mein noodles

Direction

- Mix soy sauce and sesame oil in a bowl; rub mixture over chicken breasts. Season with salt and pepper.
- Heat a large skillet over medium heat; cook marinated chicken in the hot skillet until no longer pink in the center and juices run clear, about 20 minutes. Dice chicken when cool enough to handle and transfer to a large bowl.
- Combine water, long grain and wild rice mix, and butter in a saucepan; bring to a boil. Reduce heat, cover pan, and simmer until rice is tender and liquid is absorbed, about 25 minutes.
- Mix rice, mandarin oranges, water chestnuts, green onion, celery, and almonds with diced chicken; toss well. Chill mixture in refrigerator for at least 15 minutes.
- Line a large platter with lettuce leaves; top with chicken mixture. Sprinkle noodles around salad.

Nutrition Information

- Calories: 459 calories
- Total Fat: 16.5 g
- Cholesterol: 37 mg
- Sodium: 1334 mg
- Total Carbohydrate: 56.4 g
- Protein: 22.8 g

3. Asian Chicken Salad in a Jar

"Veggies are layered with shredded chicken, Asian noodles, and a nutty dressing for an easy meal on the go."

Serving: 6 | Prep: 25 m | Ready in: 25 m

Ingredients

- 3 carrots, peeled and julienned
- 2 red bell peppers, julienned
- 3 cups chow mein noodles
- 3 cups shredded, cooked chicken breast meat
- 6 cups shredded romaine lettuce
- 6 (1-quart) jars with lids
- 1/4 cup creamy peanut butter
- 3 tablespoons water
- 2 tablespoons low-sodium soy sauce
- 1 tablespoon vegetable oil
- 1 tablespoon white sugar
- 2 1/2 teaspoons rice vinegar
- 1 teaspoon ground coriander

Direction

- Layer 1/2 cup carrots, 1/3 cup bell peppers, 1/2 cup chow mein noodles, 1/2 cup chicken, and 1 cup romaine in each jar.
- Whisk peanut butter, water, soy sauce, vegetable oil, sugar, rice vinegar, and coriander in a bowl until dressing is smooth. Chill salads and dressing, covered, until ready to serve. Serve jars with dressing on the side.

Nutrition Information

- Calories: 365 calories
- Total Fat: 20.1 g
- Cholesterol: 52 mg
- Sodium: 383 mg

- Total Carbohydrate: 22.4 g
- Protein: 24.9 g

4. Birds Nests II

"Fun treats for Springtime. You can use vanilla flavored candy coating instead of white chocolate, if you like."

Serving: 6

Ingredients

- 2 cups chow mein noodles
- 2 cups crushed cornflakes cereal
- 16 (1 ounce) squares white chocolate
- 1/3 cup chocolate covered raisins

Direction

- Place a sheet of waxed paper or foil on a large cookie sheet. In a large bowl, combine the noodles and the cereal and set aside.
- Melt white chocolate or vanilla candy-coating in a double boiler over hot water (or in the microwave). Remove from heat and pour over noodles and cereal.
- To form nests, mound 2 tablespoons of the mixture onto the prepared cookie sheet. With the back of a teaspoon, make an indentation in the center of each mound. Press 3 or 4 candies in the center of each "nest". Allow to set at room temperature until firm.

Nutrition Information

- Calories: 573 calories
- Total Fat: 32.5 g
- Cholesterol: 16 mg
- Sodium: 216 mg
- Total Carbohydrate: 65.7 g
- Protein: 7.6 g

5. Birds Nests III

"The kids can help fill the nests."

Serving: 6

Ingredients

- 4 cups chow mein noodles
- 3 cups miniature marshmallows
- 3 tablespoons butter
- 30 small jellybeans

Direction

- Line a cookie sheet with foil and grease with spray-on cooking oil.
- Pour noodles into a large bowl. Melt the butter and marshmallows over medium heat, stirring until smooth. Pour marshmallow mixture over noodles, stirring until well coated.
- Rub some butter on hands and form noodle mixture into six round balls. Place balls on prepared cookie sheet. With the back of a teaspoon, press the center of each ball to make a hollow indentation.
- Let nests set until they are firm. Fill each with small jelly beans. (Other small candies of your choice may be substituted, such as M M's, small gumdrops, chocolate covered raisins, chocolate covered peanuts, etc.)

Nutrition Information

- Calories: 307 calories
- Total Fat: 15 g
- Cholesterol: 15 mg
- Sodium: 195 mg
- Total Carbohydrate: 42.3 g
- Protein: 3 g

6. Bok Choy Salad with Chow Mein

"This is a quick bok choy salad recipe I got from my mother. I made a few modifications to the dressing to fit my own taste, but it's been a hit with my husband, and our child and frequently asked for when they see bok choy in the store. This can be served as either an appetizer or a salad for any meal. Add green onions, if desired."

Serving: 10 | Prep: 15 m | Cook: 4 m | Ready in: 29 m

Ingredients

- Crunch:
- 1 tablespoon canola oil, or as needed
- 5 tablespoons sesame seeds, or to taste
- 2 (6 ounce) packages dried chow mein noodles
- 1/4 cup chopped almonds, or to taste (optional)
- 1 1/2 tablespoons honey, or to taste (optional)
- Sauce:
- 1 cup olive oil
- 1/3 cup white sugar
- 1/2 cup apple cider vinegar
- 2 tablespoons soy sauce
- Salad:
- 1 large head bok choy, cut into 1-inch pieces

Direction

- Heat canola oil in a large skillet over medium heat. Add sesame seeds. Heat for 30 seconds; start stirring with a spatula and add chow mein noodles and almonds. Cook, stirring constantly, until seeds are dark brown, about 4 minutes. Remove from heat. Add honey; stir until crunch mixture sticks together. Pour into a bowl; cover with plastic wrap. Refrigerate until cool, about 10 minutes.
- Mix olive oil, sugar, vinegar, and soy sauce together in another bowl. Cover with plastic wrap; refrigerate dressing until cool.
- Place bok choy into a salad bowl.
- Place crunch mixture on a flat work surface. Break into smaller pieces using a meat tenderizer. Add to the bok choy; mix into the salad. Serve dressing on the side.
- Mix dressing well; serve alongside the salad.

Nutrition Information

- Calories: 456 calories
- Total Fat: 33.9 g
- Cholesterol: 0 mg
- Sodium: 463 mg
- Total Carbohydrate: 32.5 g
- Protein: 7.6 g

7. Butterscotch Crunch

"They are just what the title suggests: crunchy and butterscotch-y! They are a no-bake cookie and very easy to make. If you are a butterscotch fan this is the cookie for you."

Serving: 24 | Prep: 5 m | Cook: 5 m | Ready in: 25 m

Ingredients

- 2 cups butterscotch chips
- 1 (5 ounce) can chow mein noodles

Direction

- In a saucepan, melt the butterscotch chips over low heat, stirring frequently. When they are completely melted, remove from the heat and stir in the noodles until they are evenly coated. Drop by spoonfuls onto waxed paper. Allow cookies to set up for 20 to 25 minutes, then peel them from the waxed paper and enjoy!

Nutrition Information

- Calories: 112 calories
- Total Fat: 5.8 g
- Cholesterol: 0 mg
- Sodium: 41 mg
- Total Carbohydrate: 12.5 g
- Protein: 0.5 g

8. Cantonese Chicken Chow Mein

"Pan-fried chow mein noodles are tossed in a light Asian sauce and topped with tender slices of chicken and crisp vegetables."

Serving: 4 | Prep: 30 m | Cook: 10 m | Ready in: 55 m

Ingredients

- Marinade:
- 2 tablespoons water
- 1 teaspoon rice wine vinegar
- 1 teaspoon soy sauce
- 1 teaspoon cornstarch
- 1 teaspoon sesame oil
- 1/4 teaspoon ground black pepper
- 1 skinless, boneless chicken breast half, thinly sliced
- Seasonings:
- 1/2 cup chicken broth
- 1 tablespoon soy sauce
- 2 teaspoons oyster sauce
- 1 teaspoon rice wine vinegar
- 1 teaspoon white sugar
- 1/4 cup canola oil, divided
- 1 pound chow mein noodles
- 1 stalk celery, thinly sliced on the diagonal
- 1 carrot, cut into matchstick-size pieces
- 1/4 cup bean sprouts
- 1/4 cup thinly sliced onion
- 1 green onion, thinly sliced

Direction

- Whisk water, 1 teaspoon rice wine vinegar, 1 teaspoon soy sauce, cornstarch, sesame oil, and black pepper together in a bowl until marinade is smooth. Add chicken and marinate, about 15 minutes.
- Stir chicken broth, 1 tablespoon soy sauce, oyster sauce, 1 teaspoon rice wine vinegar, and sugar together in a bowl until seasoning mixture is well combined.
- Heat 3 tablespoons canola oil in a large skillet over medium heat; cook and stir noodles until golden brown and crisp, about 1 minute. Transfer noodles to a platter.
- Pour the remaining 1 tablespoon into skillet with the oil; cook and stir chicken over high heat until no longer pink in the center, about 5 minutes. Add seasoning mixture, celery, carrot, bean sprouts, onion, and green onion; cook and stir until sauce thickens, about 30 seconds. Pour chicken mixture over noodles.

Nutrition Information

- Calories: 519 calories
- Total Fat: 23.3 g
- Cholesterol: 81 mg
- Sodium: 703 mg
- Total Carbohydrate: 59.9 g
- Protein: 19.7 g

9. Cao Lau Vietnamese Noodle Bowl

"Cao lau is made with noodles, pork, and greens traditionally found only in the town of Hoi An, Vietnam. This recipe approximates authentic cao lau with easier-to-find ingredients. Use fresh rice noodles about the same thickness of linguine."

Serving: 6 | Prep: 20 m | Cook: 10 m | Ready in: 1 h 30 m

Ingredients

- 2 tablespoons soy sauce
- 4 cloves garlic, minced, or more to taste
- 2 teaspoons Chinese five-spice powder
- 2 teaspoons white sugar
- 1 teaspoon paprika
- 1/4 teaspoon chicken bouillon granules
- 1 1/2 pounds pork tenderloin, cut into cubes
- 2 tablespoons vegetable oil
- 2 tablespoons water
- 2 pounds fresh thick Vietnamese-style rice noodles
- 2 cups bean sprouts
- 1 cup torn lettuce leaves
- 1 bunch green onions, chopped
- 1/4 cup fresh basil leaves

- 1/4 cup fresh cilantro leaves
- 1/4 cup crispy chow mein noodles, or more to taste

Direction

- Whisk soy sauce, garlic, Chinese 5-spice, sugar, paprika, and chicken bouillon together in a large glass or ceramic bowl. Add pork cubes and toss to evenly coat. Cover the bowl with plastic wrap and marinate in the refrigerator for at least 1 hour.
- Remove pork from marinade and shake off excess. Discard remaining marinade.
- Heat oil in a large skillet or wok over medium heat. Cook and stir pork in hot oil until browned, 4 to 7 minutes. Add water; cook and stir until water evaporates and pork is cooked through, about 2 minutes more.
- Bring a large pot of water to a boil. Rinse rice noodles under cold water and gently break noodles apart. Immerse noodles in boiling water until about half tender, about 30 seconds. Add bean sprouts to the water and noodles; continue cooking until tender but still firm to the bite, about 30 seconds more. Drain.
- Combine noodles and pork mixture together in a large serving dish. Top noodles with lettuce, green onion, basil, cilantro, and crispy chow mein.

Nutrition Information

- Calories: 488 calories
- Total Fat: 8.1 g
- Cholesterol: 49 mg
- Sodium: 373 mg
- Total Carbohydrate: 78.1 g
- Protein: 23.7 g

10. Caramel Crispy Treats I

"A gooey, crunchy snack that is absolutely delicious!"

Serving: 12

Ingredients

- 3 tablespoons butter
- 2 1/2 cups miniature marshmallows
- 1 (5 ounce) can chow mein noodles
- 12 individually wrapped caramels, unwrapped
- 1 tablespoon cold water
- 2 tablespoons peanut butter

Direction

- Melt butter with marshmallows over low heat - stir until smooth.
- Add noodles - toss until coated.
- Drop spoonfuls of noodle mixture onto a greased baking sheet.
- Melt caramels with water over low heat - stir until smooth. Add peanut butter; mix well. Drizzle over treats. Chill.

Nutrition Information

- Calories: 175 calories
- Total Fat: 8.7 g
- Cholesterol: 8 mg
- Sodium: 117 mg
- Total Carbohydrate: 23.5 g
- Protein: 2.3 g

11. Carols Chow Mein Noodle Casserole

"This recipe was passed down from my aunt. It's very fast to put together, and the end result is a delicious soft noodle in the middle of the casserole with a crunchy noodle top."

Serving: 10 | Prep: 15 m | Cook: 1 h 5 m | Ready in: 1 h 35 m

Ingredients

- 1 1/2 pounds ground beef
- 1 tablespoon minced garlic
- 2 (10.75 ounce) cans condensed tomato soup
- 1 (10.75 ounce) can condensed cream of mushroom soup
- 6 stalks celery, coarsely chopped
- 1 tablespoon Worcestershire sauce
- 2 (6 ounce) packages chow mein noodles
- 2 cups water, or more as needed

Direction

- Preheat oven to 350 degrees F (175 degrees C).
- Heat a large skillet over medium-high heat. Cook and stir beef and garlic in the hot skillet until beef is browned and crumbly, 5 to 7 minutes; drain and discard grease.
- Mix beef mixture, tomato soup, cream of mushroom soup, celery, and Worcestershire sauce together in a large bowl.
- Spoon enough beef mixture into a Dutch oven to cover the bottom of the pot. Spread a layer of chow mein noodles over beef mixture, and cover noodles with another layer of the beef mixture. Continue layering process until all beef mixture and noodles are used, ending with a layer of noodles on top.
- Carefully pour water into the Dutch oven until water line is just visible below noodles. Cover the Dutch oven with a lid.
- Bake in the preheated oven for 50 minutes. Remove the lid and continue baking until top layer of noodles is crunchy, about 10 minutes. Cool for 15 minutes before serving.

Nutrition Information

- Calories: 377 calories
- Total Fat: 19.8 g
- Cholesterol: 42 mg
- Sodium: 862 mg
- Total Carbohydrate: 31.8 g
- Protein: 18.4 g

12. Chicken and Chinese Noodles Casserole

"This was one of our go-to recipes growing up. A home favorite!"

Serving: 6 | Prep: 15 m | Cook: 25 m | Ready in: 40 m

Ingredients

- cooking spray
- 1 tablespoon olive oil
- 1 small onion, diced
- 1 (10.75 ounce) can low-fat cream of mushroom soup
- 1 (10.75 ounce) can water
- 1/4 teaspoon garlic salt, or to taste
- ground black pepper to taste
- 1 roasted chicken, bones and skin removed, meat cut into cubes
- 1 (8.5 ounce) package chow mein noodles
- 1 (4 ounce) jar pimentos

Direction

- Preheat oven to 350 degrees F (175 degrees C). Prepare a casserole dish with cooking spray.
- Heat olive oil in a saucepan over medium heat; cook and stir onion in the hot oil until translucent, 5 to 7 minutes. Add soup and water; stir. Season the mixture with garlic salt and pepper.
- Layer chicken into the bottom of the prepared casserole dish; top with chow mein noodles and pimentos. Pour the mixture from the saucepan over the layers to cover.
- Bake in preheated oven until completely heated through, 20 to 30 minutes.

Nutrition Information

- Calories: 399 calories

- Total Fat: 17.5 g
- Cholesterol: 66 mg
- Sodium: 633 mg
- Total Carbohydrate: 30.3 g
- Protein: 28.9 g

13. Chinese Chicken Casserole Surprise

"Chinese-style ingredients like almonds, water chestnuts, mushrooms, celery and chow mein noodles combine with a creamy broth, soup and milk mixture - and chicken, of course - to form this casserole. The name comes from the fact that people who have it seem to be pleasantly surprised and wonder what is in it. This is a good recipe for potlucks, etc. as it can be prepared ahead of time and refrigerated or frozen until ready to bake."

Serving: 6 | Prep: 30 m | Cook: 45 m | Ready in: 1 h 15 m

Ingredients

- 2 skinless, boneless chicken breasts - cooked and cubed
- 1 cup chicken broth
- 1 (10.75 ounce) can condensed cream of mushroom soup
- 1 (5 ounce) can evaporated milk
- 1 cup sliced almonds
- 1 (4.5 ounce) can sliced mushrooms, drained
- 1 (8 ounce) can water chestnuts, drained and minced
- 1 (5 ounce) can crispy chow mein noodles
- 2/3 cup shredded Cheddar cheese
- 1 cup diced celery (optional)

Direction

- Preheat oven to 350 degrees F (175 degrees C).
- In a lightly greased 9x13 inch baking dish, combine the chicken, broth, soup, milk, almonds, mushroom pieces, water chestnuts, noodles, cheese and celery (if using). Mix well and make sure mixture is spread evenly in the dish.
- Bake in preheated oven for 45 minutes.

Nutrition Information

- Calories: 434 calories
- Total Fat: 27 g
- Cholesterol: 47 mg
- Sodium: 664 mg
- Total Carbohydrate: 28.7 g
- Protein: 21.8 g

14. Chinese Chicken Salad II

"This is a crisp lettuce salad with a zippy sweet and sour dressing. Always a hit at a gathering, but doesn't store well. Very quick to prepare at the last minute."

Serving: 9 | Prep: 15 m | Ready in: 15 m

Ingredients

- 1 head lettuce
- 1 cup chopped cooked chicken breast
- 1 (8 ounce) can chopped water chestnuts
- 1 bunch green onions, chopped
- 1 cup sliced almonds
- 1 (5 ounce) can chow mein noodles
- 1/2 cup vegetable oil
- 4 tablespoons vinegar
- 4 tablespoons white sugar
- 1/2 teaspoon salt
- 1 pinch ground black pepper
- 1 tablespoon poppy seeds

Direction

- In a small bowl, whisk together the oil, vinegar, sugar, salt, pepper, and poppy seeds, and set aside. Wash lettuce and tear into bite-sized pieces. To a large bowl, first add the lettuce, then the onions, water chestnuts, and chicken. Just before serving, top with the almonds, noodles and dressing, and toss lightly.

Nutrition Information

- Calories: 335 calories
- Total Fat: 24.1 g
- Cholesterol: 12 mg
- Sodium: 219 mg
- Total Carbohydrate: 23.6 g
- Protein: 9.2 g

15. Chinese New Year Chocolate Candy

"An easy recipe to make!"

Serving: 24 | Prep: 5 m | Cook: 30 m | Ready in: 1 h

Ingredients

- 2 cups semisweet chocolate chips
- 2 cups butterscotch chips
- 2 1/2 cups dry-roasted peanuts
- 4 cups chow mein noodles

Direction

- Butter a 9x13 inch dish.
- Melt chocolate and butterscotch chips in the top of a double boiler over simmering water. Remove from heat and stir in peanuts. Stir in noodles until all is well coated. Press into prepared dish. Chill until set; cut into squares.

Nutrition Information

- Calories: 276 calories
- Total Fat: 18.1 g
- Cholesterol: 0 mg
- Sodium: 51 mg
- Total Carbohydrate: 25.5 g
- Protein: 4.8 g

16. Chocolate Clusters

"Easy, fast, no bake, and always a favorite!!"

Serving: 12

Ingredients

- 1 cup semisweet chocolate chips
- 1 cup butterscotch chips
- 1 cup peanuts
- 1 cup chow mein noodles

Direction

- In sauce pan, over low heat, melt chocolate chips and butterscotch chips.
- Remove from heat and immediately add peanuts and chow mein noodles. Mix until well coated.
- Drop on to a wax paper lined cookie sheet until set and chilled. Enjoy!!

Nutrition Information

- Calories: 239 calories
- Total Fat: 15.4 g
- Cholesterol: 0 mg
- Sodium: 34 mg
- Total Carbohydrate: 22.7 g
- Protein: 3.8 g

17. Chocolate Spiders

"Fast, and easy. My mom used to make them all the time. These can be made for Halloween treats, or Christmas Candy."

Serving: 20 | Prep: 5 m | Cook: 25 m | Ready in: 30 m

Ingredients

- 1 pound chocolate confectioners' coating
- 1 (8.5 ounce) package chow mein noodles

Direction

- Chop the chocolate confectioners' coating and place into a heatproof bowl over simmering water. Cook, stirring occasionally until melted and smooth. Remove from heat and stir in the chow mein noodles so they are evenly distributed. Spoon out to desired size onto waxed paper. Let cool completely before storing or serving.

Nutrition Information

- Calories: 172 calories
- Total Fat: 12.7 g
- Cholesterol: 0 mg
- Sodium: 54 mg
- Total Carbohydrate: 17.6 g
- Protein: 2.8 g

18. Chocolaty Peanut Butter Haystacks

"Simple no-bake treat that kids love to eat and make."

Serving: 30 | Prep: 10 m | Cook: 5 m | Ready in: 35 m

Ingredients

- 1 cup semi-sweet chocolate chips
- 1/3 cup peanut butter
- 1/2 cup toffee baking bits (such as Heath®)
- 1 cup chow mein noodles

Direction

- Place the chocolate chips into a microwave-safe bowl and cook on High for 30 seconds; stir and repeat several times, just until the chips are melted. Add peanut butter, cook for 20 more seconds to warm the peanut butter, and mix thoroughly. Mix in the toffee bits and chow mein noodles; stir to coat the ingredients with the chocolate mixture.
- Line a baking sheet with parchment or waxed paper; drop the mixture onto the lined sheets by the tablespoon. Refrigerate until set.

Nutrition Information

- Calories: 76 calories
- Total Fat: 5 g
- Cholesterol: 3 mg
- Sodium: 39 mg
- Total Carbohydrate: 7.4 g
- Protein: 1.2 g

19. Chow Clusters

"Simple and delicious...more like candy. Peanuts work well in place of the cashews or try a combination of both!"

Serving: 18

Ingredients

- 2 cups semisweet chocolate chips
- 2 cups butterscotch chips
- 2 (5 ounce) cans chow mein noodles
- 1/2 cup cashew halves

Direction

- In a heavy saucepan, combine chocolate and butterscotch chips. Melt, stirring constantly over low heat.
- Remove when melted and add chow mein noodles. Add cashews or peanuts. Mix quickly to coat Dip out tablespoons onto wax paper. Cool. (Can also melt chips in the microwave.)

Nutrition Information

- Calories: 301 calories
- Total Fat: 17.5 g
- Cholesterol: 0 mg
- Sodium: 115 mg
- Total Carbohydrate: 34.1 g
- Protein: 2.7 g

20. Chow Mein Clusters

"Quick and easy, no-bake drop cookies."

Serving: 24 | Prep: 15 m | Ready in: 30 m

Ingredients

- 2 cups butterscotch chips
- 2 cups chow mein noodles
- 1 cup salted peanuts

Direction

- In a double boiler over simmering water, melt the butterscotch morsels, stirring frequently until smooth. Remove from heat, and stir in the chow mien noodles and peanuts.
- Drop by teaspoonfuls onto waxed paper. Refrigerate until firm.

Nutrition Information

- Calories: 136 calories
- Total Fat: 8.2 g
- Cholesterol: 0 mg
- Sodium: 81 mg
- Total Carbohydrate: 12.6 g
- Protein: 1.8 g

21. Chow Mein Noodle Bars

"I received this recipe from my grandmother and it has always been a family favorite."

Serving: 24 | Prep: 15 m | Cook: 20 m | Ready in: 40 m

Ingredients

- 1/2 cup margarine
- 1/2 cup brown sugar
- 1 cup all-purpose flour
- 1 cup semisweet chocolate chips
- 5 cups miniature marshmallows
- 1 cup creamy peanut butter
- 1/2 tablespoon light cream
- 1/2 cup brown sugar
- 4 cups chow mein noodles

Direction

- Preheat the oven to 325 degrees F (165 degrees C). Grease a 9x13 inch baking pan.
- In a medium bowl, cream together the margarine and 1/2 cup brown sugar. Stir in the flour; the mixture should be crumbly. Sprinkle over the bottom of the prepared pan and pack down to cover.
- Bake for 15 to 20 minutes in the preheated oven, until lightly toasted. Remove from the oven and immediately sprinkle with chocolate chips. When the chips have softened enough, spread them over the crust.
- In a heat-proof bowl over simmering water, or in the microwave, combine the marshmallows, peanut butter, brown sugar and light cream. Cook, stirring occasionally until melted and smooth. Remove from heat and stir in the chow mein noodles. Spread on top of the chocolate layer of the crust. Let cool before cutting into squares.

Nutrition Information

- Calories: 245 calories
- Total Fat: 13.7 g
- Cholesterol: < 1 mg
- Sodium: 137 mg
- Total Carbohydrate: 29.3 g
- Protein: 4.4 g

22. Chow Mein Noodle Casserole

"This is a very tasty dish that even my kids love! It can easily be cut in half. It uses soy sauce and chow mein noodles to give it an Asian flair."

Serving: 4 | Prep: 20 m | Cook: 20 m | Ready in: 40 m

Ingredients

- 1 pound ground beef
- 1 onion, chopped
- 2 stalks celery, chopped
- 1/2 cup slivered almonds
- 1 cup cooked rice

- 1 (10.75 ounce) can condensed cream of chicken soup
- 1/2 cup water
- 3 tablespoons soy sauce
- 5 ounces chow mein noodles

Direction

- Preheat oven to 350 degrees F (175 degrees C).
- In a large skillet over medium high heat, sauté the ground beef for 5 minutes. Add the onion and celery and sauté for 5 more minutes.
- In a separate medium bowl, combine the almonds, rice, soup, water and soy sauce. Mix together well and add to the beef mixture. Place this into a lightly greased 9x13 inch baking dish. Top with chow mein noodles.
- Bake at 350 degrees F (175 degrees C) for 20 minutes.

Nutrition Information

- Calories: 597 calories
- Total Fat: 35.5 g
- Cholesterol: 75 mg
- Sodium: 1514 mg
- Total Carbohydrate: 41.7 g
- Protein: 28.9 g

23. Chow Mein Noodle Cookie

"An easy drop cookie, perfect for the holidays."

Serving: 36

Ingredients

- 3 cups butterscotch chips
- 1 (5 ounce) can chow mein noodles
- 1 cup peanuts

Direction

- In a medium saucepan, melt butterscotch chips over low heat, stirring constantly. Stir in chow mein noodles and peanuts.
- Drop by teaspoonfuls onto foil. Let stand until cool.

Nutrition Information

- Calories: 125 calories
- Total Fat: 7.3 g
- Cholesterol: 0 mg
- Sodium: 32 mg
- Total Carbohydrate: 12.2 g
- Protein: 1.3 g

24. Chow Mein with Chicken and Vegetables

"This stir-fry combines chicken breast, bok choy, zucchini, carrots, snap peas, and chow mein noodles in a flavorful Chinese-inspired sauce."

Serving: 4 | Prep: 20 m | Cook: 15 m | Ready in: 55 m

Ingredients

- 2 teaspoons soy sauce
- 1 teaspoon cornstarch
- 1/4 teaspoon sesame oil
- 1/2 pound skinless, boneless chicken breast halves, cut into strips
- 3/4 cup chicken broth
- 2 tablespoons oyster sauce
- 3/4 teaspoon white sugar
- 1/2 pound chow mein noodles
- 1 tablespoon vegetable oil
- 1 teaspoon minced garlic
- 2 heads bok choy, chopped
- 1/2 zucchini, diced
- 10 sugar snap peas
- 1 carrot, cut into thin strips
- 2 tablespoons chopped green onion

Direction

- Whisk soy sauce, corn starch, and sesame oil together in a large bowl until smooth; add chicken strips and toss to coat. Cover and refrigerate for at least 20 minutes.

- Combine chicken broth, oyster sauce, and sugar in a small bowl and set aside.
- Bring a large pot of water to a boil. Add noodles and cook over medium heat until cooked through but still firm to the bite, 4 to 5 minutes. Drain and rinse with cold water.
- Heat vegetable oil in a large skillet. Cook and garlic in hot oil for 30 seconds; add marinated chicken. Cook and stir until browned and no longer pink in the center, 5 to 6 minutes. Remove chicken mixture to a plate. Cook and stir bok choy, zucchini, snap peas, and carrot in the hot skillet until softened, about 2 minutes. Return noodles and chicken mixture to the skillet. Pour broth mixture into noodle mixture; cook and stir until warmed through, about 2 minutes. Serve garnished with green onions.

Nutrition Information

- Calories: 526 calories
- Total Fat: 17.9 g
- Cholesterol: 30 mg
- Sodium: 992 mg
- Total Carbohydrate: 61.7 g
- Protein: 29.4 g

25. Coleslaw Gado Gado

"An Asian-style coleslaw with a spicy peanuty dressing."

Serving: 12 | Prep: 20 m | Cook: 5 m | Ready in: 2 h 25 m

Ingredients

- 1/4 cup chopped almonds
- Salad:
- 1 head cabbage, shredded
- 3 carrots, shredded
- 1 red bell pepper, thinly sliced
- 1/2 red onion, chopped
- Dressing:
- 1/3 cup olive oil
- 1/4 cup cider vinegar
- 2 tablespoons peanut butter, slightly melted
- 2 tablespoons maple syrup
- 2 tablespoons tamari (gluten-free soy sauce)
- 1 tablespoon grated fresh ginger
- 1 teaspoon sesame oil
- 1 teaspoon red pepper flakes
- 1/2 teaspoon salt
- 1 cup crispy chow mein noodles, or more to taste

Direction

- Preheat oven to 350 degrees F (175 degrees C). Spread almonds onto a baking sheet.
- Bake almonds in the preheated oven until toasted and fragrant, 5 to 10 minutes. Remove baking sheet from oven and cool almonds.
- Combine cabbage, carrots, red bell pepper, and red onion in a large bowl.
- Whisk olive oil, vinegar, peanut butter, maple syrup, tamari, ginger, sesame oil, red pepper flakes, and salt together in a bowl until dressing is smooth; pour over cabbage mixture and toss to coat. Refrigerate salad until chilled and flavors blend, about 2 hours.
- Stir toasted almonds and chow mein noodles into salad.

Nutrition Information

- Calories: 144 calories
- Total Fat: 9.5 g
- Cholesterol: 0 mg
- Sodium: 324 mg
- Total Carbohydrate: 13.2 g
- Protein: 3.4 g

26. Crunchy Fun Drops

"Your kids will love eating this delicious snack as much as they will love to help make them."

Serving: 24 | Prep: 5 m | Cook: 5 m | Ready in: 10 m

Ingredients

- 2 cups semisweet chocolate chips

- 1 cup raisins
- 1 cup dry-roasted peanuts
- 1 cup chow mein noodles

Direction

- In a large microwave safe bowl, microwave chocolate chips on high power, stirring every 30 seconds until smooth and melted. Stir in the raisins, peanuts and chow mein noodles. Roll into walnut sized balls using your hands and set onto waxed paper to cool. Chill or let sit until hard. Enjoy!

Nutrition Information

- Calories: 131 calories
- Total Fat: 7.8 g
- Cholesterol: 0 mg
- Sodium: 11 mg
- Total Carbohydrate: 16 g
- Protein: 2.4 g

27. Crunchy Lettuce

"This is a crispy and crunchy salad with bacon and toasted almonds."

Serving: 4 | Prep: 15 m | Cook: 15 m | Ready in: 1 h 30 m

Ingredients

- 6 slices bacon
- 1 head iceberg lettuce - rinsed, dried, and shredded
- 1/3 cup toasted and sliced almonds
- 1/4 cup sesame seeds, toasted
- 4 green onions, chopped
- 3/4 cup chow mein noodles
- 1/2 cup vegetable oil
- 1/4 cup white sugar
- 2 tablespoons white wine vinegar
- 1 teaspoon salt
- 1/4 teaspoon ground black pepper

Direction

- Place bacon in a large, deep skillet. Cook over medium high heat until evenly brown. Drain, crumble and set aside.
- In a salad bowl, combine the bacon, lettuce, almonds, sesame seeds, green onions and chow mien noodles; toss and refrigerate.
- In a glass jar with a tight fitting lid, combine the oil, sugar, vinegar, salt and pepper. Shake well and chill for 1 hour.
- Before serving, shake dressing and pour over salad; toss and serve.

Nutrition Information

- Calories: 555 calories
- Total Fat: 46.7 g
- Cholesterol: 15 mg
- Sodium: 956 mg
- Total Carbohydrate: 27.1 g
- Protein: 11.5 g

28. Easter Birds Nests

"Such a cute edible decoration!"

Serving: 10 | Prep: 15 m | Cook: 5 m | Ready in: 20 m

Ingredients

- 3 cups miniature marshmallows
- 1/4 cup creamy peanut butter
- 3 tablespoons butter
- 4 cups crispy chow mein noodles
- cooking spray
- 40 candy-coated milk chocolate eggs

Direction

- Cook and stir marshmallows, peanut butter, and butter in a saucepan over medium heat until the marshmallows melt completely into the mixture, about 5 minutes.
- Put chow mein noodles into a large bowl. Pour marshmallow mixture over the chow mein noodles; stir to coat.

- Spray hands with cooking spray or coat with butter so the noodles will not stick to your hands. Scoop noodle mixture from bowl with an ice cream scoop and form into balls, hollowing the center out to create the nest. Arrange 4 chocolate eggs into each nest.

Nutrition Information

- Calories: 365 calories
- Total Fat: 21.1 g
- Cholesterol: 17 mg
- Sodium: 174 mg
- Total Carbohydrate: 40.2 g
- Protein: 4.6 g

29. Edible Spiders

"A cute Halloween snack that is fun for kids to make and eat. Marshmallows grow chow mein legs and and candy coated eyes."

Serving: 24 | Prep: 30 m | Ready in: 1 h

Ingredients

- 1 cup semisweet chocolate chips
- 1 teaspoon butter
- 24 large marshmallows
- 1 (6 ounce) package chow mein noodles
- 1 (12 ounce) package mini candy-coated chocolate pieces

Direction

- In a microwave-safe bowl, combine chocolate chips and butter. Microwave until melted. Stir occasionally until chocolate is smooth. Pour chocolate into a sealable plastic bag and set aside.
- Line a cookie sheet with wax paper. Stick 4 chow mein noodles into each side of marshmallow for legs, and arrange on wax paper. Using scissors, cut one corner off the bag of melted chocolate. Drizzle over the marshmallow spiders. Attach 2 candies to each marshmallow for eyes. Chill until chocolate hardens.

Nutrition Information

- Calories: 165 calories
- Total Fat: 7.7 g
- Cholesterol: 3 mg
- Sodium: 48 mg
- Total Carbohydrate: 23.9 g
- Protein: 1.7 g

30. Five Can Casserole

"Just the thing for a quick supper."

Serving: 6 | Prep: 10 m | Cook: 25 m | Ready in: 35 m

Ingredients

- 1 (6 ounce) can chicken chunks, drained
- 1 (5 ounce) can evaporated milk
- 1 (10.75 ounce) can condensed cream of chicken soup
- 1 (10.75 ounce) can condensed cream of mushroom soup
- 1 (5 ounce) can chow mein noodles

Direction

- Preheat an oven to 350 degrees F (175 degrees C). Grease a 2-quart casserole dish.
- Stir the chicken, milk, cream of chicken soup, cream of mushroom soup, and noodles together in a mixing bowl; pour into the prepared casserole dish. Bake in the preheated oven until hot and bubbly, about 25 minutes.

Nutrition Information

- Calories: 283 calories
- Total Fat: 15 g
- Cholesterol: 28 mg
- Sodium: 1001 mg
- Total Carbohydrate: 23.6 g
- Protein: 13.4 g

31. Fresh Vegetable StirFry with Peppery Orange Beef

"Easy, tasty stir-fry recipe. Delicious and fresh taste!!! Passed down from my father. Recipe may seem long, but you can whip it up in no time. Also, feel free to use any vegetables that you like, or add bamboo shoots or water chestnuts at the end of the recipe!"

Serving: 8 | Prep: 15 m | Cook: 45 m | Ready in: 1 h

Ingredients

- 2 cups uncooked long grain white rice
- 1 quart water
- 1 tablespoon light sesame oil
- 4 cloves garlic, crushed
- 5 tablespoons butter
- 2 pounds flank steak, cut into thin strips
- salt to taste
- 4 teaspoons red pepper flakes
- 3 1/2 tablespoons teriyaki sauce
- 12 ounces fresh mushrooms, sliced
- 1 large sweet onion, sliced
- 1/2 head cabbage, sliced into strips
- 1 green bell pepper, cut into strips
- 1 red bell pepper, cut into strips
- 1 yellow bell pepper, cut into strips
- 1 teaspoon cornstarch
- 1 tablespoon brown sugar
- 1/2 cup beef broth
- 2 tablespoons orange jam
- 1 (5 ounce) can chow mein noodles
- mustard powder to taste

Direction

- In a pot, bring the rice and water to a boil. Cover, reduce heat to low, and simmer 20 minutes.
- Heat the sesame oil in a skillet over medium heat, and cook 2 cloves garlic for 2 minutes, until tender. Melt the butter in the skillet. Season the beef with salt and 2 teaspoons red pepper flakes. Cook and stir the beef in the skillet 10 minutes, until evenly brown. Reserving pan drippings, transfer the cooked beef to a bowl, and coat with 3 tablespoons teriyaki sauce.
- Melt the remaining butter in a separate skillet over medium heat, and cook the remaining garlic 2 minutes, until tender. Remove garlic, and set aside. Stir the mushrooms and onions into the skillet, and cook until onions are tender. Mix in the cabbage, green bell pepper, red bell pepper, and yellow bell pepper. Cook 3 minutes, until tender but still crisp. Remove skillet from heat, and mix in remaining 1/2 tablespoon teriyaki sauce and 1/2 the reserved pan drippings.
- Heat the remaining pan drippings in the skillet over medium heat. Mix in the remaining red pepper flakes, teriyaki sauce from the beef bowl, the reserved garlic, cornstarch, brown sugar, beef broth, and orange jam. Cook 5 minutes, until thickened. Remove garlic, and stir in the beef to coat.
- Serve the beef and vegetables, along with some of the skillet juices, over the cooked rice. Top with chow mein noodles, and sprinkle with mustard powder.

Nutrition Information

- Calories: 566 calories
- Total Fat: 22.3 g
- Cholesterol: 55 mg
- Sodium: 593 mg
- Total Carbohydrate: 67.8 g
- Protein: 24.2 g

32. Grilled Salmon Snap Peas and Spring Mix Salad with Chow Mein Noodles

"Salmon fillets are grilled and brushed with an Asian-inspired sauce then served on fresh salad greens with snap peas tossed with Asian Vinaigrette."

Serving: 4 | Prep: 20 m | Ready in: 20 m

Ingredients

- 2 tablespoons packed brown sugar
- 2 tablespoons hoisin sauce
- 2 tablespoons reduced-sodium soy sauce
- 1/4 teaspoon crushed red pepper
- 4 (4 to 6-oz each) salmon fillets
- Olive oil, as needed
- Salt and ground pepper to taste
- 1 (8.75 oz) package DOLE® Extra Veggie™ with Snap Peas
- 1/2 red bell pepper, cut into 2-inch strips
- Asian Vinaigrette*:
- 1/4 cup rice wine vinegar
- 3 tablespoons canola oil
- 2 teaspoons sesame oil
- 2 teaspoons reduced-sodium soy sauce
- 1/2 cup chow mein noodles

Direction

- Heat grill to medium-high heat.
- Whisk together brown sugar, hoisin sauce, soy sauce and crushed red pepper in small bowl until blended.
- Brush salmon with oil and season with salt and pepper, to taste. Grill 8 to 10 minutes, turning once, or until desired doneness. Generously brush both sides of fish with soy sauce mixture; cook additional 30 seconds per side.
- Combine salad blend, snap peas from pouch and red bell pepper in large bowl. Toss with Asian Vinaigrette, to taste. Divide salad mixture on 4 large plates. Top each with grilled salmon and sprinkle with chow mein noodles.
- *Asian Vinaigrette: Whisk together 1/4 cup rice wine vinegar, 3 tablespoons canola oil, 2 teaspoons sesame oil, 2 teaspoons reduced sodium soy sauce until blended. Makes about 1/2 cup.

Nutrition Information

- Calories: 386 calories
- Total Fat: 22.9 g
- Cholesterol: 51 mg
- Sodium: 874 mg
- Total Carbohydrate: 18.5 g
- Protein: 26 g

33. Happy Mountain

"Rice is topped with chicken in a cream sauce, then garnished with cheese, tomato, onion, pineapple and coconut. This melody of flavors mixed together sounds weird but the combination put together brings delicious results!!! This recipe was given to me by my aunt 20 years ago and I've been making it for my family ever since."

Serving: 4 | Prep: 15 m | Cook: 45 m | Ready in: 1 h

Ingredients

- 2 cups long grain white rice
- 4 cups water
- 1 1/2 pounds skinless, boneless chicken breast halves
- 1 (10.75 ounce) can condensed cream of chicken soup
- 3/4 cup shredded Cheddar cheese
- 3/4 cup chopped tomatoes
- 3/4 cup chopped green onions
- 1 cup pineapple chunks, drained
- 1/2 cup unsweetened flaked coconut
- 1 cup chow mein noodles

Direction

- Place rice and water into a saucepan, and bring to a boil. Reduce heat to low, cover, and simmer for 20 minutes, or until rice is tender. Set aside.
- Meanwhile, place the chicken breasts into a saucepan with enough water to cover. Bring to

a boil, and cook until tender, 20 to 30 minutes. Remove from the water, reserving liquid, and shred.
- Return the shredded chicken to the saucepan, and stir in soup. Stir in about 1 cup of the reserved water, or until the sauce reaches your desired consistency. Simmer for 15 minutes.
- To serve, place one cup of cooked rice onto a plate, spoon some of the chicken mixture over it, then top with small amounts of Cheddar cheese, tomatoes, green onions, pineapple chunks, coconut and chow mein noodles until you have a happy mountain. Now grab a fork and ENJOY!

Nutrition Information

- Calories: 866 calories
- Total Fat: 25.5 g
- Cholesterol: 125 mg
- Sodium: 780 mg
- Total Carbohydrate: 103.8 g
- Protein: 52.8 g

34. Hawaiian Haystacks

"Rice topped with creamy sauce, lots of veggies, and crunchy noodles make this a quick and easy bust still great anytime meal!"

Serving: 4 | Prep: 20 m | Cook: 20 m | Ready in: 40 m

Ingredients

- 1 tablespoon olive oil
- 4 skinless, boneless chicken breast halves, cut into small cubes
- 1/2 cup chicken broth
- 1 (10.75 ounce) can cream of mushroom soup
- 1 teaspoon dried basil
- 1 teaspoon dried parsley
- 4 cups cooked rice
- 1 cup chopped pineapple
- 1 cup chopped green bell pepper
- 1 cup shredded Cheddar cheese
- 1 cup chopped fresh tomatoes
- 1 cup chow mein noodles
- 1/2 cup toasted sliced almonds
- 1/2 cup chopped green onions
- 1/2 cup shredded coconut

Direction

- Heat olive oil in a skillet over medium heat; cook and stir chicken in the hot oil until no longer pink in the center, 5 to 7 minutes. Add chicken broth; simmer until slightly reduced, about 5 minutes. Mix cream of mushroom soup, basil, and parsley into chicken mixture until smooth; cook until warmed, about 5 minutes. Transfer chicken sauce to a small bowl.
- Spread cooked rice onto a serving platter; top with chicken sauce. Layer pineapple, green bell pepper, Cheddar cheese, tomatoes, chow mein noodles, almonds, green onions, and coconut, respectively, onto chicken sauce.

Nutrition Information

- Calories: 799 calories
- Total Fat: 32.3 g
- Cholesterol: 89 mg
- Sodium: 918 mg
- Total Carbohydrate: 87.2 g
- Protein: 39.8 g

35. Haystacks II

"These cookies are absolutely delicious."

Serving: 24

Ingredients

- 2 cups semisweet chocolate chips
- 2 cups butterscotch chips
- 12 ounces peanuts
- 5 (5 ounce) cans chow mein noodles

Direction

- Melt the chips in a saucepan on low heat. Stir in the nuts and the noodles.
- Then drop by teaspoonfuls onto waxed paper-lined cookie sheet. Cool and then store covered in the refrigerator.

Nutrition Information

- Calories: 385 calories
- Total Fat: 24.3 g
- Cholesterol: 0 mg
- Sodium: 146 mg
- Total Carbohydrate: 37.8 g
- Protein: 6.4 g

36. Haystacks IV

"Easy no bake treats made from marshmallows, butterscotch chips and chow mein noodles."

Serving: 60 | Prep: 15 m | Cook: 5 m | Ready in: 1 h

Ingredients

- 2 cups butterscotch chips
- 1 cup peanut butter
- 2 (5 ounce) cans chow mein noodles
- 4 cups miniature marshmallows

Direction

- In the microwave or over a double boiler, melt butterscotch chips and peanut butter, stirring frequently until smooth. Stir in chow mein noodles and marshmallows to blend well. Drop by heaping teaspoonfuls onto waxed paper and chill until set.

Nutrition Information

- Calories: 94 calories
- Total Fat: 5.2 g
- Cholesterol: 0 mg
- Sodium: 50 mg
- Total Carbohydrate: 9.9 g
- Protein: 1.5 g

37. Imperial Vegetables and Noodles

"Takeout-worthy stir-fry is only minutes from the table with Asian-inspired vegetables and Veggie Chick'n Tenders."

Serving: 4 | Prep: 15 m | Cook: 5 m | Ready in: 20 m

Ingredients

- 1 (500 gram) package Europe's Best® Imperial Blend vegetables
- 1 (12 ounce) package Cantonese-style steamed chow mein noodles
- 1 1/2 cups Imagine® Organic Vegetable Broth
- 2 tablespoons naturally brewed soy sauce
- 2 tablespoons cornstarch
- 1 1/2 teaspoons sesame oil
- 1 tablespoon Spectrum Naturals® Canola Oil
- 1 (170 gram) package Yves Veggie Cuisine® Chick'n or Beef Veggie Tenders
- 1 tablespoon grated fresh ginger
- 1 teaspoon minced garlic
- 1/4 cup chopped green onion

Direction

- Thaw vegetables; drain well. Set aside.
- Prepare noodles according to package directions. Set aside and keep hot.
- Prepare sauce: In a small bowl, mix together broth and soy sauce. Whisk in cornstarch. Stir in sesame oil. Set aside.
- In a large non-stick skillet over medium-high heat, heat oil. Add veggie chick'n tenders, ginger and garlic; stir-fry for 1 minute. Add vegetables; stir-fry for 2 minutes. Stir in sauce; reduce heat and simmer for about 2 minutes, until thickened.
- Pour vegetable mixture over noodles. Top with green onion. Grab your chopsticks and dig in!

Nutrition Information

- Calories: 454 calories
- Total Fat: 8.9 g
- Cholesterol: 0 mg
- Sodium: 1408 mg
- Total Carbohydrate: 67.7 g
- Protein: 23.6 g

38. Jelly Bean Nests

"Crunchy Chinese noodles and melted marshmallows make the cutest little nests for your jelly beans. Great as place markers at Easter dinner."

Serving: 12 | Prep: 25 m | Cook: 5 m | Ready in: 30 m

Ingredients

- 2 cups miniature marshmallows
- 1/4 cup butter
- 4 cups chow mein noodles

Direction

- Butter a 12 cup muffin tin.
- Combine marshmallows and butter over medium heat in a saucepan; stir until the butter and marshmallows have melted. Stir in the chow mein noodles, coat well. Butter fingers and press the mixture into the bottom and sides of the prepared muffin tin. Refrigerate until firm.

Nutrition Information

- Calories: 143 calories
- Total Fat: 8.4 g
- Cholesterol: 10 mg
- Sodium: 104 mg
- Total Carbohydrate: 15.5 g
- Protein: 1.3 g

39. Orange Chicken Stir Fry

"Chicken breast meat stir fried with orange juice and zest, soy sauce, garlic and brown sugar, topped with bean sprouts and served over crispy chow mein noodles. A healthy, zesty stir fry treat guaranteed to excite the most finicky eaters!"

Serving: 4 | Prep: 10 m | Cook: 35 m | Ready in: 45 m

Ingredients

- 1 cup orange juice
- 1 tablespoon grated orange zest
- 1/4 cup soy sauce
- 1 teaspoon salt
- 3 cloves garlic, chopped
- 1 tablespoon brown sugar
- 3 tablespoons vegetable oil
- 4 skinless, boneless chicken breast halves - cut into 1 inch cubes
- 2 tablespoons all-purpose flour
- 1 cup bean sprouts (optional)
- 1 (6 ounce) package crispy chow mein noodles

Direction

- In a small bowl combine the orange juice, orange zest, soy sauce, salt, garlic and brown sugar. Mix well.
- Heat oil in a large skillet or wok over medium high heat. When oil begins to bubble, add chicken. Sauté until cooked through (no longer pink inside), about 7 to 10 minutes.
- Add orange sauce mixture to chicken and cook until sauce begins to bubble. Add flour, a little bit at a time, until sauce has thickened to your liking. Add bean sprouts and cook for 1 minute; serve hot over chow mein noodles.

Nutrition Information

- Calories: 524 calories
- Total Fat: 25.1 g
- Cholesterol: 68 mg
- Sodium: 1749 mg
- Total Carbohydrate: 41.1 g
- Protein: 34.7 g

40. Peanut Butter Haystacks

"Delicious is all I can say."

Serving: 12

Ingredients

- 1 cup butterscotch chips
- 1/2 cup peanut butter
- 1/2 cup salted peanuts
- 2 cups chow mein noodles

Direction

- Melt butterscotch chips and peanut butter on top of a double boiler, or in a microwave. Blend together.
- Stir peanuts and noodles gently into the melted peanut butter mixture.
- Drop dough by forkfuls onto waxed paper. Cool until set.

Nutrition Information

- Calories: 219 calories
- Total Fat: 14.8 g
- Cholesterol: 0 mg
- Sodium: 147 mg
- Total Carbohydrate: 16.8 g
- Protein: 4.8 g

41. Quick Hawaiian Haystacks

"Yummy, easy-to-make meal that can feed the masses. This recipe can be modified in so many fun, different ways. If you have ideas on how to mix it up, please comment below. I'd love to try your add-ins! Add more toppings to suit your taste."

Serving: 8 | Prep: 20 m | Cook: 5 m | Ready in: 25 m

Ingredients

- 2 (10.5 ounce) cans cream of chicken soup
- 3 cooked chicken breasts, cut into bite-sized pieces
- 1/2 cup milk, or more as needed
- 4 cups cooked rice
- 1 (5 ounce) can chow mein noodles
- 1 (8 ounce) can pineapple tidbits, drained
- 1 cup shredded Cheddar cheese
- 3 stalks celery, chopped
- 2 green bell peppers, chopped
- 3 green onions, chopped
- 1/2 cup flaked coconut
- 1/2 cup slivered almonds
- 1 teaspoon soy sauce, or to taste

Direction

- Mix chicken soup and chicken together in a saucepan; stir in enough milk to make a gravy-like consistency. Cook and stir chicken sauce over medium heat until smooth and heated through, 5 to 10 minutes.
- Spoon 1/2 cup rice onto 8 plates. Layer each serving of rice with chow mein noodles, the chicken mixture, pineapple, Cheddar cheese, celery, green peppers, green onions, coconut, almonds, and a drizzle of soy sauce, respectively.

Nutrition Information

- Calories: 512 calories
- Total Fat: 23.3 g
- Cholesterol: 49 mg
- Sodium: 789 mg
- Total Carbohydrate: 52.8 g
- Protein: 23 g

42. Rocky Road Drops

"These are wonderful to give to friends as gifts. We make them every year at Christmas. You can change quantities and ingredients as needed."

Serving: 24

Ingredients

- 1 (12 ounce) package semisweet chocolate chips

- 2 cups butterscotch chips
- 2 cups raisins
- 2 cups peanuts
- 2 cups miniature marshmallows
- 4 cups chow mein noodles

Direction

- In the top of a double boiler, melt the chocolate and butterscotch chips.
- In a large bowl, combine the raisins, peanuts, marshmallows and chow mein noodles. Add melted chocolate mixture and quickly mix well.
- Drop by tablespoons onto wax paper; allow to sit until hardened.

Nutrition Information

- Calories: 308 calories
- Total Fat: 16.7 g
- Cholesterol: 0 mg
- Sodium: 55 mg
- Total Carbohydrate: 37.8 g
- Protein: 4.5 g

43. Sashimi Tuna Salad With Mint Lime Cilantro Dressing

"The closest I've been able to come in recreating one of my favorites! The salad will be fairly greasy, but that is how it is in the restaurant version as well. It just doesn't taste nearly as good with only little dressing. I usually use about 3/4 of the dressing, but you may use less or more. Enjoy!"

Serving: 2 | Prep: 30 m | Cook: 5 m | Ready in: 1 h 35 m

Ingredients

- 2 tablespoons olive oil
- 1 1/2 teaspoons lime juice
- 1 1/2 teaspoons chopped fresh cilantro
- 1/2 teaspoon garlic, minced
- 1 teaspoon chopped fresh mint
- 1/2 teaspoon lemon juice
- 1/8 teaspoon salt
- 1 1/2 cups mixed baby salad greens
- 1/2 cup torn romaine lettuce
- 2 tablespoons diced mango
- 1 1/2 teaspoons roasted peanuts
- 4 slices cucumber, quartered
- 2 tablespoons crisp chow mein noodles
- 1 (3 ounce) fresh ahi (yellowfin) tuna steak
- 1 pinch salt and ground black pepper to taste
- 1/4 avocado, sliced

Direction

- Whisk olive oil, lime juice, cilantro, garlic, mint, lemon juice, and salt in a bowl. Refrigerate salad dressing for at least 1 hour or overnight for best flavor.
- Preheat an outdoor grill for high heat and grease the grate.
- Toss salad greens, romaine lettuce, mango, peanuts, cucumber, and chow mein noodles in a salad bowl.
- Sprinkle tuna with salt and black pepper.
- Grill tuna on the preheated grill until the outside is seared and brown and the inside is still red, about 1 1/2 minutes per side for rare. Slice the grilled tuna.
- Top salad with slices of avocado and grilled tuna; drizzle with salad dressing to taste.

Nutrition Information

- Calories: 252 calories
- Total Fat: 19.3 g
- Cholesterol: 19 mg
- Sodium: 207 mg
- Total Carbohydrate: 9.3 g
- Protein: 12.4 g

44. Shrimp Chinese Chow Mein

"Shrimp, red pepper, green pepper, celery and onion in mushroom soup, served over chow mein noodles."

Serving: 6 | Prep: 15 m | Cook: 10 m | Ready in: 25 m

Ingredients

- 2 cups chopped celery
- 1 onion, diced
- 1 red bell pepper, sliced
- 1 pound fresh shrimp, peeled and deveined
- 1 (15 ounce) can mixed vegetables, drained
- 1 (10.75 ounce) can condensed cream of mushroom soup
- 1/4 cup soy sauce
- 1/2 cup green bell pepper, chopped
- 4 cups chow mein noodles

Direction

- In a large saucepan, combine celery, onions, red pepper, and shrimp. Cook over medium heat until shrimp are pink.
- Mix in canned vegetables and mushroom soup, soy sauce, and green pepper.
- Heat thoroughly. Serve over chow mein noodles.

Nutrition Information

- Calories: 335 calories
- Total Fat: 13.9 g
- Cholesterol: 115 mg
- Sodium: 1365 mg
- Total Carbohydrate: 31.9 g
- Protein: 21.2 g

45. Snow on the Mountain II

"A delicious buffet meal!"

Serving: 8 | Prep: 30 m | Cook: 10 m | Ready in: 40 m

Ingredients

- 2 cups uncooked long-grain rice
- 2 (10.75 ounce) cans condensed cream of chicken soup
- 3 cups chicken broth
- 2 (5 ounce) cans chow mein noodles
- 3 tomatoes, sliced
- 1 cup chopped celery
- 1/2 cup chopped green bell pepper
- 1/2 cup chopped green onions
- 1 (20 ounce) can pineapple chunks, drained
- 1 cup shredded Cheddar cheese
- 1/2 cup slivered almonds
- 1/2 cup shredded coconut
- 1/2 (4 ounce) jar diced pimento peppers, drained

Direction

- In a saucepan bring 4 cups water to a boil. Add rice and stir. Reduce heat, cover and simmer for 20 minutes.
- In a medium saucepan over medium heat, combine chicken soup and broth. Stir and simmer for 8 to 10 minutes, or until heated through.
- On 8 plates layer cooked rice, chow mein noodles, chicken soup mixture, tomatoes, celery, green pepper, green onion, pineapple, cheese and more chicken soup mixture. Top with almonds, coconut and pimentos.

Nutrition Information

- Calories: 626 calories
- Total Fat: 27.6 g
- Cholesterol: 21 mg
- Sodium: 762 mg
- Total Carbohydrate: 82.1 g
- Protein: 14.9 g

46. Spicy Beef and Broccoli Chow Mein

"I just mixed familiar Asian flavors together to make this oh-so-simple dish. Sometimes simplicity makes the best dishes. This is fast dinner to whip up any night to break the normal dish routine."

Serving: 2 | Prep: 10 m | Cook: 10 m | Ready in: 4 h 20 m

Ingredients

- 1/4 cup soy sauce
- 2 tablespoons oyster sauce
- 2 tablespoons hoisin sauce
- 1 tablespoon red wine vinegar
- 1 tablespoon sesame oil
- 1 tablespoon garlic powder
- 1 tablespoon honey
- 2 teaspoons chile sauce (optional)
- 1 teaspoon freshly ground black pepper
- 1/2 pound thinly-cut flat iron steaks
- 1 cup broccoli florets
- 6 ounces dried chow mein noodles
- 1 tablespoon olive oil, or more as needed
- 1/4 white onion, chopped
- 4 cloves garlic, minced, or more to taste

Direction

- Whisk soy sauce, oyster sauce, hoisin sauce, red wine vinegar, sesame oil, garlic powder, honey, chile sauce, and black pepper together in a bowl until marinade is smooth. Brush marinade onto steak strips and broccoli, reserving some for the noodles. Refrigerate for 4 hours to overnight.
- Bring a large pot of lightly salted water to a boil. Cook chow mein noodles in the boiling water, stirring occasionally until tender yet firm to the bite, about 3 minutes. Drain.
- Heat oil in a wok or deep skillet over medium heat; cook and stir onion for 3 minutes. Add garlic and beef-broccoli mixture; cook and stir until beef is cooked through, 1 to 2 minutes. Add noodles and reserved marinade; toss using tongs and cook until heated through, 1 to 2 minutes.

Nutrition Information

- Calories: 672 calories
- Total Fat: 29.9 g
- Cholesterol: 164 mg
- Sodium: 2885 mg
- Total Carbohydrate: 66.1 g
- Protein: 37.6 g

47. StirFried Shanghai Noodles

"Use the best, freshest ingredients you can find. This Shanghai noodle dish is a delicious combination of sweet, salty, spicy, and savory flavors."

Serving: 4 | Prep: 25 m | Cook: 25 m | Ready in: 50 m

Ingredients

- 1 (12 ounce) package fresh Chinese egg noodles
- 1 (8 ounce) package bean sprouts
- 2 tablespoons canola oil
- 1 chicken breast half, cut into matchstick-sized strips (optional)
- 2 stalks celery, cut into matchsticks
- 3 green onions, sliced into thin strips
- 2 cloves garlic, crushed
- 1 tablespoon XO sauce (optional)
- 4 ounces oyster mushrooms, cut into matchsticks
- 3 tablespoons mushroom-infused soy sauce
- 2 tablespoons oyster sauce
- 1 tablespoon brown sugar
- 1/2 cup unsalted chicken stock

Direction

- Bring a large pot of lightly salted water to a boil. Cook noodles in boiling water, stirring occasionally, until noodles just start to soften, 3 to 5 minutes. Drain.
- Fill a large bowl with ice and cold water. Bring a large pot of lightly salted water to a boil. Add bean sprouts and cook, uncovered, until stems start to become translucent, 2 to 3

minutes. Drain in a colander and immediately immerse in the ice water for several minutes to stop the cooking process. Drain.
- Heat oil in a wok over medium-high heat until starting to smoke. Add chicken, celery, green onions, garlic, and XO sauce. Stir-fry for 2 minutes. Add mushrooms and cook until slightly browned, 3 to 4 minutes. Add the cooked noodles, cooked bean sprouts, soy sauce, oyster sauce, and brown sugar. Cook for 3 to 5 minutes. Add chicken stock; reduce heat to low. Cover and simmer until noodles are tender yet firm to the bite, 2 to 3 minutes more.

Nutrition Information

- Calories: 432 calories
- Total Fat: 16.2 g
- Cholesterol: 69 mg
- Sodium: 1032 mg
- Total Carbohydrate: 53.3 g
- Protein: 21.3 g

48. Thai Peanut Chicken Lo Mein

"Kids love this, and we always get rave reviews and requests for the recipe. You can add additional vegetables as desired (broccoli, snow peas, etc.), though you may then need to increase the amount of peanut sauce if you add significant amounts of veggies."

Serving: 6 | Prep: 20 m | Cook: 25 m | Ready in: 45 m

Ingredients

- 7 ounces Chinese-style chow mein stir-fry noodles
- Peanut Sauce:
- 1/4 cup soy sauce
- 3 tablespoons creamy peanut butter
- 3 tablespoons vegetable oil
- 2 tablespoons white sugar
- 4 teaspoons rice wine vinegar
- 4 teaspoons sesame oil
- Stir-Fry:
- vegetable oil, divided
- 2 teaspoons sesame oil, divided
- 3 skinless, boneless chicken breast halves, cut into cubes
- 1 tablespoon minced garlic
- 1 tablespoon minced fresh ginger root
- 2 cups thinly sliced cremini mushrooms
- 2 cups bean sprouts
- 1/2 cup chopped green onion
- 1/4 cup chopped cilantro

Direction

- Bring 2 quarts lightly salted water to a boil. Cook chow mein in the boiling water, stirring occasionally, until cooked through but firm to the bite, about 12 minutes; drain.
- Whisk soy sauce, peanut butter, 4 teaspoons vegetable oil, sugar, vinegar, and 4 teaspoons sesame oil together in a bowl until smooth.
- Heat 2 teaspoons vegetable oil and 1 teaspoon sesame oil in a large skillet over medium-high heat. Sauté chicken, garlic, and ginger in hot oil until chicken is no longer pink in the center, 5 to 10 minutes. Remove chicken mixture with a slotted spoon to a bowl, retaining drippings in the skillet.
- Heat an additional 1 tablespoon vegetable oil and 1 teaspoon sesame oil in the skillet with the drippings; sauté mushrooms until fragrant, 15 to 30 seconds.
- Return the chicken to the skillet; add drained chow mein noodles, bean sprouts, and green onion. Toss mixture to distribute chicken and vegetables throughout the noodles. Drizzle peanut sauce over the noodles and toss to coat; cook until sauce is warmed, about 1 minute. Remove skillet from heat and garnish with cilantro.

Nutrition Information

- Calories: 463 calories
- Total Fat: 28.5 g
- Cholesterol: 35 mg
- Sodium: 929 mg
- Total Carbohydrate: 30.3 g
- Protein: 23 g

49. Tuna Cashew Casserole

"This is a tasty, fast, and easy casserole that every member of the family will love. My mom used to make this for us when we were kids."

Serving: 4 | Prep: 10 m | Cook: 30 m | Ready in: 40 m

Ingredients

- 1 (3 ounce) can chow mein noodles
- 1 (5 ounce) can chunk light tuna in water, drained
- 1 cup roasted salted cashews
- 1 cup diced celery
- 1 (10.75 ounce) can condensed cream of mushroom soup
- 1/4 cup water

Direction

- Preheat an oven to 375 degrees F (190 degrees C).
- Measure 1/2 cup of the chow mein noodles and set aside. Combine the remaining noodles, tuna, cashews, celery mushroom soup, and water in a 1 1/2 quart baking dish. Top with the 1/2 cup of noodles you set aside.
- Bake in the preheated oven until heated through, about 30 minutes.

Nutrition Information

- Calories: 408 calories
- Total Fat: 25.3 g
- Cholesterol: 9 mg
- Sodium: 908 mg
- Total Carbohydrate: 30 g
- Protein: 18.1 g

50. Twig Salad

"I got this recipe from a very dear friend who got it from a co-worker. We tried it and people just go crazy. It's especially great for parties and family get-togethers."

Serving: 6 | Prep: 20 m | Cook: 5 m | Ready in: 25 m

Ingredients

- 1/2 cup vegetable oil
- 1/4 cup white sugar
- 1/4 cup white vinegar
- 1/2 teaspoon salt
- 1 teaspoon salt-free herb and spice blend
- 1/4 teaspoon ground black pepper
- 1 1/2 heads iceberg lettuce, torn into bite-sized pieces
- 1 pound chopped cooked chicken breast meat
- 1 (5 ounce) can chow mein noodles
- 1 (2.25 ounce) package blanched slivered almonds
- 1/4 cup sesame seeds, lightly toasted
- 4 green onions, chopped
- 2 teaspoons poppy seeds

Direction

- In small bowl, whisk together the oil, sugar, vinegar, salt, seasoning blend, and pepper. Set aside.
- In a large bowl, combine the lettuce, chicken, chow mein noodles, almonds, sesame seeds, green onions, and poppy seeds. Toss to blend. Pour salad dressing over the salad just before serving.

Nutrition Information

- Calories: 574 calories
- Total Fat: 37.8 g
- Cholesterol: 57 mg
- Sodium: 432 mg
- Total Carbohydrate: 31 g
- Protein: 29.3 g

51. Vegetable Lo Mein Delight

"A great meal with celery, mushrooms, red bell peppers, onion, and much more."

Serving: 4 | Prep: 15 m | Cook: 15 m | Ready in: 30 m

Ingredients

- 8 ounces angel hair pasta
- 3/4 cup chicken broth
- 1/4 cup soy sauce
- 1 tablespoon cornstarch
- 2 tablespoons canola oil
- 1 3/4 cups chopped celery
- 1 3/4 cups sliced fresh mushrooms
- 1 3/4 cups sliced red bell peppers
- 1/2 cup sliced onion
- 2 cups bean sprouts
- 2 cups snow peas
- 1 cup chow mein noodles

Direction

- Bring a pot of lightly salted water to a boil. Add angel hair pasta and cook for 3 to 5 minutes or until al dente; drain.
- In a small bowl, whisk together the chicken broth, soy sauce, and cornstarch.
- Heat the oil in a wok over medium-high heat. Stir in the celery, mushrooms, peppers, and onion, and cook about 3 minutes. Add the broth mixture, bean sprouts, and snow peas. Continue to cook and stir about 5 minutes, until vegetables are tender but crisp.
- In a large bowl, toss together the cooked pasta and the vegetable mixture. Top with chow mein noodles to serve.

Nutrition Information

- Calories: 397 calories
- Total Fat: 12.6 g
- Cholesterol: 0 mg
- Sodium: 1115 mg
- Total Carbohydrate: 61.6 g
- Protein: 14.6 g

52. Yummy Bok Choy Salad

"This is hands down the best salad that I've ever had. It is definitely a family favourite, and I urge you to just give this one a try. You would think that raw baby bok choy would give this salad a bitter taste, but the dressing makes all the difference."

Serving: 4 | Prep: 20 m | Ready in: 20 m

Ingredients

- 1/2 cup olive oil
- 1/4 cup white vinegar
- 1/3 cup white sugar
- 3 tablespoons soy sauce
- 2 bunches baby bok choy, cleaned and sliced
- 1 bunch green onions, chopped
- 1/8 cup slivered almonds, toasted
- 1/2 (6 ounce) package chow mein noodles

Direction

- In a glass jar with a lid, mix together olive oil, white vinegar, sugar, and soy sauce. Close the lid, and shake until well mixed.
- Combine the bok choy, green onions, almonds, and chow mein noodles in a salad bowl. Toss with dressing, and serve.

Nutrition Information

- Calories: 458 calories
- Total Fat: 33.5 g
- Cholesterol: 0 mg
- Sodium: 868 mg
- Total Carbohydrate: 35.9 g
- Protein: 6.4 g

Chapter 2: Egg Noodles

***

53. A1 Chicken Soup

"A quick and easy chicken soup recipe for hurried cooks. Use any favorite veggies!"

Serving: 16 | Prep: 15 m | Cook: 1 h 45 m | Ready in: 2 h

Ingredients

- 2 tablespoons vegetable oil
- 2 skinless chicken leg quarters
- 1/2 cup chopped onion
- 2 quarts water
- 3 cubes chicken bouillon, crumbled
- 1 stalk celery, chopped
- 3 carrots, chopped
- 1 clove roasted garlic, minced
- salt and pepper to taste
- 1 (12 ounce) package thin egg noodles

Direction

- In a large pot over medium heat, cook chicken pieces in oil until browned on both sides. Stir in onion and cook 2 minutes more. Pour in water and chicken bouillon and bring to a boil. Reduce heat and simmer 45 minutes.
- Stir in celery, carrots, garlic, salt and pepper. Simmer until carrots are just tender. Remove chicken pieces and pull the meat from the bone. Stir the noodles into the pot and cook until tender, 10 minutes. Return chicken meat to pot just before serving.

Nutrition Information

- Calories: 119 calories
- Total Fat: 3.9 g
- Cholesterol: 26 mg
- Sodium: 241 mg
- Total Carbohydrate: 15.1 g
- Protein: 5.8 g

54. Amish Casserole

"A satisfyingly rich and hearty casserole from the Pennsylvania Dutch country."

Serving: 6 | Prep: 20 m | Cook: 35 m | Ready in: 55 m

Ingredients

- 1 pound ground beef
- 1 (10.75 ounce) can condensed tomato soup
- 1/4 cup brown sugar
- 1/8 teaspoon black pepper
- 1/4 teaspoon salt
- 1 (10.75 ounce) can condensed cream of chicken soup
- 1 (12 ounce) package wide egg noodles
- 10 slices American cheese

Direction

- Preheat the oven to 350 degrees F (175 degrees C).
- Bring a large pot of lightly salted water to a boil. Add egg noodles and cook until tender, about 7 minutes. Drain and return to the pan. Mix in the cream of chicken soup until noodles are coated.
- Crumble the ground beef into a large skillet over medium-high heat. Drain the grease, and stir in the tomato soup, brown sugar, pepper and salt. Spread half of the beef in the bottom of a greased 2 1/2 quart casserole dish. Arrange 5 slices of cheese over the beef. Top with half of the noodles, then repeat layers ending with cheese on top.
- Bake for 35 minutes in the preheated oven, until cheese is browned and sauce is bubbly.

Nutrition Information

- Calories: 630 calories
- Total Fat: 29.8 g
- Cholesterol: 141 mg
- Sodium: 1472 mg
- Total Carbohydrate: 57 g
- Protein: 33.1 g

55. Annas Amazing Easy Pleasy Meatballs over Buttered Noodles

"My friend Anna makes the most amazing and easy meatballs with gravy! Prepared in a slow cooker, this recipe couldn't be any easier! Serve over buttery hot cooked noodles and you'll have a happy crowd! Mangia!"

Serving: 24 | Prep: 15 m | Cook: 3 h | Ready in: 3 h 15 m

Ingredients

- 2 (10.75 ounce) cans condensed cream of celery soup
- 2 (10.5 ounce) cans condensed French onion soup
- 1 (16 ounce) container sour cream
- 6 pounds frozen Italian-style meatballs
- 2 (16 ounce) packages uncooked egg noodles
- 1/2 cup butter

Direction

- In a large slow cooker, mix together the cream of celery soup, French onion soup, and sour cream. Stir in the meatballs. Cook on high heat for 3-4 hours.
- Bring a large pot of lightly salted water to a boil. Add pasta and cook for 8 to 10 minutes or until al dente; drain. In a large bowl, toss the pasta with butter. Serve meatballs and sauce over the cooked pasta.

Nutrition Information

- Calories: 492 calories
- Total Fat: 25.5 g
- Cholesterol: 148 mg
- Sodium: 591 mg
- Total Carbohydrate: 38.5 g
- Protein: 25.9 g

56. Applesauce Noodle Kugel

"Tender noodles are stirred with a comforting blend of margarine, sour cream, egg substitute, sugar, lemon juice, vanilla extract, chunky applesauce, and raisins. Bake over a light sprinkling of graham cracker crumbs and top with cinnamon for a sweet treat."

Serving: 12 | Prep: 20 m | Cook: 1 h 10 m | Ready in: 1 h 30 m

Ingredients

- 1 (16 ounce) package wide egg noodles
- 1 cup reduced fat margarine
- 1/2 cup fat free sour cream
- 1 1/2 cups egg substitute
- 2 cups white sugar
- 1 teaspoon lemon juice
- 1 teaspoon vanilla extract
- 1/2 (16 ounce) jar applesauce
- 1/4 cup raisins
- 1/4 cup graham cracker crumbs (optional)
- 1 teaspoon ground cinnamon, or to taste

Direction

- Preheat oven to 350 degrees F (175 degrees C). Coat a 9x13 inch baking dish with cooking spray. Bring a large pot of lightly salted water to a boil. Cook noodles in boiling water for 8 to 10 minutes, or until al dente. Drain.
- In a large bowl, mix together margarine, sour cream, egg substitute, sugar, lemon juice, vanilla extract, and applesauce. Stir in noodles and raisins.
- Spread graham cracker crumbs on the bottom of the prepared dish. Pour the noodle mixture over the crumbs. Sprinkle top with cinnamon.
- Bake 45 to 60 minutes in the preheated oven, or until set. Cover with foil if it browns too quickly.

Nutrition Information

- Calories: 389 calories
- Total Fat: 9.8 g
- Cholesterol: 29 mg
- Sodium: 254 mg
- Total Carbohydrate: 65.2 g
- Protein: 9 g

57. Apricot Noodle Kugel

"This is an old family recipe that I recently entered in the 2001 Ventura County Fair and won 'Honorable Mention' for in the Pudding Division. There was no category for Kugel, but the judges loved it and still wanted to honor me with a ribbon! Hope you enjoy it as well."

Serving: 12 | Prep: 25 m | Cook: 45 m | Ready in: 1 h 10 m

Ingredients

- 1 (8 ounce) package wide egg noodles
- 1/4 cup butter, softened
- 1 (3 ounce) package cream cheese, softened
- 3 eggs, beaten
- 1/2 cup white sugar
- 1 teaspoon vanilla extract
- 1 cup apricot nectar
- 1 cup milk
- 1/2 cup golden raisins (optional)
- 1 1/2 cups cornflake crumbs
- 1/2 cup butter, softened
- 1/4 cup white sugar
- 1 teaspoon vanilla extract
- 1 teaspoon ground cinnamon

Direction

- Preheat oven to 350 degrees F (175 degrees C). Lightly grease a 9x9 inch baking pan.
- Bring a large saucepan of lightly salted water to a boil. Stir in egg noodles, and cook for 8 to 10 minutes or until al dente; drain.
- In a medium bowl, thoroughly mix egg noodles with 1/4 cup butter, cream cheese, eggs, 1/2 cup sugar, and vanilla. Stir in apricot nectar and milk. Mix in raisins. Transfer to the prepared baking pan.
- In a separate medium bowl, mix cornflake crumbs, 1/2 cup butter, 1/4 cup sugar, remaining vanilla, and cinnamon. Spread over the egg noodle mixture.

- Bake 45 minutes in the preheated oven, until bubbly and lightly browned.

Nutrition Information

- Calories: 352 calories
- Total Fat: 16.5 g
- Cholesterol: 102 mg
- Sodium: 219 mg
- Total Carbohydrate: 46 g
- Protein: 6.6 g

58. Artichoke Piccata

"Curb that lemony piccata craving with this vegetarian comfort food."

Serving: 2 | Prep: 5 m | Cook: 20 m | Ready in: 25 m

Ingredients

- 2 cups egg noodles
- 2 tablespoons olive oil
- 2 cloves garlic, minced
- 1 tablespoon capers with juice
- 1 (14 ounce) can quartered artichoke hearts, drained
- lemon, juiced
- 1/4 teaspoon freshly ground black pepper
- 1/3 cup Pinot Grigio wine
- 2 tablespoons butter

Direction

- Bring a pot of water to a boil. Cook egg noodles in the boiling water, stirring occasionally until tender yet firm to the bite, about 6 minutes. Drain, reserving 1/2 cup cooking water.
- Heat olive oil in a 10-inch skillet. Add garlic and capers; cook and stir until fragrant, about 1 minute. Stir in artichoke hearts, lemon juice, and pepper; cook until lemon juice evaporates, about 2 minutes.
- Pour wine into the skillet; cook until evaporated, about 3 minutes. Add butter and noodles; toss to combine. Stir in reserved cooking water; cook until sauce coats noodles, about 3 minutes.

Nutrition Information

- Calories: 482 calories
- Total Fat: 26.9 g
- Cholesterol: 62 mg
- Sodium: 950 mg
- Total Carbohydrate: 48.2 g
- Protein: 10.8 g

59. AsianInspired Vegetable Noodle Bowl

"Delicious, nutritious vegetarian noodle bowl. Lots of color and flavor. You can find the green soybeans in the freezer department of your grocery store."

Serving: 4 | Prep: 20 m | Cook: 15 m | Ready in: 35 m

Ingredients

- 1 (8 ounce) package egg noodles
- 3 1/2 cups vegetable stock
- 2 tablespoons soy sauce
- 1 tablespoon chopped fresh ginger
- 1 teaspoon Asian chile sauce
- 1 garlic clove, chopped
- 5 1/2 ounces frozen spinach, thawed
- 1 1/2 cups frozen green soybeans, thawed
- 1 red bell pepper, sliced

Direction

- Bring a large pot of water to a boil. Add noodles; cook until tender yet still firm to the bite, 1 to 2 minutes. Drain and divide among 4 large soup bowls.
- Combine vegetable stock, soy sauce, ginger, chile sauce, and garlic in a saucepan over medium heat; bring to a gentle simmer. Simmer until fragrant, about 5 minutes.
- Squeeze spinach to drain out excess moisture; coarsely chop. Add to stock with soybeans and

red bell pepper; cook until heated through, about 1 minute. Ladle over noodles.

Nutrition Information

- Calories: 410 calories
- Total Fat: 9.8 g
- Cholesterol: 47 mg
- Sodium: 910 mg
- Total Carbohydrate: 59.5 g
- Protein: 23.5 g

60. Asparagus and Ham Mac and Cheese

"This Italian-style mac and cheese is enhanced with asparagus and cooked ham."

Serving: 6 | Prep: 20 m | Cook: 50 m | Ready in: 1 h 20 m

Ingredients

- 1 stick butter
- 1 pound fresh asparagus, trimmed and cut into 1-inch pieces
- 12 ounces wide egg noodles
- 3 cups whole milk
- 1 egg
- 2 tablespoons all-purpose flour
- 1/4 teaspoon freshly ground black pepper
- 3 cups shredded Italian cheese blend, divided
- 3/4 cup finely grated Parmesan cheese, divided
- 4 ounces cooked ham, diced (optional)
- 2/3 cup Italian-seasoned bread crumbs
- 1/4 cup butter, melted

Direction

- Preheat oven to 350 degrees F (175 degrees C). Butter a 9x13-inch baking dish with 1 teaspoon butter.
- Bring a large pot of salted water to a boil; cook asparagus until tender yet firm to the bite, 2 to 3 minutes. Remove asparagus from the pot, reserving the water.
- Cook noodles in the reserved water from asparagus until tender yet firm to the bite, 6 to 8 minutes. Drain.
- Whisk milk, egg, flour, and pepper together in a bowl; stir in 2 cups Italian cheese blend and 1/2 cup Parmesan cheese, ham, and asparagus. Add noodles and toss to coat; transfer to the prepared baking dish.
- Mix bread crumbs and melted butter together in a bowl; add remaining Italian cheese blend and Parmesan cheese. Sprinkle bread crumb mixture over noodle mixture.
- Bake in the preheated oven until bubbling and top is lightly browned, 35 minutes. Let stand for 10 minutes before serving.

Nutrition Information

- Calories: 866 calories
- Total Fat: 53 g
- Cholesterol: 215 mg
- Sodium: 1310 mg
- Total Carbohydrate: 62 g
- Protein: 37.5 g

61. Awesome Chicken Noodle Soup

"Home style chicken noodle soup that really makes a wonderful side or meal, it cures what ails you. If you like lots of noodles use a whole pound of them. Serve hot with your favorite salad and bread. This freezes or doubles well."

Serving: 12 | Prep: 20 m | Cook: 2 h | Ready in: 2 h 20 m

Ingredients

- 1 gallon water
- 1 (4 pound) whole chicken, cut into pieces
- 1 large onion, peeled and halved
- 3 bay leaves
- 10 whole black peppercorns
- 2/3 bunch celery, leaves reserved
- 1 pound whole carrots
- 3 tablespoons chopped lemon grass (optional)
- 1/4 cup chicken bouillon powder
- 1 pound carrots, peeled and sliced

- 1/3 bunch celery, chopped and leaves reserved
- 1 (8 ounce) package dry egg noodles

Direction

- Place chicken and water in a large pot over high heat and bring to a boil. Reduce heat, cover and simmer, skimming fat as needed, 30 minutes.
- Place the halved onion, bay leaves, peppercorns, whole celery, whole carrots and lemon grass in the pot and simmer, covered 1 hour.
- Strain broth and reserve chicken. When chicken is cool enough to handle, remove skin and cut meat into bite-size pieces.
- Return strained stock to pot over high heat, and stir in chicken base, chopped celery and chopped carrots. Bring to a boil, then reduce heat, cover and simmer 20 minutes, or until carrots are tender.
- Chop celery leaves and stir into pot with the noodles. Simmer until noodles are cooked, about 10 minutes more. Stir in chicken and heat through.

Nutrition Information

- Calories: 303 calories
- Total Fat: 12.3 g
- Cholesterol: 81 mg
- Sodium: 864 mg
- Total Carbohydrate: 22.4 g
- Protein: 25.1 g

62. Beef and Mushroom Stroganoff Aussie Style

"Tasty beef and mushroom stroganoff. This was my favorite recipe as a kid, my Mum came up with it from the stuff that was left in the cupboard! I've since modified the ingredients to add my own personal touch."

Serving: 4 | Prep: 15 m | Cook: 45 m | Ready in: 1 h

Ingredients

- 1 tablespoon butter
- 1 onion, chopped
- 1 teaspoon minced garlic
- 8 fresh mushrooms, sliced
- 2 teaspoons curry powder
- 1 pound beef top sirloin, thinly sliced
- 2 cubes beef bouillon
- 1 1/2 cups boiling water
- 1 (6 ounce) can mushroom stems and pieces, drained
- 1/4 cup dried shiitake mushrooms
- 1 1/4 cups heavy cream
- 1 (8 ounce) package uncooked egg noodles

Direction

- Melt the butter in a large skillet over medium heat. Add the onion and garlic, and fresh mushrooms; cook until the onions are translucent. Stir in curry powder until well blended. Place the meat strips in the skillet, and fry until evenly browned.
- Dissolve the bouillon cubes in the boiling water, then stir into the skillet. Add the mushroom stems and pieces and dried shiitake mushrooms. Let the mixture simmer over medium heat until most of the liquid has evaporated, about 20 minutes.
- Meanwhile, bring a large pot of lightly salted water to a boil. Add the noodles and cook until tender, about 7 minutes. Drain.
- Reduce the heat under the skillet to low, and pour in the cream, stirring until the sauce is an even color. Simmer for about 5 minutes, but do not boil. Serve over noodles.

Nutrition Information

- Calories: 734 calories
- Total Fat: 43.8 g
- Cholesterol: 217 mg
- Sodium: 718 mg
- Total Carbohydrate: 55.8 g
- Protein: 31.7 g

63. Beef and Noodle Casserole

"This is a great recipe for busy mothers, and it's excellent with a tossed salad and French bread. It's a ground beef casserole that combines egg noodles, some sherry, and cheese in a tomato sauce base. To reduce the fat content, you may use reduced fat cheese, cut green beans, and 93% lean meat. Also, you may adjust the amount of sherry to taste."

Serving: 4 | Prep: 30 m | Cook: 30 m | Ready in: 1 h

Ingredients

- 6 ounces egg noodles
- 1 pound ground beef
- 2 (10.75 ounce) cans condensed tomato soup
- 2 tablespoons Worcestershire sauce
- 2 cloves garlic, minced
- 1/2 pound shredded Cheddar cheese
- 1/4 cup dry sherry
- 1/4 cup grated Parmesan cheese

Direction

- Preheat oven to 375 degrees F (190 degrees C).
- Cook the noodles according to package directions.
- Brown the ground beef in a large skillet over medium high heat. Stir in the tomato soup, Worcestershire sauce and garlic, bring to a boil, reduce heat to low and let simmer.
- When noodles are done, stir them and the cheese into the simmering sauce until cheese is melted. Stir the sherry into the sauce and stir for 1 minute, then place in a 2 quart casserole dish and sprinkle with the Parmesan cheese to taste.
- Bake in preheated oven for 30 minutes.

Nutrition Information

- Calories: 745 calories
- Total Fat: 38.1 g
- Cholesterol: 169 mg
- Sodium: 1540 mg
- Total Carbohydrate: 55.5 g
- Protein: 44.1 g

64. Beef and Noodles

"The best beef and egg noodles you'll ever have. Affordable, quick, and yummy! I have to give credit to my grandma. She used to cook this for her 5 kids and then later for all her grandkids."

Serving: 4 | Prep: 20 m | Cook: 1 h 10 m | Ready in: 1 h 30 m

Ingredients

- 1 pound sirloin steak, cut into 1-inch cubes
- 2 tablespoons butter
- 1 large onion, sliced
- 1 cup beef stock
- 2 bay leaves
- 1 pinch dried thyme
- salt and ground black pepper to taste
- 1 cup frozen peas
- 1 tablespoon cornstarch
- 4 cups egg noodles

Direction

- Heat a skillet over medium-high heat; cook steak, working in batches, until seared and browned on all sides, about 5 minutes. Transfer seared steak to a plate.
- Melt butter in the same skillet over medium heat and sauté onion until softened, 5 to 10 minutes. Add steak to onion and pour beef stock over steak; season with bay leaves, thyme, salt, and pepper. Bring to a boil, reduce heat to low, cover skillet with a lid, and simmer until steak is tender, 50 minutes to 1

hour 50 minutes. Stir peas and cornstarch into steak mixture; cook uncovered until liquid thickens, about 10 minutes.
- Bring a large pot of lightly salted water to a boil. Cook egg noodles in the boiling water, stirring occasionally until cooked through but firm to the bite, about 5 minutes; drain. Serve beef mixture over noodles.

Nutrition Information

- Calories: 402 calories
- Total Fat: 14.4 g
- Cholesterol: 96 mg
- Sodium: 156 mg
- Total Carbohydrate: 38.7 g
- Protein: 28.5 g

65. Beef Florentine

"This is a recipe my Mother made often. The teenagers around my house inhale it. I usually saute the onion in a little butter before adding it to the dish and I microwave the spinach."

Serving: 6 | Prep: 20 m | Cook: 25 m | Ready in: 45 m

Ingredients

- 2 cups medium egg noodles
- 1 1/2 pounds ground beef
- 2 cloves garlic, chopped
- 1 teaspoon dried oregano
- 1/2 teaspoon salt
- 1/4 teaspoon pepper
- 2 (8 ounce) cans tomato sauce
- 1/2 cup water
- 1 (10 ounce) package frozen chopped spinach, thawed and drained
- 1 (8 ounce) container cottage cheese
- 1/4 cup chopped onion
- 2 tablespoons grated Parmesan cheese
- 8 ounces shredded mozzarella cheese

Direction

- Bring a large pot of lightly salted water to a boil. Add pasta, and cook for 8 to 10 minutes or until al dente; drain.
- Preheat oven to 350 degrees F (175 degrees C).
- In a skillet over medium heat, brown the ground beef until evenly brown; drain excess fat. Season with oregano, salt and pepper. Stir in tomato sauce and water. Remove from heat, and stir in cooked noodles.
- In a medium bowl, combine spinach, cottage cheese, onion, and Parmesan cheese. Spread half of noodle mixture in a large casserole dish. Layer with all of spinach mixture, then cover with remaining noodle mixture.
- Bake in preheated oven for 15 minutes. Cover with mozzarella, and continue cooking 10 minutes, or until cheese is melted.

Nutrition Information

- Calories: 574 calories
- Total Fat: 39.4 g
- Cholesterol: 137 mg
- Sodium: 1110 mg
- Total Carbohydrate: 17.2 g
- Protein: 37.7 g

66. Beef Stroganoff in an Instant

"So fast, so few dishes, this Instant Pot® beef stroganoff tastes like you've been cooking all day! Also, there is something about dry vermouth that brings out the beef flavor, absolutely delicious. Garnish with parsley."

Serving: 8 | Prep: 15 m | Cook: 50 m | Ready in: 1 h 15 m

Ingredients

- 1 tablespoon extra-virgin olive oil
- 1 medium red onion, chopped
- 2 1/2 tablespoons Worcestershire sauce
- 3 cloves garlic, diced
- 1 teaspoon beef base (such as Better Than Bouillon®)

- 1 tablespoon ground black pepper, or to taste
- 1 teaspoon dried thyme
- 1 teaspoon salt
- 3/4 cup dry vermouth, divided
- 2 pounds New York strip steaks, cut into thin pieces
- 3 cups sliced mushrooms
- 2 cups beef broth, divided
- 1 (16 ounce) package wide egg noodles
- 2 tablespoons all-purpose flour
- 3/4 cup sour cream

Direction

- Turn on a multi-functional pressure cooker (such as Instant Pot(R)) and select Sauté function. Heat oil in the pot. Sauté onion until barely tender, about 3 minutes. Mix in Worcestershire sauce, garlic, beef base, pepper, thyme, and salt.
- Pour in 1/4 cup vermouth; deglaze the pot by scraping the bottom with a wooden spoon. Add steaks; sauté until browned, about 6 minutes. Turn off Sauté mode. Add remaining vermouth, mushrooms, and 1 1/2 cups beef broth. Mix together gently.
- Close and lock the lid. Select high pressure according to manufacturer's instructions; set timer for 10 minutes. Allow 10 to 15 minutes for pressure to build.
- Release pressure carefully using the quick-release method according to manufacturer's instructions, about 5 minutes. Unlock and remove the lid. Stir in noodles. Lock the lid and cook on high pressure until noodles are tender, about 3 minutes. Allow 5 to 10 minutes for pressure to build.
- Pour remaining 1/2 cup beef broth into a microwave-safe bowl. Microwave until hot, about 1 minute. Dissolve flour in the broth.
- Release pressure carefully using the quick-release method according to manufacturer's instructions, about 5 minutes. Open lid and stir in the beef broth mixture. Let thicken, 3 to 5 minutes. Stir again. Add sour cream; stir until completely combined.

Nutrition Information

- Calories: 521 calories
- Total Fat: 20.3 g
- Cholesterol: 116 mg
- Sodium: 659 mg
- Total Carbohydrate: 49.7 g
- Protein: 28.5 g

67. Best Beef Chow Mein

"From my experience many of the recipes I have found for chow mein and lo mein seem to be either dry or very bland. I have been working at this one and my family has decided that this is the one and I will never have to order out again."

Serving: 6 | Prep: 40 m | Cook: 20 m | Ready in: 1 h

Ingredients

- 6 cups water
- 14 ounces chow mein noodles (such as Golden Dragon®)
- 1 pound flank steak, cut into thin strips
- 6 tablespoons teriyaki sauce
- 1/4 cup soy sauce, divided
- 3 tablespoons cornstarch
- 6 cloves garlic, crushed, divided
- 1 cup water
- 1 (1.5 ounce) package chow mein sauce mix (such as Su Wong®)
- 2 tablespoons teriyaki glaze
- 1 tablespoon sriracha sauce, or more to taste
- 1/4 cup peanut oil, divided
- 1 onion, chopped
- 2 carrots, sliced
- 1 cup sliced fresh mushrooms
- 1 cup broccoli florets
- 2 stalks celery, sliced
- 8 ounces bean sprouts
- 12 fresh shrimp (optional)
- 1 1/2 cups chopped bok choy
- ground black pepper to taste

Direction

- Bring water to a boil in a large pot. Cook chow mein noodles until soft, 5 to 6 minutes. Drain and rinse with cool water.
- Mix flank steak, teriyaki sauce, 2 tablespoons soy sauce, cornstarch, and 2 cloves garlic together in a small bowl.
- Mix remaining 2 tablespoons soy sauce, 4 cloves garlic, 1 cup water, chow mein sauce mix, teriyaki glaze, and sriracha sauce in a separate bowl to make sauce.
- Preheat a wok over medium-high heat; add 2 tablespoons peanut oil. Add steak and onion; cook and stir until beef is brown and onion is translucent, about 3 minutes. Transfer to a plate.
- Pour remaining 2 tablespoons peanut oil into the wok. Add carrots, mushrooms, broccoli, and celery; cook and stir until browned, about 3 minutes.
- Return steak and onion mixture to the wok. Add noodles, sauce, bean sprouts, shrimp, bok choy; cook, stirring occasionally, until noodles are heated through and shrimp are opaque, about 4 minutes. Season with pepper.

Nutrition Information

- Calories: 500 calories
- Total Fat: 16.4 g
- Cholesterol: 54 mg
- Sodium: 1789 mg
- Total Carbohydrate: 69.9 g
- Protein: 24.8 g

68. Best Beef Stroganoff

"Thinly sliced beef in a rich creamy sour cream sauce. This recipe is how Count Stroganoff intended the dish to be made!"

Serving: 8 | Prep: 15 m | Cook: 30 m | Ready in: 45 m

Ingredients

- 1 (16 ounce) package egg noodles
- 2 tablespoons butter, softened
- 2 onions, finely chopped
- 2 cloves garlic, minced
- 1 (8 ounce) package fresh mushrooms, thinly sliced
- 1 pound beef loin steak, cut into thin strips
- 1 (14 ounce) can beef consomme
- 1/4 cup Burgundy wine (optional)
- 3 tablespoons lemon juice
- 2 tablespoons all-purpose flour
- 2 tablespoons cold water, or as needed
- 1 (8 ounce) container sour cream

Direction

- Bring a large pot of lightly salted water to a boil. Add noodles and cook 5 to 7 minutes or until al dente; drain.
- Melt butter in a large saucepan over medium-high heat. Stir in onions and garlic, and cook until slightly tender. Mix in mushrooms, and continue cooking 2 minutes. Place steak strips in saucepan and cook about 1 minute. Mix in consomme, Burgundy and lemon juice. Bring to a boil.
- In a small bowl, thoroughly blend flour with cold water until smooth. Reduce saucepan heat to low. While stirring constantly, slowly pour flour mixture into saucepan. Gradually return to boil while stirring rapidly, until sauce is thick and smooth. Cover saucepan and continue cooking 5 minutes, stirring occasionally. Remove from heat, let cool slightly and stir in sour cream. Serve over cooked egg noodles.

Nutrition Information

- Calories: 403 calories
- Total Fat: 17.2 g
- Cholesterol: 91 mg
- Sodium: 229 mg
- Total Carbohydrate: 42.4 g
- Protein: 18.6 g

69. Best Tuna Casserole

"This is a tuna casserole that even my picky family loves! The potato chips give the casserole a crunchy crust."

Serving: 6 | Prep: 15 m | Cook: 20 m | Ready in: 35 m

Ingredients

- 1 (12 ounce) package egg noodles
- 1/4 cup chopped onion
- 2 cups shredded Cheddar cheese
- 1 cup frozen green peas
- 2 (5 ounce) cans tuna, drained
- 2 (10.75 ounce) cans condensed cream of mushroom soup
- 1/2 (4.5 ounce) can sliced mushrooms
- 1 cup crushed potato chips

Direction

- Bring a large pot of lightly salted water to a boil. Cook pasta in boiling water for 8 to 10 minutes, or until al dente; drain.
- Preheat oven to 425 degrees F (220 degrees C).
- In a large bowl, thoroughly mix noodles, onion, 1 cup cheese, peas, tuna, soup and mushrooms. Transfer to a 9x13 inch baking dish, and top with potato chip crumbs and remaining 1 cup cheese.
- Bake for 15 to 20 minutes in the preheated oven, or until cheese is bubbly.

Nutrition Information

- Calories: 595 calories
- Total Fat: 26.1 g
- Cholesterol: 99 mg
- Sodium: 1061 mg
- Total Carbohydrate: 58.1 g
- Protein: 32.1 g

70. Broccoli Noodles and Cheese Casserole

"This is a quick and easy recipe if you are in a hurry -- just noodles, broccoli, cottage cheese and Cheddar. My daughter loves it. It's always a hit."

Serving: 8 | Cook: 30 m | Ready in: 30 m

Ingredients

- 1 (16 ounce) package egg noodles
- 1 head broccoli, cut into florets
- 2 cups cottage cheese
- 2 cups shredded Cheddar cheese

Direction

- Preheat oven to 350 degrees F (175 degrees C). Bring a large pot of lightly salted water to a boil. Add pasta and cook for 8 to 10 minutes or until al dente; drain.
- Steam broccoli until bright green and tender, 5 to 10 minutes. Combine broccoli, pasta and cottage cheese in 2 quart baking dish; mix well.
- Sprinkle pasta mixture with Cheddar cheese and bake for 8 to 10 minutes, until cheese is bubbly.

Nutrition Information

- Calories: 374 calories
- Total Fat: 14.8 g
- Cholesterol: 78 mg
- Sodium: 407 mg
- Total Carbohydrate: 39.5 g
- Protein: 21 g

71. Buffalo Ranch Pasta

"A delicious alternative to wings all in one pot. Enjoy with a cool drink... you'll need it!"

Serving: 4 | Prep: 10 m | Cook: 32 m | Ready in: 42 m

Ingredients

- 2 skinless, boneless chicken breast halves

- 1 yellow onion, thinly sliced
- 1/4 pound bacon, chopped
- 1/2 pound wide egg noodles
- 1/2 cup ranch dressing
- 1/4 cup cream cheese
- 2 tablespoons hot sauce

Direction

- Bring a pot of water to a boil; add chicken and cook until chicken is no longer pink in the center, 10 to 15 minutes. An instant-read thermometer inserted into the center should read at least 165 degrees F (74 degrees C). Remove chicken from pot and place on a work surface; shred using 2 forks.
- Heat a skillet over medium-high heat; cook and stir onion and bacon until onion is tender and bacon is cooked through, about 5 minutes.
- Bring a large pot of lightly salted water to a boil. Cook noodles in the boiling water, stirring occasionally until tender yet firm to the bite, about 7 minutes. Drain, reserving some of the water.
- Mix noodles, chicken, onion-bacon mixture, ranch dressing, cream cheese, and hot sauce together in the pot. Add reserved water if sauce needs to be thinned.

Nutrition Information

- Calories: 635 calories
- Total Fat: 37.4 g
- Cholesterol: 125 mg
- Sodium: 795 mg
- Total Carbohydrate: 47.8 g
- Protein: 25.7 g

72. Burgundy Stroganoff

"This recipe is one of our family favorites!! Beef strips are simmered in a Burgundy wine sauce, then served hot over noodles."

Serving: 6 | Prep: 20 m | Cook: 1 h | Ready in: 1 h 20 m

Ingredients

- 2 tablespoons margarine
- 2 pounds beef round steak, cut into thin strips
- 1/4 cup all-purpose flour for dusting
- 1 medium onion, sliced
- 1 cup beef broth
- 1/2 cup Burgundy wine
- 3 tablespoons tomato paste
- 1/2 teaspoon ground thyme
- 1 (12 ounce) package wide egg noodles
- 3/4 cup sour cream

Direction

- Melt margarine in a large skillet over medium heat. Add beef strips, and fry until browned. Stir in onion and cook, stirring, for 3 minutes, or until softened. Sprinkle flour over the meat, and stir into the pan juices until blended. Gradually mix in the beef broth, Burgundy, tomato paste and thyme. Reduce heat to low, and simmer for 40 to 45 minutes.
- During the last 15 minutes of the cooking, bring a large pot of lightly salted water to a boil. Add egg noodles, and cook until tender, about 7 minutes.
- Remove the burgundy beef from the heat and stir in sour cream. Serve over hot egg noodles.

Nutrition Information

- Calories: 520 calories
- Total Fat: 21.3 g
- Cholesterol: 113 mg
- Sodium: 306 mg
- Total Carbohydrate: 48.9 g
- Protein: 28.6 g

73. Busy Mom Lasagna

"I'm not sure where this recipe originated, but it's been in my family a long time, and we just love it! It's simple and quite tasty for the amount of effort it requires. We try lots of new recipes, but this one is definitely an old favorite that we keep pulling out."

Serving: 8 | Prep: 15 m | Cook: 4 h 5 m | Ready in: 4 h 20 m

Ingredients

- 1 pound ground beef
- 1/2 cup diced onion
- 1 (16 ounce) jar spaghetti sauce, or more to taste
- 1/2 (8 ounce) package cream cheese, softened
- 1/2 (8 ounce) container sour cream
- cooking spray
- 1 (12 ounce) package wide egg noodles
- 1 1/2 cups shredded mozzarella cheese
- 1 1/2 cups shredded Cheddar cheese

Direction

- Heat a large skillet over medium heat. Cook and stir beef and onion in the hot skillet until beef browns and onion softens, 5 to 7 minutes. Drain and discard grease.
- Add spaghetti sauce, cream cheese, and sour cream to the skillet. Mix well.
- Spray a 5-quart slow cooker with cooking spray. Layer noodles, beef mixture, and cheeses in the slow cooker. Repeat layers as necessary until cooker is full.
- Cover and cook on High for 2 hours. Switch to Low and cook until noodles are soft and cheeses are melted, about 2 hours more.

Nutrition Information

- Calories: 533 calories
- Total Fat: 28.3 g
- Cholesterol: 128 mg
- Sodium: 583 mg
- Total Carbohydrate: 40.4 g
- Protein: 28.5 g

74. Butter Garlic Cabbage and Kluski Noodles

"Buttery, garlicky cabbage and noodles! I have found this to work with other vegetables as well. Instead of cabbage, use spinach, collards, or any other leafy vegetable that wilts well. What doesn't taste good with garlic and butter?"

Serving: 6 | Prep: 20 m | Cook: 20 m | Ready in: 40 m

Ingredients

- 1 (12 ounce) package kluski noodles
- 3 tablespoons butter
- 2 tablespoons butter
- 1 sweet onion, finely chopped
- 1 tablespoon minced garlic
- 1 pinch crushed red pepper flakes
- 1/2 teaspoon dried Italian herb seasoning
- 1 large head cabbage, cored and finely chopped
- 1/4 cup water
- 3 tablespoons butter (optional)
- salt and ground black pepper to taste
- 1 pinch garlic powder, or to taste (optional)

Direction

- Fill a large pot with lightly salted water and bring to a rolling boil. Stir in kluski noodles and return to a boil. Cook kluski noodles uncovered, stirring occasionally, until tender but still slightly firm, 7 to 10 minutes. Drain well. Return to pot and stir in 3 tablespoons butter until butter has melted and coated the noodles. Set noodles aside.
- Melt 2 tablespoons butter in a large pot over medium heat; cook and stir sweet onion in butter until translucent, about 5 minutes. Add garlic; cook and stir until fragrant, about 30 seconds.
- Thoroughly mix in crushed red pepper flakes and Italian seasoning. Stir cabbage and water into onion mixture until well combined. Cover and cook, stirring often, until cabbage is tender and reduced in volume by about half, 15 to 20 minutes. There should be a small amount of liquid left in pot.

- Gently stir the buttered kluski noodles into the cabbage mixture until well combined. For a more buttery flavor, stir in 3 more tablespoons butter if desired; season to taste with salt, black pepper, and garlic powder.

Nutrition Information

- Calories: 416 calories
- Total Fat: 18.1 g
- Cholesterol: 88 mg
- Sodium: 160 mg
- Total Carbohydrate: 55.1 g
- Protein: 11.2 g

75. Cabbage and Noodles

"Cabbage and noodles, cooked with bacon, is comfort food supreme, great for a chilly day."

Serving: 4 | Prep: 10 m | Cook: 35 m | Ready in: 45 m

Ingredients

- 1 (8 ounce) package egg noodles
- 3 tablespoons butter
- 1/2 pound bacon
- 1 onion, chopped
- 1 small head cabbage, chopped
- 1 dash garlic salt

Direction

- Fill a large pot with lightly salted water and bring to a rolling boil over high heat. Stir in the egg noodles; return to a boil. Cook, uncovered, stirring occasionally, until the noodles are cooked through, but still firm to the bite, about 5 minutes. Drain; return to the pot and stir in the butter.
- Meanwhile, place the bacon in a large, deep skillet, and cook over medium-high heat, turning occasionally, until evenly browned, about 10 minutes. Drain the bacon slices on a paper towel-lined plate.
- Place the onion into the skillet with the bacon grease, and cook and stir over medium heat until the onion begins to soften, about 2 minutes. Stir in the cabbage, and cook and stir until wilted, about 5 minutes. Chop the bacon, add it to the skillet, and cook until the cabbage is tender, about 10 minutes. Stir in the noodles, and continue cooking just until heated through.

Nutrition Information

- Calories: 447 calories
- Total Fat: 19.1 g
- Cholesterol: 90 mg
- Sodium: 616 mg
- Total Carbohydrate: 53.1 g
- Protein: 17.5 g

76. Cabbage Balushka or Cabbage and Noodles

"This Hungarian favorite is cabbage, onions, and egg noodles cooked in butter. Salt and pepper to taste. So easy, so good."

Serving: 6 | Prep: 15 m | Cook: 10 m | Ready in: 25 m

Ingredients

- 1 (16 ounce) package egg noodles
- 1/2 cup butter
- 1 large onion, chopped
- 1 head cabbage, cored and chopped
- salt and ground black pepper to taste

Direction

- Fill a large pot with lightly salted water and bring to a rolling boil. Stir in egg noodles and return to a boil. Cook noodles uncovered, stirring occasionally, until tender but still slightly firm, about 5 minutes. Drain well.
- Melt butter in a large skillet or wok over medium heat; cook and stir onion until browned, about 8 minutes.
- Cook and stir cabbage into onions until cabbage has wilted, another 5 to 8 minutes.

- Gently stir cooked noodles into cabbage mixture; season with salt and black pepper to taste.

Nutrition Information

- Calories: 482 calories
- Total Fat: 18.9 g
- Cholesterol: 103 mg
- Sodium: 161 mg
- Total Carbohydrate: 67 g
- Protein: 13.5 g

77. Campbells Kitchen Beef Stroganoff

"Always a family favorite, this classic dish of quickly sauteed beef and onion in a creamy mushroom sauce is perfect over hot cooked noodles. Garnish with fresh parsley for a colorful table presence and serve with a family favorite green vegetable."

Serving: 4 | Cook: 25 m | Ready in: 25 m

Ingredients

- 1 pound boneless beef sirloin steak or beef top round steak
- 2 tablespoons vegetable oil
- 1 medium onion, chopped
- 1 (10.75 ounce) can Campbell's® Condensed Cream of Mushroom Soup or Campbell's® Condensed 98% Fat Free Cream of Mushroom Soup
- 1/2 teaspoon paprika
- 1/2 cup sour cream or yogurt
- 4 cups hot cooked medium egg noodles
- Chopped fresh parsley

Direction

- Slice beef into very thin strips.
- Heat half the oil in skillet over medium-high heat. Cook beef until browned, stirring often. Set beef aside.
- Add remaining oil. Add onion and cook over medium heat until tender. Pour off fat.
- Add soup and paprika. Heat to a boil. Stir in sour cream and return beef to skillet. Heat through. Serve over noodles. Sprinkle with parsley.

78. Cheesy Goulash

"This is a recipe that my sister and I always begged my mother to make. It was our favorite and now it is my children's favorite, too. Very basic ingredients combine for a wonderful and tasty dish."

Serving: 6 | Prep: 15 m | Cook: 40 m | Ready in: 55 m

Ingredients

- 1 (10 ounce) package broad egg noodles, cooked, rinsed, drained (Kosher for Passover)
- 1 pound ground beef
- 3 tablespoons vegetable oil
- 5 medium potatoes, cubed
- 1 medium onion, minced
- 1 (10 ounce) can tomato sauce
- 16 ounces processed cheese, cubed

Direction

- Bring a large pot of lightly salted water to a boil. Add pasta and cook for 8 to 10 minutes or until al dente; drain, and set aside.
- Brown ground beef in a large skillet over medium high heat, stirring to crumble; drain, and set aside. Heat oil in a separate skillet over medium high heat. Cook potatoes for 2 minutes, then stir in onion. Continue cooking until well browned, then carefully drain excess oil.
- Combine potatoes with ground beef mixture, and stir in tomato sauce and cubed cheese. When cheese has melted, stir in noodles and continue cooking 15 minutes more. Serve immediately.

Nutrition Information

- Calories: 748 calories
- Total Fat: 36.8 g

- Cholesterol: 145 mg
- Sodium: 1249 mg
- Total Carbohydrate: 68.7 g
- Protein: 36.2 g

79. Chef Johns Turkey Noodle Casserole

"This delicious casserole is for leftover leftovers. I don't know about you, but after a few days of eating Thanksgiving leftovers, no matter how tasty they originally were, I want something that makes me forget there's even turkey in it. Since ingredients like garam masala, spicy cheese, and peppers aren't typically used in the meal, they work wonderfully here to disguise the last of a holiday bird."

Serving: 6 | Prep: 15 m | Cook: 40 m | Ready in: 55 m

Ingredients

- 12 ounces egg noodles
- 3 tablespoons butter
- 3 tablespoons flour
- 3 1/2 cups cold milk
- 1 (10 ounce) can condensed cream of mushroom soup
- 1/2 cup diced red bell pepper
- 1/2 cup diced green bell pepper
- 1/4 cup chopped green onions
- 1 teaspoon garam masala
- 1 teaspoon dried tarragon
- 1 cup shredded pepperjack cheese
- 1 teaspoon salt, or to taste
- 3 cups cubed skinless cooked turkey
- 5 ounces crushed potato chips

Direction

- Preheat oven to 350 degrees F (175 degrees C).
- Bring a large pot of lightly salted water to a boil. Cook egg noodles in boiling water, stirring occasionally until almost cooked through and still firm to the bite, about 4 minutes. Drain.
- Melt butter in a large saucepan over medium heat. Whisk in flour; cook, stirring, until mixture is light golden, about 3 minutes.
- Pour milk into butter and flour mixture, whisking constantly. Stir in cream of mushroom soup, red bell pepper, green bell pepper, green onions, garam masala, and dried tarragon. Bring mixture to a simmer, cook for 2 minutes. Remove from heat.
- Stir in pepperjack cheese until cheese is melted and incorporated.
- Stir pepperjack cheese mixture, turkey meat, and noodles in a large bowl until evenly incorporated. Pour mixture into a large casserole dish. Sprinkle chips on top, pressing down slightly with the tines of a fork. Bake in the preheated oven until casserole top is golden brown and sauce is bubbling, about 30 minutes.

Nutrition Information

- Calories: 736 calories
- Total Fat: 33.4 g
- Cholesterol: 150 mg
- Sodium: 1113 mg
- Total Carbohydrate: 67.3 g
- Protein: 41 g

80. Chicken and Cold Noodles with Spicy Sauce

"This is a good summertime meal, and can be made ahead."

Serving: 4

Ingredients

- 6 cups water
- 1 whole bone-in chicken breast, with skin
- 6 ounces dry Chinese noodles
- 1 teaspoon sesame oil
- 1/4 cup tahini
- 3 tablespoons water
- 1 tablespoon sesame oil
- 2 teaspoons chili oil (optional)

- 3 tablespoons soy sauce
- 2 tablespoons red wine vinegar
- 1/4 cup peanut oil
- 2 tablespoons minced garlic

Direction

- In large saucepan over medium high heat, bring 6 cups water to boil. Add chicken breast, and return to boil. Reduce heat to low. Simmer, uncovered, about 15 minutes. Remove meat from broth, and set aside to cool.
- Bring broth to boil again, and add noodles. Cook, stirring occasionally, 5 to 7 minutes. Drain, reserving broth for another use if desired. Rinse noodles under cold running water until chilled. Drain again, and transfer to serving bowl. Toss lightly with 1 teaspoon sesame oil.
- Cut or pull chicken meat into fine shreds, discarding skin and bones. Set aside.
- Combine tahini and 3 tablespoons water, stirring to blend. Add chili oil, soy sauce, vinegar, 1 tablespoon sesame oil, peanut oil, and garlic. Mix well.
- Arrange the chicken on top of noodles in serving dish. Spoon sauce over all.

Nutrition Information

- Calories: 542 calories
- Total Fat: 35.6 g
- Cholesterol: 46 mg
- Sodium: 752 mg
- Total Carbohydrate: 37.2 g
- Protein: 23.3 g

81. Chicken and Noodle Casserole

"This is a great one-dish meal that's delicious and filling."

Serving: 8

Ingredients

- 2 boneless chicken breast halves, cooked and cubed
- 1 (16 ounce) package wide egg noodles
- 1 (15 ounce) can mixed vegetables
- 1 cup frozen broccoli
- 1 (10.75 ounce) can condensed cream of potato soup
- 1 (10.75 ounce) can condensed cream of broccoli soup
- 1/4 teaspoon dried thyme
- 1 teaspoon salt
- 1 teaspoon ground black pepper
- 1/2 cup milk
- 2 cups shredded Colby cheese

Direction

- Cook noodles according to package directions. Drain.
- In a 2 quart saucepan, mix cooked chicken, cream of potato soup, cream of broccoli soup, milk, mixed vegetables, broccoli, salt, pepper, and thyme. Cook over medium heat until broccoli is cooked. Mix with egg noodles. Spread into a greased 9 x 13 inch pan. Cover.
- Bake at 350 degrees F (175 degrees C) for 20 minutes. Cover with Colby cheese, and bake uncovered for an additional 15 minutes.

Nutrition Information

- Calories: 464 calories
- Total Fat: 15.8 g
- Cholesterol: 99 mg
- Sodium: 1089 mg
- Total Carbohydrate: 54.4 g
- Protein: 25.2 g

82. Chicken Chow Mein West Indian Style

"In the West Indies we eat chicken chow mein with lots of chile. It's usually served with plain rice. This dish has tons of flavor and is a bit different from what you'd get in a Chinese restaurant."

Serving: 4 | Prep: 35 m | Cook: 25 m | Ready in: 1 h

Ingredients

- 1 (8 ounce) package egg noodles
- 1/2 cup vegetable oil for frying, or as needed
- 2 chile peppers, chopped
- 1 onion, finely chopped
- 1 clove garlic, minced
- 1 (1 1/2 inch) piece ginger root, cut into strips
- 5 tablespoons dark soy sauce
- 2 skinless, boneless chicken breast halves, chopped
- 1 green bell pepper, cut into strips
- 2 large carrots, cut into strips
- 1 tablespoon ground white pepper
- 5 tablespoons dark soy sauce
- 1/4 cup chopped fresh cilantro, or more to taste
- salt to taste (optional)
- 4 green onions, finely chopped

Direction

- Bring a large pot of lightly salted water to a boil. Cook egg noodles in the boiling water, stirring occasionally until cooked through but firm to the bite, about 5 minutes. Drain.
- Heat vegetable oil in a large pot over medium heat. Add chile peppers, onion, garlic, and ginger; cook until fragrant, 2 to 3 minutes. Add 5 tablespoons dark soy sauce; fry for 1 more minute.
- Cook and stir chicken in the onion mixture over high heat until chicken is no longer pink in the center, 5 to 7 minutes. Add green bell pepper and carrots and cook until softened, about 5 more minutes.
- Gently fold noodles into chicken mixture. Mix in white pepper, 5 more tablespoons dark soy sauce, and cilantro until heated through, about 5 minutes. Sprinkle with green onion to serve.

Nutrition Information

- Calories: 380 calories
- Total Fat: 7 g
- Cholesterol: 81 mg
- Sodium: 2328 mg
- Total Carbohydrate: 55.5 g
- Protein: 24.6 g

83. Chicken I Hate You

"Chicken chunks with Alfredo noodles, asparagus, tomatoes and mushrooms (sprinkled, of course, with some grated Parmesan cheese). Why the name? One time my husband came home late from work without calling me, so instead of the dinner I was going to prepare he got this recipe. When he asked me 'What's for dinner?', I said 'Chicken I hate you!' - and a new dish was born! It's great."

Serving: 4 | Prep: 20 m | Cook: 25 m | Ready in: 45 m

Ingredients

- 1 pound skinless, boneless chicken breast meat - cut into chunks
- 1 tablespoon vegetable oil
- 1 (4.5 ounce) package Alfredo sauce egg noodles mix
- 1 (10 ounce) can canned asparagus, drained
- 1 (16 ounce) can Italian-style diced tomatoes, drained
- 1 (4.5 ounce) can mushrooms, drained
- 1 tablespoon grated Parmesan cheese

Direction

- Heat oil in a large skillet over medium high heat. Add chicken and sauté until cooked through and juices run clear.
- Meanwhile, prepare Alfredo noodles according to package directions; when finished, stir in cooked chicken, asparagus,

tomatoes and mushrooms. Sprinkle with cheese and serve.

Nutrition Information

- Calories: 337 calories
- Total Fat: 9.5 g
- Cholesterol: 102 mg
- Sodium: 1161 mg
- Total Carbohydrate: 26.7 g
- Protein: 34.6 g

84. Chicken Livers Stroganoff

"A different and delicious way to enjoy chicken livers. To make this dish healthier, I like to use yolkless noodles. I have made this for many of my friends over the past 20 years, and have always received rave reviews, even from some who thought that they would not like chicken livers."

Serving: 6 | Prep: 15 m | Cook: 25 m | Ready in: 40 m

Ingredients

- 3 tablespoons olive oil
- 1 pound chicken livers, rinsed and trimmed
- 2 cups chopped onion
- 4 ounces sliced fresh mushrooms
- 1 tablespoon paprika
- 1/3 cup dry sherry
- 1 1/2 cups sour cream
- salt and pepper to taste
- 1 (12 ounce) package medium egg noodles

Direction

- Bring a large pot of lightly salted water to a boil. Add noodles, and cook until tender, about 8 minutes. Drain, and set aside.
- While the noodles are getting started, heat olive oil in a large heavy skillet. Add onions, and cook, stirring until tender, about 5 minutes. Add mushrooms, and continue cooking for a few minutes, until starting to brown. Add the chicken livers, and season with paprika, salt and pepper. Cook for 8 to 10 minutes, until livers are nicely browned on the outside, but still slightly pink in the center. Do not over cook - the livers will become tough and leathery.
- Remove the skillet from the heat, and gradually whisk in the sherry, then the sour cream until well blended. Serve over hot egg noodles.

Nutrition Information

- Calories: 521 calories
- Total Fat: 25.2 g
- Cholesterol: 333 mg
- Sodium: 178 mg
- Total Carbohydrate: 49.4 g
- Protein: 23.5 g

85. Chicken Noodle Casserole I

"Creamy chicken and noodle casserole topped with crushed crackers. Wonderful as leftovers topped with melted cheese!"

Serving: 6 | Prep: 30 m | Cook: 30 m | Ready in: 1 h

Ingredients

- 4 skinless, boneless chicken breast halves
- 6 ounces egg noodles
- 1 (10.75 ounce) can condensed cream of mushroom soup
- 1 (10.75 ounce) can condensed cream of chicken soup
- 1 cup sour cream
- salt to taste
- ground black pepper to taste
- 1 cup crumbled buttery round crackers
- 1/2 cup butter

Direction

- Poach chicken in a large pot of simmering water. Cook until no longer pink in center, about 12 minutes. Remove from pot and set aside. Bring chicken cooking water to a boil and cook pasta in it. Drain. Cut chicken into small pieces, and mix with noodles.

- In a separate bowl, mix together mushroom soup, chicken soup, and sour cream. Season with salt and pepper. Gently stir together cream soup mixture with the chicken mixture. Place in a 2 quart baking dish.
- Melt butter in a small saucepan, and remove from heat. Stir in crumbled crackers. Top casserole with the buttery crackers.
- Bake at 350 degrees F (175 degrees C) for about 30 minutes, until heated through and browned on top.

Nutrition Information

- Calories: 542 calories
- Total Fat: 34.2 g
- Cholesterol: 133 mg
- Sodium: 895 mg
- Total Carbohydrate: 35.5 g
- Protein: 23.3 g

86. Chicken Noodle Casserole II

"A mixture of chicken, soup, milk, peas and carrots baked with egg noodles, cheese and bread. My husband hates tuna, so I improvised my mom's tuna casserole recipe. Both he and my brother-in-law love it!"

Serving: 4 | Prep: 30 m | Cook: 30 m | Ready in: 1 h

Ingredients

- 1 (8 ounce) package egg noodles, cooked
- 2 skinless, boneless chicken breast halves - cut into cubes
- 1 tablespoon minced onion
- 1 (10.75 ounce) can condensed cream of chicken soup
- 1 1/4 cups milk
- 1 (14.5 ounce) can peas and carrots, drained
- salt and pepper to taste
- paprika to taste
- 1 teaspoon chili powder
- 4 slices Monterey Jack cheese
- 4 slices soft white bread, cubed

Direction

- Preheat oven to 350 degrees F (175 degrees C). Spread cooked egg noodles in a 9x13 inch baking dish and set aside.
- In a large skillet over medium high heat, sauté cubed chicken meat with onion for about 7 to 10 minutes, or until chicken is cooked through and no longer pink inside. Add the soup, milk, peas and carrots and stir together. Season with salt and pepper, paprika and chili powder to taste. Stir until just bubbly and remove from heat.
- Stir chicken mixture into noodles in baking dish until well combined; top with cheese slices, then bread cubes.
- Bake at 350 degrees F (175 degrees C) for about 30 minutes or until bread is toasted; serve hot.

Nutrition Information

- Calories: 463 calories
- Total Fat: 17.6 g
- Cholesterol: 88 mg
- Sodium: 1165 mg
- Total Carbohydrate: 45.2 g
- Protein: 31.7 g

87. Chicken Noodle Soup

"This soup is delicious, and very easy to make. It is a wonderful soup to prepare for friends or neighbors that you would like to cook for."

Serving: 10

Ingredients

- 4 cups chopped, cooked chicken meat
- 1 cup chopped celery
- 1/4 cup chopped carrots
- 1/4 cup chopped onion
- 1/4 cup butter
- 8 ounces egg noodles
- 12 cups water

- 9 cubes chicken bouillon
- 1/2 teaspoon dried marjoram
- 1/2 teaspoon ground black pepper
- 1 bay leaf
- 1 tablespoon dried parsley

Direction

- In a large stock pot, sauté celery and onion in butter or margarine.
- Add chicken, carrots, water, bouillon cubes, marjoram, black pepper, bay leaf, and parsley. Simmer for 30 minutes.
- Add noodles, and simmer for 10 more minutes.

Nutrition Information

- Calories: 227 calories
- Total Fat: 8.1 g
- Cholesterol: 74 mg
- Sodium: 1124 mg
- Total Carbohydrate: 18.2 g
- Protein: 19.2 g

88. Chicken Noodle Soup III

"In Asia, there are different kinds of 'noodle soup'. Noodle soup is more a noodle dish rather than a soup dish. This one is a great comfort food on a cold day. Light and healthy as well. Quantities are arbitrary. Adjust to own taste. Very important to add the shallots as they give the fragrance and flavor. Instead of egg noodles, sometimes I use macaroni. You can also use soy sauce instead of the salt. If you are adventurous, eat with chopped hot chile pepper or add some cayenne pepper to make the soup spicy."

Serving: 6 | Prep: 10 m | Cook: 20 m | Ready in: 30 m

Ingredients

- 12 shallots, thinly sliced
- 1/4 cup vegetable oil
- 6 ounces egg noodles
- 1 cup bean sprouts
- 3 quarts chicken broth
- 3 cups shredded, cooked chicken breast meat
- 1/2 cup chopped green onion
- salt and pepper to taste

Direction

- In a small skillet over medium heat, cook shallots in oil until brown and fragrant. Remove from heat and set aside.
- Bring a large pot of water to a boil. Cook noodles in boiling water until just tender, 8 to 10 minutes; drain and rinse under cold water. Set aside.
- Bring a small pot of water to a boil; have ready a bowl of ice water. Blanch bean sprouts by plunging them into boiling water for 1 minute, then into cold water. Drain and set aside.
- In a large saucepan over medium heat, bring chicken broth to a simmer.
- Divide noodles evenly between 6 bowls. Top with bean sprouts and shredded chicken. Pour the heated broth into the bowls. Drizzle with the shallot mixture and garnish with the green onion. Season with salt and pepper. Serve at once.

Nutrition Information

- Calories: 384 calories
- Total Fat: 15.9 g
- Cholesterol: 73 mg
- Sodium: 61 mg
- Total Carbohydrate: 35.7 g
- Protein: 25.3 g

89. Chicken Tetrazzini II

"A crunchy cornflake topping adds a new twist to the usual tetrazzini recipes!"

Serving: 6

Ingredients

- 2 skinless, boneless chicken breast halves
- 1 stalk celery
- 1 (4.5 ounce) can sliced mushrooms
- 1 (12 fluid ounce) can evaporated milk

- 8 ounces processed cheese food (eg. Velveeta)
- 1/2 cup butter
- 1/3 cup dry sherry
- 1 pinch salt
- 1 pinch ground black pepper
- 1/4 cup cornflakes cereal
- 1 pinch paprika
- 3/4 (12 ounce) package egg noodles, cooked and drained

Direction

- Boil chicken breasts and celery in 4 cups of water for about 30 minutes. Remove from heat and remove chicken from water to cool. When chicken is cooled, shred and set aside.
- In a large skillet, melt butter or margarine. Drain mushrooms, reserving liquid, and add to skillet. Heat thoroughly, seasoning with salt and pepper. Add evaporated milk, reserved mushroom liquid and sherry, stirring well. Add cheese a few slices at a time until thoroughly melted and blended. Add shredded chicken and bring to a slow boil.
- Preheat oven to 350 degrees (175 C). Grease a 9x13x2 glass baking dish. Put in noodles at about a 1 1/2 inch depth and pour chicken mixture over noodles. Stir to coat. Top with cornflake crumbs and paprika, cover dish and bake for 25 minutes. Uncover dish and bake for 5 more minutes. Serve warm.

Nutrition Information

- Calories: 532 calories
- Total Fat: 26.5 g
- Cholesterol: 133 mg
- Sodium: 985 mg
- Total Carbohydrate: 45.2 g
- Protein: 27.4 g

90. Chili Casserole

"A simple casserole with a little zing! The zing comes from the taco sauce. This is a great dish for when you do not have much time to make dinner, but you want something that has substance and will fill you up! You can use any kind of cheese on top."

Serving: 6 | Prep: 20 m | Cook: 20 m | Ready in: 40 m

Ingredients

- 1 1/2 pounds ground beef
- 1/2 cup chopped onion
- 3 stalks celery, chopped
- 1 (15 ounce) can chili
- 1 (14.5 ounce) can peeled and diced tomatoes with juice
- 1/4 cup taco sauce
- 1 (15 ounce) can corn
- 1 (8 ounce) package egg noodles
- 1/4 cup shredded Cheddar cheese

Direction

- Preheat oven to 350 degrees F (175 degrees C).
- In a large skillet over medium high heat, sauté the beef and onion for 5 to 10 minutes, or until meat is browned and onion is tender; drain fat. Add the celery, chili, tomatoes, taco sauce and corn. Heat thoroughly, reduce heat to low and allow to simmer.
- Meanwhile, prepare the noodles according to package directions. When cooked, place them in a 9x13 inch baking dish. Pour the meat mixture over the noodles, stirring well. Top with the cheese.
- Bake at 350 degrees F (175 degrees C) for 20 minutes, or until cheese is completely melted and bubbly.

Nutrition Information

- Calories: 671 calories
- Total Fat: 37.7 g
- Cholesterol: 145 mg
- Sodium: 843 mg
- Total Carbohydrate: 52.3 g
- Protein: 31.9 g

91. Chili Casserole with Egg Noodles

"This recipe is similar in flavor to my chili recipe. I came up with it one night when I had a craving for chili. Because the kids will not eat beans, I substituted pasta and they loved it!"

Serving: 6 | Prep: 15 m | Cook: 35 m | Ready in: 50 m

Ingredients

- 1 (12 ounce) package wide egg noodles
- 1 pound ground beef
- 1 onion, chopped
- 3 cloves garlic, minced
- 2 (15 ounce) cans tomato sauce
- 1 (8 ounce) can tomato sauce
- 15 fluid ounces water
- 1 cup red wine
- 1 tablespoon ground cumin
- 1 teaspoon dried oregano
- 1/2 teaspoon cayenne pepper
- 1 cup shredded sharp Cheddar cheese

Direction

- Preheat an oven to 350 degrees F (175 degrees C). Grease a 9x14 inch baking dish.
- Fill a large pot with lightly-salted water and bring to a boil; stir in the egg noodles and return to a boil. Stirring occasionally, boil uncovered until the pasta is cooked yet still firm to the bite, about 5 minutes. Drain well in a colander set in the sink.
- Place a large skillet over medium-high heat; cook and stir the ground beef in the skillet until completely browned. Add the onion and garlic; continue cooking and stirring until the onion is translucent. Pour all of the tomato sauce, water, and red wine into the mixture. Season with cumin, oregano, and cayenne pepper. Bring the mixture to a simmer. Mix the cooked pasta into the sauce; transfer the mixture to the prepared baking dish. Sprinkle the Cheddar cheese over the top of the pasta and sauce.
- Bake in the preheated oven until the cheese is melted and the sauce has absorbed into the dish, about 20 minutes.

Nutrition Information

- Calories: 510 calories
- Total Fat: 20 g
- Cholesterol: 111 mg
- Sodium: 1129 mg
- Total Carbohydrate: 49 g
- Protein: 27.6 g

92. Classic Beef Stroganoff

"This hearty comfort food is great when the weather turns."

Serving: 8 | Prep: 15 m | Cook: 40 m | Ready in: 55 m

Ingredients

- 2 pounds beef stew meat, cut across the grain into 1/4x1/2-inch strips
- 2 teaspoons salt
- 2 teaspoons ground black pepper
- 1 teaspoon Spanish paprika
- 1/4 cup butter
- 1 1/2 onions, minced
- 1 1/2 pounds sliced fresh mushrooms
- 1 (10.5 ounce) can condensed beef broth, divided
- 1/3 cup dry white wine
- 6 cloves garlic, minced
- 3 tablespoons ketchup
- salt and ground black pepper to taste
- 1 (16 ounce) package broad egg noodles
- 3 tablespoons all-purpose flour
- 1 cup sour cream
- 1 pinch paprika, for garnish

Direction

- Season beef with salt, pepper, and Spanish paprika.
- Melt butter in a large skillet over medium heat. Sauté onions and mushrooms in melted butter until onions are tender, 5 to 7 minutes; transfer to a bowl, retaining some of the butter in the skillet.
- Cook and stir beef in retained butter until lightly browned, 5 to 7 minutes.
- Stir 2/3 cup beef broth, white wine, garlic, and ketchup into the beef mixture; season with salt and pepper. Place a cover on the skillet and cook mixture at a simmer for 15 minutes.
- Bring a large pot of lightly salted water to a boil. Cook egg noodles in the boiling water, stirring occasionally until cooked through but firm to the bite, about 5 minutes; drain.
- Whisk remaining beef broth and flour together in a bowl; add to beef mixture. Bring the mixture to a boil, stirring continually, and boil for 1 minute. Reduce heat to low, add sour cream, and stir until smoothly incorporated. Ladle over egg noodles and garnish with paprika.

Nutrition Information

- Calories: 543 calories
- Total Fat: 21.3 g
- Cholesterol: 135 mg
- Sodium: 887 mg
- Total Carbohydrate: 53.1 g
- Protein: 33.9 g

93. Classic Beef Stroganoff in a Slow Cooker

"This classic beef stroganoff recipe uses ingredients commonly kept on hand for an easy and delicious family meal."

Serving: 4 | Prep: 15 m | Cook: 8 h | Ready in: 8 h 25 m

Ingredients

- 1 pound top round steak, trimmed
- 1 (8 ounce) package sliced fresh mushrooms
- 1 cup chopped onion
- 2 tablespoons Dijon mustard
- 2 tablespoons chopped fresh parsley
- 3 cloves garlic, minced
- 1/2 teaspoon salt
- 1/2 teaspoon dried dill
- 1/2 teaspoon freshly ground black pepper
- 1/3 cup all-purpose flour (spooned and leveled)
- 1 cup fat-free reduced-sodium beef broth
- 1 (8 ounce) container reduced-fat sour cream
- 2 cups hot cooked egg noodles

Direction

- Cut steak diagonally across the grain into 1/4-inch thick slices. Place steak, mushrooms, onion, mustard, parsley, garlic, salt, dill, and black pepper into a 3-quart slow cooker; stir well.
- Place flour in a small bowl; gradually add broth, stirring with a whisk until blended. Add to slow cooker; stir well. Cover with the lid; cook on High for 1 hour. Reduce heat to Low and cook until steak is tender, 7 to 8 hours.
- Turn slow cooker off and remove lid. Allow stroganoff to stand for 10 minutes. Stir in sour cream. Serve over noodles.

Nutrition Information

- Calories: 441 calories
- Total Fat: 16.8 g
- Cholesterol: 105 mg
- Sodium: 560 mg
- Total Carbohydrate: 38.9 g

- Protein: 32.6 g
- Cholesterol: 83 mg
- Sodium: 29 mg
- Total Carbohydrate: 19 g
- Protein: 5.8 g

94. Classic Lukshen Noodle Kugel

"Most kugels are loaded with sugar and dairy products. This simple family favorite is savory and is the prefect accompaniment to roast chicken."

Serving: 9 | Prep: 10 m | Cook: 50 m | Ready in: 1 h

Ingredients

- 1 (8 ounce) package egg noodles
- 1/3 cup vegetable oil, divided
- 1 onion, chopped
- 3 eggs, beaten
- salt and black pepper to taste

Direction

- Fill a large pot with lightly salted water and bring to a rolling boil over high heat. Once the water is boiling, stir in the egg noodles, and return to a boil. Cook the pasta uncovered, stirring occasionally, until the pasta has cooked through, but is still firm to the bite, about 5 minutes. Drain well in a colander set in the sink.
- Preheat an oven to 350 degrees F (175 degrees C).
- Heat 1 tablespoon of the vegetable oil in a skillet over medium heat. Stir in the onion; cook and stir until the onion has softened and turned translucent, about 5 minutes. Reduce heat to medium-low, and continue cooking and stirring until the onion is golden brown, 10 to 15 minutes more. Combine the noodles, onion, eggs, remaining vegetable oil, salt, and pepper in a large bowl. Pour mixture into an 8-inch square pan.
- Bake in the preheated oven until firm, about 35 minutes.

Nutrition Information

- Calories: 196 calories
- Total Fat: 10.8 g

95. Company Casserole

"Egg noodles and beef in a tomato and mushroom sauce with cottage and Cheddar cheese."

Serving: 5 | Prep: 20 m | Cook: 30 m | Ready in: 50 m

Ingredients

- 1 (8 ounce) package egg noodles
- 1 pound lean ground beef
- 1 onion, chopped
- 2 (7 ounce) cans tomato sauce with mushrooms
- 1 teaspoon salt
- 1/4 teaspoon black pepper
- 1/4 teaspoon ground cinnamon
- 1 cup cottage cheese
- 1/2 cup chopped green onions
- 1/2 cup shredded Cheddar cheese

Direction

- Preheat oven to 350 degrees F (175 degrees C). Bring a large pot of lightly salted water to a boil. Add pasta and cook for 8 to 10 minutes or until al dente; drain.
- In a skillet over medium heat, brown the ground beef with the onion until no pink shows; drain. Mix in 1 of the cans of tomato sauce, salt, pepper and cinnamon. Pour into shallow 3 quart casserole baking dish.
- Pour in noodles in an even layer. Top with cottage cheese; sprinkle with onions and Cheddar cheese. Pour on remaining can of tomato sauce.
- Bake in a preheated oven for 30 minutes.

Nutrition Information

- Calories: 467 calories
- Total Fat: 20.7 g

- Cholesterol: 106 mg
- Sodium: 1182 mg
- Total Carbohydrate: 39.1 g
- Protein: 31 g

96. Corned Beef Noodle Casserole

"A sure fire hit at family reunions and potlucks."

Serving: 5

Ingredients

- 1 (8 ounce) package wide egg noodles
- 1 (12 ounce) can corned beef
- 4 ounces processed cheese food (eg. Velveeta)
- 1 (10.75 ounce) can condensed cream of chicken soup
- 1 cup milk
- 1/2 cup chopped onion
- 1 cup seasoned dry bread crumbs

Direction

- Preheat oven to 350 degrees F (175 degrees C).
- Cook noodles until tender and drain.
- Combine noodles, corned beef, cheese, cream of chicken soup, milk and onion. Pour into a 2 quart casserole dish. Top with buttered bread crumbs.
- Bake at 350 degrees F (175 degrees C) for 45 minutes.

Nutrition Information

- Calories: 561 calories
- Total Fat: 20 g
- Cholesterol: 114 mg
- Sodium: 1619 mg
- Total Carbohydrate: 58.3 g
- Protein: 35.1 g

97. Cowgirl Beef Stroganoff

"My cowboy's cute description of a great woman is that 'she has got biscuit dough on her bridle reins!' So, gals, your secret weapon is your slow cooker! Set it and forget it! You can be in two places at one time. This freezes well."

Serving: 6 | Prep: 10 m | Cook: 6 h 10 m | Ready in: 6 h 20 m

Ingredients

- 1 (10.75 ounce) can golden mushroom soup (such as Campbell's®)
- 1 (10.75 ounce) can water
- 1/2 cup chopped onion
- 2 tablespoons Worcestershire sauce
- 1 (1 ounce) package dry onion soup mix
- 2 pounds cubed beef stew meat, trimmed
- 1 (4 ounce) package cream cheese
- 1/2 cup sour cream
- 1 tablespoon butter
- 1 (4 ounce) package sliced fresh mushrooms
- 1 (12 ounce) package egg noodles

Direction

- Stir golden mushroom soup, water, onion, Worcestershire sauce, and onion soup mix together in a slow cooker; add beef and stir to coat.
- Cook on Low for 6 hours.
- Stir cream cheese and sour cream into the beef mixture.
- Melt butter in a skillet over medium heat. Cook and stir mushrooms in melted butter until tender, 3 to 5 minutes; add to beef mixture.
- Bring a large pot of lightly salted water to a boil. Cook egg noodles in the boiling water, stirring occasionally until cooked through but firm to the bite, about 5 minutes. Drain. Ladle beef mixture over noodles to serve.

Nutrition Information

- Calories: 838 calories
- Total Fat: 46.4 g
- Cholesterol: 215 mg

- Sodium: 1018 mg
- Total Carbohydrate: 51.1 g
- Protein: 51.8 g

98. Cream of Broccoli Cheese Soup I

"Our favorite anytime soup. Very quick and easy."

Serving: 7 | Prep: 5 m | Cook: 25 m | Ready in: 30 m

Ingredients

- 2/3 cup chopped onion
- 1 tablespoon margarine
- 5 cups chicken broth
- 1 (8 ounce) package wide egg noodles
- 1 (10 ounce) package frozen chopped broccoli
- 1 clove garlic, minced
- 6 cups milk
- 12 ounces shredded American cheese

Direction

- In a large saucepan, sauté onion and garlic in butter or margarine over medium heat till tender.
- Add broth, and bring to a boil. Reduce heat, and add noodles. Cook for 3 to 4 minutes. Stir in broccoli. Cover, and cook for 5 minutes.
- Stir in milk and cheese. Heat slowly, stirring, till cheese melts. DO NOT BOIL. Serve immediately.

Nutrition Information

- Calories: 483 calories
- Total Fat: 24 g
- Cholesterol: 97 mg
- Sodium: 1450 mg
- Total Carbohydrate: 37.6 g
- Protein: 26.7 g

99. Creamy Beef Stroganoff

"I have been making this recipe for almost 20 years. It was the recipe my mom always made for us. Now my kids love it, too! It's always a hit, even with friends and family who do not normally care for Stroganoff. Goes great with rolls. Also, I have tried using reduced-fat and fat-free sour cream. Turns out okay with reduced fat but I did not like it with the fat-free sour cream."

Serving: 8 | Prep: 10 m | Cook: 1 h | Ready in: 1 h 10 m

Ingredients

- 1 1/2 pounds ground beef
- 1 teaspoon seasoned salt
- 1 onion, finely chopped
- 1/4 teaspoon ground nutmeg
- 1/4 teaspoon ground cloves
- 2 cups hot water
- 1/4 cup all-purpose flour
- 2 (10.75 ounce) cans golden mushroom soup (such as Campbell's®)
- 1 (16 ounce) container sour cream
- 1/4 cup dried parsley
- 2 teaspoons dry mustard
- 2 teaspoons salt, or to taste
- 2 teaspoons ground black pepper, or to taste
- 1 (16 ounce) package egg noodles

Direction

- Crumble ground beef into a large skillet over medium heat; sprinkle with seasoned salt. Cook and stir until completely browned, 7 to 10 minutes. Drain excess grease from skillet and return to heat. Stir onion, nutmeg, and cloves into the beef.
- Whisk hot water and flour together in a bowl until smooth; pour over beef mixture and mix. Stir mushroom soup into the beef mixture. Place a cover on the skillet. Reduce heat to medium-low. Stirring occasionally, cook at a simmer until thickened, about 30 minutes.
- Whisk sour cream, parsley, and dry mustard together in a bowl. Stir sour cream mixture into the beef mixture; season with salt and black pepper. Continue cooking at a simmer uncovered until hot, 15 to 20 minutes.

- Bring a large pot of lightly salted water to a boil. Cook egg noodles in the boiling water until cooked through but firm to the bite, about 5 minutes; drain. Transfer noodles to a large bowl. Ladle beef mixture over the noodles and mix.

Nutrition Information

- Calories: 571 calories
- Total Fat: 26.9 g
- Cholesterol: 127 mg
- Sodium: 1334 mg
- Total Carbohydrate: 55.1 g
- Protein: 26.4 g

100. Creamy Buffalo Chicken Noodle Soup

"All of the classics of a creamy chicken noodle soup paired with buffalo chicken. This soup is the perfect fusion of comfort food and sports bar fare. It's sure to warm you up on those chilly winter nights."

Serving: 4

Ingredients

- 1 (8 ounce) package extra-wide egg noodles
- 2 tablespoons butter
- 1 medium onion, chopped
- 3 stalks celery, chopped
- 3 carrots, peeled and chopped
- 1 clove garlic, chopped
- 1/4 cup flour
- 1 (32 ounce) carton Swanson® Chicken Broth
- 1 pound cooked chicken breast meat, chopped
- 1/3 cup hot pepper sauce
- 1 teaspoon dried parsley flakes
- 1 cup half-and-half
- crumbled blue cheese (optional)
- ranch-flavored croutons (optional)

Direction

- Cook egg noodles as directed on package, drain.
- Melt butter in a large sauce pan over medium heat. Add onion, celery, and carrots and cook until softened, 10 to 12 minutes. Add garlic and cook until fragrant, 1 minute. Stir in flour and cook until mixture is thickened and beginning to brown, about 4 minutes.
- Pour in Swanson(R) Chicken Broth; add chicken, hot pepper sauce, and parsley and bring to a boil. Reduce heat and simmer 10 minutes. Stir in cream and cooked noodles; continue cooking until soup is heated through, about 3 more minutes.
- Garnish with blue cheese crumbles and/or ranch flavored croutons if desired.

Nutrition Information

- Calories: 639 calories
- Total Fat: 24.8 g
- Cholesterol: 175 mg
- Sodium: 1648 mg
- Total Carbohydrate: 59.1 g
- Protein: 44 g

101. Creamy Cabbage with Noodles

"A terrific side dish that pairs well with ham, pork roast or chops, or kielbasa. Easy and comforting!"

Serving: 4 | Prep: 30 m | Cook: 30 m | Ready in: 1 h

Ingredients

- 5 tablespoons butter, divided
- 1/2 medium head cabbage, cut into 1-inch chunks
- 1 large onion, cut into 1-inch chunks
- 1 teaspoon Diamond Crystal® Kosher Salt
- 1 teaspoon ground black pepper
- 1 cup heavy cream
- 1 cup chicken broth
- 2 tablespoons all-purpose flour

- 8 ounces dried egg noodles

Direction

- Preheat oven to 325 degrees F. Grease a 2-quart casserole dish with 1 tablespoon butter.
- Melt 2 tablespoons butter over medium high heat in large sauté pan. Add cabbage and onions and season; season with 1 teaspoon Diamond Crystal(R) Kosher Salt and 1 teaspoon black pepper. Stir; cover and cook for until cabbage and onions are soft, about 10 minutes.
- Sprinkle in flour, stir. Cook 2 more minutes. Slowly stir in broth and cream; simmer until slightly thickened, about 2 minutes.
- Bring a large pot of lightly salted water to a boil. Cook egg noodles in the boiling water, stirring occasionally until cooked through but firm to the bite, about 5 minutes. Drain.
- Add cooked noodles to cabbage mixture. Stir to combine. Transfer to prepared casserole dish. Dot with 2 tablespoons butter.
- Cover and bake until mixture is hot and bubbly, about 30 minutes.

Nutrition Information

- Calories: 610 calories
- Total Fat: 39.2 g
- Cholesterol: 168 mg
- Sodium: 879 mg
- Total Carbohydrate: 55.2 g
- Protein: 11.9 g

102. Creamy Chicken Cordon Bleu Casserole

"This is a second version of another member's yummy casserole. It has all the creamy and wonderful flavor of chicken cordon bleu with a little of the fat and hassle removed."

Serving: 8 | Prep: 20 m | Cook: 35 m | Ready in: 55 m

Ingredients

- 1 (8 ounce) package wide egg noodles
- 2 cups chopped cooked chicken breast
- 8 ounces cooked ham, cubed
- 8 ounces Swiss cheese, cubed
- 1 (10.75 ounce) can reduced-fat, reduced-sodium cream of chicken soup (such as Campbell's® Healthy Request)
- 1/2 cup 2% milk
- 1/2 cup light sour cream
- 2 tablespoons butter
- 1/3 cup seasoned bread crumbs
- 1/4 cup grated Parmesan cheese

Direction

- Preheat oven to 350 degrees F (175 degrees C). Lightly grease a 9x13-inch casserole dish.
- Bring a large pot of lightly salted water to a boil. Cook egg noodles in the boiling water, stirring occasionally until cooked through but firm to the bite, about 5 minutes. Drain and transfer noodles to the prepared casserole dish; top with chicken, ham, and Swiss cheese.
- Mix cream of chicken soup, milk, and sour cream together in a bowl; spoon soup mixture over noodle mixture.
- Melt butter in a skillet over medium heat; cook and stir bread crumbs and Parmesan cheese in the melted butter until crumbs are coated with butter and cheese, 2 to 3 minutes. Sprinkle bread crumb mixture over casserole.
- Bake in the preheated oven until casserole is bubbling and lightly browned, about 30 minutes. Allow casserole to cool for 10 minutes before serving.

Nutrition Information

- Calories: 455 calories
- Total Fat: 23.6 g
- Cholesterol: 110 mg
- Sodium: 687 mg
- Total Carbohydrate: 29.9 g
- Protein: 29.5 g

103. Creamy Chicken Egg Noodle Soup

"I made up this recipe when I got sick of the bland, over-salted ones from stores and cans. It's creamy but very light. Sooo delicious!"

Serving: 4 | Prep: 20 m | Cook: 1 h 12 m | Ready in: 1 h 32 m

Ingredients

- 8 cups chicken stock
- 1/2 bulb garlic
- 4 whole black peppercorns
- 1 bay leaf
- 1 yellow onion, diced
- 2 large carrots, diced
- 2 large stalks celery, diced
- 8 sprigs fresh thyme, tied together with kitchen twine
- 1 teaspoon salt
- 1/2 teaspoon Italian seasoning
- 1/2 teaspoon dried celery leaves
- 1/4 teaspoon fresh cracked black pepper
- 2 cups egg noodles
- 1 cup corn
- 2 cups diced cooked rotisserie chicken
- 1/2 cup heavy whipping cream

Direction

- Bring chicken stock, garlic bulb, peppercorns, and bay leaf to a boil in a large pot. Reduce heat and simmer, covered, until flavors combine, about 35 minutes. Strain out garlic bulb, peppercorns, and bay leaf from the stock.
- Stir onion, carrots, celery, thyme, salt, Italian seasoning, celery leaves, and black pepper into the stock. Simmer over medium-low heat until carrots are tender, about 18 minutes. Bring to a gentle boil; stir in egg noodles and corn. Cook until noodles are tender yet still firm to the bite, about 8 minutes. Discard thyme bundle.
- Stir chicken and cream into the pot; simmer until heated through, about 3 minutes.

Nutrition Information

- Calories: 347 calories
- Total Fat: 14.6 g
- Cholesterol: 58 mg
- Sodium: 2029 mg
- Total Carbohydrate: 51.7 g
- Protein: 10.7 g

104. Creamy Scallion and White Bean Pasta

"An easy pasta dish you can make with ingredients right out of the pantry. Great for a last-minute supper or as a side dish to meat, poultry or fish."

Serving: 6 | Prep: 10 m | Cook: 26 m | Ready in: 36 m

Ingredients

- 1 tablespoon vegetable oil
- 2 bunches green onions, chopped
- 1/3 cup whole milk
- 1 (15.5 ounce) can small white beans
- salt and ground black pepper to taste
- 1 (12 ounce) package egg noodles

Direction

- Heat oil in a skillet over medium heat; stir in green onions. Cook and stir until wilted, 3 to 5 minutes. Increase heat to medium-high. Pour in milk; cook until milk starts to bubble. Reduce heat and simmer until mixture thickens, 7 to 10 minutes. Add beans, salt, and pepper. Simmer until sauce thickens to a stew-like consistency, about 10 minutes.

- Bring a large pot of lightly salted water to a boil. Cook egg noodles in the boiling water, stirring occasionally, until tender yet firm to the bite, about 6 minutes. Drain and return to pot. Stir in the sauce and serve.

Nutrition Information

- Calories: 350 calories
- Total Fat: 5.5 g
- Cholesterol: 48 mg
- Sodium: 59 mg
- Total Carbohydrate: 61.4 g
- Protein: 15 g

105. Creamy Shrimp Casserole

"My grandmother's special recipe and a family favorite in our house. Shrimp, egg noodles, peas and a few mushrooms layered in creamy sauce. Although this recipe yields quite a bit, my family of 4 usually devours the whole dish in one sitting."

Serving: 8 | Prep: 20 m | Cook: 1 h 15 m | Ready in: 1 h 35 m

Ingredients

- 1 pound shrimp, peeled and deveined
- 1 teaspoon salt
- 3 cups wide egg noodles
- 2 tablespoons butter
- 1 1/2 tablespoons all-purpose flour
- 2 1/2 cups milk
- 1/2 cup heavy cream
- salt and ground black pepper to taste
- 1 cup frozen green peas, thawed
- 1 (4.5 ounce) can sliced mushrooms, drained (optional)
- 1 cup crushed buttery round crackers
- 1 tablespoon cold butter, thinly sliced

Direction

- Preheat oven to 350 degrees F (175 degrees C). Lightly grease a 3-quart casserole dish.
- Fill a large pot with water, and bring to a boil over high heat. Stir in the shrimp, reduce heat to a simmer, and cook the shrimp until opaque and bright pink, about 3 minutes. Remove the shrimp to a bowl with a slotted spoon. Return the water to a full rolling boil over high heat, and stir in the noodles. Cook until the noodles are tender, about 8 minutes; drain in a colander set in the sink.
- Melt 2 tablespoons of butter in a saucepan over medium heat, and stir the flour into the butter to make a paste. Remove the pan from the heat; slowly whisk in the milk and cream until smooth. Season to taste with salt and black pepper. Return the sauce to the heat, lower heat to a simmer, and whisk constantly until the sauce thickens, about 5 minutes.
- Place noodles into the prepared casserole dish, and top with peas, mushrooms, and cooked shrimp. Pour the sauce over the casserole, and sprinkle the crushed cracker crumbs evenly over the top. Dot the top of the casserole with about 6 thin slices of butter.
- Bake in the preheated oven until the cracker topping is crisp and golden brown, about 1 hour.

Nutrition Information

- Calories: 263 calories
- Total Fat: 11.9 g
- Cholesterol: 126 mg
- Sodium: 614 mg
- Total Carbohydrate: 22.9 g
- Protein: 15.9 g

106. Creamy Swiss Chicken Casserole

"Cheesy chicken breasts and a smooth mushroom sauce are served over egg noodles."

Serving: 4 | Prep: 15 m | Cook: 30 m | Ready in: 45 m

Ingredients

- 1 (10.75 ounce) can condensed cream of chicken soup
- 1/4 cup milk

- 4 skinless, boneless chicken breast halves
- 4 slices Swiss cheese
- 1 (4 ounce) can sliced mushrooms (optional)
- 1 (10 ounce) package uncooked egg noodles

Direction

- Preheat oven to 375 degrees F (190 degrees C). Lightly grease an 8x8 inch casserole dish.
- In a bowl, mix the soup and milk. Arrange chicken breast halves in the casserole dish. Top each breast half with a slice of cheese. Pour soup and milk over the chicken. Sprinkle with mushrooms.
- Bake 30 minutes in the preheated oven, or until sauce is bubbly and chicken juices run clear.
- Bring a large pot of lightly salted water to a boil. Add noodles and cook for 8 to 10 minutes, until al dente; drain. Serve chicken and mushroom sauce over the cooked noodles.

Nutrition Information

- Calories: 566 calories
- Total Fat: 19.2 g
- Cholesterol: 152 mg
- Sodium: 748 mg
- Total Carbohydrate: 53.8 g
- Protein: 43 g

107. Dianes Beef Stroganoff

"A traditional family favorite for holidays and birthdays. Serve with warm crusty Italian bread. This recipe can be easily adapted to the slow cooker."

Serving: 10 | Prep: 20 m | Cook: 3 h 5 m | Ready in: 3 h 25 m

Ingredients

- 2 tablespoons olive oil
- 1/4 cup butter
- 1/2 cup all-purpose flour
- 1 teaspoon salt
- 2 teaspoons ground black pepper
- 2 1/2 pounds beef stew meat, cubed
- 1 cup white wine
- 1 large onion, cut into 1/4-inch strips
- 1 large clove garlic, minced
- 1/2 cup ketchup
- 1/2 cup Worcestershire sauce
- 4 (4 ounce) cans button mushrooms, undrained
- 1 (16 ounce) container sour cream
- 1 (16 ounce) package wide egg noodles

Direction

- Heat olive oil and butter in a large, heavy pot or Dutch oven over medium heat. Combine flour, salt, and black pepper in a bowl and toss beef stew meat in seasoned flour. Brown the beef in the hot oil and butter, stirring often, and remove meat from pan.
- Pour white wine into pan and scrape up and dissolve any small bits of browned food; stir onion and garlic into white wine. Cook until onion is translucent, stirring often, about 5 minutes. Return browned beef to pan. Stir ketchup, Worcestershire sauce, and juice from canned mushrooms with beef mixture. Reduce heat to low, cover pan, and simmer until beef is tender, about 3 hours.
- Mix button mushrooms and sour cream into beef mixture and heat through, about 5 minutes.
- Bring a large pot of lightly salted water to a boil. Cook egg noodles in the boiling water, stirring occasionally, until cooked through but firm to the bite, about 5 minutes. Drain. Serve Stroganoff over cooked egg noodles.

Nutrition Information

- Calories: 618 calories
- Total Fat: 34.7 g
- Cholesterol: 127 mg
- Sodium: 769 mg
- Total Carbohydrate: 45.4 g
- Protein: 27 g

108. Easy and Quick Beef Stroganoff

"Easy and quick, this beef stroganoff is so good, so fast. Even easier of you prepare the meat ahead of time. Kids love it."

Serving: 6 | Prep: 10 m | Cook: 29 m | Ready in: 39 m

Ingredients

- 1 pound ground beef
- 1/2 teaspoon dried onion flakes, or to taste (optional)
- 1/2 teaspoon garlic powder, or to taste
- ground black pepper to taste
- 1/2 (16 ounce) package egg noodles
- 2 cups water
- 2 cubes beef bouillon
- 1/4 cup all-purpose flour
- 1 (16 ounce) container sour cream
- 1/4 cup ketchup
- 1/4 cup vinegar

Direction

- Season beef lightly with dried onion, garlic powder, and black pepper. Heat a large skillet over medium-high heat. Cook and stir meat in the hot skillet until browned and crumbly, 5 to 7 minutes. Drain and discard grease.
- Fill a large pot with lightly salted water and bring to a rolling boil. Stir in egg noodles and return to a boil. Cook noodles uncovered, stirring occasionally, until tender yet firm to the bite, about 6 minutes. Drain.
- Combine water and bouillon cubes in a microwave-safe measuring cup. Cook in the microwave until boiling, about 6 minutes. Crush cubes and stir broth until dissolved.
- Pour broth into a deep saucepan over medium-high heat. Add flour gradually, whisking in until bubbly and thick, about 1 minute. Reduce heat and add sour cream, ketchup, and vinegar. Whisk until smooth, about 1 minute. Add beef and cook until heated through, about 5 minutes more. Pour beef sauce over noodles and toss to coat.

Nutrition Information

- Calories: 488 calories
- Total Fat: 29.4 g
- Cholesterol: 111 mg
- Sodium: 382 mg
- Total Carbohydrate: 34.4 g
- Protein: 21 g

109. Easy and Quick Halushki

"Polish dish combining bacon, fried cabbage and egg noodles."

Serving: 6 | Prep: 10 m | Cook: 20 m | Ready in: 30 m

Ingredients

- 1 pound bacon
- 1 onion, diced
- 1 (16 ounce) package egg noodles
- 1 head cabbage, sliced
- salt and ground black pepper to taste

Direction

- Snip bacon into small pieces with a scissors and cook in a large skillet over medium heat until crisp, stirring often, about 10 minutes. Cook and stir onion with bacon until translucent, about 5 more minutes; set bacon and onion aside, leaving drippings in the skillet.
- Bring a large pot of lightly salted water to a boil. Cook egg noodles in the boiling water, stirring occasionally until cooked through but firm to the bite, about 5 minutes. Drain.
- Transfer bacon and onion mixture with drippings into the pot used to cook the noodles and cook and stir cabbage until coated with drippings. Cover pot and cook until cabbage is tender, 10 to 12 minutes, stirring occasionally. Gently stir in noodles and season to taste with salt and black pepper.

Nutrition Information

- Calories: 698 calories
- Total Fat: 37.6 g
- Cholesterol: 114 mg
- Sodium: 709 mg
- Total Carbohydrate: 68.7 g
- Protein: 22.3 g

110. Easy Beef Stroganoff

"Easy to make. Reheats well. Very good, this is a favorite in our house. Total preparation time is 30 minutes!"

Serving: 8 | Prep: 10 m | Cook: 20 m | Ready in: 30 m

Ingredients

- 1 (12 ounce) package egg noodles, cooked and drained
- 6 ounces fresh mushrooms, sliced
- 1 onion, chopped
- 1/4 cup butter
- 2 pounds lean ground beef
- 4 tablespoons all-purpose flour
- 2 cups beef broth
- 1 cup sour cream
- salt and black pepper to taste

Direction

- Bring a large pot of water to a boil. Cook egg noodles in boiling water until done, about 8 minutes. Drain.
- Meanwhile, prepare the sauce. In a large skillet, cook mushrooms and onions in 2 tablespoons of butter over medium heat until soft; remove from pan.
- Using the same pan, melt remaining butter. Cook ground beef in melted butter until browned. Mix in flour. Stir in beef broth, and cook until slightly thickened. Add mushroom and onion mixture; stir in sour cream. Season to taste with salt and pepper. Continue cooking until sauce is hot, but not boiling. Serve sauce over egg noodles.

Nutrition Information

- Calories: 602 calories
- Total Fat: 37.4 g
- Cholesterol: 148 mg
- Sodium: 633 mg
- Total Carbohydrate: 36.1 g
- Protein: 28.9 g

111. Easy Beef Strogonoff

"This used to be my favorite dish growing up. I never knew it was so easy to make. Growing up CAN be fun!"

Serving: 3 | Prep: 10 m | Cook: 10 m | Ready in: 20 m

Ingredients

- 1 pound ground beef
- 1/2 teaspoon garlic powder
- 1/2 teaspoon salt
- 1/2 teaspoon ground black pepper
- 1 cube beef bouillon
- 1 medium onion, chopped
- 8 ounces fresh mushrooms, sliced
- 1 pint sour cream
- 4 ounces egg noodles, cooked and drained

Direction

- In a large skillet brown beef in oil over medium high heat. When meat is browned, drain excess fat from skillet. Add garlic powder, salt and pepper and stir in.
- Add bouillon, onion and mushrooms to skillet and sauté until onions are translucent. Remove from heat (very important) and add sour cream. Stir all together and serve over hot cooked egg noodles.

Nutrition Information

- Calories: 977 calories
- Total Fat: 74.4 g
- Cholesterol: 228 mg
- Sodium: 789 mg
- Total Carbohydrate: 39.9 g

- Protein: 38.3 g

112. Easy Cheesy Tuna Noodle Casserole

"This is the best tuna noodle casserole! My family and friends always request it! And, best of all, it is easy!"

Serving: 6 | Prep: 10 m | Cook: 40 m | Ready in: 50 m

Ingredients

- 2 (10 ounce) packages egg noodles
- 1 tablespoon olive oil
- 1 tablespoon salt
- 1 (8 ounce) package processed cheese food (such as Velveeta®), cut into cubes
- 3 (5 ounce) cans chunk light tuna in water, drained
- 1 (15 ounce) can peas, drained (optional)
- 2 (10.75 ounce) cans condensed cream of celery soup
- 1 (10.75 ounce) can condensed cream of mushroom soup
- 1 teaspoon ground black pepper
- 1 cup grated Parmesan cheese

Direction

- Bring a large pot of lightly salted water to a boil. Cook egg noodles in the boiling water, stirring occasionally until cooked through but firm to the bite, about 5 minutes. Drain noodles and return to the pot. Pour olive oil and salt over the drained noodles; stir.
- Preheat oven to 350 degrees F (175 degrees C).
- Put processed cheese food cubes into a large, microwave-safe bowl. Heat in microwave, stirring every 30 seconds, until melted and smooth, 3 to 5 minutes; pour over noodles and add tuna, peas, celery soup, mushroom soup, and black pepper. Stir to coat noodles completely; pour into a large casserole dish. Sprinkle Parmesan cheese over the top of the noodle mixture to cover completely.
- Bake in preheated oven until Parmesan cheese just begins to brown, 20 to 30 minutes.

Nutrition Information

- Calories: 754 calories
- Total Fat: 28.6 g
- Cholesterol: 140 mg
- Sodium: 3491 mg
- Total Carbohydrate: 80.4 g
- Protein: 43.3 g

113. Easy Ham and Noodles

"Great for leftover ham. This is easy to make with ingredients you probably already have in the kitchen. Try adding peas or other vegetables, if desired."

Serving: 4 | Prep: 10 m | Cook: 30 m | Ready in: 40 m

Ingredients

- 2 cups cooked egg noodles
- 1 cup cubed, cooked ham
- 1/2 cup cubed Cheddar cheese
- 1 (10.75 ounce) can condensed cream of mushroom soup
- 1/2 (10.75 ounce) can milk

Direction

- Preheat oven to 375 degrees F (190 degrees C).
- Place the noodles, ham, cheese, soup and milk in a 9x9 inch casserole dish and mix well.
- Bake at 375 degrees F (190 degrees C) for 25 to 30 minutes.

Nutrition Information

- Calories: 318 calories
- Total Fat: 15 g
- Cholesterol: 63 mg
- Sodium: 1098 mg
- Total Carbohydrate: 27.4 g
- Protein: 17.9 g

114. Easy Noodle Kugel

"This is a yummy version of noodle kugel (noodle pudding) that has been in our family for years. So easy to make and so tasty!"

Serving: 12 | Prep: 20 m | Cook: 1 h | Ready in: 1 h 20 m

Ingredients

- 1 (8 ounce) package wide egg noodles
- 1/2 cup butter, melted
- 2 cups small curd cottage cheese
- 1 teaspoon salt
- 1 1/2 cups applesauce
- 1 1/2 cups white sugar
- 1 teaspoon ground cinnamon
- 6 eggs, beaten

Direction

- Preheat oven to 350 degrees F (175 degrees C). Lightly oil a 9x13-inch baking dish.
- Fill a large pot with lightly salted water and bring to a rolling boil over high heat. Once the water is boiling, stir in the egg noodles, and return to a boil. Cook the pasta uncovered, stirring occasionally, until the pasta has cooked through, but is still firm to the bite, 4 to 5 minutes. Drain well.
- Melt butter in the pot, and stir together the drained noodles, cottage cheese, salt, and applesauce. Mix in the sugar and cinnamon. Add the beaten eggs; stir to blend all ingredients. Pour mixture into prepared baking dish.
- Bake until top is very brown, about 1 hour.

Nutrition Information

- Calories: 324 calories
- Total Fat: 12.7 g
- Cholesterol: 135 mg
- Sodium: 440 mg
- Total Carbohydrate: 43.1 g
- Protein: 10.6 g

115. Easy Polish Noodles

"Growing up in South Bend, Indiana, Polish dinner buffets are extremely common at weddings and funerals. Polish noodles are a staple at these events and served alongside Polish sausage, green beans, mashed potatoes and chicken gravy, and fried chicken. While at a Polish meat market, an elderly Polish lady passed this recipe on to me upon request."

Serving: 6 | Prep: 5 m | Cook: 35 m | Ready in: 40 m

Ingredients

- 1 (49.5 fluid ounce) can chicken broth
- 1/2 cup water, or as desired
- 1 tablespoon chicken soup base, or more to taste
- 1 (16 ounce) package kluski noodles

Direction

- Combine chicken broth, water, and chicken base in a 6-quart saucepan and bring to a boil. Add kluski noodles, reduce heat, and simmer until liquid is completely absorbed, 30 to 40 minutes.

Nutrition Information

- Calories: 310 calories
- Total Fat: 4.1 g
- Cholesterol: 69 mg
- Sodium: 1515 mg
- Total Carbohydrate: 54.8 g
- Protein: 12.1 g

116. Easy Slow Cooker Stroganoff

"Was in a hurry one day and threw this all together in the slow cooker. When I got home I was so surprised because it tastes like beef stroganoff made the hard way. So much simpler. I love this on a big piece of butter bread like an open-faced stroganoff sandwich."

Serving: 6 | Prep: 15 m | Cook: 8 h | Ready in: 8 h 15 m

Ingredients

- 2 (10.75 ounce) cans cream of mushroom soup
- 1 (8 ounce) package sliced fresh mushrooms (optional)
- 1/2 cup butter
- 1 small onion, chopped
- 3 pounds beef tips, cut into bite-size pieces
- 1 (8 ounce) package wide egg noodles

Direction

- Mix cream of mushroom soup, mushrooms, butter, and onion in a slow cooker; add beef tips.
- Cook for 8 hours on Low.
- Bring a large pot of lightly salted water to a boil. Cook egg noodles in the boiling water, stirring occasionally until cooked through but firm to the bite, about 5 minutes. Drain.
- Serve beef tips and sauce over cooked egg noodles.

Nutrition Information

- Calories: 663 calories
- Total Fat: 36.1 g
- Cholesterol: 170 mg
- Sodium: 857 mg
- Total Carbohydrate: 35.8 g
- Protein: 47.8 g

117. Easy Turkey Tetrazzini

"An easy, quick turkey dish that turns precooked turkey into a family favorite."

Serving: 6 | Prep: 20 m | Cook: 25 m | Ready in: 45 m

Ingredients

- 1 (8 ounce) package cooked egg noodles
- 2 tablespoons butter
- 1 (6 ounce) can sliced mushrooms
- 1 teaspoon salt
- 1/8 teaspoon pepper
- 2 cups chopped cooked turkey
- 1 (10.75 ounce) can condensed cream of celery soup
- 1 cup sour cream
- 1/2 cup grated Parmesan cheese

Direction

- Bring a large pot of lightly salted water to a boil. Add pasta and cook for 8 to 10 minutes or until al dente; drain. Preheat oven to 375 degrees F (190 degrees C).
- Melt butter in a large heavy skillet. Sauté mushrooms for 1 minute. Season with salt and pepper, and stir in turkey, condensed soup, and sour cream. Place cooked noodles in a 9x13 inch baking dish. Pour sauce mixture evenly over the top. Sprinkle with Parmesan cheese.
- Bake in preheated oven for 20 to 25 minutes, or until sauce is bubbling.

Nutrition Information

- Calories: 411 calories
- Total Fat: 20.1 g
- Cholesterol: 105 mg
- Sodium: 1082 mg
- Total Carbohydrate: 33.5 g
- Protein: 24 g

118. Easy Weeknight Beef Stroganoff

"Try this easy version of a fabulous dish ready in minutes!"

Serving: 4 | Prep: 10 m | Ready in: 20 m

Ingredients

- 1 pound cooked seasoned frozen beef strips, thawed
- 1 (9 ounce) pouch Progresso™ Recipe Starters™ creamy portabella mushroom cooking sauce
- 1/2 cup sour cream
- Hot cooked noodles (optional)

Direction

- Brown beef strips in 1 tablespoon oil in nonstick skillet; cook 1 to 2 minutes.
- Stir in cooking sauce and sour cream. Simmer 8 minutes or until sauce thickens, stirring occasionally.
- Serve over noodles.

Nutrition Information

- Calories: 310 calories
- Total Fat: 18.7 g
- Cholesterol: 83 mg
- Sodium: 1018 mg
- Total Carbohydrate: 9.5 g
- Protein: 27.5 g

119. Egg Noodles

"This is your basic old fashioned recipe for egg noodles, just like grammy used to make! Try making them next time you prepare your favorite soup or stew. Don't forget that fresh pasta cooks much quicker than dried! You may use a dough hook attachment on your electric mixer or your hands to make the pasta dough."

Serving: 7 | Prep: 15 m | Cook: 3 m | Ready in: 33 m

Ingredients

- 2 1/2 cups all-purpose flour
- 1 pinch salt
- 2 eggs, beaten
- 1/2 cup milk
- 1 tablespoon butter

Direction

- In a large bowl, stir together the flour and salt. Add the beaten egg, milk, and butter. Knead dough until smooth, about 5 minutes. Let rest in a covered bowl for 10 minutes.
- On a floured surface, roll out to 1/8 or 1/4 inch thickness. Cut into desired lengths and shapes.
- Allow to air dry before cooking.
- To cook fresh pasta, in a large pot with boiling salted water cook until al dente.

Nutrition Information

- Calories: 206 calories
- Total Fat: 3.8 g
- Cholesterol: 59 mg
- Sodium: 40 mg
- Total Carbohydrate: 35 g
- Protein: 7 g

120. Egg Noodles with Spinach

"A wonderful side dish to ramp up plain buttered egg noodles. We love it with Salisbury steak, chicken, or pork."

Serving: 4 | Prep: 10 m | Cook: 15 m | Ready in: 25 m

Ingredients

- 8 ounces wide egg noodles
- 1/4 cup butter
- 1 onion, diced
- 1 clove garlic, minced
- 4 ounces baby spinach leaves
- salt and ground black pepper to taste

Direction

- Bring a large pot of lightly salted water to a boil. Cook egg noodles in the boiling water, stirring occasionally until cooked through but firm to the bite, about 8 minutes; drain and return noodles to pot.
- While the noodles boil, melt butter in a skillet over medium-high heat. Sauté onion and garlic in melted butter until lightly browned and soft, about 8 minutes. Stir baby spinach into the onion mixture; sauté until the spinach is just barely wilted, about 2 minutes.
- Stir spinach mixture into the noodles; season with salt and pepper.

Nutrition Information

- Calories: 335 calories
- Total Fat: 14.1 g
- Cholesterol: 78 mg
- Sodium: 117 mg
- Total Carbohydrate: 43.8 g
- Protein: 9.2 g

121. Emilys Super Eggplant Sauce

"This recipe makes a large amount of sweet, hearty tomato sauce, featuring eggplant, green pepper, onion, and garlic. Serve over egg noodles for a delicious dinner for six."

Serving: 6 | Prep: 15 m | Cook: 30 m | Ready in: 45 m

Ingredients

- 1/2 cup olive oil
- 1 large eggplant, cut into 1/2 inch cubes
- 1 large green bell pepper, chopped
- 1 large onion, chopped
- 2 cloves garlic, minced
- 1 (28 ounce) can diced tomatoes
- 1 (6 ounce) can tomato paste
- 1 tablespoon sugar
- 1 cup water
- 1 (16 ounce) package uncooked egg noodles

Direction

- Heat olive oil in a large skillet over medium heat. Cook eggplant, bell pepper, onion, and garlic until soft and tender, stirring often.
- Meanwhile, bring a large pot of lightly salted water to a boil. Add egg noodles and cook for 8 to 10 minutes, or until al dente; drain, and set aside.
- When done, transfer vegetables to a large stock pot. Stir in the diced tomatoes, tomato paste, sugar, and water. Simmer for 15 to 20 minutes, stirring occasionally. Serve hot over egg noodles.

Nutrition Information

- Calories: 513 calories
- Total Fat: 22.2 g
- Cholesterol: 54 mg
- Sodium: 442 mg
- Total Carbohydrate: 67.4 g
- Protein: 12.1 g

122. Fairy Godmother Rice

"My grandfather's second wife (hence the recipe name) served this to us when we first met her. We've loved her ever since! A tasty side dish that's perfect with any dinner."

Serving: 6 | Prep: 15 m | Cook: 45 m | Ready in: 1 h

Ingredients

- 1/2 cup butter
- 5 ounces thin egg noodles
- 2 cups uncooked instant rice
- 2 (1 ounce) packages dry onion soup mix
- 4 cups vegetable broth
- 1 (5 ounce) can water chestnuts, drained and sliced
- soy sauce to taste

Direction

- Preheat oven to 350 degrees F (175 degrees C). Grease a 2 quart casserole dish.
- Melt butter in a large skillet over medium heat. Brown noodles in the butter.
- In a large bowl combine browned noodles, rice, soup mix, broth, water chestnuts and soy sauce. Mix well and transfer to prepared casserole dish.
- Bake for 45 minutes, or until liquid has been absorbed and casserole is browned and crispy on top.

Nutrition Information

- Calories: 402 calories
- Total Fat: 17.6 g
- Cholesterol: 58 mg
- Sodium: 1249 mg
- Total Carbohydrate: 54.5 g
- Protein: 6.7 g

123. Firehouse Haluski

"This is a quick easy lunch, and cheap too. I make this at the fire station and it is very filling. Serve sprinkled with Romano cheese with bread."

Serving: 6 | Prep: 25 m | Cook: 35 m | Ready in: 1 h

Ingredients

- 1 (12 ounce) package kluski noodles
- 2 heads cabbage, cored and cut into bite-size pieces
- 1 onion, chopped
- 1/4 cup water
- 1 pound kielbasa sausage, diced
- 1/4 cup vegetable oil
- 1 tablespoon mustard seeds
- salt and ground black pepper to taste
- 4 eggs, beaten

Direction

- Bring a large pot of lightly salted water to a boil and cook kluski noodles until tender, about 8 minutes. Drain, chop noodles into small pieces, and set aside.
- Cook cabbage and onion, covered, in a large pot with water over medium heat until tender, 8 to 10 minutes. Heat vegetable oil in a large skillet over medium heat and transfer cabbage and onion into skillet with a slotted spoon. Cook in the hot oil until vegetables begin to brown, about 10 minutes; stir in kielbasa and continue to cook until sausage is heated through. Stir mustard seeds into cabbage mixture; season to taste with salt and black pepper. Stir chopped kluski into the mixture.
- Pour eggs over the noodle mixture and stir until eggs are set, 3 to 5 minutes.

Nutrition Information

- Calories: 722 calories
- Total Fat: 38.8 g
- Cholesterol: 225 mg
- Sodium: 753 mg
- Total Carbohydrate: 68.5 g
- Protein: 27.5 g

124. Fruit Kugel

"We make kugel every year for Passover, and this sweet noodle casserole is one of our favorites! This dish is just as good cold as it is hot."

Serving: 8 | Prep: 20 m | Cook: 20 m | Ready in: 40 m

Ingredients

- 1 (24 ounce) package wide egg noodles
- 2 eggs
- 1 teaspoon ground cinnamon
- 1/2 teaspoon vanilla extract
- 1 (14 ounce) can crushed pineapple
- 8 ounces raisins
- 1 apple, cored and diced
- 2 tablespoons pareve margarine, cut into small pieces (optional)
- 1 (12 ounce) jar apricot preserves

Direction

- Preheat oven to 350 degrees F (175 degrees C).
- Bring a large pot of lightly salted water to a boil. Cook egg noodles in the boiling water, stirring occasionally, until cooked through but firm to the bite, about 5 minutes. Drain and let noodles cool.
- Beat eggs with cinnamon and vanilla extract in a large bowl; gently stir in noodles. Mix pineapple, raisins, and apple into noodle mixture. Transfer mixture into a large casserole dish and scatter pieces of margarine over the noodle mixture. Spread apricot preserves over the casserole.
- Bake in the preheated oven until noodles on top are golden brown and preserves are bubbling, about 15 minutes. Cool slightly before serving.

Nutrition Information

- Calories: 563 calories
- Total Fat: 8.5 g
- Cholesterol: 107 mg
- Sodium: 80 mg
- Total Carbohydrate: 114.1 g
- Protein: 12.6 g

125. Funfetti Spaghetti

"Take a traditional classic noodle kugel and transform it into a delicious (and oft-requested) kids' favorite. It is incredibly easy to make and tastes so good! Sprinkle with additional Funfetti® to serve."

Serving: 8 | Prep: 15 m | Cook: 55 m | Ready in: 1 h 10 m

Ingredients

- 1 (16 ounce) package thin egg noodles
- 3/4 cup melted unsalted butter
- 2 pounds cottage cheese
- 1 1/2 cups white sugar
- 1 1/2 cups applesauce
- 4 eggs
- 1 cup raisins
- 2 teaspoons vanilla extract
- 2 teaspoons ground black pepper
- 1 cup cake mix with candy bits (such as Pillsbury® Funfetti®), or more to taste
- 1 teaspoon ground cinnamon, or to taste
- 1 teaspoon white sugar, or to taste

Direction

- Bring a large pot of lightly salted water to a boil. Cook egg noodles in the boiling water, stirring occasionally until cooked through but firm to the bite, 5 to 7 minutes. Drain and transfer noodles to a large bowl.
- Preheat oven to 350 degrees F (175 degrees C).
- Stir butter into noodles until evenly coated. Add cottage cheese, 1 1/2 cups sugar, applesauce, eggs, raisins, vanilla extract, and black pepper and mix well; fold in cake mix with candy bits. Pour noodle mixture into a 9x13-inch baking dish. Sprinkle cinnamon and 1 teaspoon sugar over noodle mixture. Cover baking dish with aluminum foil.

- Bake in the preheated oven for 30 minutes. Remove foil and continue baking until golden brown, 20 to 30 minutes more.

Nutrition Information

- Calories: 815 calories
- Total Fat: 28.9 g
- Cholesterol: 203 mg
- Sodium: 616 mg
- Total Carbohydrate: 114.7 g
- Protein: 26.8 g

126. Garlic Chive Chicken

"These flavorful chicken breasts are bathed in a lemony garlic butter. Easy to make, they are great for a light dinner."

Serving: 4 | Prep: 15 m | Cook: 1 h | Ready in: 1 h 15 m

Ingredients

- 1 head garlic
- 1 (8 ounce) package egg noodles
- 1 cup chicken broth
- 1 lemon, zested and juiced
- 1/4 teaspoon salt
- 1/4 teaspoon ground black pepper
- 2 teaspoons olive oil
- 4 skinless, boneless chicken breast halves
- 2 tablespoons all-purpose flour
- 4 tablespoons butter
- 1/3 cup chopped fresh chives

Direction

- Preheat oven to 400 degrees F (200 degrees C). Wrap the garlic head in foil, and bake 30 minutes, until cloves are soft. Remove from heat, and cool enough to handle.
- Bring a large pot of lightly salted water to a boil. Add egg noodles and cook for 6 to 8 minutes or until al dente; drain.
- Slice off the top of the garlic head, and squeeze the softened cloves into a medium bowl. Mix in the chicken broth, lemon zest, lemon juice, salt, and pepper.
- Heat the olive oil in a skillet over medium heat. Lightly coat the chicken breast halves with flour, and cook in the skillet about 10 minutes on each side, until lightly browned. Set chicken aside, retaining skillet juices. Stir in the garlic mixture, and bring to a boil. Reduce heat, and return chicken to the skillet. Continue cooking the chicken about 5 minutes on each side, until no longer pink and juices run clear. Remove chicken, and arrange on plates over the egg noodles.
- Mix the butter into the garlic sauce mixture in the skillet until melted, and stir in the chives. Spoon the sauce over the chicken and egg noodles to serve.

Nutrition Information

- Calories: 477 calories
- Total Fat: 19.4 g
- Cholesterol: 132 mg
- Sodium: 287 mg
- Total Carbohydrate: 46 g
- Protein: 31.2 g

127. Goulash I

"This is a quick and easy dinner, I can usually whip it up in 20 minutes and then serve with fresh bread."

Serving: 6 | Prep: 10 m | Cook: 10 m | Ready in: 20 m

Ingredients

- 3 cups dry egg noodles
- 1 pound ground beef
- 1 medium onion, chopped
- salt to taste
- ground black pepper to taste
- garlic salt to taste
- 1 (15 ounce) can corn
- 1 (15 ounce) can kidney beans
- 1 (10.75 ounce) can condensed tomato soup

Direction

- Bring a large pot of lightly salted water to a boil. Add pasta and cook for 8 to 10 minutes or until al dente; drain.
- In a large skillet, over medium heat, brown the ground beef and onion together. Drain off the grease. Add salt, pepper, and garlic salt to taste.
- Stir in the corn, kidney beans, and tomato soup. Stir in the cooked egg noodles and mix thoroughly.

Nutrition Information

- Calories: 453 calories
- Total Fat: 22.5 g
- Cholesterol: 78 mg
- Sodium: 658 mg
- Total Carbohydrate: 43.5 g
- Protein: 21.1 g

128. Grandma Earharts Pepper Pot Casserole

"My Grandma Earhart was a wonderful cook. There wasn't anything she made that my family and I didn't love. This casserole of hers was one of my favorites. I hope you will try her casserole recipe and will love it as much as I do. Bon appetite!"

Serving: 6 | Prep: 25 m | Cook: 50 m | Ready in: 1 h 15 m

Ingredients

- 1 tablespoon vegetable oil
- 2 tablespoons butter
- 1 onion, chopped
- 1/2 cup sliced celery
- 1/2 green bell pepper, chopped
- 1 pound bulk pork sausage
- 1 (28 ounce) can whole peeled tomatoes, chopped
- 1/2 teaspoon garlic powder
- 1 teaspoon dried basil
- 1/2 teaspoon dried sage
- 1 tablespoon Worcestershire sauce
- 1 (8 ounce) package egg noodles
- 1 cup grated Cheddar cheese

Direction

- Preheat oven to 350 degrees F (175 degrees C).
- Heat the vegetable oil with butter in a large skillet over medium heat, and cook the onion, celery, and green pepper until the vegetables are tender, stirring occasionally, about 8 minutes. Mix in the pork sausage, and cook until the meat is browned, breaking it up into crumbles as it cooks, about 8 more minutes. Drain off excess grease. Stir in the tomatoes, garlic powder, basil, sage, and Worcestershire sauce, mixing until well combined.
- Fill a large pot with lightly salted water and bring to a rolling boil over high heat. Once the water is boiling, stir in the egg noodles, and return to a boil. Cook the pasta uncovered, stirring occasionally, until the pasta has cooked through, but is still firm to the bite, about 5 minutes. Drain well in a colander set in the sink. Mix the noodles gently into the pork mixture, and place into a 9x12-inch baking dish. Sprinkle the top with Cheddar cheese.
- Bake in the preheated oven until the cheese is bubbling and browned, 30 to 40 minutes.

Nutrition Information

- Calories: 510 calories
- Total Fat: 30.5 g
- Cholesterol: 105 mg
- Sodium: 1052 mg
- Total Carbohydrate: 37.7 g
- Protein: 21.9 g

129. Grandmas Dried Beef Casserole

"This was my favorite meal when staying with Grandpa and Grandma. Hope you enjoy!"

Serving: 8 | Cook: 30 m | Ready in: 30 m

Ingredients

- 1/4 cup margarine
- 1/4 cup all-purpose flour
- 2 cups milk
- 4 ounces processed cheese food, cubed
- 1 (8 ounce) package uncooked egg noodles
- 1 (10.75 ounce) can cream of mushroom soup
- 4 ounces dried beef, chopped
- 1 cup crushed plain potato chips

Direction

- Preheat the oven to 350 degrees F (175 degrees C).
- Bring a large pot of lightly salted water to a boil. Add the egg noodles, and cook until tender, about 8 minutes. Drain and transfer to a greased 9x13 inch baking dish.
- Melt the margarine in a saucepan over medium heat. Whisk in the flour using a fork so that no lumps form. Gradually stir in the milk. Bring to a simmer, stirring constantly, then add the cheese. Cook and stir until smooth. Stir in the cream of mushroom soup, and then the dried beef. Stir into the noodles in the casserole dish, and top with crushed potato chips.
- Bake for 30 minutes in the preheated oven, until the sauce is thick and bubbling, and top is toasted.

Nutrition Information

- Calories: 333 calories
- Total Fat: 17.2 g
- Cholesterol: 48 mg
- Sodium: 952 mg
- Total Carbohydrate: 31.3 g
- Protein: 13.7 g

130. Grandmas Ground Beef Casserole

"As the title suggests, this was my Grandmother's recipe. I've tweaked the amount of cheese and sour cream depending on what I've got in the fridge and it always turns out great! My mother has suggested this was made up as a way to use up ingredients in the fridge."

Serving: 6 | Prep: 20 m | Cook: 55 m | Ready in: 1 h 15 m

Ingredients

- 1 pound ground beef
- 1 teaspoon white sugar
- 1 teaspoon salt
- 1 teaspoon garlic salt
- 2 (15 ounce) cans tomato sauce
- 1 (8 ounce) package egg noodles
- 1 cup sour cream
- 1 (3 ounce) package cream cheese
- 1 large white onion, diced
- 1/2 cup shredded sharp Cheddar cheese, or more to taste

Direction

- Heat a large skillet over medium-high heat. Cook and stir beef in the hot skillet until browned and crumbly, 5 to 7 minutes; drain and discard grease. Mix sugar, salt, garlic salt and tomato sauce into ground beef; simmer until flavors blend, about 20 minutes. Remove from heat, cover skillet, and cool to room temperature.
- Bring a large pot of lightly salted water to a boil. Cook egg noodles in the boiling water, stirring occasionally until cooked through but firm to the bite, about 5 minutes. Drain and cool slightly.
- Preheat oven to 350 degrees F (175 degrees C). Grease a 9x13-inch casserole dish.
- Mix sour cream, cream cheese, and onion in a bowl.
- Scoop half the noodles into the prepared casserole dish; top with half the sour cream mixture. Spoon half the ground beef mixture

atop sour cream layer. Repeat layering with remaining ingredients. Top casserole with Cheddar cheese.
- Bake in the preheated oven until Cheddar cheese has browned, 25 to 30 minutes.

Nutrition Information

- Calories: 519 calories
- Total Fat: 29.8 g
- Cholesterol: 120 mg
- Sodium: 1597 mg
- Total Carbohydrate: 39.4 g
- Protein: 24.5 g

131. Grandmas Hamburger Hot Dish

"My grandma made this recipe using the old stand-by hamburger and cream soups. We always ate it up!"

Serving: 6 | Prep: 15 m | Cook: 1 h 5 m | Ready in: 1 h 20 m

Ingredients

- 1 (8 ounce) package egg noodles
- 1 pound ground beef
- 1 onion, chopped
- 1 cup diced celery
- 1 (10.75 ounce) can condensed cream of mushroom soup
- 1 (10.75 ounce) can condensed cream of chicken soup
- 1 (4.5 ounce) can mushrooms
- 1/2 cup milk
- 1/2 cup salted cashews

Direction

- Preheat oven to 350 degrees F (175 degrees C). Butter a casserole dish. Arrange noodles in prepared dish.
- Heat a large skillet over medium-high heat. Cook and stir beef, onion, and celery in the hot skillet until beef is browned and crumbly, 5 to 7 minutes; drain and discard grease. Stir cream of mushroom soup, cream of chicken soup, mushrooms, and milk into beef mixture until evenly combined; pour over noodles into prepared dish. Cover dish with aluminum foil.
- Bake in the preheated oven for 30 minutes. Remove foil and sprinkle cashews over mixture; continue baking until bubbling, about 30 minutes more.

Nutrition Information

- Calories: 483 calories
- Total Fat: 25.2 g
- Cholesterol: 83 mg
- Sodium: 900 mg
- Total Carbohydrate: 41.7 g
- Protein: 22.9 g

132. Grandmas Noodle Pudding Kugel

"My grandma gave me her recipe for this family favorite. We always ate this at Hanukkah dinner, but I could really eat it for any meal, anytime!"

Serving: 6 | Prep: 15 m | Cook: 35 m | Ready in: 50 m

Ingredients

- 1 (8 ounce) package broad egg noodles
- 2 tablespoons butter
- 3 eggs, separated
- 1 cup white sugar
- 1 1/2 teaspoons ground cinnamon
- 2 apples - peeled, cored and chopped
- 1/4 cup raisins
- 1/2 cup chopped almonds

Direction

- Preheat oven to 350 degrees F (175 degrees C). Grease a 2-quart casserole dish.
- Fill a large pot with lightly salted water and bring to a rolling boil. Stir in the egg noodles, and return to a boil. Cook uncovered, stirring occasionally, until the noodles have cooked through, but are still firm to the bite, about 5

minutes. Drain well. Place cooked noodles into a mixing bowl.
- With an electric mixer, beat egg whites in a bowl until they form stiff peaks; set egg whites aside. Whisk the egg yolks together in a bowl until smooth, and mix in the sugar until well combined. Pour egg yolk mixture over the noodles, and mix in the cinnamon, apples, raisins, and almonds. Gently fold in the beaten egg whites, trying to keep as much volume as possible. Pour the kugel into the prepared baking dish.
- Bake in the preheated oven until the kugel is browned and the center is set, about 30 minutes.

Nutrition Information

- Calories: 434 calories
- Total Fat: 12.1 g
- Cholesterol: 135 mg
- Sodium: 71 mg
- Total Carbohydrate: 74 g
- Protein: 10.5 g

133. Grandmas Noodles I

"My grandmother made these noodles almost every Sunday for dinner. They are eaten over mashed potatoes. They are simple to make with a pasta machine and are still very much in demand in my family."

Serving: 6

Ingredients

- 4 cups all-purpose flour
- 4 eggs, lightly beaten
- 1 teaspoon salt

Direction

- Put all ingredients in the pasta machine. Let dry an hour or so.
- Add noodles to boiling chicken stock. Cook for ten to fifteen minutes.

Nutrition Information

- Calories: 351 calories
- Total Fat: 4.1 g
- Cholesterol: 124 mg
- Sodium: 436 mg
- Total Carbohydrate: 63.8 g
- Protein: 12.8 g

134. Grandmas Noodles II

"Homemade soup noodles."

Serving: 4

Ingredients

- 1 egg, beaten
- 1/2 teaspoon salt
- 2 tablespoons milk
- 1 cup sifted all-purpose flour
- 1/2 teaspoon baking powder (optional)

Direction

- Combine egg, salt, milk. Add flour. (For thicker noodles add baking powder to flour before mixing.) Separate into two balls.
- Roll out dough, and let stand for 20 minutes.
- Cut into strips and spread to dry--dust with a little flour. Let dry for approximately 2 hours.
- Drop into hot soup--cook for about 10 minutes.

Nutrition Information

- Calories: 136 calories
- Total Fat: 1.7 g
- Cholesterol: 47 mg
- Sodium: 373 mg
- Total Carbohydrate: 24.5 g
- Protein: 5.1 g

135. Grilled Chicken Noodle Soup

"This is a quick chicken noodle soup with mushrooms, peas and carrots. Chopped chicken breast is sauteed to bring out its best flavor. Egg noodles are suggested, but use any noodle that you like."

Serving: 6 | Prep: 30 m | Cook: 1 h | Ready in: 1 h 30 m

Ingredients

- 1 tablespoon vegetable oil
- 3 skinless, boneless chicken breast halves - cut into bite size pieces
- 1 cup sliced carrots
- 1/3 cup frozen green peas
- 4 cups chicken broth
- 1 cup chopped celery
- 1/2 red onion, chopped
- 3/4 cup chopped fresh mushrooms
- 1 cup uncooked egg noodles

Direction

- Heat oil in a medium skillet over medium high heat. Fry chicken pieces in the oil until slightly browned and the juices run clear. Remove from the pan and drain on a paper towel.
- In a large saucepan or Dutch oven, heat chicken broth over medium heat. Add the carrots, peas, celery, onion and mushrooms. Bring to a boil, then reduce heat and let simmer for 20 to 25 minutes. Add the noodles and cook for 10 more minutes or until noodles are al dente.

Nutrition Information

- Calories: 133 calories
- Total Fat: 3.4 g
- Cholesterol: 40 mg
- Sodium: 81 mg
- Total Carbohydrate: 9.4 g
- Protein: 15.7 g

136. Ground Beef Mexican Style

"Spicy ground beef casserole - it is sort of an enchilada in a bowl without the tortillas! To vary the amount of spiciness, add mild, medium, or hot salsa."

Serving: 4 | Prep: 10 m | Cook: 30 m | Ready in: 40 m

Ingredients

- 1 pound ground beef
- 1 cup salsa
- 1/2 cup water
- 1 green bell pepper, chopped
- 1 bunch green onions, chopped
- 1 (8 ounce) package wide egg noodles
- 1/2 cup sour cream
- 1/2 cup shredded Cheddar cheese
- 1 tomato, chopped

Direction

- In a large nonstick skillet, cook and stir ground beef until browned. Drain off excess fat.
- Stir in salsa and water. Simmer for 10 minutes.
- Meanwhile, cook pasta in boiling water until al dente. Drain.
- Stir in green pepper and onions, and continue simmering until veggies are crisp/tender. Stir in noodles and sour cream. Sprinkle grated cheese on top, and cover pan until the cheese melts. Sprinkle chopped tomatoes on the top, and serve.

Nutrition Information

- Calories: 732 calories
- Total Fat: 43.7 g
- Cholesterol: 171 mg
- Sodium: 592 mg
- Total Carbohydrate: 52.1 g
- Protein: 33.8 g

137. Ground Turkey Noodle Bake

"A satisfying casserole using ground turkey, egg noodles, and plenty of cheese."

Serving: 6 | Prep: 15 m | Cook: 35 m | Ready in: 50 m

Ingredients

- 3 cups wide egg noodles
- 1 pound ground turkey
- 1 onion, chopped
- 1 (15 ounce) can tomato sauce
- 1 teaspoon Italian seasoning
- 1/2 cup milk
- 4 ounces cream cheese
- 1 tablespoon minced fresh parsley
- 1 clove garlic, minced
- 1 1/4 cups shredded part-skim mozzarella cheese

Direction

- Preheat oven to 375 degrees F (190 degrees C). Lightly grease an 8-inch square baking dish.
- Bring a large pot of lightly salted water to a boil. Cook egg noodles in boiling water, stirring occasionally until cooked through but firm to the bite, about 5 minutes; drain.
- Heat a large skillet over medium-high heat and stir in turkey and onion. Cook and stir until turkey mixture is crumbly, evenly browned, and no longer pink, about 10 minutes; drain. Stir in tomato sauce and Italian seasoning; bring to a boil. Reduce heat to low, cover, and simmer for 10 minutes.
- Combine milk, cream cheese, parsley, and garlic in a small saucepan. Cook and stir over medium heat until cream cheese is melted, about 5 minutes.
- Toss noodles with cream cheese mixture; transfer to prepared baking dish. Top with turkey mixture and sprinkle with mozzarella cheese.
- Bake in preheated oven until cheese is melted, 15 to 30 minutes.

Nutrition Information

- Calories: 346 calories
- Total Fat: 17.4 g
- Cholesterol: 109 mg
- Sodium: 625 mg
- Total Carbohydrate: 21.5 g
- Protein: 26.7 g

138. Gunk on Noodles

"My mother came up with this wonderfully simple dish on a snowy Michigan night when all she had on hand was a pound of ground beef. My father and I just loved it, and when Dad asked her what it was called she laughed and said 'Gunk on Noodles.' The silly name stuck, and I've been making it for my family for 25 years. A quick meal made with items we all have on hand."

Serving: 4 | Prep: 15 m | Cook: 25 m | Ready in: 40 m

Ingredients

- 1 (8 ounce) package uncooked egg noodles
- 1 pound ground beef
- 1 small onion, chopped
- 1 clove garlic, minced
- 1 (6 ounce) can tomato paste
- 1 (4 ounce) can sliced mushrooms with juice
- 1 teaspoon sugar
- 1 tablespoon butter
- 1 teaspoon Worcestershire sauce
- salt and pepper to taste

Direction

- Bring a large pot of lightly salted water to a boil. Place the egg noodles in the pot, cook 6 to 8 minutes, until al dente, and drain.
- In a large skillet over medium-high heat, cook the ground beef 10 minutes, or until evenly brown. Mix in the onion and garlic, and cook until onion is tender. Mix in the tomato paste, mushrooms and juice, sugar, butter, and Worcestershire sauce. Season with salt and pepper. Continue to cook and stir 5 minutes, until bubbly and heated through. Serve over the cooked noodles.

Nutrition Information

- Calories: 475 calories
- Total Fat: 19.4 g
- Cholesterol: 117 mg
- Sodium: 564 mg
- Total Carbohydrate: 47.9 g
- Protein: 28 g

139. Ham and Swiss Casserole

"This is one of the only casseroles that my picky husband will eat."

Serving: 4 | Prep: 15 m | Cook: 30 m | Ready in: 45 m

Ingredients

- 2 cups egg noodles
- 2 tablespoons vegetable oil
- 1 cup chopped onions
- 1 (6 ounce) can mushrooms, drained
- 1 cup diced cooked ham
- 1 cup diced Swiss cheese
- 1 teaspoon salt
- 1/2 teaspoon ground black pepper
- 2 eggs
- 1/4 cup milk
- 1/4 cup grated Parmesan cheese

Direction

- Bring a large pot of lightly salted water to a boil. Add egg noodles and cook for 8 to 10 minutes or until al dente; drain.
- Preheat oven to 400 degrees F (200 degrees C).
- Toss drained noodles with 2 teaspoons of the oil. Heat remaining oil in a skillet and sauté onion over medium heat until soft. Combine noodles, onion, mushrooms, ham, Swiss cheese, salt and pepper. Transfer to a greased 3 quart casserole dish. In a bowl mix together egg and milk; pour over noodle mixture. Sprinkle with parmesan cheese.
- Bake in a preheated oven for 30 minutes.

Nutrition Information

- Calories: 432 calories
- Total Fat: 28 g
- Cholesterol: 163 mg
- Sodium: 1491 mg
- Total Carbohydrate: 21 g
- Protein: 24.7 g

140. Hamburger Casserole

"This is a quick and easy way to prepare dinner for the family. It's a hamburger casserole with a Mexican flair. Try it with some shredded cheese sprinkled on top."

Serving: 6 | Prep: 20 m | Cook: 20 m | Ready in: 40 m

Ingredients

- 1 pound ground beef
- 1 onion, chopped
- 1 stalk celery, chopped
- 8 ounces egg noodles
- 1 (15 ounce) can chili
- 1 (14.5 ounce) can peeled and diced tomatoes
- 1 (15 ounce) can whole kernel corn, drained
- 1/4 cup salsa
- 1 (1 ounce) package taco seasoning mix

Direction

- Preheat oven to 250 degrees F (120 degrees C).
- In a large skillet over medium heat, combine the ground beef, onion and celery and sauté for 10 minutes, or until the meat is browned and the onion is tender. Drain the fat and set aside.
- In a separate saucepan, cook noodles according to package directions. When cooked, drain the water and stir in the meat mixture, chili, tomatoes, corn, taco sauce and taco seasoning mix. Mix well and place entire mixture into a 10x15 baking dish.
- Bake at 250 degrees F (120 degrees C) for 20 minutes, or until thoroughly heated.

Nutrition Information

- Calories: 554 calories
- Total Fat: 26.3 g
- Cholesterol: 108 mg
- Sodium: 1155 mg
- Total Carbohydrate: 56.1 g
- Protein: 24.7 g

141. Hamburger Noodle Casserole

"Easy casserole."

Serving: 8 | Prep: 10 m | Cook: 55 m | Ready in: 1 h 5 m

Ingredients

- 2 pounds ground beef
- 1 onion, chopped
- 2 cups sour cream
- 2 cups canned whole kernel corn, drained
- 1 (10.75 ounce) can cream of mushroom soup
- 1 (10.75 ounce) can cream of chicken soup
- 1 (6 ounce) package egg noodles
- salt and ground black pepper to taste
- 1 (32 ounce) bag shredded Cheddar cheese

Direction

- Preheat oven to 325 degrees F (165 degrees C).
- Cook and stir beef and onion together in a large skillet over medium-high heat until the beef is browned and crumbly, 5 to 7 minutes; drain and discard grease.
- Stir ground beef mixture, sour cream, corn, mushroom soup, chicken soup, and egg noodles together in a large bowl; season with salt and pepper and spread the mixture into a 13x8-inch baking dish.
- Bake in preheated oven until the egg noodles are tender, about 45 minutes. Sprinkle cheese over the top of the casserole and continue baking until the cheese is melted, 10 to 15 minutes more.

Nutrition Information

- Calories: 978 calories
- Total Fat: 69.1 g
- Cholesterol: 236 mg
- Sodium: 1443 mg
- Total Carbohydrate: 34.7 g
- Protein: 55.1 g

142. Haviland Glop

"This is a clan favorite from the early years. Everyone in the family makes it and has been enjoying it since childhood. It's quick, cheap and gets better after reheating. Great for the college students!"

Serving: 8 | Prep: 15 m | Cook: 20 m | Ready in: 35 m

Ingredients

- 1 (8 ounce) package dry egg noodles
- 1 pound lean ground beef
- 1 (10.75 ounce) can condensed tomato soup
- 1 (10.5 ounce) can condensed vegetable soup
- salt to taste
- ground black pepper to taste
- 8 slices processed American cheese

Direction

- Bring a large pot of lightly salted water to a boil. Add dry egg noodles and cook for 8 to 10 minutes, or until al dente; drain.
- Preheat oven to 350 degrees F (175 degrees C).
- In a large skillet over medium heat, brown the ground beef; drain fat. Stir in tomato and vegetable soups, salt and pepper. Mix in the noodles and cook for 10 minutes.
- Transfer mixture to an 11x7 inch baking dish and layer with cheese. Bake in the preheated oven 20 minutes, or until cheese is melted and lightly brown.

Nutrition Information

- Calories: 365 calories
- Total Fat: 18.7 g

- Cholesterol: 86 mg
- Sodium: 915 mg
- Total Carbohydrate: 26.7 g
- Protein: 22.3 g

143. Hearty Chicken and Noodle Casserole

"Chicken, mixed vegetables, noodles and cheese are brought together in this rich and crowd-pleasing casserole."

Serving: 4 | Prep: 10 m | Cook: 25 m | Ready in: 35 m

Ingredients

- 1 (10.75 ounce) can Campbell's® Condensed Cream of Mushroom Soup (Regular, 98% Fat Free or 25% Less Sodium)
- 1/2 cup milk
- 1/4 teaspoon ground black pepper
- 1 cup frozen mixed vegetables
- 2 cups cubed, cooked chicken
- 2 cups medium egg noodles, cooked and drained
- 1/4 cup grated Parmesan cheese
- 1/2 cup shredded Cheddar cheese

Direction

- Stir soup, milk, black pepper, vegetables, chicken, noodles and Parmesan cheese in 1 1/2-quart casserole.
- Bake at 400 degrees F for 25 minutes or until hot. Stir.
- Top with the Cheddar cheese.

144. Hearty Chicken Vegetable Soup I

"This thick and hearty chicken soup makes a great meal on those cold winter days. Try different types of pasta like bow ties, elbow macaroni, shells, rotini, spiral etc. This soup can not be beat when served with fresh thick sliced bread on the side!!"

Serving: 40 | Prep: 15 m | Cook: 1 h 40 m | Ready in: 1 h 55 m

Ingredients

- 1 (3 pound) whole chicken
- 1 onion, cut into thick slices
- 5 stalks celery, thickly sliced
- 1 tablespoon salt
- 1 teaspoon packed fresh basil leaves
- 1 teaspoon coarse ground black pepper
- 5 carrots, sliced
- 1 yellow squash, thinly sliced
- 1 zucchini, thinly sliced
- 1 pound fresh mushrooms, sliced
- 1 red bell pepper, sliced
- 12 ounces fresh tortellini pasta
- 2 tablespoons chicken soup base
- 2 cups uncooked egg noodles

Direction

- Place chicken, onion, celery, salt, basil, and pepper in a 10 quart stock pot. Fill stock pot with water until ingredients are fully covered and bring to a boil. Let simmer for 1 and 1/2 hours or until chicken is tender.
- Remove chicken from pot with slotted spoon and set aside for later.
- Add carrots, squash, zucchini, mushrooms, red pepper, tortellini, chicken soup base and uncooked noodles to stock pot and increase temperature to medium heat.
- While noodles and vegetables are cooking, tear chicken apart from bones. Cut up into pieces and add to soup in stock pot. Be sure to add additional water if ingredients are not fully covered. Bring to a boil, then reduce to a simmer for about 10 minutes or just until noodles are cooked. Enjoy

Nutrition Information

- Calories: 80 calories
- Total Fat: 3.2 g
- Cholesterol: 19 mg
- Sodium: 328 mg
- Total Carbohydrate: 6.3 g
- Protein: 6.6 g

145. Hearty Sausage Soup II

"A meal all by itself."

Serving: 8 | Prep: 25 m | Cook: 1 h 10 m | Ready in: 1 h 35 m

Ingredients

- 2 tablespoons olive oil
- 1 (1 pound) package smoked sausage, chopped
- 2 onions, chopped
- 1 green bell pepper, chopped
- 2 cloves garlic, minced
- 10 cups water
- 3 cups chopped cabbage
- 2 carrots, thinly sliced
- 1 (15.5 ounce) can diced tomatoes
- 1 (6 ounce) can tomato paste
- 4 beef bouillon cubes
- 1 teaspoon seasoned salt
- 1/2 teaspoon dried thyme leaves
- 1 dash cayenne pepper
- 2 small zucchini, chopped
- 1 (15 ounce) can kidney beans, rinsed and drained
- 1 (8 ounce) package thin egg noodles
- grated Parmesan cheese

Direction

- Heat the olive oil in a large stockpot over medium-high heat; cook the sausage, onions, bell pepper, and garlic in the hot oil until the onion is tender, 5 to 7 minutes. Add the water, cabbage, carrots, diced tomatoes, tomato paste, beef bouillon cubes, seasoned salt, thyme, and cayenne pepper to the stockpot and bring to a boil. Reduce heat to medium-low, place a cover on the stockpot, and cook the soup at a simmer for 45 minutes. Stir the zucchini and beans into the soup; cook another 10 minutes.
- Bring a large pot with lightly salted water to a rolling boil. Cook the egg noodles in boiling water until cooked yet firm to the bite, about 5 minutes. Drain and stir into the soup. Ladle the soup into bowls, and top with Parmesan cheese to serve.

Nutrition Information

- Calories: 481 calories
- Total Fat: 24.2 g
- Cholesterol: 61 mg
- Sodium: 1951 mg
- Total Carbohydrate: 43.8 g
- Protein: 22.9 g

146. Hearty Tuna Casserole

"This isn't your Grandma's tuna casserole, but it is sure to please everybody in the family."

Serving: 6 | Prep: 15 m | Cook: 45 m | Ready in: 1 h

Ingredients

- 3 cups uncooked egg noodles
- 2 (5 ounce) cans tuna, drained
- 1/2 cup chopped celery
- 1/3 cup chopped green onions
- 1/3 cup sour cream
- 2 teaspoons prepared mustard
- 1/2 cup mayonnaise
- 1/2 teaspoon dried thyme
- 1/4 teaspoon salt
- 1 small zucchini, sliced
- 1 cup shredded Monterey Jack cheese
- 1 tomato, chopped

Direction

- Preheat oven to 350 degrees F (175 degrees C). Grease a 2 quart casserole dish.
- Bring a large pot of salted water to a boil, add noodles, and cook until al dente; drain.
- In a large mixing bowl, combine noodles, tuna, celery, and green onion. Stir in sour cream, mustard, and mayonnaise. Season with salt and thyme. Spoon 1/2 of the noodle mixture into the prepared casserole dish. Arrange a layer of zucchini over the mixture. Top with the remaining noodles, followed by a layer of zucchini. Top the entire casserole with cheese.
- Bake in preheated oven for 30 minutes, or until hot and bubbly. Sprinkle the casserole with tomatoes before serving.

Nutrition Information

- Calories: 356 calories
- Total Fat: 24.5 g
- Cholesterol: 56 mg
- Sodium: 364 mg
- Total Carbohydrate: 15.7 g
- Protein: 18.8 g

147. Hillbilly Casserole

"This recipe has been in my family since I was very young. It is very quick and easy. Perfect for a busy family! Even my picky two year old likes it!"

Serving: 12 | Prep: 15 m | Cook: 25 m | Ready in: 40 m

Ingredients

- 1 (8 ounce) package uncooked egg noodles
- 1 (10.75 ounce) can condensed tomato soup
- 1 (11 ounce) can Mexican-style corn
- 1 medium onion, finely chopped
- 1 (10.75 ounce) can condensed cream of mushroom soup
- 16 slices American cheese

Direction

- Bring a large pot of lightly salted water to a boil. Add the egg noodles and cook until tender, about 7 minutes. Drain, and set aside.
- Preheat the oven to 350 degrees F (175 degrees C).
- In a large bowl, mix together the tomato soup, corn, onion, and cream of mushroom soup. Stir in the cooked noodles until well coated. Transfer to a 9x13 inch baking dish. Place slices of cheese to cover the top.
- Bake for 25 minutes in the preheated oven, or until cheese is melted and lightly browned.

Nutrition Information

- Calories: 275 calories
- Total Fat: 14.7 g
- Cholesterol: 51 mg
- Sodium: 961 mg
- Total Carbohydrate: 24.5 g
- Protein: 12.5 g

148. Holiday Apricot Kugel

"I first came across this recipe while visiting my wife's family in Buck's County, PA. It goes great with Thanksgiving dinner as a side dish. The original recipe was savory and comes from Eastern Europe and dates back more than 1,000 years. This particular recipe is most likely a variation of a recipe brought over to the new world by German/Dutch immigrants."

Serving: 18 | Prep: 7 m | Cook: 1 h 8 m | Ready in: 1 h 25 m

Ingredients

- 1 (16 ounce) package wide egg noodles
- 1 (18 ounce) jar apricot preserves (such as SMUCKER'S® Apricot Preserves)
- 6 eggs, beaten
- 1 cup melted butter
- 1/2 cup white sugar
- 1 teaspoon vanilla extract
- 1 pinch salt

- 1 (16 ounce) container cottage cheese
- 2 cups shredded Cheddar cheese

Direction

- Preheat oven to 375 degrees F (190 degrees C). Grease a 9x12 inch baking dish.
- Bring a large pot of lightly salted water to a boil. Add egg noodles and cook for 8 to 10 minutes or until al dente; drain.
- In a large bowl, stir together the apricot preserves, eggs, butter, sugar, vanilla extract, and salt, and mix to thoroughly combine. Fold in the cottage cheese and noodles, and spoon the mixture into the prepared baking dish.
- Bake in the preheated oven until the center of the kugel is cooked and set, about 50 minutes. Remove the kugel and top with Cheddar cheese, return to the oven, and bake until the cheese is browned and bubbling, about 10 minutes. Let the kugel rest for 10 minutes before serving.

Nutrition Information

- Calories: 377 calories
- Total Fat: 18.3 g
- Cholesterol: 127 mg
- Sodium: 291 mg
- Total Carbohydrate: 42.5 g
- Protein: 12.2 g

149. Home Made Chicken Noodle Soup

"This is an easy-to-make recipe from my Hungarian mother. No stock, no bouillon, and some peppercorn and parsnip are used for a bit of bite. If you don't have a metal tea-ball or herb bag, you can seal the peppercorn in a piece of cheesecloth tied with some kitchen twine. This way we get all of the pepper and none of the hassle. Keep noodles and soup separate until serving. If you mix the noodles in with the broth, they will get soggy and overcooked. If you have leftovers, store the noodles and soup separate or make a new batch of noodles the next day."

Serving: 6 | Prep: 20 m | Cook: 1 h | Ready in: 1 h 20 m

Ingredients

- 1 whole chicken
- 1 large onion, peeled and root trimmed
- water to cover
- 1 tablespoon whole black peppercorns
- 4 carrots, peeled and sliced
- 4 parsnips, peeled and sliced
- 1 cup diced celery
- 1 (16 ounce) package egg noodles
- 2 tablespoons chopped fresh parsley, or to taste
- salt to taste

Direction

- Place chicken and whole onion into the bottom of a large pot. Pour enough water over the chicken to cover completely. Put peppercorns in a metal tea ball; add to the pot.
- Bring water to a boil, reduce heat to medium-low, and cook at a simmer until the chicken until no longer pink and is falling off the bone, 40 to 60 minutes. An instant-read thermometer inserted into the thickest part of the thigh, near the bone should read 165 degrees F (74 degrees C).
- Remove chicken from the broth with a slotted spoon to a bowl; set aside to cool.
- Remove the onion and give it a squeeze to get as much of the flavor as possible. Discard the onion.
- Stir carrots, parsnips, and celery into the broth; bring to a boil and cook vegetables until

tender, 10 to 15 minutes. Remove and discard peppercorns.
- While the vegetables boil, bring a large pot of lightly salted water to a boil. Cook egg noodles in the boiling water, stirring occasionally until cooked through but firm to the bite, about 5 minutes. Drain. Divide between 6 soup bowls.
- Remove meat from chicken and discard bones. Cut meat into bite-size chunks and stir into vegetable mixture with parsley. Season with salt. Ladle soup over noodles to serve.

Nutrition Information

- Calories: 823 calories
- Total Fat: 46.5 g
- Cholesterol: 135 mg
- Sodium: 444 mg
- Total Carbohydrate: 71.2 g
- Protein: 29.9 g

150. Homemade Noodles

"Easy, homemade noodles for two."

Serving: 2

Ingredients

- 1 cup all-purpose flour
- 1 egg
- 1 pinch salt

Direction

- Mix all ingredients. Roll thin with flour, then roll like a jelly roll. Cut into 1/2 inch strips. Let dry.
- Drop into hot chicken broth. Boil for 15 minutes.

Nutrition Information

- Calories: 263 calories
- Total Fat: 3.1 g
- Cholesterol: 93 mg
- Sodium: 36 mg
- Total Carbohydrate: 47.9 g
- Protein: 9.6 g

151. Hong Kong Style Chicken Chow Mein

"A delicious chow mein with crispy noodles."

Serving: 4 | Prep: 20 m | Cook: 22 m | Ready in: 42 m

Ingredients

- 14 ounces skinless, boneless chicken breast, thinly sliced
- 1 egg white, beaten
- 2 teaspoons cornstarch
- 1 teaspoon sesame oil
- 1 (8 ounce) package Chinese egg noodles
- 2 tablespoons vegetable oil, or as needed
- 1/2 cup chicken broth
- 3 spring onions, chopped, or to taste
- 1 1/2 tablespoons light soy sauce
- 1 tablespoon rice wine (sake)
- 1/2 teaspoon ground white pepper
- 1/2 teaspoon ground black pepper
- 1 tablespoon cornstarch
- 2 teaspoons water
- 2 tablespoons oyster sauce
- 1 cup fresh bean sprouts, or to taste

Direction

- Mix chicken with egg white, 2 teaspoons cornstarch, and sesame oil in a bowl.
- Bring a large pot of water to a boil. Add egg noodles; cook until soft, about 4 minutes. Drain. Spread out on paper towels to remove excess moisture.
- Heat vegetable oil in a wok over medium heat. Cook and stir noodles in the hot oil until golden brown, 3 to 5 minutes per side. Drain on paper towels.
- Stir chicken into the wok; cook, stirring frequently, until white, about 2 minutes. Transfer to a bowl using a slotted spoon.

- Pour chicken stock into the wok; stir in spring onions, soy sauce, rice wine, white pepper, and black pepper.
- Mix 1 tablespoon cornstarch and water together in a small bowl until smooth. Pour into the wok. Stir in oyster sauce. Add chicken and bean sprouts; cook and stir until chicken is tender and sauce is thickened, about 5 minutes. Serve over noodles.

Nutrition Information

- Calories: 419 calories
- Total Fat: 12.5 g
- Cholesterol: 61 mg
- Sodium: 579 mg
- Total Carbohydrate: 49.1 g
- Protein: 30.4 g

152. Hot Dog Noodle Casserole

"Spinach, egg noodles and a creamy hot dog mixture is topped with peas and crumbled bacon. What a casserole! This is a recipe I received in German class 24 years ago. It looks unusual, but it is very delicious. I don't know where the teacher found the recipe. Drop biscuits go well with this casserole."

Serving: 9 | Prep: 20 m | Cook: 1 h | Ready in: 1 h 20 m

Ingredients

- 1 (10 ounce) package frozen chopped spinach, thawed
- 1 (8 ounce) package wide egg noodles
- 1 (10.75 ounce) can cream of mushroom soup
- 1/2 cup milk
- 1/2 cup sour cream
- 1 pound hot dogs, sliced into circles
- 1 pound frozen green peas, thawed
- 4 slices bacon, fried and crumbled

Direction

- Prepare spinach according to package directions. Drain and spread in the bottom of a lightly greased 9x13-inch baking dish.
- Bring a large pot of lightly salted water to a boil. Add egg noodles and cook for 8 to 10 minutes or until al dente. Drain and place on top of spinach in baking dish.
- Preheat oven to 350 degrees F (175 degrees C).
- In a large bowl combine the soup, milk, sour cream and hot dogs. Mix together and place mixture on top of noodles.
- Cover dish with aluminum foil and bake at 350 degrees F (175 degrees C) for about 45 minutes, or until heated through. Sprinkle with peas and bacon and heat in oven until peas are just hot.

Nutrition Information

- Calories: 381 calories
- Total Fat: 23 g
- Cholesterol: 62 mg
- Sodium: 914 mg
- Total Carbohydrate: 29.2 g
- Protein: 15.2 g

153. Hungarian Goulash III

"This is the Hungarian goulash my mother made and her mother made; it's the only one I know"

Serving: 6 | Prep: 10 m | Cook: 2 h 45 m | Ready in: 2 h 55 m

Ingredients

- cooking spray
- 1 pound beef stew meat, cut into cubes
- 1 small yellow onion, chopped
- 1 1/2 cups water
- 1/2 cup ketchup
- 3 tablespoons Worcestershire sauce
- 3/4 teaspoon distilled white vinegar
- 2 tablespoons brown sugar
- 1 1/2 teaspoons paprika
- 1 teaspoon salt
- 1/2 teaspoon dry mustard
- 1 (16 ounce) package egg noodles

Direction

- Prepare a large pot with cooking spray and place over medium heat; cook the beef stew meat in the pot until completely browned on all sides, 5 to 7 minutes. Add the onions; cook and stir until the onions begin to soften, about 5 minutes. Stir the water, ketchup, Worcestershire sauce, vinegar, brown sugar, paprika, salt, and mustard into the beef and onion mixture. Place a cover on the pot, reduce heat to low, and simmer the mixture until the beef is tender, about 2 1/2 hours.
- Bring a large pot of lightly salted water to a rolling boil. Cook the egg noodles at a boil until cooked through yet firm to the bite, about 5 minutes; drain. Serve the goulash over the noodles.

Nutrition Information

- Calories: 528 calories
- Total Fat: 18.1 g
- Cholesterol: 113 mg
- Sodium: 755 mg
- Total Carbohydrate: 65.8 g
- Protein: 25 g

154. Italian Casserole

"This was a recipe of my Aunt Ethel's -- egg noodles in a tomato, ground beef sauce. She said, 'It is so good, don't change a thing!' And she was right."

Serving: 4 | Prep: 20 m | Cook: 3 h 20 m | Ready in: 3 h 40 m

Ingredients

- 3/4 pound lean ground beef
- 1 onion, chopped
- 1 (28 ounce) can whole peeled tomatoes, chopped
- 1 (6 ounce) can tomato paste
- 1 teaspoon salt
- 1 tablespoon dried parsley
- 1/2 teaspoon garlic salt
- black pepper to taste
- 8 ounces wide egg noodles
- 1 (12 ounce) package process sharp cheddar cheese singles

Direction

- In large skillet, brown ground beef and onion. Stir in tomatoes, tomato paste, salt, parsley, garlic salt and pepper, and simmer over low heat for 3 hours.
- Preheat oven to 350 degrees F (175 degrees C). Bring a large pot of lightly salted water to a boil. Add pasta and cook for 8 to 10 minutes or until al dente; drain.
- In a 2 quart casserole dish, combine noodles and meat mixture. Top with cheese slices and bake for 15 to 20 minutes, or until cheese is melted.

Nutrition Information

- Calories: 739 calories
- Total Fat: 39 g
- Cholesterol: 164 mg
- Sodium: 2572 mg
- Total Carbohydrate: 62.1 g
- Protein: 41.2 g

155. Italian Style Pot Roast

"If you are a pot roast enthusiast, this is definitely one to add to your collection. The meat is simmered in a tomato sauce, and served over hot noodles."

Serving: 8 | Prep: 10 m | Cook: 2 h 40 m | Ready in: 2 h 50 m

Ingredients

- 3 1/2 pounds boneless chuck roast
- 2 tablespoons vegetable oil
- 1 (14.5 ounce) can stewed tomatoes
- 1 1/2 cups pizza sauce
- 1/2 cup grated Parmesan cheese
- 4 teaspoons Worcestershire sauce
- 2 cloves garlic, minced
- 2 teaspoons salt

- 2 teaspoons dried oregano
- 1/2 teaspoon ground black pepper
- 1/2 pound fresh mushrooms, sliced
- 3 tablespoons cornstarch
- 3 tablespoons water
- 1 (12 ounce) package egg noodles

Direction

- Heat a Dutch oven over medium-high heat, and brown meat on all sides in hot oil.
- In large bowl combine tomatoes, pizza sauce, cheese, Worcestershire sauce, garlic, salt, oregano, and pepper. Pour over meat. Cover and simmer over medium heat for 2 hours, turning meat each half hour.
- Remove meat from pan, and cool slightly. Skim fat from pan juices. Measure juices, and add enough water to make 6 cups liquid. Return liquid to Dutch oven. Blend cornstarch and 3 tablespoons cold water; stir into pan juices. Cook and stir till thickened and bubbly.
- Slice meat thinly against the grain. Return meat to pot, and add mushrooms. Simmer for 30 minutes longer.
- Cook pasta in a large pot of boiling water until done. Drain. To serve, place meat slices over hot noodles, and pour some sauce over. Pass remaining sauce.

Nutrition Information

- Calories: 742 calories
- Total Fat: 42.9 g
- Cholesterol: 182 mg
- Sodium: 1208 mg
- Total Carbohydrate: 42.5 g
- Protein: 44.8 g

156. ItalianStyle Pot Roast with Carrots and Fennel

"Pot roast seasoned with herbs and garlic cooks in a pressure cooker with a traditional pasta sauce, broth, carrots, fennel wedges, and onions."

Serving: 6 | Prep: 10 m | Cook: 40 m | Ready in: 1 h 5 m

Ingredients

- 1 teaspoon dried Italian seasoning, crushed
- 2 cloves garlic, minced
- 1/2 teaspoon salt
- 1/2 teaspoon pepper
- 1 (2 1/2 pound) boneless beef chuck pot roast
- 6 medium carrots, peeled and cut into 1 1/2-inch pieces
- 1 medium bulb fennel, trimmed and cut into wedges
- 1 large yellow onion, cut into chunks
- 1 (24 ounce) jar RAGÚ® Old World Style® Traditional Sauce, divided
- 1 cup reduced-sodium beef broth
- 6 ounces dried egg noodles, cooked according to package directions
- 2 tablespoons chopped fresh Italian parsley

Direction

- Combine Italian seasoning, garlic, salt, and pepper. Sprinkle over the pot roast; rub in with your fingers.
- In a 6-qt. electric pressure cooker combine carrots, fennel and onion. Top with pot roast. Pour 14 oz. RAGÚ® Old World Style® Traditional Sauce over the meat. Pour broth over all.
- Lock lid in place. Set cooker on high pressure to cook 40 minutes. Let stand to release pressure for 15 minutes. Carefully open steam vent to release remaining pressure.
- Remove meat and vegetables from sauce to a serving platter. Spoon some warmed RAGÚ® Old World Style® Traditional Sauce over meat and hot cooked noodles. Garnish with parsley. Serve with warmed sauce.

Nutrition Information

- Calories: 445 calories
- Total Fat: 22.9 g
- Cholesterol: 94 mg
- Sodium: 761 mg
- Total Carbohydrate: 30.8 g
- Protein: 27.9 g

157. Jaeger Schnitzel

"This is wonderful. Breaded and fried cubed pork with mushrooms and hunter gravy over a bed of noodles. Serve with a salad and a hunk of thick crusty bread."

Serving: 8 | Prep: 30 m | Cook: 2 h | Ready in: 2 h 30 m

Ingredients

- 2 pounds boneless pork chops, cubed
- oil for frying
- 2 eggs, beaten
- plain bread crumbs
- 3 (1 ounce) packages dry mushroom gravy mix
- 1 pound fresh mushrooms, coarsely chopped
- 1 (16 ounce) package dry egg noodles

Direction

- Pound out cubed pork, and cut in half.
- Heat oil in a large skillet or Dutch oven over medium heat. Dip pork in egg, then bread crumbs, and place in hot oil. Cook, turning, until golden brown. Remove to a warm plate.
- Prepare gravy mix according to package directions. Stir in mushrooms, and cook with gravy.
- Meanwhile, bring a large pot of lightly salted water to a boil. Add the egg noodles, and cook until al dente, about 8 to 10 minutes; drain.
- Serve pork over noodles and smother with gravy.

Nutrition Information

- Calories: 455 calories
- Total Fat: 9.1 g
- Cholesterol: 169 mg
- Sodium: 828 mg
- Total Carbohydrate: 53.5 g
- Protein: 38.6 g

158. JayBeez Beef Stroganoff

"One of my favorite firehouse comfort foods during the colder months is beef stroganoff that uses cream of mushroom soup. Savory sauce full of flavor, satisfying the palate and the appetite!"

Serving: 8 | Prep: 10 m | Cook: 35 m | Ready in: 50 m

Ingredients

- 1 1/2 pounds beef top sirloin, thinly sliced
- 1 1/2 tablespoons steak seasoning
- 2 tablespoons olive oil
- 2 tablespoons butter
- 1 (8 ounce) package baby bella mushrooms, thinly sliced
- 1 small onion, finely chopped
- 4 cups water
- 1 tablespoon beef soup base (such as L.B. Jamison's®)
- 1 teaspoon beef soup base (such as L.B. Jamison's®)
- 1 (8 ounce) container sour cream
- 1 (10.5 ounce) can condensed cream of mushroom soup
- 1 (8 ounce) package egg noodles
- 1 cup frozen peas, thawed (optional)
- 1/2 cup chopped fresh flat-leaf parsley, or to taste (optional)

Direction

- Mix beef and steak seasoning together in a bowl.
- Heat olive oil in a 5-quart pot over medium-high heat. Add beef in a single layer; cook, turning once, until just browned on both sides, 5 to 7 minutes. Transfer to a plate using tongs; cover with aluminum foil and keep warm.

- Combine butter with the drippings in the pot and melt over medium heat. Add mushrooms and onion; cook and stir until mushrooms brown and onion softens, 7 to 9 minutes. Stir in water and bring to a simmer. Add 1 tablespoon plus 1 teaspoon soup base; mix well.
- Place sour cream in a bowl. Ladle in 1/2 cup of the simmering mushroom-soup base mixture. Beat with a whisk to combine. Set aside until the final step.
- Stir cream of mushroom soup and egg noodles into the pot and mix well. Bring to a boil and reduce heat. Simmer, uncovered, stirring occasionally, until noodles are tender yet firm to the bite and liquid is mostly reduced to sauce, 10 to 15 minutes.
- Stir cooked beef and any accumulated liquid into the sauce. Return to a simmer. Remove from heat; stir in sour cream mixture. Add peas. Let sit until heated through, 5 to 7 minutes. Top with parsley.

Nutrition Information

- Calories: 395 calories
- Total Fat: 21 g
- Cholesterol: 80 mg
- Sodium: 1237 mg
- Total Carbohydrate: 28.8 g
- Protein: 22.9 g

159. Johnny Marzetti III

"An easy school version of Johnny Marzetti. To freeze, don't add the cheese or bake ahead of time. Use your choice of elbow or egg noodles."

Serving: 6 | Prep: 30 m | Cook: 40 m | Ready in: 1 h 10 m

Ingredients

- 8 ounces pasta
- 1 pound lean ground beef
- 1 cup chopped onion
- 2 cups chopped celery
- salt and ground black pepper to taste
- 1 (10.75 ounce) can condensed tomato soup
- 1 (8 ounce) can tomato sauce
- 1 cup water
- 2 cups shredded sharp Cheddar cheese

Direction

- In a large pot with boiling salted water cook pasta until al dente. Drain.
- Meanwhile, in a large skillet cook ground beef until no pink remains. Add onions and celery and cook until they are softened. Add salt and pepper to taste. Stir in tomato soup, tomato sauce, and water. Simmer for 10 minutes.
- In a casserole dish, mix together the cooked and drained pasta with the meat mixture.
- Bake in a preheated 350 degree F (175 degree C) oven for 20 to 30 minutes. Sprinkle the top with grated Cheddar cheese and continue to cook until cheese is melted, about 3 to 5 minutes.

Nutrition Information

- Calories: 553 calories
- Total Fat: 32.7 g
- Cholesterol: 132 mg
- Sodium: 859 mg
- Total Carbohydrate: 33.5 g
- Protein: 31 g

160. Johnny Marzetti IV

"I first had this over 13 years ago when my son was born. My brother, who is great cook, gave me this recipe. It is an easy dish that can be made ahead and refrigerated."

Serving: 4

Ingredients

- 1 (8 ounce) package wide egg noodles
- 1 pound lean ground beef
- 1 onion, chopped
- 1 (4.5 ounce) can sliced mushrooms

- 1 pinch garlic salt
- ground black pepper to taste
- 1 1/2 tablespoons white sugar
- 1 tablespoon Worcestershire sauce
- 2 (15 ounce) cans tomato sauce
- 8 ounces sharp Cheddar cheese, shredded

Direction

- Cook pasta in a large pot of boiling salted water until al dente. Drain.
- In a large skillet, cook ground beef, onion, and mushrooms. Drain grease. Mix in garlic salt, ground black pepper, sugar, Worcestershire sauce, and tomato sauce. Simmer for 30 minutes.
- In a greased 2 quart casserole dish, layer half of the cooked egg noodles, then half of the sauce mixture, followed by half of the grated cheese. Repeat.
- Bake in a preheated 375 degree (190 degree C) oven for 20 to 30 minutes.

Nutrition Information

- Calories: 834 calories
- Total Fat: 45.2 g
- Cholesterol: 192 mg
- Sodium: 1802 mg
- Total Carbohydrate: 61.6 g
- Protein: 45.8 g

161. Kohlrabi and Egg Noodles

"This is a recipe that my husband introduced me to from my mother-in-law. It is a Hungarian dish; it is really easy and really good. I like No Yolks® noodles."

Serving: 8 | Prep: 5 m | Cook: 15 m | Ready in: 20 m

Ingredients

- 4 cups egg noodles (such as No Yolks®)
- 2 tablespoons butter or margarine
- 3 cups grated kohlrabi
- salt and ground black pepper to taste

Direction

- Bring a large pot of lightly salted water to a boil. Cook egg noodles in boiling water, stirring occasionally, until cooked through yet firm to the bite, about 5 minutes; drain.
- Melt butter in a skillet over medium heat. Add kohlrabi, season with salt and pepper, and cook until the kohlrabi is tender, 7 to 10 minutes. Stir the drained egg noodles into the kohlrabi; cook and stir until the noodles are slightly fried, 5 to 7 minutes.

Nutrition Information

- Calories: 105 calories
- Total Fat: 3.9 g
- Cholesterol: 21 mg
- Sodium: 109 mg
- Total Carbohydrate: 15.1 g
- Protein: 3 g

162. Kugel

"This is a wonderful side dish generally made for Jewish holidays. Your guests cannot guess the ingredient used for the topping. Very rich!"

Serving: 9 | Prep: 30 m | Cook: 1 h | Ready in: 1 h 30 m

Ingredients

- 1 (8 ounce) package large egg noodles
- 6 tablespoons butter, sliced
- 6 eggs, separated
- 1/2 cup white sugar
- 3/4 (8 ounce) package cream cheese, softened
- 4 tablespoons sour cream
- 1 (16 ounce) package cottage cheese, creamed
- 1 pinch salt
- 4 tablespoons butter, melted
- 1/4 cup white sugar
- 1/3 cup graham cracker crumbs

Direction

- Preheat oven to 350 degrees F (175 degrees C). Grease a 9x13 inch glass baking dish.
- Bring a large pot of lightly salted water to a boil. Add pasta and cook for 8 to 10 minutes or until al dente; drain and stir in 6 tablespoons sliced butter.
- In a medium bowl beat egg yolks with sugar and cream cheese; stir into noodles and add sour cream, cottage cheese and salt. Beat egg whites until stiff and fold into mixture. Transfer mixture to prepared dish.
- In a small bowl combine melted butter, 1/4 cup sugar, and graham cracker crumbs. Sprinkle over noodle mixture.
- Bake in preheated oven for 1 hour.

Nutrition Information

- Calories: 454 calories
- Total Fat: 27.8 g
- Cholesterol: 207 mg
- Sodium: 420 mg
- Total Carbohydrate: 37.1 g
- Protein: 15.2 g

163. Lazygirls Ground Turkey Stroganoff

"A creamy and delicious seasoned ground turkey mixture is served over hot egg noodles."

Serving: 4 | Prep: 15 m | Cook: 20 m | Ready in: 35 m

Ingredients

- 1 (8 ounce) package uncooked egg noodles
- 1 tablespoon vegetable oil
- 1 pound ground turkey
- 1 tablespoon minced onion
- 1 cube chicken bouillon, crumbled
- 1 (10.75 ounce) can condensed cream of mushroom soup
- 1/2 cup water
- 1 tablespoon paprika
- salt to taste

Direction

- Bring a pot of lightly salted water to a boil. Place the egg noodles in the pot, cook 6 to 8 minutes, until al dente, and drain.
- Heat the oil in a skillet over medium heat. Place the turkey and onion in the skillet and cook until turkey is evenly brown and onion is tender. Mix in the bouillon.
- Stir the cream of mushroom soup and water into the skillet. Cook and stir until heated through. Season with paprika and salt. Serve over the cooked egg noodles.

Nutrition Information

- Calories: 463 calories
- Total Fat: 19.6 g
- Cholesterol: 125 mg
- Sodium: 852 mg
- Total Carbohydrate: 41.8 g
- Protein: 30.5 g

164. Lemon Chicken and Veggie Pasta

"This can be a little spicy depending on the heat of the chiles in the can. Ro-Tel® tends to be milder than Hatch® brand. You can also substitute asparagus, zucchini, and Cajun seasoning with broccoli, snap peas, and ginger for an Asian flavor."

Serving: 5 | Prep: 30 m | Cook: 25 m | Ready in: 55 m

Ingredients

- 1 teaspoon lemon pepper
- 1/2 teaspoon dried thyme
- 1/2 teaspoon dried parsley
- 1/4 teaspoon dried rosemary
- 1/4 teaspoon Cajun seasoning
- 1/4 teaspoon coarsely ground black pepper
- 1 tablespoon olive oil
- 5 large chicken tender strips

- 1 (10 ounce) can diced tomatoes with green chile peppers (such as Hatch®)
- 1 onion, quartered
- 1 cup (1 1/2-inch) sliced asparagus
- 6 baby carrots, thinly sliced
- 1 zucchini, halved and sliced
- 6 baby bella mushrooms, sliced
- 3 small bell peppers, sliced
- 2 large cloves garlic, minced
- 1 cup chicken broth
- 1/2 lemon, juiced
- 1/4 teaspoon lemon zest
- 1 (12 ounce) package no-yolk egg noodles
- 1 ounce grated Parmesan cheese
- 1 ounce shredded mozzarella cheese

Direction

- Mix lemon pepper, thyme, parsley, rosemary, Cajun seasoning, and black pepper in a small bowl.
- Rub olive oil over chicken tenders.
- Arrange chicken tenders in a large skillet over medium heat; season with half the seasoning mixture. Cook chicken until halfway cooked, about 5 minutes. Flip and season the other sides with the remaining seasoning mixture; cook until chicken is no longer pink in the center and juices run clear, about 5 more minutes. Remove cooked chicken from skillet.
- Mix tomatoes with green chile peppers, onion, asparagus, carrots, zucchini, mushrooms, bell peppers, and garlic in the same skillet; cook until vegetables are softened, 3 to 4 minutes. Add chicken broth, lemon juice, lemon zest, and chicken tenders to the vegetable mixture. Reduce heat to medium-low, cover, and simmer for 10 minutes.
- Bring a large pot of lightly salted water to a boil. Cook egg noodles in the boiling water, stirring occasionally until cooked through but firm to the bite, about 10 minutes. Drain and return noodles to pot. Add Parmesan cheese and mozzarella cheese; toss until cheeses melt. Transfer noodles to 5 serving bowls; top each with 1 chicken tender and 1/5 the vegetable mixture.

Nutrition Information

- Calories: 531 calories
- Total Fat: 11.6 g
- Cholesterol: 130 mg
- Sodium: 784 mg
- Total Carbohydrate: 67.5 g
- Protein: 40.5 g

165. Lloyds Healthy Chicken Zoopa

"This is a throw together soup that is satisfying and maybe even healthy. When you first saute the veggies in oil, you are making a 'moughe'. This is my own word, actually stolen from my daughter Amy (then 3 years old)!"

Serving: 5 | Prep: 30 m | Cook: 45 m | Ready in: 1 h 15 m

Ingredients

- 2 tablespoons vegetable oil
- 2 cloves garlic, minced
- 2 cups chopped onion
- 1 red bell pepper, chopped
- 1 green bell pepper, chopped
- 2 cups chopped celery
- 1 cup julienned carrots
- 1 cup minced leek (optional)
- 4 cups chicken stock
- salt and pepper to taste
- 1/4 teaspoon hot pepper sauce
- 1/4 teaspoon soy sauce (optional)
- 6 ounces spinach, rinsed
- 1/2 cup egg noodles
- 1/2 pound skinless, boneless chicken breast halves, cut into bite size pieces

Direction

- Heat oil in a large soup pot over medium heat. Add garlic, onion, red bell pepper, green bell pepper, celery, carrot and leek. Sauté until onions are translucent and balance of veggies has been tossed through with hot oil. Add

stock and season with salt and pepper to taste. If using hot pepper sauce and soy sauce, add now. Bring soup to a simmer and allow to simmer over low heat for about 40 minutes.
- Add spinach and cover pot. (Note: Volume of spinach will appear to be too great for the pot; don't worry, just put it in - within a few minutes it will be reduced to size). Stir soup; add noodles. Stir again and add chicken strips. Make sure soup is still simmering. Exactly 5 minutes later, you will have a terrific hot soup. Serve hot!

Nutrition Information

- Calories: 198 calories
- Total Fat: 7.3 g
- Cholesterol: 30 mg
- Sodium: 649 mg
- Total Carbohydrate: 20 g
- Protein: 14.5 g

166. Lokshin Kugel Noodle Pudding

"This is a side dish commonly served with roasted chicken for Friday night (Shabbat) dinner. It doesn't have to accompany chicken only, but, as my mother once told us, when she was a child, chicken and noodles were more affordable than other foods. This is a great accompaniment to any meat."

Serving: 8 | Prep: 30 m | Cook: 1 h | Ready in: 1 h 30 m

Ingredients

- 1 (12 ounce) package thin egg noodles
- 6 onions, diced
- 1/8 cup vegetable oil for frying
- salt and pepper to taste
- 4 eggs
- 1/4 cup dry bread crumbs
- paprika to taste

Direction

- Preheat oven to 350 degrees F (175 degrees C). Grease a 9 x 13 baking dish. Bring a large pot of lightly salted water to a boil. Add pasta and cook for 8 to 10 minutes or until al dente; drain.
- While pasta is cooking, in medium saucepan, cook onions in oil over medium heat. Season with salt and pepper, and cook until brown and soft.
- In very large mixing bowl, combine pasta, onions, eggs, bread crumbs and salt and pepper to taste. Mix thoroughly. Pour into baking dish and sprinkle paprika over the top. Sprinkle with oil, if desired, and bake 50 to 60 minutes, until top is crispy and golden.

Nutrition Information

- Calories: 228 calories
- Total Fat: 5.3 g
- Cholesterol: 123 mg
- Sodium: 107 mg
- Total Carbohydrate: 36.2 g
- Protein: 9.3 g

167. Louisiana Crawfish YaYa Pasta

"This cheesy, creamy, rich crawfish pasta is found at every family gathering in the New Orleans area - a great addition to your seafood recipe box and a great way to try crawfish!"

Serving: 4 | Prep: 30 m | Cook: 15 m | Ready in: 45 m

Ingredients

- 3/4 (12 ounce) package egg noodles
- 1/2 cup butter
- 1/2 cup chopped onion
- 1/4 cup minced green bell pepper
- 1 clove garlic, minced
- 2 tablespoons chopped fresh parsley
- 1 (16 ounce) package cooked and peeled whole crawfish tails

- 2 tablespoons Cajun seasoning blend (such as Tony Chachere's®), or to taste
- 1/2 cup heavy cream
- 1/3 cup sliced fresh mushrooms (optional)
- 3/4 cup shredded Cheddar cheese, divided
- 1/3 cup sliced green onions

Direction

- Bring a large pot of lightly-salted water to a rolling boil; stir in the egg noodles and return to a boil. Cook the pasta uncovered, stirring occasionally, until the pasta has cooked through but is still firm to the bite, about 5 minutes. Drain well in a colander set in the sink.
- Meanwhile, melt the butter in a large skillet over medium heat. Stir in the chopped onion, green pepper, garlic, and parsley. Cook and stir until the onion has softened and turned translucent, about 5 minutes. Add the crawfish tails and Cajun seasoning; simmer 5 minutes longer.
- Pour in the heavy cream, mushrooms, and 1/2 cup of Cheddar cheese; stir until the cheese has melted. Toss the pasta with the crawfish sauce and green onions; sprinkle with the remaining Cheddar cheese.

Nutrition Information

- Calories: 741 calories
- Total Fat: 45.2 g
- Cholesterol: 298 mg
- Sodium: 1105 mg
- Total Carbohydrate: 51.4 g
- Protein: 33 g

168. Lynns Easy Noodle Pudding

"This pudding is super easy to make, a great dish to bring along for a pot luck, and can be served warm, cold, or reheated. It was my late Mom's recipe that she brought to everyone's home. She was always begged by family and friends to PLEASE make this. It was, and still is, a staple at the holiday table for us."

Serving: 12 | Prep: 20 m | Cook: 55 m | Ready in: 1 h 25 m

Ingredients

- 1 (16 ounce) package egg noodles
- 2 cups sour cream
- 2 cups creamy whipped cottage cheese
- 1 cup white sugar, divided
- 2 eggs, beaten
- 1 cup raisins
- 1/2 cup butter
- 1 teaspoon ground cinnamon

Direction

- Bring a large pot of lightly salted water to a boil. Stir in egg noodles and cook until al dente, 10 to 12 minutes. Drain.
- Preheat oven to 350 degrees F (175 degrees C). Lightly grease 13x9 inch baking dish.
- Toss the cooked noodles with the sour cream, cottage cheese, 1/2 cup sugar, eggs, and raisins until well blended. Pour the noodle mixture into the prepared pan. Dot the top with small pieces of butter.
- Mix the remaining 1/2 cup sugar with the cinnamon. Sprinkle over the noodles.
- Bake in preheated oven until top is lightly brown, about 45 minutes. Remove from oven and cool 10 minutes to set pudding before serving.

Nutrition Information

- Calories: 451 calories
- Total Fat: 19.9 g
- Cholesterol: 108 mg
- Sodium: 229 mg
- Total Carbohydrate: 57.4 g
- Protein: 12.7 g

169. Mama Longs Goulash Soup

"My mother received this recipe while briefly living in Germany many years ago. A hearty stew that can easily be modified by adding veggies of your choice! I can eat this stew all year long!"

Serving: 4 | Prep: 20 m | Cook: 2 h 35 m | Ready in: 2 h 55 m

Ingredients

- 1 tablespoon olive oil
- 1 pound beef stew meat, cubed
- 1/2 onion, chopped
- 4 cups water
- 1 (8 ounce) can tomato sauce
- 3 tablespoons paprika
- 1 tablespoon vinegar
- 1 tablespoon Worcestershire sauce
- 2 teaspoons chopped garlic
- 2 beef bouillon cubes
- 1 teaspoon dry mustard
- 1/2 teaspoon lemon juice
- 1 bay leaf
- 2 potatoes, peeled and cubed
- 1 (8 ounce) package wide egg noodles

Direction

- Heat olive oil in a large pot over medium heat; cook and stir beef and onion in hot oil until meat is browned, about 10 minutes. Add water, tomato sauce, paprika, vinegar, Worcestershire sauce, garlic, beef bouillon, mustard, lemon juice, and bay leaf. Reduce heat, cover, and simmer over low heat until beef is very tender, 2 to 3 hours.
- Stir potatoes into soup and continue to simmer until potatoes are tender, about 30 minutes more. For a thicker soup, leave the pot uncovered; for a thinner soup, replace lid.
- Bring a large pot of lightly salted water to a boil. Cook egg noodles in the boiling water, stirring occasionally until cooked through but firm to the bite, about 5 minutes. Drain.
- Serve soup over egg noodles in bowls.

Nutrition Information

- Calories: 590 calories
- Total Fat: 22.4 g
- Cholesterol: 110 mg
- Sodium: 839 mg
- Total Carbohydrate: 67.5 g
- Protein: 30.8 g

170. Marchetti

"Delicious!!! Ingredients you usually have on hand, easy to make, and mmmm mmmm so good! Makes a big casserole to feed a big family or split it in two and freeze half for later. This is my favorite recipe and is very good with a tossed salad and garlic bread. Enjoy!"

Serving: 12 | Prep: 30 m | Cook: 30 m | Ready in: 1 h

Ingredients

- 1/3 (16 ounce) package dry egg noodles
- 1 1/2 pounds ground beef
- 1 onion, chopped
- 1 (10.75 ounce) can condensed tomato soup
- 1 (10.75 ounce) can condensed cream of mushroom soup
- 1 (4 ounce) jar sliced mushrooms
- 1 1/2 cups processed American cheese, shredded
- 1/4 teaspoon garlic powder
- salt and pepper to taste

Direction

- Bring a large pot of lightly salted water to a boil. Add pasta and cook for 8 to 10 minutes or until al dente; drain. Preheat oven to 350 degrees F (175 degrees C.)
- Place ground beef and onion in a large, deep skillet. Cook over medium high heat until meat is evenly brown, and onion is tender. Drain excess fat. Stir in noodles, condensed tomato soup, condensed mushroom soup, sliced mushrooms and 1 cup cheese. Season

with garlic powder, salt and pepper. Pour into a 9x13 inch baking dish. Sprinkle top with remaining 1/2 cup cheese.
- Bake in preheated oven for 30 minutes.

Nutrition Information

- Calories: 322 calories
- Total Fat: 22 g
- Cholesterol: 72 mg
- Sodium: 597 mg
- Total Carbohydrate: 15.5 g
- Protein: 15.4 g

171. Marcias Company Casserole

"This is a wonderful casserole my mother served often. It was always a hit with everyone who tried it - especially the men!"

Serving: 8 | Prep: 30 m | Cook: 40 m | Ready in: 1 h 10 m

Ingredients

- 1 (8 ounce) package egg noodles
- 1 tablespoon margarine
- 1 pound ground beef chuck
- 2 (8 ounce) cans tomato sauce
- 1 cup cottage cheese
- 1 (8 ounce) package cream cheese, softened
- 1/4 cup sour cream
- 1/3 cup chopped green onions
- 1 tablespoon finely chopped green bell pepper
- 2 tablespoons margarine, melted

Direction

- Preheat oven to 350 degrees F (175 degrees C). Lightly grease a 2 quart casserole dish. Bring a large pot of lightly salted water to a boil. Add pasta and cook for 8 to 10 minutes or until al dente; drain.
- Heat 1 tablespoon margarine in a large heavy skillet over medium-high heat. Cook ground beef until evenly brown. Stir in tomato sauce; remove from heat. In a medium bowl, combine cottage cheese, cream cheese, sour cream, green onion and green pepper.
- Spread 1/2 the cooked noodles in the casserole dish. Cover with cheese mixture, then the remaining noodles. Pour melted margarine over the noodles. Spoon meat sauce on top and spread to cover noodles.
- Bake in preheated oven for 30 minutes.

Nutrition Information

- Calories: 433 calories
- Total Fat: 28 g
- Cholesterol: 102 mg
- Sodium: 586 mg
- Total Carbohydrate: 25.2 g
- Protein: 20.5 g

172. Marks Cabbage and Hamburger Delight

"My husband calls this extreme Hamburger Helper® and says it is an awesome dish for a cold night as a yummy comfort food!!"

Serving: 6 | Prep: 15 m | Cook: 30 m | Ready in: 45 m

Ingredients

- 1 tablespoon butter
- 1/2 head cabbage, chopped
- 1 cup chicken broth
- 3/4 cup heavy whipping cream
- 1 teaspoon salt, or to taste
- 1 teaspoon ground black pepper, or to taste
- 1 pound ground beef
- 1 onion, chopped
- 2 tablespoons smoked paprika
- 1 teaspoon dry mustard powder
- 2 cups uncooked egg noodles

Direction

- Melt the butter in a large skillet over medium heat. Stir in the cabbage, and cook until just wilted, about 5 minutes. Pour in the chicken

broth, and bring to a simmer. Cook until slightly reduced, about 10 minutes more. Stir in the cream, and season with salt and pepper. Keep the cabbage hot over low heat while preparing the ground beef.
- Heat a Dutch oven or large skillet over medium-high heat and stir in the ground beef. Cook and stir until the beef is crumbly and no longer pink. Add the onion, and cook until tender, about 5 minutes. Stir in the smoked paprika and mustard. Stir in the cabbage mixture and egg noodles; season to taste with salt and pepper. Cover, and cook over low heat until the noodles are tender, about 10 minutes. Pour in water as needed so the noodles do not become dry.

Nutrition Information

- Calories: 352 calories
- Total Fat: 23 g
- Cholesterol: 102 mg
- Sodium: 479 mg
- Total Carbohydrate: 20.7 g
- Protein: 17.3 g

173. Meatballs in Sour Cream Gravy

"If you like olives and dill you will like this. The surprise in this is the olive in the center of the meatball!"

Serving: 8 | Prep: 20 m | Cook: 25 m | Ready in: 45 m

Ingredients

- 1 (16 ounce) package uncooked wide egg noodles
- 2 pounds ground beef
- 1 1/2 teaspoons salt, divided
- 1/4 teaspoon pepper
- 2 eggs, beaten
- 1 cup chopped onion
- 2 (4.25 ounce) cans pitted black olives
- 3 tablespoons vegetable oil
- 3 tablespoons all-purpose flour
- 1/2 cup water
- 2 cups sour cream
- 1 teaspoon dried dill weed

Direction

- Bring a large pot of lightly salted water to a boil. Place egg noodles in the pot, cook for 8 to 10 minutes, until al dente, and drain.
- In a bowl, mix the beef, 1 1/4 teaspoons salt, pepper, eggs, and onion. Form into small meatballs around the olives.
- Heat the oil in skillet over medium heat, and cook the meatballs until evenly brown. Remove meatballs from skillet, reserving oil; set meatballs aside, and keep warm.
- Stir the flour into the reserved oil in the skillet. Gradually mix in water to form a thick gravy. Stir in sour cream, dill, and remaining 1/4 teaspoon salt, and cook until heated through. Pour over the meatballs, and serve over cooked egg noodles.

Nutrition Information

- Calories: 632 calories
- Total Fat: 37.8 g
- Cholesterol: 181 mg
- Sodium: 817 mg
- Total Carbohydrate: 43.3 g
- Protein: 29.5 g

174. Modern Jewish Low Fat Kugel

"This noodle kugel is a sweet casserole that feels like comfort food (especially if you are of Jewish heritage) yet is low fat and lower sugar than the average sweet kugel. I use the low-fat dairy and egg substitute to give it a richer flavor, but it tastes great made with nonfat ingredients as well. Enjoy! I developed it in honor of my beloved Grandma Sylvia."

Serving: 12 | Prep: 20 m | Cook: 1 h | Ready in: 1 h 20 m

Ingredients

- cooking spray

- 1 (16 ounce) package yolk-free egg noodles
- 1 (16 ounce) container low-fat sour cream
- 1 (16 ounce) container low-fat cottage cheese
- 1 (8 ounce) can crushed pineapple in juice, undrained
- 3 eggs, lightly beaten
- 1/2 cup orange juice
- 1/2 cup dried cranberries
- 5 tablespoons butter, melted
- 1/4 cup white sugar
- 1/4 cup applesauce
- 1/2 orange, zested
- 2 teaspoons vanilla extract
- 2 teaspoons ground cinnamon

Direction

- Preheat oven to 375 degrees F (190 degrees C). Spray a 9x13-inch baking dish with cooking spray.
- Bring a large pot of lightly salted water to a boil. Cook egg noodles in the boiling water, stirring occasionally until cooked through but firm to the bite, about 5 minutes. Drain.
- Gently stir egg noodles, sour cream, cottage cheese, pineapple with juice, eggs, orange juice, cranberries, melted butter, sugar, applesauce, orange zest, vanilla extract, and cinnamon together in a large bowl until thoroughly combined. Spoon the noodle mixture into prepared baking dish.
- Bake in the preheated oven until kugel is set and browned on top, 60 to 75 minutes.

Nutrition Information

- Calories: 332 calories
- Total Fat: 11.3 g
- Cholesterol: 75 mg
- Sodium: 239 mg
- Total Carbohydrate: 43.7 g
- Protein: 12.9 g

175. Mom Sykes Hungarian Goulash

"The lemon flavor gives you a pleasant surprise in this tender goulash served over egg noodles."

Serving: 4 | Prep: 20 m | Cook: 1 h 30 m | Ready in: 1 h 50 m

Ingredients

- 3 tablespoons butter
- 2 pounds cubed beef stew meat
- 1 pinch caraway seeds (optional)
- 1 pound onion, sliced
- 2 teaspoons paprika
- 1 clove garlic, minced
- 1 tablespoon lemon zest
- 1 (6 ounce) can tomato paste
- 1 (10.5 ounce) can beef consomme
- 1 (10 ounce) package broad egg noodles, cooked, rinsed, drained (Kosher for Passover)

Direction

- Melt butter in a large pot over medium heat. Add the stew meat, caraway seeds, onion and paprika. Cook and stir until the meat is browned, and the onions are translucent. Add the garlic and lemon zest, and cook for about a minute, then stir in the tomato paste and beef consomme, adding water if necessary to cover the meat. Cover, and simmer over medium-low heat for 1 1/2 hours.
- Just before the meat is done cooking, bring a large pot of salted water to a boil. Add egg noodles, and cook until tender, about 8 minutes. Drain and serve the goulash spooned over the egg noodles.

Nutrition Information

- Calories: 1132 calories
- Total Fat: 61.3 g
- Cholesterol: 282 mg
- Sodium: 801 mg
- Total Carbohydrate: 70.5 g
- Protein: 73.2 g

176. Moms Casserole

"This recipe is easy to make and feeds a crowd. Great to freeze also! This can be made more low-calorie by using ground turkey, fat free sour cream and low-calorie cream cheese. Serve with garlic bread and salad, if desired."

Serving: 11 | Prep: 25 m | Cook: 45 m | Ready in: 1 h 10 m

Ingredients

- 12 ounces wide egg noodles
- 1 pound lean ground beef
- 1 onion, chopped
- 1 clove garlic, chopped
- 1 (8 ounce) can tomato sauce
- 8 ounces cream cheese, softened
- 1 cup sour cream
- 6 green onions, chopped
- 1 cup shredded Cheddar cheese

Direction

- Bring a large pot of lightly salted water to a boil. Add pasta and cook for 8 to 10 minutes or until al dente; drain.
- In a large skillet over medium heat, cook hamburger, onion and garlic; add tomato sauce and simmer for a few minutes.
- In a small bowl, combine cream cheese, sour cream and green onions; mix well.
- Preheat oven to 350 degrees F (175 degrees C).
- In a lightly greased 9x13 inch baking dish, spread 1/4 cup of meat mixture on bottom. Layer with some egg noodles, cream cheese mixture and meat sauce. Repeat layers ending with meat sauce; top with Cheddar cheese.
- Bake in preheated oven for 30 to 45 minutes or until bubbly; serve.

Nutrition Information

- Calories: 396 calories
- Total Fat: 24.9 g
- Cholesterol: 99 mg
- Sodium: 279 mg
- Total Carbohydrate: 26.1 g
- Protein: 16.9 g

177. Mrs Strongs Casserole

"My grandmother got this recipe from an old neighbor, it's a lot like lasagna...but a lot better! It's absolutely delicious. Try it yourself!"

Serving: 6 | Prep: 25 m | Cook: 20 m | Ready in: 45 m

Ingredients

- 1 pound lean ground beef
- 1 clove garlic, crushed
- salt to taste
- 1 teaspoon white sugar
- 1 (15 ounce) can tomato sauce
- 1 (8 ounce) package egg noodles
- 6 green onions, chopped
- 1 (3 ounce) package cream cheese, softened
- 2 tablespoons sour cream
- 1 cup shredded Cheddar cheese

Direction

- Place ground beef in a large, deep skillet. Cook over medium high heat until evenly brown. Stir in crushed garlic, salt, sugar and tomato sauce; cover and simmer for 15 to 20 minutes
- Bring a large pot of lightly salted water to a boil. Add noodles and cook for 8 to 10 minutes or until al dente; drain and set aside.
- Preheat oven to 350 degrees F (175 degrees C).
- In a small bowl combine green onions, cream cheese and sour cream. In a 9x13 inch baking dish, place 1/3 of the noodles, cheese mixture, and tomato sauce; repeat twice. Sprinkle Cheddar cheese on top of the casserole.
- Bake in preheated oven for 20 minutes or until bubbly; serve.

Nutrition Information

- Calories: 489 calories
- Total Fat: 29.9 g
- Cholesterol: 121 mg
- Sodium: 588 mg

- Total Carbohydrate: 30 g
- Protein: 24.8 g

178. Mums DairyFree Stroganoff

"Easy and delicious dairy-free stroganoff. Red wine adds a bit of zest. Started off making my mum's recipe and added my own pizzazz."

Serving: 6 | Prep: 5 m | Cook: 25 m | Ready in: 30 m

Ingredients

- 1 (16 ounce) package ground turkey
- 2 teaspoons garlic powder
- 2 teaspoons onion powder
- 1 (16 ounce) package egg noodles
- 1/8 cup Merlot wine
- 1/2 teaspoon salt
- 1/2 teaspoon ground black pepper
- 1/2 teaspoon Italian seasoning
- 2 drops liquid smoke flavoring, or to taste (optional)
- 1 (10 ounce) can golden mushroom soup (such as Campbell's®)

Direction

- Heat a large skillet over medium-high heat. Sauté turkey in the hot skillet until starting to brown, about 3 minutes. Add garlic powder and onion powder. Cook and stir until turkey is mostly browned and slightly pink, 3 to 5 minutes more.
- Fill a large pot with lightly salted water and bring to a rolling boil. Stir in egg noodles and return to a boil. Cook pasta uncovered, stirring occasionally, until tender yet firm to the bite, about 6 minutes. Drain.
- Pour Merlot into the skillet with the turkey. Let simmer until reduced to your liking, stirring occasionally, about 5 minutes. Add salt, pepper, Italian seasoning, and liquid smoke; mix thoroughly. Stir in mushroom gravy; let simmer until stroganoff is thickened, at least 5 minutes.

Nutrition Information

- Calories: 442 calories
- Total Fat: 10.7 g
- Cholesterol: 121 mg
- Sodium: 588 mg
- Total Carbohydrate: 58.5 g
- Protein: 26.6 g

179. Mushroom Tuna Noodle Casserole

"A very easy casserole made with ingredients you probably already have on hand. This was a family favorite as I was growing up."

Serving: 6 | Prep: 15 m | Cook: 45 m | Ready in: 1 h

Ingredients

- 5 cups dry egg noodles
- 1 (10.75 ounce) can condensed cream of mushroom soup
- 1 cup milk
- 1 1/2 cups water
- 2 (12 ounce) cans tuna, drained and flaked
- 1 (10 ounce) package frozen green peas
- 1 (10 ounce) package frozen carrots
- 2 (15 ounce) cans sliced potatoes, drained
- salt to taste
- ground black pepper to taste
- paprika to taste
- 3/4 cup dry bread crumbs

Direction

- Preheat oven to 350 degrees F (175 degrees C).
- Bring a large pot of lightly salted water to a boil. Add pasta and cook for 8 to 10 minutes or until al dente; drain.
- In a mixing bowl combine soup, milk, and water. Pour a small amount of the mixture into a 9x13 inch baking dish; enough to just cover the bottom.
- Layer the cooked noodles, flaked tuna, peas, carrots, and potatoes until all used up. Pour

the remaining soup mixture over the layers. Sprinkle with salt, pepper, and paprika. Lightly coat the entire casserole with bread crumbs.
- Cover and bake in preheated oven for 45 minutes.

Nutrition Information

- Calories: 414 calories
- Total Fat: 7.5 g
- Cholesterol: 60 mg
- Sodium: 609 mg
- Total Carbohydrate: 46.1 g
- Protein: 39.1 g

180. NeverFail Chicken Noodle Soup

"I created this recipe for my 5 children. They loved canned soup, but the sodium content is far too high. They all love this soup. It's hearty enough for a satisfying meal, yet light enough to be part of an overall healthy eating plan."

Serving: 16 | Prep: 20 m | Cook: 1 h 20 m | Ready in: 1 h 55 m

Ingredients

- 3 quarts water
- 1 (2 to 3 pound) whole fryer chicken
- 1 large whole onion
- 3 sprigs fresh rosemary
- 1 pound baby carrots, minced
- 6 stalks celery, minced
- 1 clove garlic, minced
- 1 tablespoon sea salt
- 1 (12 ounce) package egg noodles
- 1 (10 ounce) bag fresh spinach, chopped

Direction

- Combine water, chicken, whole onion, and rosemary in a large stockpot; bring to a rolling boil and cook until chicken is no longer pink at the bone and the juices run clear, about 1 hour. An instant-read thermometer inserted into the thickest part of the thigh, near the bone should read 165 degrees F (74 degrees C). Remove stockpot from heat and allow chicken to cool until easily handled, about 15 minutes.
- Remove chicken and onion from stockpot. Remove chicken meat from bones and chop or shred meat; discard carcass and skin. Chop onion if desired. Return chicken meat and onion to stockpot with water.
- Mix carrots, celery, garlic, and sea salt with the chicken mixture; bring to a boil and cook until carrots and celery are tender, 10 to 15 minutes. Reduce heat to medium-low; add egg noodles and cook until noodles are cooked through but firm to the bite, about 5 minutes. Add spinach to soup and cook until wilted, 1 to 2 minutes.

Nutrition Information

- Calories: 190 calories
- Total Fat: 6.1 g
- Cholesterol: 49 mg
- Sodium: 412 mg
- Total Carbohydrate: 19.7 g
- Protein: 13.8 g

181. NO YOLKS Beef Noodle Casserole

"Perfect for chilly evenings, this hearty ground beef casserole made with always smooth, firm and delicious NO YOLKS® Noodles will warm the soul."

Serving: 4 | Prep: 10 m | Cook: 30 m | Ready in: 40 m

Ingredients

- 6 ounces NO YOLKS® Extra Broad Noodles
- 1 pound ground beef
- 1 small onion, chopped
- 1 clove garlic, minced
- 1/2 teaspoon oregano
- 1/2 teaspoon salt
- 1 (15 ounce) can tomato sauce
- 1/3 cup water
- 1 cup shredded Cheddar cheese

Direction

- Prepare noodles according to package directions.
- Preheat oven to 375 degrees F.
- Heat a large skillet over medium heat and brown beef with onion, garlic, oregano and salt. Stir in tomato sauce, water and cooked noodles. Pour into casserole dish and top with shredded Cheddar cheese.
- Bake 20 minutes or until casserole is bubbling.

Nutrition Information

- Calories: 644 calories
- Total Fat: 34.5 g
- Cholesterol: 135 mg
- Sodium: 1309 mg
- Total Carbohydrate: 39.6 g
- Protein: 42 g

182. NO YOLKS Lamb Stew

"Tender chunks of lamb spiced with fresh herbs are served over delicious NO YOLKS® Noodles that are always smooth, firm and delicious."

Serving: 4 | Prep: 10 m | Cook: 1 h 15 m | Ready in: 1 h 25 m

Ingredients

- 6 ounces NO YOLKS® Dumplings
- 1 tablespoon olive oil
- 1 pound lamb stew meat in 1 1/2-inch chunks
- 2 leeks, white part only, chopped
- 2 cloves garlic, minced
- 1/3 cup dry red wine
- 1 (14.5 ounce) can crushed tomatoes
- 1 cup beef broth
- 1/4 teaspoon pepper
- 1 teaspoon crushed dried rosemary
- 1 teaspoon salt
- 2 cups frozen cut green beans, thawed

Direction

- Prepare noodles according to package directions.
- Heat oil in large heavy-bottomed pot over medium heat. Add lamb, half at a time, and brown on all sides. Remove when done. Add leeks, garlic and wine to pot and scrape up browned bits on bottom of pot. Cook for 2 minutes, stirring occasionally. Add tomatoes, broth, pepper and rosemary. Bring to a simmer. Return lamb to pot. Cover and cook over low heat for 1 hour. Stir in green beans and salt.
- Serve over noodles.

Nutrition Information

- Calories: 475 calories
- Total Fat: 16.4 g
- Cholesterol: 64 mg
- Sodium: 994 mg
- Total Carbohydrate: 50.2 g
- Protein: 27.1 g

183. NO YOLKS Luscious Kugel

"Always smooth, firm and delicious NO YOLKS® Noodles hold together this perfect holiday side dish or dessert with sweet, creamy custard."

Serving: 10 | Prep: 15 m | Cook: 1 h | Ready in: 1 h 25 m

Ingredients

- 8 ounces NO YOLKS® Extra Broad Noodles
- 1 (8 ounce) package low-fat cream cheese, at room temperature
- 2 tablespoons unsalted butter, melted
- 1 cup sugar
- 4 large eggs
- 1 1/2 cups reduced-fat milk
- 1/2 cup raisins
- 1 cup cornflakes cereal
- 2 tablespoons sugar
- 1/4 teaspoon cinnamon

Direction

- Prepare noodles according to package directions.
- Preheat oven to 350 degrees F.
- Combine cream cheese, butter and sugar in bowl of electric mixer. Cream at medium speed, scraping down bowl occasionally. Add eggs, one at a time and beat in. Add milk, a little at a time. Remove bowl from mixer. Stir in noodles and raisins. Spoon mixture into greased deep, 3-quart baking pan. Sprinkle corn flakes over noodle mixture. Combine remaining sugar and cinnamon and sprinkle over corn flakes.
- Bake 1 hour or until pudding is firm and knife inserted near center comes out clean. Remove from oven. Let set for 10 minutes before slicing.

Nutrition Information

- Calories: 321 calories
- Total Fat: 8.9 g
- Cholesterol: 95 mg
- Sodium: 148 mg
- Total Carbohydrate: 50.9 g
- Protein: 9.9 g

184. NO YOLKS Noodles Romanoff

"Creamy and comforting, this easy NO YOLKS® noodles Romanoff is sure to please the whole family."

Serving: 6 | Prep: 10 m | Cook: 20 m | Ready in: 30 m

Ingredients

- 12 ounces NO YOLKS® Extra Broad Noodles
- 2 cups sour cream
- 4 ounces half-and-half
- 1 teaspoon Worcestershire sauce
- 1/4 cup finely chopped green onions
- 2 tablespoons chopped parsley
- 1/2 teaspoon salt
- 1/4 teaspoon garlic powder
- 1/4 teaspoon pepper
- 1/4 cup grated Parmesan cheese

Direction

- Prepare noodles according to package directions; drain.
- In a large saucepan, combine sour cream, half-and-half and Worcestershire sauce. Stir over low heat until smooth and just warm. Add onions, parsley, salt, garlic powder and pepper. Stir in noodles. Serve topped with Parmesan cheese.

Nutrition Information

- Calories: 420 calories
- Total Fat: 19.9 g
- Cholesterol: 44 mg
- Sodium: 335 mg
- Total Carbohydrate: 46.5 g
- Protein: 12.5 g

185. NO YOLKS Tuna Noodle Casserole

"Nothing says comfort like a golden, bubbly, delicious tuna casserole made with always smooth, firm and delicious NO YOLKS® Noodles."

Serving: 6 | Prep: 10 m | Cook: 20 m | Ready in: 40 m

Ingredients

- 6 ounces NO YOLKS® Extra Broad Noodles
- 1 tablespoon olive oil
- 1 (8 ounce) package sliced fresh mushrooms
- 2 ribs celery, chopped
- 1 1/2 cups frozen peas, thawed
- 1 small onion, chopped
- 1 teaspoon garlic powder
- 1 quart vegetable broth
- Dash Worcestershire sauce
- 1 sprig fresh thyme
- 1 (8 ounce) package light cream cheese, softened

- 3 tablespoons all-purpose flour
- 2 (5 ounce) cans tuna, drained and flaked
- 1 cup shredded Cheddar cheese
- Fresh ground black pepper to taste (optional)
- Topping:
- 1 cup panko bread crumbs
- 1 tablespoon butter, melted
- Salt and pepper, to taste

Direction

- Combine topping ingredients and set aside.
- Preheat oven to 400 degrees F. Add olive oil to a 7-quart stock pot, and sauté mushrooms, celery, onions and garlic powder for 3-4 minutes over medium heat. Add broth, Worcestershire sauce and thyme sprig and bring to a boil, stirring occasionally. Add cream cheese and noodles, stirring until creamy and smooth. Sprinkle flour over top of mixture. Stir and cook for 2 minutes, or until mixture begins to thicken. Fold in tuna and peas. Season with salt and pepper.
- Pour into a 3-quart casserole dish. Sprinkle on Cheddar cheese and topping mixture. Bake uncovered 15 minutes. Remove from oven and let stand 10 minutes.

Nutrition Information

- Calories: 483 calories
- Total Fat: 19 g
- Cholesterol: 59 mg
- Sodium: 762 mg
- Total Carbohydrate: 51.1 g
- Protein: 29.9 g

186. NoFuss Turkey Noodle Soup

"Make good use of your leftover dark meat without the fuss of boiling the carcass. Simply pick through the carcass before you toss the bird and save the meat for a quick next-day soup. Serve with warm bread for a great hot meal on a cold winter day. I substitute fresh herbs wherever possible, but for a quick meal after the intense preparation of a whole turkey, dried herbs do nicely. If you don't have chipotle chili powder, regular chili powder can be substituted. The chipotle provides a very light smoky flavor in the background. White meat can be used, but your broth will be less flavorful. Leftovers freeze well. Use whatever type pasta you prefer."

Serving: 6 | Prep: 20 m | Cook: 45 m | Ready in: 1 h 5 m

Ingredients

- 1 (32 fluid ounce) container chicken stock
- 1 teaspoon dried summer savory
- 1 teaspoon dried basil
- 1/2 teaspoon dried thyme
- 1/8 teaspoon chipotle chile powder
- 1 teaspoon salt
- 1/2 teaspoon coarse ground black pepper
- 1 tablespoon dried parsley
- 1/4 cup sherry
- 2 carrots, thinly sliced
- 1 tablespoon butter
- 2 stalks celery, sliced
- 1 onion, chopped
- 1 tablespoon minced garlic
- 1 pound cubed cooked dark-meat turkey
- 1 (8 ounce) package egg noodles
- salt and ground black pepper to taste

Direction

- Combine chicken stock, summer savory, basil, thyme, chipotle powder, salt, black pepper. parsley, and sherry in a stock pot; bring to a boil. Add carrots, reduce heat to medium-low, and cook until carrots are tender, 5 to 7 minutes.
- Melt butter in a skillet. Cook and stir celery, onion, and garlic in hot butter until onions are translucent, about 5 minutes; stir into stock mixture. Add turkey, reduce heat to low, and

cook at a simmer until turkey is hot and has flavored the soup, about 30 minutes.
- Bring a large pot of lightly salted water to a boil. Cook egg noodles in the boiling water, stirring occasionally until cooked through but firm to the bite, about 5 minutes; drain and add to soup. Season with salt and black pepper to serve.

Nutrition Information
- Calories: 328 calories
- Total Fat: 7.9 g
- Cholesterol: 94 mg
- Sodium: 1003 mg
- Total Carbohydrate: 34 g
- Protein: 28.6 g

187. Noodle Kugel Dairy

"This is a slightly sweet noodle pudding. It can be served as a side dish, at brunch, or after a fast such as Yom Kippur."

Serving: 8 | Prep: 15 m | Cook: 45 m | Ready in: 1 h 10 m

Ingredients
- 8 ounces wide egg noodles
- 2 extra-large eggs
- 1/4 cup white sugar
- 3 tablespoons butter, melted
- 1 cup low-fat whipped cottage cheese
- 8 ounces sour cream
- 1 pinch salt and ground black pepper to taste
- 2 tablespoons brown sugar, or to taste

Direction
- Fill a large pot with lightly salted water and bring to a rolling boil over high heat. Once the water is boiling, stir in the egg noodles, and return to a boil. Cook the pasta uncovered, stirring occasionally, until the pasta has cooked through, but is still firm to the bite, about 5 minutes. Drain well in a colander set in the sink.
- Preheat oven to 350 degrees F (175 degrees C). Spray a 1-quart baking dish with nonstick cooking spray.
- In a bowl, mix together the eggs with white sugar until thoroughly combined, then stir in the melted butter, whipped cottage cheese, sour cream, salt, and pepper. Lightly mix in the noodles; spoon the kugel into the prepared baking dish. Sprinkle the top with brown sugar.
- Bake in the preheated oven until the top has browned, about 40 minutes. Cool for 10 minutes before serving.

Nutrition Information
- Calories: 287 calories
- Total Fat: 13.2 g
- Cholesterol: 103 mg
- Sodium: 163 mg
- Total Carbohydrate: 31.6 g
- Protein: 10.7 g

188. Noodle Pudding

"This noodle pudding is a family favorite. The recipe has been passed to many friends. It can also be frozen and it travels well. Can be baked for 30 minutes, allowed to cool and then be frozen. Cut into serving size pieces before freezing. Defrost after freezing and then bake at 350 degrees for 30 minutes or until hot."

Serving: 20 | Prep: 30 m | Cook: 1 h | Ready in: 1 h 45 m

Ingredients
- 1 (16 ounce) package wide egg noodles
- 1 (16 ounce) package cottage cheese
- 1 (8 ounce) package cream cheese
- 1 pint sour cream
- 1 teaspoon vanilla extract
- 1 cup white sugar
- 6 eggs, beaten
- 1/2 cup butter, melted
- 2 cups graham cracker crumbs
- 1/2 cup butter, melted

- 1/2 cup white sugar

Direction

- Preheat oven to 350 degrees F (175 degrees C). Grease a large casserole dish.
- Bring a large pot of lightly salted water to a boil. Add egg noodles and cook for 8 to 10 minutes or until al dente; drain.
- Blend together cottage cheese and cream cheese until smooth. Mix in sour cream, vanilla, sugar and eggs. When noodles are done stir together 1/2 cup butter and noodles in a large bowl. Combine cheese mixture and noodles; Blend well. Place all in one large casserole dish.
- To make the topping: Mix together graham cracker crumbs, butter and sugar until it looks like large crumbs. Sprinkle evenly over top of noodle mixture.
- Bake at 350 degrees for 15 minutes. Lower oven to 325 degrees and continue baking for 45 minutes more. Allow to cool before cutting and serve warm.

Nutrition Information

- Calories: 386 calories
- Total Fat: 22.4 g
- Cholesterol: 122 mg
- Sodium: 276 mg
- Total Carbohydrate: 37.6 g
- Protein: 9.5 g

189. Noodles

"This is my sister's recipe which she cooked at a daycare she worked at years ago...it serves many, and kids love it! It is absolutely delicious."

Serving: 6 | Cook: 15 m | Ready in: 15 m

Ingredients

- 1 (16 ounce) package wide egg noodles
- 2 (5 ounce) cans chunk chicken, drained
- 2 (10.75 ounce) cans condensed cream of mushroom soup
- 1/2 teaspoon garlic salt
- 1/2 teaspoon ground black pepper

Direction

- Bring a large pot of lightly salted water to a boil. Add pasta and cook for 8 to 10 minutes or until al dente; drain.
- Return pasta to pot with chicken, soup, garlic salt and pepper over medium heat. Heat through, 5 minutes.

Nutrition Information

- Calories: 423 calories
- Total Fat: 13.6 g
- Cholesterol: 83 mg
- Sodium: 1054 mg
- Total Carbohydrate: 54 g
- Protein: 20.4 g

190. Noodles Marmaduke

"This is an easy Stroganoff dish made with Burgundy wine. Simple, delicious and quick to make."

Serving: 4 | Prep: 20 m | Cook: 40 m | Ready in: 1 h

Ingredients

- 1/4 cup butter
- 1/2 cup sliced onion
- 1 clove garlic, minced
- 8 ounces fresh mushrooms, sliced
- 1 pound ground beef
- 1/2 cup Burgundy wine
- 3 tablespoons lemon juice
- 1 (10.5 ounce) can condensed beef consomme
- 1/2 teaspoon salt
- 1/4 teaspoon ground black pepper
- 2 cups medium egg noodles
- 1 cup sour cream
- 1 tablespoon chopped fresh parsley for garnish

Direction

- Melt the butter in a large skillet over medium heat. Add the onions, garlic and mushrooms; cook and stir until lightly browned. Crumble in the ground beef, and cook until no longer pink. Drain excess grease.
- Stir in the Burgundy wine, scraping any bits of food from the bottom of the pan to flavor the sauce. Then stir in the lemon juice, beef consomme, salt and pepper. Simmer uncovered for 15 minutes.
- Mix the uncooked noodles into the skillet. Cover, and simmer for 10 minutes, or until noodles are tender. Remove from the heat and stir in the sour cream. Sprinkle parsley over the top and serve.

Nutrition Information

- Calories: 555 calories
- Total Fat: 38.1 g
- Cholesterol: 141 mg
- Sodium: 721 mg
- Total Carbohydrate: 22 g
- Protein: 26.6 g

191. Noodles Mexicana

"This has come to be my favorite winter comfort food. Ground beef, black olives, tomatoes, chili beans, noodles, and corn make for a great stew like meal. Serve with sour cream and tortilla chips! YUM!"

Serving: 8 | Prep: 15 m | Cook: 30 m | Ready in: 45 m

Ingredients

- 1 pound ground beef
- 1 onion, chopped
- 2 cloves garlic, minced
- 1 (11 ounce) can whole kernel corn, with liquid
- 1 (2.25 ounce) can sliced black olives, with liquid
- 1 (14.5 ounce) can tomatoes with juice, chopped
- 1 (15 ounce) can chili beans, drained
- 1/2 cup chopped green onions
- 1 (1.25 ounce) package taco seasoning mix
- 1/2 teaspoon salt
- 1 (16 ounce) package uncooked egg noodles
- 1/2 cup sour cream, for topping

Direction

- In a large skillet over medium heat, cook the ground beef, onion, and garlic until beef is evenly brown. Drain.
- Mix the corn, olives, tomatoes, chili beans, and green onions into the skillet. Season with taco seasoning and salt. Cover, and cook 15 minutes.
- Mix the egg noodles into the skillet. Cover, and continue cooking 12 minutes, or until egg noodles are tender. Top each serving with a dollop of sour cream.

Nutrition Information

- Calories: 443 calories
- Total Fat: 14.3 g
- Cholesterol: 82 mg
- Sodium: 1013 mg
- Total Carbohydrate: 60.1 g
- Protein: 21 g

192. Noodles Napoli

"This is a hearty family dish that my mother made for us on chilly nights! The Italian sausage makes it extra special."

Serving: 5

Ingredients

- 1 pound lean ground beef
- 1/2 pound Italian sausage
- 1 onion, chopped
- 1 clove crushed garlic
- 1 (8 ounce) package wide egg noodles
- 1 (4 ounce) jar diced pimento peppers, drained
- 1 (16 ounce) can crushed tomatoes
- 1 (8 ounce) can tomato sauce

- 2 cups water
- 1 cup shredded Cheddar cheese

Direction

- Mix beef and sausage into 1 or 2 flat patties. In a large skillet over medium to medium-high heat, salt patties and brown well on each side. Remove meat and set aside.
- Sauté onion and garlic in the drippings. Remove with a slotted spoon and add to the platter with the meat.
- In the drippings, carefully brown a single layer of the raw noodles until golden, remove and do another layer until all are done.
- Return all the noodles to the skillet with the garlic, onions, peppers, crushed tomatoes, tomato sauce and water. Break the meat patty into large chunks, gently stir all together and simmer 1/2 hour or so. Add a little water as the noodles absorb the juices. This should not be soupy, just thick and dry. Stir in the grated cheese and let it melt into the sauce. It sticks easily at this point, so don't overcook. This reheats well in a slow cooker or casserole.

Nutrition Information

- Calories: 599 calories
- Total Fat: 29.5 g
- Cholesterol: 139 mg
- Sodium: 940 mg
- Total Carbohydrate: 45.9 g
- Protein: 37.8 g

193. Noodles Riviera

"My Mom's recipe for Noodles Riviera. It is like lasagna with sour cream. You can use ground turkey in place of ground beef if you prefer."

Serving: 9 | Prep: 15 m | Cook: 1 h 10 m | Ready in: 1 h 25 m

Ingredients

- 1 tablespoon olive oil
- 1 pound extra lean ground beef
- 1/2 teaspoon ground dried thyme
- 1 (1.5 ounce) envelope spaghetti sauce seasoning mix
- 1 (6 ounce) can tomato paste
- 3 cups water
- salt and black pepper to taste
- 1 (8 ounce) package egg noodles
- 1 (3 ounce) package cream cheese, softened
- 1 tablespoon chopped fresh parsley
- 1/4 cup grated Parmesan cheese
- 1 (8 ounce) container sour cream
- 1 cup shredded mozzarella cheese, divided

Direction

- Heat the olive oil in a large skillet over medium-high heat and stir in the ground beef. Cook and stir until the beef is crumbly, evenly browned, and no longer pink, 5 to 7 minutes. Drain and discard any excess grease, then stir in the thyme, spaghetti sauce mix, tomato paste, and water; season to taste with salt and pepper. Bring to a simmer, then reduce heat to medium-low, cover, and simmer 25 minutes, stirring occasionally.
- Preheat an oven to 350 degrees F (175 degrees C). Grease a 9x13 inch baking dish.
- While the meat is simmering, fill a large pot with lightly salted water and bring to a rolling boil over high heat. Once the water is boiling, stir in the egg noodles, and return to a boil. Cook the pasta uncovered, stirring occasionally, until the pasta has cooked through, but is still firm to the bite, about 5 minutes. Drain well in a colander set in the sink.
- Mix the cream cheese with the parsley and Parmesan cheese in a bowl until the cream cheese is no longer lumpy. Stir in the sour cream and 3/4 of the shredded mozzarella until evenly combined. Pour half of the drained egg noodles into the prepared baking dish, followed by half of the meat sauce. Spread half of the sour cream mixture over the meat sauce. Repeat the layers with the remaining egg noodles, meat sauce, and sour

cream mixture. Sprinkle with the remaining mozzarella cheese.
- Bake in the preheated oven until the mozzarella cheese is bubbly and golden brown, about 35 minutes.

Nutrition Information

- Calories: 336 calories
- Total Fat: 16.5 g
- Cholesterol: 84 mg
- Sodium: 744 mg
- Total Carbohydrate: 26.2 g
- Protein: 20.9 g

194. Noodles Romanoff

"A creamy family favorite. Very good with meat loaf."

Serving: 6 | Prep: 10 m | Cook: 10 m | Ready in: 20 m

Ingredients

- 1 (8 ounce) package egg noodles
- 2 cups sour cream
- 1/2 cup grated Parmesan cheese, divided
- 1 tablespoon chopped fresh chives
- 1/2 teaspoon salt
- 1/8 teaspoon ground black pepper
- 2 tablespoons butter

Direction

- Bring a large pot of lightly salted water to a boil. Add noodles and cook for 8 to 10 minutes or until al dente; drain.
- While noodles are cooking, combine the sour cream, 1/4 cup cheese, chives, salt and pepper in a medium bowl. Mix together.
- Stir butter into drained noodles, then stir in sour cream mixture. Place on a warm platter and sprinkle with remaining 1/4 cup cheese.

Nutrition Information

- Calories: 363 calories
- Total Fat: 24.2 g
- Cholesterol: 78 mg
- Sodium: 394 mg
- Total Carbohydrate: 27.1 g
- Protein: 9.9 g

195. One Dish Chicken Noodles

"Combination of wide egg noodles, chicken cubes, peas and chicken gravy."

Serving: 6

Ingredients

- 1 pound skinless, boneless chicken breast meat
- 2 (12 ounce) jars chicken gravy
- 1 (12 ounce) package egg noodles
- 3 cups frozen green peas, thawed

Direction

- Heat oil in large skillet. Cube chicken into bite size pieces and brown in hot oil. Meanwhile, in a large saucepan, boil noodles in water until soft, then drain. Add hot cooked noodles to chicken in skillet and pour in gravy and peas. Stir together until ingredients are covered/coated with gravy. Cover skillet, reduce heat to medium low and let simmer for 10 minutes until gravy and peas are hot. Serve directly from the skillet.

Nutrition Information

- Calories: 450 calories
- Total Fat: 9.3 g
- Cholesterol: 100 mg
- Sodium: 650 mg
- Total Carbohydrate: 57.7 g
- Protein: 31.2 g

196. One Skillet Cheesy Hamburger and Egg Noodle

"Easy to make, delicious hamburger recipe. The egg noodles instead of the traditional pasta make for a tastier substitute."

Serving: 6 | Prep: 10 m | Cook: 22 m | Ready in: 32 m

Ingredients

- 1 (8 ounce) package egg noodles
- 1 1/2 pounds ground beef
- salt and ground black pepper to taste
- 1 (14.5 ounce) can chicken broth
- 1 (10.75 ounce) can condensed cream of chicken soup
- 1/2 cup sour cream
- 4 ounces processed cheese (such as Velveeta®)
- 1/2 teaspoon chopped fresh rosemary
- 1/2 teaspoon chopped fresh thyme

Direction

- Fill a large pot with lightly salted water and bring to a rolling boil. Cook egg noodles at a boil until tender yet firm to the bite, about 6 minutes. Drain.
- Heat a large non-stick skillet over medium heat. Cook and stir ground beef, seasoning with salt and pepper, until no longer pink in the center, about 8 minutes. An instant-read thermometer inserted into the center should read at least 160 degrees F (70 degrees C). Drain; reserve drippings in the skillet.
- Reduce heat to medium-low. Pour chicken broth, chicken soup, sour cream, cheese, rosemary, and thyme into the skillet. Cook and stir, seasoning with salt and pepper, until well combined and the cheese is melted, 5 to 7 minutes. Reduce heat to low. Stir in the egg noodles and ground beef; cook until evenly mixed, 3 to 5 minutes.

Nutrition Information

- Calories: 521 calories
- Total Fat: 29.8 g
- Cholesterol: 128 mg
- Sodium: 950 mg
- Total Carbohydrate: 32.9 g
- Protein: 28.8 g

197. OnePot Ground Beef Stroganoff

"My family loved the boxed version of this ground beef stroganoff, but we have done away with processed foods. I created this out of necessity, and they don't miss the box at all! It's creamy and delicious!"

Serving: 4 | Prep: 5 m | Cook: 15 m | Ready in: 20 m

Ingredients

- 1 pound ground beef
- 1 1/2 tablespoons cornstarch
- 1 1/2 teaspoons salt
- 1 1/2 teaspoons dried parsley
- 1 teaspoon garlic powder
- 1 teaspoon onion powder
- 1 3/4 cups milk
- 1 1/4 cups beef stock
- 1 (8 ounce) package egg noodles
- 1/2 cup sour cream
- 1/4 cup freshly grated Parmesan cheese

Direction

- Heat a large skillet over medium-high heat. Cook and stir beef in the hot skillet until browned and crumbly, 5 to 7 minutes. Drain and discard grease.
- Combine cornstarch, salt, parsley, garlic powder, and onion powder in a small bowl.
- Pour cornstarch mixture, milk, beef stock, and egg noodles into the skillet of beef. Bring to a boil. Cover and reduce heat. Simmer, stirring occasionally, until noodles are tender, about 5 minutes. Stir in sour cream and Parmesan cheese; do not return to a boil.

Nutrition Information

- Calories: 586 calories
- Total Fat: 26.1 g
- Cholesterol: 144 mg
- Sodium: 1113 mg

- Total Carbohydrate: 51.2 g
- Protein: 34.9 g

198. Pappardelle Pasta with California Walnut Pesto

"Walnuts, parsley, grated cheese, garlic, and olive oil make a deliciously different pesto tossed with fresh, tender pappardelle pasta and topped with toasted California walnuts."

Serving: 16 | Prep: 20 m | Cook: 3 m | Ready in: 30 m

Ingredients

- 3 1/2 cups California walnuts, toasted
- 4 cups Italian parsley leaves, packed
- 2 cups Parmigiano-Reggiano cheese, freshly grated
- 4 cloves garlic
- 1 1/2 cups extra virgin olive oil
- salt and pepper to taste
- 4 pounds fresh pappardelle pasta
- Toppings:
- 1 1/2 cups California walnuts, toasted, chopped
- Parmigiano-Reggiano cheese (optional)

Direction

- Place half of the walnuts, parsley, cheese and garlic in food processor; process until finely chopped.
- With motor running, slowly pour in half of the oil; puree until smooth. Transfer to bowl and repeat with remaining ingredients, making a total of 2 batches. Season with salt and pepper; set aside. (Makes approximately 4 cups).
- Cook pasta in boiling salted water until al dente, about 3 to 4 minutes. Drain, reserving some of the cooking water. For each serving, toss 2 cups cooked pasta with 1/4 cup Walnut Pesto adding some of the reserved cooking water as required to thin the pesto; toss well to coat evenly.
- Transfer to warm pasta bowl; sprinkle with 1 tablespoon chopped walnuts and shaved or grated cheese, as desired. Serve immediately.

Nutrition Information

- Calories: 879 calories
- Total Fat: 49.8 g
- Cholesterol: 9 mg
- Sodium: 179 mg
- Total Carbohydrate: 87 g
- Protein: 23.6 g

199. Pasta With Spinach Sauce

"A wonderful sauce if you want to get your kids to eat spinach! Kids love this recipe, and the short cooking time guarantees a quick fix for lunch. Preparation time: As fast as your pasta water takes to cook!"

Serving: 4

Ingredients

- 1 tablespoon olive oil
- 1 onion, chopped
- 2 tablespoons minced garlic
- 2 (10 ounce) packages frozen chopped spinach, thawed
- 3 tablespoons sour cream
- 1 (10.75 ounce) can condensed cream of celery soup
- 1/2 cup grated Parmesan cheese
- 1 cup chopped ham
- 8 ounces spaghetti

Direction

- Cook noodles in a large pot of boiling water until al dente. Drain.
- Meanwhile prepare the sauce. Heat oil in a medium saucepan over medium heat. Add onions, and ham if desired. Cook until onion is transparent, 2 to 3 minutes. Add garlic, and cook for 30 seconds. Stir in thawed spinach. Mix in sour cream, cream of celery soup, and

- Parmesan cheese. Reduce heat to low, and heat through.
- Serve spinach sauce over spaghetti or egg noodles.

Nutrition Information

- Calories: 468 calories
- Total Fat: 16.5 g
- Cholesterol: 39 mg
- Sodium: 1224 mg
- Total Carbohydrate: 59.2 g
- Protein: 22.9 g

200. Pasta With Veggies In a Tahini and Yogurt Sauce

"A creamy garlic sauce and a medley of vegetables served over egg noodles make a superb one dish meal. Of course if you were looking for something a little more elaborate, a Greek salad, thick slabs of feta cheese, and warm pita bread are wonderful accompaniments."

Serving: 6 | Prep: 15 m | Cook: 10 m | Ready in: 25 m

Ingredients

- 1 (16 ounce) package wide egg noodles
- 3 tablespoons tahini
- 1 lemon, juiced
- 1 1/4 cups water
- 3 cloves garlic, minced
- 1 cup yogurt, drained
- 1/4 teaspoon hot pepper sauce
- 1/4 cup olive oil
- 1 large red bell pepper, thinly sliced
- 1 zucchini, thinly sliced
- salt to taste
- ground black pepper to taste

Direction

- Cook noodles in a large pot of boiling water until al dente. Drain.
- Meanwhile, mix together tahini, lemon juice, and water until smooth. Add garlic, yogurt, and pepper sauce.
- In a medium skillet, heat oil over medium high heat. Sauté red pepper and zucchini in oil for 2 to 3 minutes, or until tender crisp. Add tahini sauce, and heat through. Season to taste with salt and pepper. Do not boil or overcook: this sauce curdles easily. Toss noodles with sauce.

Nutrition Information

- Calories: 456 calories
- Total Fat: 18.3 g
- Cholesterol: 68 mg
- Sodium: 47 mg
- Total Carbohydrate: 61.4 g
- Protein: 14.4 g

201. Pastira Macaroni Cake

"This is a sort of Italian version of custard, made with macaroni."

Serving: 20

Ingredients

- 5 eggs
- 1 1/2 cups white sugar
- 1 pound ricotta cheese
- 1 teaspoon salt
- 1 cup milk
- 1 teaspoon vanilla extract
- 2 tablespoons butter
- 1/4 pound thin egg noodles

Direction

- Beat eggs and sugar, add Ricotta, milk, and vanilla. Mix thoroughly.
- Cook macaroni, drain, put in large mixing bowl and melt butter over top.
- Add egg/Ricotta mixture, stirring in thoroughly. Pour into thoroughly buttered 6x10 inch pan.

- Bake for 1 hour at 350 degrees F (175 degrees C), let cool, then refrigerate before serving.

Nutrition Information

- Calories: 146 calories
- Total Fat: 4.7 g
- Cholesterol: 62 mg
- Sodium: 177 mg
- Total Carbohydrate: 20.9 g
- Protein: 5.4 g

202. Pecan Noodle Kugel

"Noodle kugel coated with a brown sugar/pecan mixture hot out of the oven is sweet enough it could also work as a dessert. This is an old family recipe guaranteed to be loved by all!"

Serving: 8 | Prep: 10 m | Cook: 1 h 20 m | Ready in: 1 h 30 m

Ingredients

- 1 (16 ounce) package broad egg noodles
- 4 eggs
- 1/4 cup melted butter, divided
- 1 cup brown sugar, divided
- 1 pinch salt
- 1/2 cup chopped pecans

Direction

- Fill a large pot with lightly salted water and bring to a rolling boil over high heat. Once the water is boiling, stir in the egg noodles, and return to a boil. Cook the pasta uncovered, stirring occasionally, until the pasta has cooked through, but is still firm to the bite, about 5 minutes. Drain well in a colander set in the sink.
- Preheat an oven to 325 degrees F (165 degrees C).
- Beat eggs in a large bowl. Beat in half of the melted butter, then stir in half of the brown sugar and a pinch of salt. Stir in the noodles, making sure the noodles are evenly coated. Spread the remaining butter on the bottom of a deep baking dish. Sprinkle the remaining brown sugar in the baking dish, patting the sugar up the sides. Spread pecans over the brown sugar. Pour noodle mixture over the sugar.
- Bake in the preheated oven until firm, about 1 hour and 15 minutes. Run a paring knife between the kugel and the edge of the baking dish. Hold the pan on its side and gently tap the sides of the pan against the counter to loosen it. Cover the baking dish with a large platter and invert it to tip the kugel out of the baking dish and onto the plate.

Nutrition Information

- Calories: 418 calories
- Total Fat: 15.6 g
- Cholesterol: 155 mg
- Sodium: 93 mg
- Total Carbohydrate: 58.8 g
- Protein: 11.8 g

203. Pepperoni Pizza Casserole

"A cheesy casserole with all of your favorite pizza toppings. I like to serve this with a salad and garlic bread. The leftovers are great. I have prepared this in advance and then taken it to potlucks in a slow cooker the next day."

Serving: 8 | Prep: 15 m | Cook: 45 m | Ready in: 1 h

Ingredients

- 1 pound ground beef
- 1 (8 ounce) package uncooked egg noodles
- 1 (16 ounce) jar spaghetti sauce, or as needed
- 1 (2.25 ounce) can sliced black olives, drained
- 1 (2.5 ounce) can sliced mushrooms, drained
- 1 (8 ounce) package sliced pepperoni, coarsely chopped
- 20 ounces shredded mozzarella cheese, divided

Direction

- Preheat oven to 375 degrees F (190 degrees C).

- Cook the ground beef in a skillet over medium heat until no longer pink, breaking the meat apart into crumbles as it cooks, about 10 minutes.
- Bring a large pot of lightly salted water to a rolling boil. Cook the egg noodles in the boiling water until cooked through yet slightly firm, about 5 minutes; drain.
- Mix the noodles with the spaghetti sauce, black olives, mushrooms, pepperoni, and half the mozzarella cheese in a large mixing bowl; spoon the mixture into a 9x13-inch baking dish and top with remaining half of the mozzarella cheese. Cover the dish with foil.
- Bake in the preheated oven until the casserole is bubbling, 30 to 45 minutes.

Nutrition Information

- Calories: 586 calories
- Total Fat: 33.9 g
- Cholesterol: 134 mg
- Sodium: 1276 mg
- Total Carbohydrate: 30.6 g
- Protein: 38.2 g

204. Pineapple Kugel

"Although it is sweet enough for dessert, this noodle dish is usually served as a side dish. It's fluffy, creamy, and wonderful!"

Serving: 8

Ingredients

- 1 (8 ounce) package wide egg noodles
- 6 eggs
- 5 tablespoons unsalted butter, melted
- 1/2 cup white sugar
- 1 (8 ounce) can crushed pineapple, with juice
- 1 1/4 teaspoons vanilla extract
- 1 teaspoon ground cinnamon
- 1 (8 ounce) can sliced pineapple, drained
- 1/4 cup candied cherries (optional)

Direction

- Boil noodles in boiling salted water just until softened; do not cook through. Rinse, and drain.
- Beat the eggs with the melted butter. Mix in sugar, crushed pineapple with juice, vanilla, and cinnamon. Stir in the noodles. Spread into a greased 9 x 13 inch baking pan. Place pineapple rings decoratively over the top. Place a cherry in the center of each ring if desired
- Bake at 350 degrees F (175 degrees C) for 50 minutes, or until golden.

Nutrition Information

- Calories: 327 calories
- Total Fat: 12.2 g
- Cholesterol: 182 mg
- Sodium: 65 mg
- Total Carbohydrate: 46.2 g
- Protein: 8.9 g

205. Plantation

"A delicious creamy ground beef dinner with noodles and corn topped with cheese."

Serving: 8 | Prep: 10 m | Cook: 20 m | Ready in: 30 m

Ingredients

- 1 (10 ounce) package egg noodles
- 2 pounds ground beef
- 1 pinch onion powder to taste
- 1 pinch garlic powder to taste
- 1 pinch salt and pepper to taste
- 1 (8 ounce) package cream cheese
- 1 (10.75 ounce) can cream of mushroom soup
- 1 (10 ounce) can whole kernel corn, drained
- 1 (5 ounce) can evaporated milk
- 1 (8 ounce) package shredded mozzarella cheese

Direction

- Bring a large pot of lightly salted water to a boil. Add noodles, and cook until tender, about 7 minutes. Drain.
- Meanwhile, crumble the ground beef into a large skillet over medium-high heat. Season with onion powder, garlic powder, salt and pepper; cook and stir until evenly browned. Drain off grease.
- Stir the cream cheese and cream of mushroom soup into the ground beef until well blended. Mix in the drained noodles and corn. Stir in evaporated milk to reach your desired consistency. Top with mozzarella cheese, and serve.

Nutrition Information

- Calories: 587 calories
- Total Fat: 33.4 g
- Cholesterol: 148 mg
- Sodium: 679 mg
- Total Carbohydrate: 37.1 g
- Protein: 34.9 g

206. Polish Cabbage Noodles

"Sauteed cabbage and onions with noodles, a perfect last minute meatless meal!!"

Serving: 5

Ingredients

- 1 medium head shredded cabbage
- 2 red onions, cut into strips
- 1/2 cup butter
- 1 (16 ounce) package wide egg noodles
- salt to taste
- ground black pepper to taste

Direction

- Cook pasta in a large pot of boiling salted water.
- Meanwhile, heat butter or margarine in a skillet over medium heat. Sauté cabbage and onions until tender.
- Drain pasta, and return to the pot. Add cabbage and onion mixture to the noodles, and toss. Season with salt and pepper to taste.

Nutrition Information

- Calories: 570 calories
- Total Fat: 22.6 g
- Cholesterol: 124 mg
- Sodium: 184 mg
- Total Carbohydrate: 78.5 g
- Protein: 15.7 g

207. Polish Chop Suey

"Great good mood food and easy to prepare. Polish and German decedents will appreciate this blend of flavors. Try pork steaks in place of the kielbasa for a different flavor combination."

Serving: 8 | Prep: 10 m | Cook: 1 h 10 m | Ready in: 1 h 20 m

Ingredients

- 1 (16 ounce) package kluski noodles
- 2 (16 ounce) packages kielbasa sausage
- 1 (10.75 ounce) can condensed cream of mushroom soup
- 1 (1 ounce) package dry onion soup mix
- 3 (10.75 ounce) cans water
- 1 (14.5 ounce) can sauerkraut, drained

Direction

- Preheat oven to 350 degrees F (175 degrees C).
- Bring a large pot of lightly salted water to a boil. Cook kluski noodles in the boiling water, stirring occasionally, until cooked through but firm to the bite, about 5 minutes; drain.
- Heat a skillet over medium heat. Cook sausages in the skillet until browned, about 5 minutes; cut into bite-size pieces.

- Stir mushroom soup, onion soup mix, and water together in a large baking dish; add kluski noodles, sausage, and sauerkraut. Cover dish with aluminum foil.
- Bake in preheated oven for 1 hour to 90 minutes.

Nutrition Information

- Calories: 617 calories
- Total Fat: 35.8 g
- Cholesterol: 122 mg
- Sodium: 1932 mg
- Total Carbohydrate: 50 g
- Protein: 23.1 g

208. Polish Noodles

"This recipe combines sage sausage, cabbage, and noodles. Simple and DELISH! This is my husband's grandma's recipe, and my husband's favorite. I couldn't ask for an easier favorite. It's better when served the next day, or cooled for at least an hour, then reheated."

Serving: 8 | Prep: 10 m | Cook: 45 m | Ready in: 55 m

Ingredients

- 1 (8 ounce) package kluski noodles
- 2 (12 ounce) packages sage pork sausage
- 1 green pepper, diced
- 1 onion, diced
- 4 cups water, or as needed
- 1 large head cabbage, chopped
- salt and pepper to taste
- 1/2 cup sour cream (optional)

Direction

- Bring a pot of lightly salted water to a rolling boil over high heat. Stir in the egg noodles, and return to a boil. Cook, uncovered, stirring occasionally, until the pasta is cooked through, but still firm to the bite, about 5 minutes. Drain.
- Meanwhile, heat a large skillet over medium-high heat and stir in the sausage, green pepper, and onion. Cook and stir until the sausage is crumbly, evenly browned, and no longer pink, about 10 minutes. Drain and discard any excess grease.
- Bring the 4 cups of water to a boil in a large pot. Stir in the cabbage, the sausage mixture, and the noodles. Simmer over medium-low heat, stirring occasionally, until the cabbage is tender, about 30 minutes. Add water while cooking if needed; the mixture should not be dry. Season to taste with salt and pepper. Garnish with sour cream if desired.

Nutrition Information

- Calories: 402 calories
- Total Fat: 22.5 g
- Cholesterol: 78 mg
- Sodium: 791 mg
- Total Carbohydrate: 32.7 g
- Protein: 18.1 g

209. Polish Noodles Cottage Cheese and Noodles

"This simple recipe came from the Polish side of my family. We simply called it 'cottage cheese and noodles' or 'lazy man pierogies.' It's a great comfort food and can be made with any kind of noodle. It could be a side dish, but we always enjoyed it as a meal."

Serving: 6 | Prep: 10 m | Cook: 20 m | Ready in: 30 m

Ingredients

- 1/2 cup butter
- 1 small onion, diced
- 1 (16 ounce) package egg noodles
- 1 (16 ounce) package cottage cheese
- 1/2 cup sour cream
- 1/2 teaspoon sea salt
- 1/4 teaspoon ground black pepper

Direction

- Melt butter in a saucepan over medium heat. Cook and stir onion in melted butter until softened, 7 to 10 minutes.
- Bring a large pot of lightly salted water to a boil. Cook egg noodles in the boiling water, stirring occasionally until cooked through but firm to the bite, about 5 minutes. Drain and return to the pot.
- Stir butter and onion mixture, cottage cheese, sour cream, sea salt, and black pepper into the noodles. Place the pot over medium heat; cook and stir until heated through and warm, 5 to 8 minutes.

Nutrition Information

- Calories: 545 calories
- Total Fat: 26.1 g
- Cholesterol: 123 mg
- Sodium: 584 mg
- Total Carbohydrate: 57.2 g
- Protein: 20.8 g

210. Poor Mans Stroganoff

"This is a recipe I came up with when I was helping to raise 6 kids. Every penny counted. You can add onions if desired."

Serving: 4 | Prep: 10 m | Cook: 20 m | Ready in: 30 m

Ingredients

- 1 (12 ounce) package egg noodles
- 1 pound ground beef
- 1 teaspoon Greek seasoning (such as Cavender's®)
- salt and ground black pepper to taste
- 1 teaspoon vegetable oil
- 1 (16 ounce) package sliced fresh mushrooms
- 1 pint sour cream

Direction

- Bring a large pot of lightly salted water to a boil. Cook egg noodles in the boiling water, stirring occasionally, until cooked through but firm to the bite, about 5 minutes; drain.
- Heat a large skillet over medium-high heat. Cook and stir beef in the hot skillet until browned and crumbly, 5 to 7 minutes; drain and discard grease. Season beef with Greek seasoning, salt, and pepper.
- Heat vegetable oil in a separate skillet over medium heat. Cook and stir mushrooms in hot oil until tender, about 5 minutes; add to ground beef.
- Stir sour cream into ground beef mixture; cook and stir until hot, about 5 minutes. Serve over egg noodles.

Nutrition Information

- Calories: 810 calories
- Total Fat: 43.1 g
- Cholesterol: 192 mg
- Sodium: 268 mg
- Total Carbohydrate: 68.8 g
- Protein: 38.2 g

211. Porkolt Hungarian Stew Made With Pork

"A flavorful stew, Pörkölt is redolent with the fragrance of paprika and bell peppers. It has few ingredients, and is surprisingly easy to make. Save time by using boneless pork chops and cubing them after they are browned. There should be enough salt in the canned tomatoes to season the stew, but if not, add more to your taste. Use best-quality, real Hungarian paprika for best results. We prefer to serve it with noodles, but galuska (Hungarian dumplings) or rice are good, too."

Serving: 14 | Prep: 20 m | Cook: 1 h 55 m | Ready in: 2 h 15 m

Ingredients

- 5 slices bacon, diced

- 2 large onions, diced
- 1/4 cup Hungarian paprika
- 1 1/2 teaspoons garlic powder
- 1/4 teaspoon ground black pepper
- 5 pounds boneless pork chops, trimmed
- 1 large yellow bell pepper, seeded and diced
- 2 (14 ounce) cans diced tomatoes, with liquid
- 2/3 cup beef broth
- 2 cups reduced-fat sour cream
- 2 (6 ounce) packages wide egg noodles

Direction

- Place the bacon in a large, deep skillet, and cook over medium-high heat until evenly browned, about 10 minutes. Drain, and reserve the drippings. Add the onions to the bacon and cook together until the onion is translucent. Remove skillet from heat and stir the paprika, garlic powder, and pepper into the bacon mixture. Transfer the mixture into a large stockpot.
- Heat a small amount of the reserved bacon drippings in the skillet again over medium-high heat. Cook the pork chops in batches in the hot drippings until evenly browned on both sides. Use additional bacon drippings for each batch as needed. Remove the pork chops to a cutting board and blot excess fat off the surface of the chops with a paper towel; cut into bite-sized cubes and stir into the bacon mixture.
- Heat a small amount of the bacon drippings in the skillet; cook and stir the bell pepper in the hot drippings until softened and fragrant; drain on a plate lined with paper towels. Stir the cooked pepper into the bacon mixture.
- Pour the tomatoes with liquid and beef broth into a stockpot and place the pot over medium-high heat. Bring to a simmer and reduce heat to medium-low. Cook until the stew begins to thicken, stirring occasionally, about 90 minutes. Stir the sour cream into the stew just before serving.
- Bring a pot with lightly-salted water and bring to a rolling boil; add the egg noodles to the water and return to a boil. Cook uncovered, stirring occasionally, until the pasta has cooked through, but is still firm to the bite, about 5 minutes. Drain well in a colander set in the sink. Ladle the stew over the drained noodles to serve.

Nutrition Information

- Calories: 323 calories
- Total Fat: 13.2 g
- Cholesterol: 86 mg
- Sodium: 349 mg
- Total Carbohydrate: 22.9 g
- Protein: 26.9 g

212. Quick and Easy Chicken and Stuffing Casserole

"This is so good, it should be illegal. Everyone in my family loves it. Even my picky 3 year old!"

Serving: 8 | Prep: 15 m | Cook: 35 m | Ready in: 50 m

Ingredients

- 9 ounces egg noodles
- 2 (10.5 ounce) cans cream of chicken soup
- 1 cup sour cream
- 3 cups cubed cooked chicken
- 1 (6 ounce) package stuffing mix
- 2 cups chicken broth
- 3/4 cup butter

Direction

- Bring a large pot of lightly salted water to a boil. Cook egg noodles in the boiling water, stirring occasionally until cooked through but firm to the bite, about 5 minutes. Drain.
- Preheat oven to 350 degrees F (175 degrees C). Grease a 9x13-inch baking dish.
- Mix cream of chicken soup and sour cream together in a bowl; stir in chicken and noodles. Spoon mixture into the prepared baking dish; sprinkle with stuffing mix.

- Combine chicken broth and butter in a saucepan over medium heat until butter is melted; pour over stuffing layer.
- Bake in the preheated oven until casserole is bubbling and stuffing is browned, about 30 minutes.

Nutrition Information

- Calories: 585 calories
- Total Fat: 33.7 g
- Cholesterol: 132 mg
- Sodium: 1243 mg
- Total Carbohydrate: 45.5 g
- Protein: 24.3 g

213. Quick and Easy Chicken Noodle Soup

"When you don't have time to make your soup totally from scratch, this is a very easy, very good substitute."

Serving: 6 | Prep: 10 m | Cook: 20 m | Ready in: 30 m

Ingredients

- 1 tablespoon butter
- 1/2 cup chopped onion
- 1/2 cup chopped celery
- 4 (14.5 ounce) cans chicken broth
- 1 (14.5 ounce) can vegetable broth
- 1/2 pound chopped cooked chicken breast
- 1 1/2 cups egg noodles
- 1 cup sliced carrots
- 1/2 teaspoon dried basil
- 1/2 teaspoon dried oregano
- salt and pepper to taste

Direction

- In a large pot over medium heat, melt butter. Cook onion and celery in butter until just tender, 5 minutes. Pour in chicken and vegetable broths and stir in chicken, noodles, carrots, basil, oregano, salt and pepper. Bring to a boil, then reduce heat and simmer 20 minutes before serving.

Nutrition Information

- Calories: 161 calories
- Total Fat: 6.1 g
- Cholesterol: 46 mg
- Sodium: 1357 mg
- Total Carbohydrate: 12.1 g
- Protein: 13.4 g

214. Quick and Easy Goulash

"A homemade meal easy enough for a busy college student! Hearty beef and cheese with noodles and corn."

Serving: 4 | Prep: 20 m | Cook: 10 m | Ready in: 30 m

Ingredients

- 1 (12 ounce) package egg noodles
- 1 pound lean ground beef
- 1 (26 ounce) jar spaghetti sauce
- 1 (15.25 ounce) can whole kernel corn
- 1 onion, chopped
- 1 cup shredded Cheddar cheese

Direction

- Bring a large pot of lightly salted water to a boil. Add egg noodles and cook for 8 to 10 minutes or until al dente; drain.
- In a skillet over medium heat, brown the beef; drain.
- Heat through over medium the beef, spaghetti sauce, corn, chopped onion and cheese.

Nutrition Information

- Calories: 885 calories
- Total Fat: 35.2 g
- Cholesterol: 163 mg
- Sodium: 1314 mg
- Total Carbohydrate: 101.1 g
- Protein: 42.8 g

215. Quick and Zesty Vegetable Soup

"A vegetable soup recipe that is very tasty and very easy and quick."

Serving: 8

Ingredients

- 1 pound ground beef
- 1/2 cup chopped onion
- salt and pepper to taste
- 2 (14.5 ounce) cans stewed tomatoes
- 2 cups frozen mixed vegetables
- 1/2 cup egg noodles
- 1/2 teaspoon dried oregano

Direction

- In a large stock pot, brown beef and onion. Cook until onion is tender, and drain any grease. Season to taste with salt and pepper.
- Stir in stewed tomatoes, vegetables, egg noodles and oregano. Bring to a boil; reduce heat, cover and simmer for 15 minutes, or until noodles are tender. Serve hot.

Nutrition Information

- Calories: 242 calories
- Total Fat: 15.6 g
- Cholesterol: 50 mg
- Sodium: 283 mg
- Total Carbohydrate: 14.5 g
- Protein: 12.2 g

216. Quick Chicken and Noodles

"This is one of my kids' favorite recipes - mine too, since it takes about 30 minutes to make."

Serving: 8

Ingredients

- 4 skinless, boneless chicken breasts
- 1/4 teaspoon garlic powder
- 2 cups chicken broth
- 1/2 teaspoon dried basil
- 1/8 teaspoon ground black pepper
- 2 cups frozen mixed vegetables, thawed
- 1 (16 ounce) package wide egg noodles

Direction

- In a medium skillet, sauté chicken breasts over medium high heat for about 10 minutes, or until browned. If the chicken sticks at all, you can add a little of the broth. When chicken is browned, remove from skillet and cut into 1 inch cubes. Sprinkle with garlic powder.
- In the same skillet heat the broth, basil, pepper and vegetables. Bring to a boil. Stir in the uncooked noodles and return the chicken to the skillet. Reduce heat to low. Cover skillet and simmer all together, stirring occasionally, for 10 minutes or until chicken meat is no longer pink and noodles are soft. Serve.

Nutrition Information

- Calories: 307 calories
- Total Fat: 3.4 g
- Cholesterol: 81 mg
- Sodium: 69 mg
- Total Carbohydrate: 45.5 g
- Protein: 22.9 g

217. Quick Meatball Stroganoff

"This is a recipe I came up because my family loves stroganoff. It was a hit with everyone."

Serving: 4 | Prep: 5 m | Cook: 55 m | Ready in: 1 h

Ingredients

- 8 ounces broad egg white noodles (such as No Yolks®)
- 1 tablespoon vegetable oil
- 1/2 onion, chopped
- 2 teaspoons minced garlic
- 1 (10.75 ounce) can condensed cream of mushroom soup
- 1/2 cup milk
- 1 tablespoon Worcestershire sauce
- 15 frozen beef meatballs, or more to taste
- 3/4 cup sour cream
- salt and ground black pepper to taste

Direction

- Bring a large pot of lightly salted water to a boil. Add noodles and cook, stirring occasionally, until tender yet firm to the bite, 10 to 12 minutes. Drain.
- Heat oil in a large skillet over medium-high heat. Add onion and garlic; cook and stir until onion is almost soft, about 3 minutes. Reduce heat to medium and pour in cream of mushroom soup, milk, and Worcestershire sauce; stir until blended.
- Stir meatballs into the skillet. Reduce heat to low and simmer, covered, until tender, 35 to 40 minutes. Stir in sour cream, salt, and pepper. Cook until flavors combine, about 2 minutes.
- Serve meatballs over noodles.

Nutrition Information

- Calories: 656 calories
- Total Fat: 31.5 g
- Cholesterol: 109 mg
- Sodium: 769 mg
- Total Carbohydrate: 60.5 g
- Protein: 29.7 g

218. Regular Chicken Soup

"A simple, hearty chicken soup with noodles. It's perfect for a chilly winter afternoon."

Serving: 6 | Prep: 30 m | Cook: 2 h 30 m | Ready in: 3 h

Ingredients

- 3 skinless, boneless chicken breast halves
- 8 cups water
- 10 carrots, peeled and sliced
- 6 stalks celery, thinly sliced
- 1 onion, diced
- 8 cubes chicken bouillon
- 1 (12 ounce) package uncooked egg noodles

Direction

- In a large saucepan, boil the chicken until tender and no longer pink. Drain and dice.
- Return diced chicken to the large saucepan. Mix together the water, carrots, celery, onion, chicken bouillon and egg noodles. Boil the mixture approximately 15 minutes, stirring occasionally. Reduce heat and simmer at least 2 hours before serving.

Nutrition Information

- Calories: 348 calories
- Total Fat: 3.8 g
- Cholesterol: 82 mg
- Sodium: 1689 mg
- Total Carbohydrate: 54.1 g
- Protein: 23.9 g

219. Reuben Casserole with Egg Noodles

"Here is a clever twist on a traditional deli sandwich! Reuben casserole."

Serving: 8 | Prep: 15 m | Cook: 50 m | Ready in: 1 h 5 m

Ingredients

- 1 (16 ounce) package egg noodles
- 1/2 cup thousand island salad dressing, or to taste
- 1/2 cup mayonnaise, or to taste
- 1 pound thickly sliced deli-style corned beef, cut into 1-inch squares
- 12 ounces sauerkraut
- 6 ounces shredded Swiss cheese
- 6 ounces shredded Cheddar cheese

Direction

- Preheat oven to 325 degrees F (165 degrees C).
- Bring a large pot of lightly salted water to a boil. Cook egg noodles in the boiling water, stirring occasionally, until cooked through but firm to the bite, about 5 minutes; drain, reserving a few tablespoons of the water. Transfer noodles and reserved water to a large bowl.
- Mix salad dressing and mayonnaise into the noodles about a tablespoon each at a time, stirring to coat the noodles, until the mixture has a creamy texture to your liking. Add corned beef, sauerkraut, Swiss cheese, and Cheddar cheese to the noodles; stir. Pour the mixture into a 13x9-inch baking dish.
- Bake in preheated oven until the cheese melts completely and the casserole is hot in the center, 45 minutes to 1 hour.

Nutrition Information

- Calories: 638 calories
- Total Fat: 36.7 g
- Cholesterol: 136 mg
- Sodium: 1483 mg
- Total Carbohydrate: 47.8 g
- Protein: 30.4 g

220. Reuben Hot Dish

"Sauerkraut, corned beef, Swiss cheese, and rye bread are combined in a casserole version of a deli favorite."

Serving: 10 | Prep: 20 m | Cook: 1 h 10 m | Ready in: 1 h 30 m

Ingredients

- 2 (10.75 ounce) cans condensed cream of mushroom soup
- 1 1/2 cups milk
- 1/4 cup finely chopped onion
- 12 ounces deli sliced corned beef, chopped
- 3 tablespoons prepared mustard
- 2 (16 ounce) cans sauerkraut, drained and rinsed
- 1 (8 ounce) package uncooked egg noodles
- 2 cups shredded Swiss cheese
- 2 tablespoons butter, melted
- 3/4 cup cubed rye bread

Direction

- Preheat oven to 250 degrees F (120 degrees C). Arrange bread cubes in a single layer on a baking sheet. Toast until dry. Crush, and reserve. Increase oven temperature to 350 degrees F (175 degrees C).
- In a medium bowl, mix together the soup, milk, onion, corned beef, and mustard. Set aside.
- Spread sauerkraut evenly in the bottom of a lightly greased 9x13 inch baking dish. Spread uncooked noodles over sauerkraut. Spoon soup mixture over noodles, and sprinkle with cheese. In a small bowl, mix melted butter with rye bread crumbs, and sprinkle mixture over cheese.
- Cover, and bake in preheated oven for 50 minutes. Remove cover, and bake an additional 10 minutes.

Nutrition Information

- Calories: 363 calories

- Total Fat: 17 g
- Cholesterol: 67 mg
- Sodium: 1682 mg
- Total Carbohydrate: 33.9 g
- Protein: 19.6 g

221. Reuben Mac and Cheese

"I just love the Reuben sandwich so I wanted to create a casserole version. It turned out delicious! My son came home from football practice and brought a friend who dove into it as soon as he saw it. Yum! I served it with some steamed green beans and coleslaw mixed with thousand island dressing and toasted, buttered rye bread."

Serving: 8 | Prep: 15 m | Cook: 45 m | Ready in: 1 h

Ingredients

- 3 slices rye bread, torn
- 1/3 cup panko bread crumbs
- 1 (16 ounce) package egg noodles
- 3 tablespoons butter
- 1 cup chopped onion
- 1 teaspoon salt
- 1/2 teaspoon ground black pepper
- 1/4 cup spicy brown mustard
- 3 tablespoons all-purpose flour
- 3 cups hot milk
- 3 cups shredded Swiss cheese, or more to taste - divided
- 1 1/2 cups sauerkraut, drained (reserve juice)
- 1/2 pound deli sliced corn beef, or more to taste
- 3 tablespoons butter, melted

Direction

- Preheat oven to 350 degrees F (175 degrees C). Butter a 2-quart casserole dish.
- Place torn rye bread into a food processor and pulse several times to make crumbs; combine rye crumbs with panko crumbs in a bowl and set aside.
- Bring a large pot of lightly salted water to a boil. Cook egg noodles in the boiling water, stirring occasionally until cooked through but firm to the bite, about 5 minutes. Drain noodles and set aside.
- Melt 3 tablespoons butter in a large saucepan over medium heat; cook and stir onion until lightly browned, about 15 minutes. Season with salt and black pepper; stir in brown mustard. Remove from heat, stir in flour until smooth, and gradually whisk in milk. Sauce will thicken. Whisk 1 1/2 cup Swiss cheese into the sauce, stirring until the cheese has melted and the sauce is smooth. Stir sauerkraut with about 1 tablespoon of reserved juice and corned beef into the cheese sauce.
- Transfer cooked noodles to the prepared casserole dish and pour in the sauce; stir to combine. Sprinkle remaining 1 1/2 cup Swiss cheese in an even layer over the top.
- Bake casserole in the preheated oven until bubbling, about 20 minutes. Remove casserole from oven and set the oven to broil.
- Stir 3 tablespoons melted butter into the reserved rye and panko crumbs until thoroughly combined and sprinkle top of casserole with rye crumb mixture. Return to oven and broil until the crumbs are golden brown, about 2 more minutes. Watch carefully to prevent burning.

Nutrition Information

- Calories: 583 calories
- Total Fat: 27.6 g
- Cholesterol: 127 mg
- Sodium: 1230 mg
- Total Carbohydrate: 56.6 g
- Protein: 28.6 g

222. Reuben Noodle Bake

"Satisfying, tasty and filling! A breeze to make. Using the Reuben ingredients and adding noodles really works. You can substitute Thousand Island dressing for the mayonnaise for added zip."

Serving: 8 | Prep: 5 m | Cook: 1 h 10 m | Ready in: 1 h 15 m

Ingredients

- 8 ounces egg noodles
- 4 tablespoons butter, melted
- 1 (20 ounce) can sauerkraut, drained and rinsed
- 1 pound corned beef
- 1/2 cup mayonnaise
- 2 cups shredded Swiss cheese
- 1 tomato, sliced
- 1/2 cup crushed saltine crackers
- 1/4 teaspoon caraway seed

Direction

- Preheat oven to 350 degrees F (175 degrees C).
- Bring a large pot of lightly salted water to a boil. Add pasta and cook for 8 to 10 minutes or until al dente; drain. Toss with half the melted butter and place in a 9x13 baking dish.
- Spread sauerkraut over the noodles; cover evenly with corned beef. Spread mayonnaise over beef and top with the shredded Swiss and tomato slices.
- In a small bowl, toss together crushed crackers and caraway seed with remaining melted butter. Sprinkle crumb mixture over Swiss and tomato.
- Bake in preheated oven 1 hour, until bubbly and golden.

Nutrition Information

- Calories: 447 calories
- Total Fat: 31 g
- Cholesterol: 90 mg
- Sodium: 966 mg
- Total Carbohydrate: 26.6 g
- Protein: 16.3 g

223. Rushin Casserole

"This recipe is adapted from one I found in a Georgian/Russian cookbook. The original recipe was more complex, and called for other ingredients like lamb -- which my family won't eat. This version is a big favorite in our home. The yogurt sauce can be as garlicky as your family likes. We usually go for lots, but we've had guests who like it with plain yogurt."

Serving: 6 | Prep: 15 m | Cook: 30 m | Ready in: 45 m

Ingredients

- 1 (16 ounce) package wide egg noodles
- 4 cups plain yogurt
- 2 cloves garlic, minced
- 1 pound ground beef
- 1 onion, chopped
- 2 teaspoons ground cinnamon
- 1 lemon, juiced
- 1/2 teaspoon salt

Direction

- Bring a large pot of lightly salted water to a boil. Add noodles and cook for 8 to 10 minutes or until al dente. Drain, and transfer to a serving dish. While the pasta is cooking, mix together the yogurt and garlic in a medium bowl. Cover, and refrigerate until serving.
- In a large skillet over medium heat, brown the ground beef with the onion. Season with cinnamon while cooking. Drain off excess grease, and stir in lemon juice and salt. Adjust seasoning to taste. Toss the meat mixture with noodles, and serve hot with cold yogurt sauce spooned over.

Nutrition Information

- Calories: 538 calories
- Total Fat: 14.8 g
- Cholesterol: 118 mg
- Sodium: 369 mg
- Total Carbohydrate: 69.2 g
- Protein: 32.3 g

224. Sarahs Tofu Noodle Soup

"Tastes just like chicken noodle soup but with tofu. I add raisins to this soup, just like grandma used to."

Serving: 4 | Prep: 15 m | Cook: 40 m | Ready in: 55 m

Ingredients

- 2 tablespoons butter
- 2 cups sliced carrots
- 1 1/2 cups chopped onion
- 1 1/2 cups chopped celery
- 1 1/2 teaspoons minced garlic
- 12 cups vegetarian chicken-flavored broth
- 2 cups egg noodles
- 1 (14 ounce) container extra-firm tofu, drained and cubed
- 1/4 cup raisins
- 1/2 teaspoon dried basil
- 1/2 teaspoon dried oregano
- 1/4 teaspoon poultry seasoning
- 1/4 teaspoon dried thyme
- 1/4 teaspoon dried rosemary
- 1/4 teaspoon dried marjoram
- 1/4 teaspoon black pepper
- 1/4 cup cornstarch
- 3 tablespoons cold water

Direction

- Melt the butter in a stockpot over medium heat. Stir in the carrots, onion, celery, and garlic and cook until just tender, about 10 minutes.
- Pour in the broth and bring to a boil over high heat. Once boiling, add the noodles, tofu, raisins, basil, oregano, poultry seasoning, thyme, rosemary, marjoram, and pepper. Dissolve the cornstarch and water in a small bowl. Stir the cornstarch mixture into the soup. Return soup to a boil, then reduce heat to medium-low, cover, and simmer for 30 minutes.

Nutrition Information

- Calories: 358 calories
- Total Fat: 12.9 g
- Cholesterol: 29 mg
- Sodium: 1484 mg
- Total Carbohydrate: 49 g
- Protein: 17.1 g

225. Sauerbraten Beef in Gingersnap Gravy

"Sauerbraten but easier!"

Serving: 6 | Prep: 15 m | Cook: 7 h 15 m | Ready in: 7 h 30 m

Ingredients

- 2 pounds cubed beef stew meat
- 1 cup chopped onion
- 1 cup beef broth
- 1 cup red wine vinegar
- 2 bay leaves
- 3 cups egg noodles
- 3/4 cup crushed gingersnap cookies
- 2 tablespoons brown sugar
- 2 tablespoons chopped fresh parsley

Direction

- Combine beef stew meat, onion, beef broth, vinegar, and bay leaves in a slow cooker.
- Cook on Low for 7 to 9 hours.
- Bring a large pot of lightly salted water to a boil. Cook egg noodles in the boiling water, stirring occasionally until tender yet firm to the bite, 4 to 5 minutes. Drain.
- Remove bay leaves from beef mixture; stir in crushed gingersnaps and brown sugar. Cook beef mixture on Low until thickened, about 15 minutes. Serve sauerbraten over egg noodles and garnish with parsley.

Nutrition Information

- Calories: 607 calories
- Total Fat: 32.7 g
- Cholesterol: 147 mg

- Sodium: 276 mg
- Total Carbohydrate: 31.6 g
- Protein: 43.9 g

226. Sausage Apples and Noodles

"This is more of a dessert than anything. This Pennsylvania-Dutch meal is a favorite at our family potlucks and will fill you up quickly. It also makes great leftovers for lunches."

Serving: 6 | Prep: 20 m | Cook: 40 m | Ready in: 1 h

Ingredients

- 1 (8 ounce) package wide egg noodles
- 1 1/2 pounds sweet Italian sausage, sliced
- 3/4 cup white sugar
- 1 teaspoon ground cinnamon
- 2 tablespoons butter, melted
- 4 apples - peeled, cored, and thinly sliced
- 2 tablespoons butter, cut into pieces

Direction

- Preheat an oven to 350 degrees F (175 degrees C).
- Fill a large pot with lightly salted water and bring to a rolling boil over high heat. Once the water is boiling, stir in the egg noodles, and return to a boil. Cook the pasta uncovered, stirring occasionally, until the pasta has cooked through, but is still firm to the bite, about 5 minutes. Drain well in a colander set in the sink.
- Place a large skillet over medium-high heat; cook the sausages until completely cooked, 5 to 7 minutes.
- Stir together the sugar and cinnamon in a small bowl.
- Pour the melted butter into the bottom of a 9x13 inch baking dish; layer half of the cooked egg noodles into the bottom of the dish; top with half of the sausage slices and half of the apple slices; sprinkle about half of the cinnamon-sugar mix over the dish. Repeat layers with remaining noodles, sausage, apples, and cinnamon-sugar. Dot with the butter pieces.
- Bake in the preheated oven until the apples are soft, 30 to 45 minutes.

Nutrition Information

- Calories: 626 calories
- Total Fat: 30.8 g
- Cholesterol: 96 mg
- Sodium: 1007 mg
- Total Carbohydrate: 68 g
- Protein: 20.6 g

227. Scarletts Chicken Cacciatore

"A great chicken dish full of veggies. You can have it for dinner tonight, or freeze it for later."

Serving: 6 | Prep: 30 m | Cook: 40 m | Ready in: 1 h 10 m

Ingredients

- 1 tablespoon vegetable oil
- 1 pound skinless, boneless chicken breast halves, cubed
- 1 small onion, diced
- 1/2 green bell pepper, diced
- 2 cups sliced fresh mushrooms
- 1 clove garlic, crushed
- 1 (28 ounce) can Italian-style crushed tomatoes
- 2 tablespoons chopped fresh parsley
- 1 teaspoon salt
- 1/4 teaspoon ground black pepper
- 2 teaspoons Italian seasoning
- 1 teaspoon dried basil
- 1 (8 ounce) package egg noodles
- 1/2 cup grated Parmesan cheese

Direction

- Heat the oil in a large skillet over medium heat, and cook and stir the chicken, onion, green pepper, mushrooms, and garlic until the chicken is no longer pink inside, 10 to 15 minutes. Stir in the crushed tomatoes, parsley,

salt, pepper, Italian seasoning, and basil, bring the mixture to a boil, and reduce heat. Cover the skillet and simmer for 30 minutes.
- While the chicken mixture is simmering, fill a large pot with lightly salted water and bring to a rolling boil over high heat. Once the water is boiling, stir in the egg noodles, and return to a boil. Cook the noodles uncovered, stirring occasionally, until cooked through but still firm to the bite, about 5 minutes. Drain well in a colander set in the sink.
- Serve the chicken cacciatore over the hot cooked noodles. Sprinkle with Parmesan cheese before serving.

Nutrition Information

- Calories: 329 calories
- Total Fat: 8.1 g
- Cholesterol: 76 mg
- Sodium: 836 mg
- Total Carbohydrate: 37.8 g
- Protein: 24.8 g

228. Sensational Chicken Noodle Soup

"Sometimes you just want a good, old-fashioned chicken noodle soup...no fancy ingredients...just great flavor. Give this version a try...all you need is 6 ingredients and 35 minutes to make a home-style soup that you'll really enjoy."

Serving: 4 | Prep: 10 m | Ready in: 35 m

Ingredients

- 4 cups Swanson® Chicken Broth or Swanson® Certified Organic Chicken Broth or Swanson® Natural Goodness® Chicken Broth
- Generous dash ground black pepper
- 1 medium carrot, peeled and sliced
- 1 stalk celery, sliced
- 1/2 cup uncooked medium egg noodles
- 1 cup shredded cooked chicken or turkey

Direction

- Heat the broth, 1 generous dash ground black pepper, carrot and celery in a 2-quart saucepan over medium-high heat to a boil.
- Stir the noodles and chicken in the saucepan. Reduce the heat to medium. Cook for 10 minutes or until the noodles are tender, stirring occasionally.

229. Sensational Turkey Noodle Soup

"Here is a great idea for that leftover turkey! Combine it with a few simple ingredients to make a sensational soup that's incredibly good. It's a breeze to prepare, but one taste guarantees that this will become a soup time favorite recipe."

Serving: 4 | Prep: 10 m | Cook: 15 m | Ready in: 25 m

Ingredients

- 3 1/2 cups Swanson® Chicken Broth or Swanson® Natural Goodness® Chicken Broth or Swanson® Certified Organic Chicken Broth
- 1 medium carrot, peeled and sliced
- 1 stalk celery, sliced
- 1/2 cup uncooked medium egg noodles
- 1 cup cubed cooked turkey or chicken

Direction

- Heat the broth, 1/8 teaspoon black pepper, carrot and celery in a 3-quart saucepan over medium-high heat to a boil.
- Stir the noodles and turkey in the saucepan. Reduce the heat to medium. Cook for 10 minutes or until the noodles are tender.

Nutrition Information

- Calories: 94 calories
- Total Fat: 2.4 g
- Cholesterol: 35 mg
- Sodium: 884 mg
- Total Carbohydrate: 6 g

- Protein: 12 g

230. ShowOff Stroganoff

"This recipe was handed down over several generations. Simply delicious! Serve over hot egg noodles. Enjoy!"

Serving: 6 | Prep: 15 m | Cook: 40 m | Ready in: 55 m

Ingredients

- 5 tablespoons olive oil, or more as needed
- 2 ounces butter
- 1 cup all-purpose flour
- salt and ground black pepper to taste
- 1 pound beef chuck steak, cut across the grain into 1 1/2-inch-thin strips
- 1 (8 ounce) package button mushrooms
- 1/2 cup dry red cooking wine
- 1/2 cup beef broth
- 1 (8 ounce) package egg noodles
- 1 (15 ounce) jar Holland-style pearl onions, drained
- 1 1/2 cups sour cream

Direction

- Heat olive oil and butter together in a skillet over low heat until smooth.
- Whisk flour, salt, and pepper together in a shallow bowl. Coat beef strips in flour mixture, gently shaking off any excess flour.
- Increase heat under skillet to medium. Add beef to skillet and cook and stir until browned, 1 to 2 minutes per side. Mix mushrooms into beef, adding more oil if pan is dry; cook and stir until mushrooms are lightly browned, about 5 minutes.
- Pour wine into the skillet and bring to a boil while scraping the browned bits of food off of the bottom of the pan with a wooden spoon; continue cooking until liquid is reduced by half, 5 to 10 minutes. Add beef broth and return to a boil.
- Cover skillet and cook until beef is tender, 20 to 25 minutes.
- Bring a large pot of lightly salted water to a boil. Cook egg noodles in the boiling water, stirring occasionally until cooked through but firm to the bite, about 5 minutes. Drain.
- Mix onions into beef mixture; cook and stir until onions are warmed, 3 to 5 minutes. Remove skillet from heat and gently stir sour cream into beef mixture; serve over noodles.

Nutrition Information

- Calories: 683 calories
- Total Fat: 40.9 g
- Cholesterol: 111 mg
- Sodium: 314 mg
- Total Carbohydrate: 58.4 g
- Protein: 20.5 g

231. Shrimp and Asparagus

"This recipe is a delicious option for shrimp. Shrimp sauteed with asparagus and mushrooms, tossed with egg noodles."

Serving: 8 | Prep: 20 m | Cook: 30 m | Ready in: 50 m

Ingredients

- 1 pound fresh asparagus
- 1 (16 ounce) package egg noodles
- 4 cloves garlic, minced
- 1/2 cup extra virgin olive oil
- 1 cup butter
- 1 tablespoon lemon juice
- 1 pound medium shrimp - peeled and deveined
- 1 pound fresh mushrooms, thinly sliced
- 1/2 cup grated Parmesan cheese
- salt and pepper to taste

Direction

- In a small saucepan, boil or steam asparagus in enough water to cover until tender; chop and set aside.

- Bring a large pot of salted water to full boil, place the pasta in the pot and return to a rolling boil; cook until al dente. Drain well.
- In a large saucepan, sauté garlic in the olive oil over medium-low heat until the garlic is golden brown.
- Place butter and lemon juice in the saucepan. Heat until the butter has melted. Place the shrimp in the saucepan and cook until the shrimp turns pink. Place the mushrooms and asparagus into the saucepan, cook until mushrooms are tender.
- Toss the shrimp and vegetable mixture with the egg noodles and sprinkle with Parmesan cheese. Salt and pepper to taste. Serve immediately.

Nutrition Information

- Calories: 653 calories
- Total Fat: 42.2 g
- Cholesterol: 199 mg
- Sodium: 340 mg
- Total Carbohydrate: 45.4 g
- Protein: 24.7 g

232. Silvers Savory Chicken and Broccoli Casserole

"This is an easy to make recipe that is great for potlucks, church gatherings, holidays, or outside gatherings. It is also a non-hassle recipe for you working folks, single folks, or even for kids to make! You can even make it ahead of time by preparing the casserole and then freezing it - for up to 3months! My family loves this casserole and we change things around in it, by adding or taking out different things. Have fun with it, and I would love to hear comments on what worked for you and what changes you made! Serve with dinner rolls or French bread and a salad!"

Serving: 6 | Prep: 20 m | Cook: 20 m | Ready in: 40 m

Ingredients

- 6 ounces egg noodles
- 3 tablespoons butter
- 1 yellow onion, chopped
- 1/4 cup all-purpose flour
- 1 1/2 cups chicken broth
- 3/4 cup milk
- salt and pepper to taste
- 5 cups cooked, shredded chicken breast meat
- 1 (10 ounce) package chopped frozen broccoli, thawed
- 1 cup shredded Cheddar cheese
- 1 cup shredded provolone cheese

Direction

- Bring a large pot of lightly salted water to a boil. Add pasta and cook for 6 to 8 minutes or until al dente; drain. Preheat oven to 400 degrees F (200 degrees C.) Grease a 9x13 inch casserole dish.
- Melt butter in a large saucepan over medium heat. Sauté onion until tender, about 3 minutes. Mix in flour. Gradually stir in chicken broth. Slowly stir in milk, and cook, stirring, until sauce begins to thicken. Season with salt and pepper.
- Place cooked noodles in the bottom of casserole dish. Arrange cooked chicken in an even layer over noodles. Place broccoli over the chicken. Pour sauce evenly over the broccoli. Combine cheeses, and sprinkle half over the casserole.
- Bake in preheated oven for 20 minutes, or until the cheese melts. Remove from oven, and sprinkle with remaining cheese. Allow to set for 5 minutes, until cheese melts.

Nutrition Information

- Calories: 580 calories
- Total Fat: 28.6 g
- Cholesterol: 164 mg
- Sodium: 453 mg
- Total Carbohydrate: 30.1 g
- Protein: 49.4 g

233. Simple Beef Stroganoff

"This is a very simple and quick beef stroganoff that can be made after a busy day at work. It uses ground beef and mushroom soup!"

Serving: 4 | Prep: 20 m | Cook: 10 m | Ready in: 30 m

Ingredients

- 1 (8 ounce) package egg noodles
- 1 pound ground beef
- 1 (10.75 ounce) can fat free condensed cream of mushroom soup
- 1 tablespoon garlic powder
- 1/2 cup sour cream
- salt and pepper to taste

Direction

- Prepare the egg noodles according to package directions and set aside.
- In a separate large skillet over medium heat, sauté the ground beef over medium heat for 5 to 10 minutes, or until browned. Drain the fat and add the soup and garlic powder. Simmer for 10 minutes, stirring occasionally.
- Remove from heat and combine the meat mixture with the egg noodles. Add the sour cream, stirring well, and season with salt and pepper to taste.

Nutrition Information

- Calories: 679 calories
- Total Fat: 40.5 g
- Cholesterol: 159 mg
- Sodium: 660 mg
- Total Carbohydrate: 48.2 g
- Protein: 28.7 g

234. Simple Beef Tips and Noodles

"This is one of my family favorites; it's a great starter recipe for using a pressure cooker. It is wonderful any time of year, but we like it best in the cooler weather. Very quick and easy to make after a day at work. It can also be made in a slow cooker."

Serving: 4 | Prep: 20 m | Cook: 30 m | Ready in: 1 h 5 m

Ingredients

- 2 tablespoons vegetable oil
- 1 pound cubed beef stew meat
- 1 large onion, diced
- 2 cloves garlic, minced
- 1 (8 ounce) package sliced button mushrooms
- 1 (32 ounce) carton beef stock
- salt to taste
- ground black pepper to taste
- 1 (8 ounce) package wide egg noodles
- 3 tablespoons cornstarch
- 1/2 cup cold water

Direction

- Heat oil in the pressure cooker over medium-high heat and stir in beef cubes. Cook until the beef is browned on all sides; remove beef and set it aside. Drain and discard excess grease.
- Lower the heat to medium and add onion; cook and stir until onion has softened and turned translucent, about 5 minutes. Stir in garlic and mushrooms and continue to cook about 5 minutes more, until garlic is fragrant but not brown.
- Pour in beef stock, beef stew meat, and any accumulated drippings; season with salt and pepper. Return to high heat, seal the lid, and bring to full pressure.
- Reduce the heat to low, maintaining full pressure, and cook for 20 minutes.
- While the stew is cooking, bring a large pot of lightly salted water to a boil. Stir in noodles and cook until tender, stirring often, about 8 minutes. Drain and set aside.
- Remove the pressure cooker from the heat and allow the pressure to drop naturally. Dissolve cornstarch into 1/2 cup of cold water. When the pressure has dropped, remove the lid and

whisk in the cornstarch mixture. Bring the beef and mushrooms back to a boil and cook, stirring constantly, for 2 minutes or until the sauce has thickened. Pour the beef over the noodles and serve.

Nutrition Information

- Calories: 518 calories
- Total Fat: 17.1 g
- Cholesterol: 107 mg
- Sodium: 151 mg
- Total Carbohydrate: 54.8 g
- Protein: 35 g

235. Simple Hamburger Stroganoff

"I've always loved the taste of a good Stroganoff, but I hated the expense and preparation of beef tips or steak or roast beef to make it. So I created my own creamy Stroganoff."

Serving: 6 | Prep: 20 m | Cook: 10 m | Ready in: 30 m

Ingredients

- 1 (16 ounce) package egg noodles
- 1 pound lean ground beef
- 1 (.75 ounce) packet dry brown gravy mix
- 1 (8 ounce) package cream cheese
- 1 (6 ounce) can chopped mushrooms, with liquid
- 1/2 cup milk
- 1 (8 ounce) container sour cream
- 2 (10.75 ounce) cans condensed cream of mushroom soup

Direction

- Bring a large pot of lightly salted water to a boil. Add egg noodles and cook for 8 to 10 minutes or until al dente; drain.
- In a skillet over medium heat, brown the ground beef until no pink shows, about 5 minutes; drain fat.
- Mix brown gravy, cream cheese, and mushrooms with hamburger, stirring until cream cheese melts. Add milk, sour cream, and mushroom soup to cooked pasta. Blend hamburger mixture with pasta.

Nutrition Information

- Calories: 735 calories
- Total Fat: 42 g
- Cholesterol: 159 mg
- Sodium: 1134 mg
- Total Carbohydrate: 60.9 g
- Protein: 28.9 g

236. Slow Cooker Beef Stew II

"Easy, quick and delicious. This stew is cooked in the slow cooker, so all you have to do is heat up some egg noodles and you've got dinner!"

Serving: 6 | Prep: 5 m | Cook: 10 h 30 m | Ready in: 10 h 35 m

Ingredients

- 2 pounds stew meat, trimmed and cubed
- 3 (10.75 ounce) cans condensed cream of chicken soup
- 1 (16 ounce) package egg noodles

Direction

- Spray the inside of a slow cooker with the vegetable cooking spray. Add the meat and the soups to the slow cooker.
- Cook on low setting for 8 to 10 hours.
- Prepare noodles according to package directions.
- When stew is ready, pour over the noodles and serve hot.

Nutrition Information

- Calories: 752 calories
- Total Fat: 34.9 g
- Cholesterol: 176 mg
- Sodium: 1095 mg
- Total Carbohydrate: 64.1 g

- Protein: 43.2 g

237. Slow Cooker Beef Stroganoff II

"A delicious beef stroganoff recipe for the slow cooker. This one uses round steak and golden mushroom soup mixed with egg noodles and sour cream. Very simple to assemble and the slow cooker does the work for you."

Serving: 6 | Prep: 10 m | Cook: 8 h 40 m | Ready in: 8 h 50 m

Ingredients

- 2 tablespoons vegetable oil
- 1 1/2 pounds round steak, cubed
- 1/4 cup all-purpose flour for coating
- 2 (10.75 ounce) cans condensed golden mushroom soup
- 3 1/2 cups water
- 3 cubes beef bouillon
- 1 cup sour cream
- 1 (16 ounce) package egg noodles

Direction

- Heat oil in a large skillet over medium high heat. Roll the beef in flour and sauté in the hot oil until well browned, about 5 minutes.
- Transfer the meat to the slow cooker and top with the soup, water and bouillon.
- Cook on high setting for 8 hours. Stir in the sour cream during the last 30 minutes.
- Cook the egg noodles according to package directions. Serve the meat over the noodles.

Nutrition Information

- Calories: 719 calories
- Total Fat: 32.8 g
- Cholesterol: 149 mg
- Sodium: 1058 mg
- Total Carbohydrate: 66.1 g
- Protein: 38.6 g

238. Slow Cooker Chicken and Noodles

"This is a wonderfully easy soup to cook while at work or on a busy day! This can be 'soupy' with more broth; or sometimes I like to thicken the juice with a little water and cornstarch mixture and let cook till thick. Then it is good served over mashed potatoes! Enjoy!!"

Serving: 6 | Prep: 30 m | Cook: 8 h | Ready in: 8 h 30 m

Ingredients

- 4 skinless, boneless chicken breast halves
- 6 cups water
- 1 onion, chopped
- 2 stalks celery, chopped (optional)
- salt and pepper to taste
- 1 (12 ounce) package frozen egg noodles

Direction

- Place chicken, water, onion and salt and pepper to taste into a slow cooker. Add celery if desired. Set temperature to low and cook for 6 to 8 hours.
- When chicken is tender, remove from the slow cooker and tear or chop into bite-sized pieces. Set aside in a small casserole dish to keep warm. Turn the slow cooker up to high heat and stir in the frozen egg noodles. Cook until noodles are tender then return the chicken pieces to the broth. Adjust seasonings to taste.

Nutrition Information

- Calories: 311 calories
- Total Fat: 3.5 g
- Cholesterol: 93 mg
- Sodium: 81 mg
- Total Carbohydrate: 42 g
- Protein: 26.4 g

239. Smoked Paprika Goulash for the Slow Cooker

"This is a very rich and flavorful beef dish with a thick, red, smoky tasting sauce. Great for making a day ahead and reheating. Instead of noodles, you can serve over rice or potatoes."

Serving: 8

Ingredients

- 1 tablespoon vegetable oil
- 3 onions, sliced
- 3 cloves garlic, chopped
- 1/4 cup smoked Spanish paprika
- 2 teaspoons kosher salt
- 1 teaspoon coarsely ground black pepper
- 3 pounds lean beef stew meat, cut into 1-inch cubes
- 3 tablespoons vegetable oil, divided
- 1 1/2 cups water
- 1 (6 ounce) can tomato paste
- 1 (10 ounce) package egg noodles
- 1/2 cup sour cream (optional)
- 8 sprigs fresh parsley (optional)

Direction

- Heat 1 tablespoon oil in a large skillet over medium-high heat. Cook and stir onions until they soften and begin to brown at the edges, 8 to 10 minutes. Add the garlic and cook for one minute. Transfer mixture to a slow cooker. Cover and set cooker to Low.
- Mix together paprika, salt, and pepper in a large bowl. Toss the meat cubes in the paprika mixture until evenly coated.
- Heat one tablespoon of the oil in the skillet over medium-high heat. Put a third of the beef cubes into the skillet and cook until nicely browned on all sides. Transfer to the slow cooker. Pour 2 tablespoons of water into the skillet and scrape the browned bits from the pan; pour liquid into the slow cooker. This prevents the paprika from burning when you brown the next batches of beef. Add another tablespoon of oil to the skillet and cook the next batch the same way; repeat for the third batch.
- Stir the tomato paste and the rest of the water into the slow cooker; cover. Cook on High for 4 to 5 hours (or on Low for 6 to 9 hours).
- Fill a large pot with lightly salted water and bring to a rolling boil over high heat. Stir in the egg noodles, and cook uncovered, stirring occasionally, until the noodles have cooked through, but are still firm to the bite, about 5 minutes. Drain.
- Serve goulash over noodles with a dollop of sour cream and a sprig of parsley.

Nutrition Information

- Calories: 642 calories
- Total Fat: 28 g
- Cholesterol: 182 mg
- Sodium: 795 mg
- Total Carbohydrate: 38 g
- Protein: 59.1 g

240. Spicy and Creamy Chicken Pasta

"A delicious spicy, but not too spicy, creamy chicken pasta! Easy to make! Serve with crescent rolls."

Serving: 6 | Prep: 15 m | Cook: 25 m | Ready in: 1 h 40 m

Ingredients

- 1/4 cup cider vinegar
- 1/4 cup vegetable oil
- 2 teaspoons seasoned salt
- 1 teaspoon red pepper flakes
- 1 teaspoon monosodium glutamate (such as Ac'cent®) (optional)
- 1/2 teaspoon ground black pepper
- 1/4 teaspoon salt
- 4 skinless, boneless chicken breast halves - cut into chunks
- 2 tablespoons vegetable oil
- 1 cup heavy whipping cream

- 1 (8 ounce) package egg noodles

Direction

- Mix cider vinegar, 1/4 cup vegetable oil, seasoned salt, red pepper flakes, monosodium glutamate, black pepper, and salt in a resealable plastic bag. Place chicken pieces into marinade, seal bag, and marinate in refrigerator for 1 hour.
- Heat 2 tablespoons vegetable oil in a large skillet over medium heat. Remove chicken from marinade; discard used marinade. Cook chicken in hot oil until browned and no longer pink inside, about 10 minutes. Stir frequently. Transfer chicken to a bowl with a slotted spoon, leaving accumulated juices in skillet.
- Whisk whipping cream into pan juices and cook until cream has started to thicken, about 5 minutes. Stir chicken back into skillet and reduce heat to low. Simmer chicken in cream sauce until sauce is thick, 15 to 20 minutes.
- Bring a large pot of lightly salted water to a boil. Cook egg noodles in the boiling water, stirring occasionally until cooked through but firm to the bite, about 5 minutes. Drain. Gently stir cooked noodles into skillet with chicken and cream sauce.

Nutrition Information

- Calories: 494 calories
- Total Fat: 31.9 g
- Cholesterol: 130 mg
- Sodium: 548 mg
- Total Carbohydrate: 28.4 g
- Protein: 22.5 g

241. Spicy Noodles Malay Style

"Spicy and simply devilish, a kick start on Malay cuisine. Remember to set water at the side 'cause you're on fire!!!"

Serving: 4 | Prep: 15 m | Cook: 35 m | Ready in: 50 m

Ingredients

- 1 (12 ounce) package uncooked egg noodles
- 3 tablespoons olive oil
- 1 teaspoon finely chopped garlic
- 1/2 bunch fresh spinach, stems removed, chopped
- 1/4 cup chile paste
- 3 tablespoons ketchup
- 1 egg
- 1/2 teaspoon white sugar
- 1/4 cup water
- salt and pepper to taste
- 1/2 cup fresh bean sprouts
- 1/2 cup green peas

Direction

- Bring a large pot of water to a boil, cook the egg noodles 6 to 8 minutes, until al dente, and drain.
- Heat the oil in a skillet over medium heat, and sauté the garlic about 1 minute. Stir in the spinach, and cook about 1 minute. Mix in the cooked egg noodles, chile paste, and ketchup, and toss until well coated.
- Make a hole in the center of the noodle mixture. Place the egg in the center, and scramble, tossing with the noodles just before egg is finished cooking.
- Mix the sugar and enough water to keep the mixture moist into the skillet. Season with salt and pepper. Continue to cook, stirring constantly, about 6 minutes. Toss in the sprouts and peas, and cook and stir about 4 minutes, until heated through.

Nutrition Information

- Calories: 506 calories
- Total Fat: 17.4 g
- Cholesterol: 117 mg
- Sodium: 346 mg

- Total Carbohydrate: 76.7 g
- Protein: 16.2 g

242. Spinach Cheese Pasta

"My children love spinach because of this dish! Makes a fast, easy, and delicious supper. Add slices of grilled chicken breast if you have meat lovers in the family. My husband and mother love it, too!"

Serving: 8 | Prep: 15 m | Cook: 10 m | Ready in: 25 m

Ingredients

- 1 (16 ounce) package extra wide egg noodles
- 1/3 cup extra virgin olive oil
- 2 cloves garlic, pressed
- 1 1/2 (10 ounce) packages frozen chopped spinach
- 1 (8 ounce) container cottage cheese
- 1 (3 ounce) package finely grated Parmesan cheese

Direction

- Bring a large pot of lightly salted water to a boil. Add egg noodles and cook for 8 to 10 minutes or until al dente. Drain, and return to the pot.
- Heat the olive oil in a skillet, and cook the garlic and spinach 3 to 5 minutes, until well coated. Transfer to the pot with the drained pasta. Toss in the cottage cheese. Top with Parmesan cheese to serve.

Nutrition Information

- Calories: 368 calories
- Total Fat: 16.8 g
- Cholesterol: 54 mg
- Sodium: 320 mg
- Total Carbohydrate: 38.9 g
- Protein: 15.9 g

243. Spinach Kugel

"My grandmother always made this wonderful kugel at every family dinner. It is moist and delicious and VERY easy to make!"

Serving: 18 | Prep: 20 m | Cook: 1 h 10 m | Ready in: 1 h 30 m

Ingredients

- 1 (16 ounce) package egg noodles
- 6 eggs, beaten
- 8 ounces butter, melted
- 1 (16 ounce) container sour cream
- 2 (1 ounce) envelopes dry onion soup mix
- 1 teaspoon black pepper
- 4 (10 ounce) boxes frozen chopped spinach, thawed and drained

Direction

- Preheat oven to 350 degrees F (175 degrees C). Grease a 9x13 inch baking dish.
- Fill a large pot with lightly salted water; bring to a rolling boil over high heat. Stir in the egg noodles, and return to a boil. Cook the pasta until cooked through, but is still firm to the bite, about 5 minutes. Drain well in a colander set in the sink.
- Combine the eggs, melted butter, sour cream, soup mix, and pepper in a large bowl. Stir in the cooked noodles, and drained spinach. Spoon into prepared baking dish.
- Bake in preheated oven until hot and golden brown, about 60 minutes. Cover dish with aluminum foil if kugel begins to brown too quickly.

Nutrition Information

- Calories: 287 calories
- Total Fat: 18.4 g
- Cholesterol: 113 mg
- Sodium: 432 mg
- Total Carbohydrate: 23.6 g
- Protein: 8.8 g

244. Spring Vegetable Soup

"It's so good on a chilly spring night and even better with a grilled sandwich for lunch the next day. By the way, you can omit any veggies you chose, but don't use canned vegetables. I promise you it's just better this way."

Serving: 6 | Prep: 15 m | Cook: 45 m | Ready in: 1 h

Ingredients

- 1 tablespoon vegetable oil
- 1/2 cup chopped onion
- 1 clove garlic, minced
- 1 medium potato, peeled and chopped
- 1/2 cup chopped broccoli
- 1/2 cup frozen corn
- 1/2 cup torn spinach
- 1/2 cup chopped fresh mushrooms
- 1/2 cup chopped carrots
- 1/4 cup chopped cabbage
- 2 (32 fluid ounce) containers chicken broth
- 6 ounces egg noodles
- 1 cup canned white beans

Direction

- Heat the oil in a large pot over medium heat, and cook the onion and garlic until tender. Mix in potato, broccoli, corn, spinach, mushrooms, carrots, and cabbage. Pour in chicken broth and bring to a boil. Reduce heat to low. Simmer 20 minutes, until potato is tender.
- Stir egg noodles and white beans into the pot, and continue cooking 7 minutes, or until noodles are tender and beans are heated through.

Nutrition Information

- Calories: 245 calories
- Total Fat: 4.9 g
- Cholesterol: 28 mg
- Sodium: 1452 mg
- Total Carbohydrate: 41 g
- Protein: 9.8 g

245. Steves Chicken Noodle Soup

"Easily made, this is a wonderfully flavorful chicken noodle soup that will cure any common disease and make your guests happy."

Serving: 12 | Prep: 20 m | Cook: 1 h | Ready in: 1 h 20 m

Ingredients

- 3 tablespoons vegetable oil
- 2 onions, diced
- 6 stalks celery, diced
- 6 carrot, diced
- 3/4 tablespoon chopped fresh rosemary
- 3/4 tablespoon chopped fresh tarragon
- 3/4 tablespoon chopped fresh thyme
- 3/4 tablespoon chopped Italian flat leaf parsley
- 4 quarts low-fat, low sodium chicken broth
- 3 1/2 cups cubed skinless, boneless chicken breast meat
- 1 (16 ounce) package egg noodles
- salt and pepper to taste

Direction

- In a large skillet over medium heat, cook onions in oil until translucent. Stir in celery, carrot, rosemary, tarragon, thyme and parsley and cook, covered, until vegetables are soft, 5 to 10 minutes.
- Transfer vegetable mixture to a large pot and pour in chicken broth. Simmer over low heat, covered, for 30 minutes.
- Stir in chicken breast pieces and egg noodles and simmer, covered, 30 minutes more. Season with salt and pepper.

Nutrition Information

- Calories: 276 calories
- Total Fat: 6.6 g
- Cholesterol: 65 mg
- Sodium: 593 mg
- Total Carbohydrate: 29.9 g
- Protein: 23.2 g

246. Stroganoff Soup

"Homemade stroganoff turned soup."

Serving: 5 | Prep: 20 m | Cook: 2 h | Ready in: 2 h 20 m

Ingredients

- 1 (16 ounce) package dry egg noodles
- 1 1/2 pounds round steak, cut into small pieces
- 1 small yellow onion, diced
- 2 (10.75 ounce) cans condensed cream of mushroom soup
- 2 2/3 cups water
- 1 (16 ounce) container sour cream
- 1 teaspoon steak sauce

Direction

- Bring a large pot of lightly salted water to a boil. Add egg noodles and cook for 8 to 10 minutes, or until al dente; drain and rinse under hot water.
- In a large skillet, brown the round steak pieces with the onion to desired doneness.
- In a slow cooker, combine the soup, 2 2/3 cup (or 2 soup cans) of water, sour cream and steak sauce. Mix until smooth. Add cooked steak pieces, onions and cooked noodles. Cook on low for 2 hours, or to desired taste and consistency.

Nutrition Information

- Calories: 754 calories
- Total Fat: 38.6 g
- Cholesterol: 152 mg
- Sodium: 903 mg
- Total Carbohydrate: 70 g
- Protein: 31.6 g

247. Sues Minestrone

"This is a good make-ahead recipe. In fact, I usually let it sit in the fridge for a few days before I reheat it! Feel free to experiment with the mixed vegetables. I use the Italian-style mixed veggies. Serve with warmed foccacia or French bread for dipping."

Serving: 8 | Cook: 40 m | Ready in: 40 m

Ingredients

- 1 pound ground beef
- 8 slices turkey bacon
- 1 (10.5 ounce) can beef broth
- 1 (11.5 ounce) can condensed bean with bacon soup
- 3 3/4 cups water
- 1 (8 ounce) can tomato sauce
- 1 tablespoon dried basil
- 1 tablespoon dried oregano
- 1 (10 ounce) package frozen mixed vegetables
- 1 (8 ounce) package egg noodles

Direction

- In a large pot over high heat, combine the meat, bacon, consomme, soup, water, tomato sauce, basil and oregano. Bring to a boil and reduce heat to low. Cover and simmer for 10 minutes.
- Add the vegetables and simmer for another 20 to 30 minutes. Add the egg noodles and simmer uncovered for another 10 minutes.

Nutrition Information

- Calories: 436 calories
- Total Fat: 23.2 g
- Cholesterol: 98 mg
- Sodium: 966 mg
- Total Carbohydrate: 34.7 g
- Protein: 22.4 g

248. Super Easy Ground Beef Stroganoff

"I love warm meals during cold months. This ground beef stroganoff is one of our family favorites. Add a dollop of sour cream and enjoy."

Serving: 4 | Prep: 10 m | Cook: 23 m | Ready in: 33 m

Ingredients

- 5 teaspoons beef bouillon granules
- 5 cups boiling water
- 1/2 teaspoon onion powder, or to taste, divided (optional)
- 1/2 teaspoon dried minced onion, or to taste (optional)
- 1 pinch garlic powder, or to taste (optional)
- 1 (10 ounce) package egg noodles, or more to taste
- 1 cup frozen peas
- 1 tablespoon butter
- 1/2 white onion, chopped
- 1/2 pound ground beef
- 1 dash ground black pepper
- 1/4 cup all-purpose flour, or more as needed

Direction

- Dissolve bouillon in the boiling water in a large bowl; pour a portion of the broth into another pot for boiling the noodles.
- Bring the broth in the pot to a boil and add onion powder, dried onion, and garlic powder. Add egg noodles; bring back to a boil. Cook until tender yet firm to the bite, about 12 minutes. Drain. Stir in frozen peas and cover.
- Melt butter in a saucepan over medium-high heat. Sauté onions until translucent, about 5 minutes. Add ground beef; cook and stir until no longer pink, 5 to 7 minutes. Add remaining onion powder and pepper. Stir in flour and mix well, 2 to 3 minutes. Add the reserved broth. Bring to a boil. Cook, stirring to avoid clumps, until beef sauce is thickened, 5 to 7 minutes.
- Serve meat sauce over a plate of noodles.

Nutrition Information

- Calories: 519 calories
- Total Fat: 21.5 g
- Cholesterol: 116 mg
- Sodium: 636 mg
- Total Carbohydrate: 59.3 g
- Protein: 21.1 g

249. Susans Beef Stroganoff

"Easy recipe to follow. I like to add sour cream to the top just before serving."

Serving: 4 | Prep: 10 m | Cook: 1 h 45 m | Ready in: 1 h 55 m

Ingredients

- 1 pound beef stew meat, sliced thinly
- 1 onion, chopped
- 2 cups water
- 2 cubes beef bouillon (such as Oxo®), crumbled
- 1 (10.75 ounce) can cream of mushroom soup
- 1 (16 ounce) package egg noodles

Direction

- Heat a large skillet over medium heat. Cook beef in hot skillet, stirring occasionally, until some of the fat from the meat renders, 1 to 2 minutes; add onion and sauté the mixture until the beef is completely browned, about 5 minutes more.
- Pour water into the skillet; add beef bouillon. Reduce heat to low and cook mixture at a simmer until the liquid is mostly evaporated, about 90 minutes.
- Stir cream of mushroom soup into the beef mixture; continue cooking until heated through, 5 to 7 minutes.
- Bring a large pot of lightly salted water to a boil. Cook egg noodles in the boiling water, stirring occasionally until cooked through but firm to the bite, about 5 minutes; drain. Divide

noodles between 4 plates and spoon beef mixture over the noodles.

Nutrition Information

- Calories: 667 calories
- Total Fat: 16 g
- Cholesterol: 154 mg
- Sodium: 999 mg
- Total Carbohydrate: 90.5 g
- Protein: 38.8 g

250. Swiss Cheese Noodle Bake

"Using broad egg noodles and Swiss cheese, this layered pasta dish is a delicious change from the normal pasta dish! It's a family favorite! Can be made ahead of time, and refrigerated until ready to cook. freezes well."

Serving: 8 | Prep: 20 m | Cook: 50 m | Ready in: 1 h 15 m

Ingredients

- 1 pound ground beef
- 1 pound bulk Italian sausage
- 2 (26 ounce) jars chunky style pasta sauce (such as Prego®)
- 1 (16 ounce) package broad egg noodles
- 3 (8 ounce) packages sliced Swiss cheese (such as Sargento®)

Direction

- Preheat oven to 350 degrees F (175 degrees C). Grease a 9x13 inch baking dish.
- Cook ground beef and sausage in a large, deep skillet until well browned, about 5 minutes. Drain fat. Stir in pasta sauce. Bring to a simmer.
- While sauce is simmering, bring a large pot of salted water to a boil over high heat. Stir in the egg noodles. Boil until cooked through, but is still firm to the bite, about 5 minutes. Drain well.
- Spoon half of the meat sauce into the prepared baking dish. Top with half of the cooked noodles, and 1 1/2 packages of cheese slices. Repeat with remaining sauce, noodles, and cheese.
- Place uncovered dish in preheated oven. Bake, until cheese is melted and browned, about 40 minutes. Let stand 5 minutes before serving.

Nutrition Information

- Calories: 951 calories
- Total Fat: 50.6 g
- Cholesterol: 186 mg
- Sodium: 1427 mg
- Total Carbohydrate: 71.2 g
- Protein: 50.9 g

251. Swiss Steak Italian Style

"A new twist on the classic Swiss taste. Marinara sauce and red wine makes this steak recipe stand out with style!"

Serving: 5 | Prep: 15 m | Cook: 45 m | Ready in: 1 h

Ingredients

- 1 pound round steak, cut into pieces
- 3 tablespoons all-purpose flour
- 1 teaspoon salt
- 1/4 teaspoon ground black pepper
- 3 tablespoons vegetable oil
- 3/4 cup chopped onion
- 2 (16 ounce) jars spaghetti sauce
- 1/2 cup red wine
- 2 cups thinly sliced celery
- 1 cup sliced green bell pepper
- 1 (12 ounce) package egg noodles

Direction

- Dredge steak in flour, salt and pepper. Heat a large skillet on medium high heat. Add oil to hot pan. Add meat and sauté until browned. Stir in onion and sauté. Stir in marinara sauce and wine and bring to boil. Add celery and green pepper; stir. Reduce heat, cover and simmer for 45 minutes.

- Heat a large pot of water to a boil and cook noodles until al dente. Remove from heat and drain.
- Serve meat sauce over noodles.

Nutrition Information

- Calories: 705 calories
- Total Fat: 24.8 g
- Cholesterol: 115 mg
- Sodium: 1302 mg
- Total Carbohydrate: 81.4 g
- Protein: 33.5 g

252. Swiss Steak Quick and Easy

"My mother has been making this Swiss steak for years. It is wonderful, and can be made either on the stove top or -- when you don't have a lot of time but want a hearty meal ready when you come home -- in the crock pot. Serve over a bed of egg noodles or rice with a hunk of thick crusty bread."

Serving: 6 | Prep: 20 m | Cook: 1 h | Ready in: 1 h 20 m

Ingredients

- 1 tablespoon vegetable oil
- 2 pounds cube steaks, pounded thin and cut into bite-size pieces
- 1 1/2 tablespoons all-purpose flour
- 1 medium onion, chopped
- 1 pound mushrooms, sliced
- salt and pepper to taste
- 1 (1.2 ounce) package brown gravy mix
- 2 (14.5 ounce) cans stewed tomatoes
- 1 (12 ounce) package egg noodles

Direction

- Heat oil in a Dutch oven over medium heat. Dredge steak strips in flour. Working in batches, place strips in hot oil. Fry until browned on both sides. Remove to a warm platter. When all meat is browned, return meat to Dutch oven, and stir in onions, mushrooms, salt, pepper, gravy mix, and stewed tomatoes. Bring to a boil, then simmer about 30 to 45 minutes.
- About 20 minutes before steak is finished, fill a large pot with water and bring to a boil. Add pasta, and cook until al dente, about 8 to 10 minutes; drain.
- Serve Swiss steak over noodles.

Nutrition Information

- Calories: 471 calories
- Total Fat: 13.7 g
- Cholesterol: 84 mg
- Sodium: 630 mg
- Total Carbohydrate: 58.2 g
- Protein: 29.8 g

253. Tallerine

"This recipe is so quick and delicious. It's been in my family for years! I serve it with garlic bread or Mexican cornbread."

Serving: 5

Ingredients

- 1 (12 ounce) package egg noodles
- 1 pound lean ground beef
- 1 pinch seasoning salt
- 1 pinch freshly ground black pepper
- 1 pinch garlic powder
- 1 (11 ounce) can Mexican-style corn
- 1 (10 ounce) can diced tomatoes with green chile peppers
- 1/2 pound processed cheese food (eg. Velveeta), sliced

Direction

- In a large pot with boiling salted water cook egg noodles until al dente. Drain well.
- Meanwhile, in a large skillet cook meat with seasoning salt, black pepper, and garlic powder until brown. Add the cans of Mexican-style corn, tomatoes with green chilies and mix well.

- Pour mixture into casserole dish prepared with butter spray. Arrange sliced processed cheese food on top. Cover with aluminum foil.
- Bake in a preheated 375 degree F (190 degrees C) oven for 20 to 30 minutes. Stir and serve.

Nutrition Information

- Calories: 656 calories
- Total Fat: 26.6 g
- Cholesterol: 144 mg
- Sodium: 1407 mg
- Total Carbohydrate: 66.7 g
- Protein: 36.5 g

254. Tasty Turkey Tetrazzini

"Creamy, cheesy and loaded with turkey and veggies, this turkey tetrazzini with egg noodles will please the heartiest of appetites."

Serving: 10 | Prep: 20 m | Cook: 1 h | Ready in: 1 h 20 m

Ingredients

- For topping:
- 3 Sister Schubert's Dinner Yeast Rolls, defrosted and coarsely crumbled
- 1/2 cup grated or shaved Parmesan cheese
- 2 tablespoons parsley
- 3 tablespoons olive oil
- 1 teaspoon Italian herb blend
- For filling:
- 1 (16 ounce) package Reames Noodles, cooked, drained and rinsed
- 2 teaspoons vegetable oil
- 1 cup chopped onion
- 1 cup diced yellow squash
- 1 cup peas, defrosted
- 3 cups diced cooked turkey meat
- 2 cups prepared Alfredo sauce
- 1/2 cup grated Parmesan cheese

Direction

- Preheat oven to 350 degrees F. Butter a 9 x 13-inch dish.
- For topping, combine all ingredients and set aside.
- For filling, heat oil in a sauté pan, add onions and cook for 3 to 4 minutes or until they are soft. Add yellow squash and sauté for 3 to 4 minutes. Transfer to large bowl and add remaining ingredients and toss gently. Place mixture into prepared pan. Cover with topping and bake 30 to 35 minutes or until thoroughly heated. Serve.

Nutrition Information

- Calories: 485 calories
- Total Fat: 26.6 g
- Cholesterol: 111 mg
- Sodium: 730 mg
- Total Carbohydrate: 38.1 g
- Protein: 23.6 g

255. Tex Mex Shark and Shrimp

"This is a great spicy recipe for shark and shrimp. You can probably get non-seafood eaters to enjoy this! I did!"

Serving: 6 | Prep: 15 m | Cook: 23 m | Ready in: 40 m

Ingredients

- 1 (16 ounce) package uncooked wide egg noodles
- 1 teaspoon olive oil
- 1 pound shark steaks, cut into chunks
- 1 pound frozen medium shrimp
- 1 (14.5 ounce) can diced tomatoes and green chiles
- 2 cups shredded mozzarella cheese
- ground black pepper to taste

Direction

- Bring a large pot of lightly salted water to a boil. Add egg noodles, cook for 6 to 8 minutes, until al dente, and drain.
- Heat the olive oil in a skillet over medium heat. Mix in the shark, shrimp, and tomatoes

with green chiles. Cover, and cook 15 minutes, or until shark is easily flaked with a fork.
- Serve the shark mixture over the cooked egg noodles. Sprinkle with mozzarella cheese, and season with pepper.

Nutrition Information

- Calories: 528 calories
- Total Fat: 14.8 g
- Cholesterol: 232 mg
- Sodium: 706 mg
- Total Carbohydrate: 50.6 g
- Protein: 46.3 g

256. The Best Ever Classic Jewish Noodle Kugel

"This is the classic noodle kugel that my mom always made for Shabbat dinner. It is incredibly easy to make and tastes so good!"

Serving: 12 | Prep: 10 m | Cook: 1 h | Ready in: 1 h 10 m

Ingredients

- 1 (16 ounce) package egg noodles
- 1/2 cup margarine
- 4 eggs, beaten
- 1 cup white sugar
- 1 1/2 cups applesauce
- 1 teaspoon vanilla extract
- ground cinnamon, for dusting

Direction

- Preheat an oven to 350 degrees F (175 degrees C).
- Fill a large pot with lightly salted water and bring to a rolling boil over high heat. Once the water is boiling, stir in the egg noodles, and return to a boil. Cook the pasta uncovered, stirring occasionally, until the pasta has cooked through, but is still firm to the bite, about 5 minutes. Drain well in a colander set in the sink.
- Place noodles in a large bowl. Mix margarine into the noodles until melted. Stir in the eggs, sugar, applesauce, and vanilla extract. Pour noodle mixture into a 9x13 inch baking pan, then sprinkle with cinnamon. Cover baking pan with aluminum foil.
- Bake in the preheated oven for 30 minutes. Uncover the kugel and bake until golden brown, 20 to 30 minutes.

Nutrition Information

- Calories: 313 calories
- Total Fat: 10.8 g
- Cholesterol: 93 mg
- Sodium: 119 mg
- Total Carbohydrate: 47 g
- Protein: 7.5 g

257. Three Cheese Noodle Bake

"After searching for years, I have found the ultimate mac-and-cheese recipe. Use low fat or fat free ingredients if desired. Tastes great either way. For variation, omit Worcestershire sauce, and add 1 tablespoon yellow or brown mustard."

Serving: 6

Ingredients

- 2 cups egg noodles
- 1 cup cottage cheese
- 1/2 cup sour cream
- 3 tablespoons grated Parmesan cheese
- 1 egg
- 2 cups shredded Cheddar cheese
- 1 teaspoon Worcestershire sauce
- 1/4 cup milk
- 1/4 teaspoon salt
- 1/4 teaspoon ground black pepper
- 3 tablespoons butter

Direction

- Cook noodles al dente. Drain and rinse. Set aside.

- In a large mixing bowl, mix together cottage cheese, sour cream, parmesan, 1 egg, 1 cup cheddar cheese, Worcestershire sauce, milk, butter or margarine, and salt and pepper. Stir in cooked noodles. Spread into a 9 inch square baking dish, top with remaining shredded cheese.
- Bake at 300 degrees F (150 degrees C) for one hour, or until set.

Nutrition Information

- Calories: 360 calories
- Total Fat: 26.3 g
- Cholesterol: 114 mg
- Sodium: 600 mg
- Total Carbohydrate: 12.2 g
- Protein: 18.9 g

258. Throw Together Mexican Casserole

"Ground beef, olives, egg noodles, corn, taco sauce and seasoning give this throw together casserole it's South-of-the-border flavor."

Serving: 4 | Prep: 5 m | Cook: 30 m | Ready in: 35 m

Ingredients

- 1 pound ground beef
- 1 (15 ounce) can sweet corn, drained
- 1 cup mild, chunky salsa
- 1/4 cup sliced black olives
- 3 1/2 cups cooked egg noodles
- 1 (15.25 ounce) can kidney beans, drained and rinsed
- 1/4 cup taco sauce
- 1 (1.25 ounce) package taco seasoning mix
- 1/2 cup tomato sauce

Direction

- Preheat oven to 325 degrees F (165 degrees C).
- In a skillet over medium heat, cook the ground beef until evenly brown; drain.
- In a 9x13 inch baking dish combine the beef, corn, salsa, olives, cooked noodles, beans, taco sauce, seasoning mix and tomato sauce.
- Bake in the preheated oven for 1/2 hour, or until cooked through.

Nutrition Information

- Calories: 663 calories
- Total Fat: 21.8 g
- Cholesterol: 109 mg
- Sodium: 1960 mg
- Total Carbohydrate: 84.7 g
- Protein: 34.4 g

259. Thyme Salmon with Sage Pasta

"This is a family favorite! It's also a great recipe for entertaining as well."

Serving: 6 | Prep: 20 m | Cook: 25 m | Ready in: 1 h 15 m

Ingredients

- 1 1/2 pounds skinned salmon fillet, cut into 4-inch pieces
- 2 tablespoons extra virgin olive oil
- 4 cloves garlic, crushed
- salt to taste
- 1 teaspoon dried thyme leaves
- 1 (12 ounce) package egg noodles
- 2 tablespoons salted butter
- 1/2 cup chopped fresh sage
- 2 cloves crushed garlic
- 1 tablespoon extra-virgin olive oil
- 2 cups frozen peas, thawed
- 1 lime, juiced
- 1 1/2 teaspoons salt
- 1 lime, juiced

Direction

- Place the salmon pieces into a mixing bowl. Drizzle with 2 tablespoons of extra virgin olive

oil, then toss with 4 cloves of crushed garlic. Refrigerate at least 30 minutes.
- Preheat an oven to 350 degrees F (175 degrees C).
- Line a baking sheet with aluminum foil. Place the salmon onto the foil, and season with salt and thyme. Fold the foil over the salmon to form a sealed pouch. Bake in the preheated oven until the salmon is no longer translucent in the center, 15 to 20 minutes.
- Meanwhile, fill a large pot with lightly salted water and bring to a rolling boil over high heat. Once the water is boiling, stir in the egg noodles, and return to a boil. Cook the pasta uncovered, stirring occasionally, until the pasta has cooked through, but is still firm to the bite, about 5 minutes. Drain well in a colander set in the sink, then return to the cooking pot.
- Melt the butter in a small saucepan over medium heat. Cook until the butter has browned lightly. Stir in the sage and garlic until the sage has wilted. Stir in 1 tablespoon of olive oil, the frozen peas, the juice of 1 lime, and 1 1/2 teaspoons of salt. Stir into the pasta, and place into a serving bowl. Remove the salmon from the foil, and place onto the pasta. Squeeze another lime over top to serve.

Nutrition Information
- Calories: 527 calories
- Total Fat: 20.1 g
- Cholesterol: 108 mg
- Sodium: 725 mg
- Total Carbohydrate: 50.8 g
- Protein: 35.3 g

260. Tofu Noodle Soup

"A simple and delicious twist on the traditional chicken noodle soup."

Serving: 8 | Prep: 20 m | Cook: 30 m | Ready in: 50 m

Ingredients
- 1 tablespoon vegetable oil
- 4 cups quartered red potatoes
- 1 (14 ounce) package extra-firm tofu, cubed
- 1 sweet yellow onion, chopped
- 2 carrots, chopped
- 2 stalks celery, chopped
- 2 cloves garlic, minced
- 4 cups water
- 2 cubes vegetable bouillon
- 1 (12 ounce) package fine egg noodles
- 1 1/2 cups broccoli florets
- 1 cup frozen peas
- 2 tablespoons chopped fresh parsley
- 1/2 teaspoon ground black pepper, or to taste

Direction
- Heat vegetable oil in a large stockpot over medium heat; stir in potatoes, tofu, yellow onion, carrots, celery, and garlic. Cook and stir until vegetables are soft, about 10 minutes.
- Pour water into stockpot, and add vegetable bouillon cubes; cover and bring to boil. Stir in egg noodles, broccoli florets, peas, parsley, and pepper; reduce heat to low, cover, and simmer until egg noodles are cooked through and broccoli is tender, about 15 minutes.

Nutrition Information
- Calories: 305 calories
- Total Fat: 6.2 g
- Cholesterol: 35 mg
- Sodium: 71 mg
- Total Carbohydrate: 50.6 g
- Protein: 13.3 g

261. Traditional Apple Noodle Kugel

"Sweet apple and noodle dish of east European origin. Kugels can be made in many flavors, both sweet and savory. Serve either warm or cold, as a side dish or a dessert. Like lasagna, kugel tastes better the day after it is made. Jonagold and Rome Beauty are two apple varieites ideal for this dish."

Serving: 9 | Prep: 20 m | Cook: 50 m | Ready in: 1 h 10 m

Ingredients

- 4 cups egg noodles
- 1 (8 ounce) package cream cheese, softened
- 1/4 cup brown sugar, or more to taste
- 1 (16 ounce) package cottage cheese
- 1 egg
- 2 egg whites
- 1 teaspoon vanilla extract
- 1/2 teaspoon ground cinnamon
- 1/4 teaspoon ground nutmeg
- 2 firm, tart apples - cored, quartered, and thinly sliced

Direction

- Preheat oven to 350 degrees F (175 degrees C). Lightly grease an 8-inch square pan.
- Bring a large pot of lightly salted water to a boil. Cook egg noodles in the boiling water, stirring occasionally until cooked through but firm to the bite, about 5 minutes. Drain.
- Beat cream cheese and brown sugar together in a bowl using an electric mixer until smooth and creamy; beat in cottage cheese, egg, egg whites, vanilla extract, cinnamon, and nutmeg until well combined. Fold noodles and apples into cheese mixture by hand; spread into the prepared pan.
- Bake in the preheated oven until kugel is lightly browned and firm, 45 to 50 minutes.

Nutrition Information

- Calories: 248 calories
- Total Fat: 12.3 g
- Cholesterol: 70 mg
- Sodium: 300 mg
- Total Carbohydrate: 22.5 g
- Protein: 12.1 g

262. Tuna Cheese Mac

"A delightfully cheesy combination of tuna, egg noodles, and Cheddar cheese."

Serving: 5 | Prep: 5 m | Cook: 20 m | Ready in: 25 m

Ingredients

- 1 cup uncooked egg noodles
- 2 1/2 cups sharp Cheddar cheese, shredded
- 1/4 cup milk
- 1/4 cup butter
- 1/3 cup cottage cheese
- 2 tablespoons sour cream
- 1 (12 ounce) can tuna, drained
- 1 1/2 cups green peas

Direction

- Bring a large pot of lightly salted water to a boil. Add pasta and cook for 8 to 10 minutes or until al dente; drain.
- In a saucepan over medium heat, combine cheddar cheese, milk, butter, cottage cheese, and sour cream; stir until melted.
- Pour cooked noodles into the cheese mixture and stir until well mixed. Stir in canned tuna and green peas; heat thoroughly.

Nutrition Information

- Calories: 535 calories
- Total Fat: 35.2 g
- Cholesterol: 129 mg
- Sodium: 648 mg
- Total Carbohydrate: 13.7 g
- Protein: 40.3 g

263. Tuna Delicious

"A rich 'n creamy tuna pasta... try it.. that's all I can say!"

Serving: 4 | Prep: 20 m | Cook: 15 m | Ready in: 35 m

Ingredients

- 1 (8 ounce) package egg noodles
- 1 tablespoon vegetable oil
- 1 onion, chopped
- 1 (6 ounce) can tuna, drained
- 1 (10.75 ounce) can condensed cream of mushroom soup
- 1 (8 ounce) container sour cream

Direction

- Bring a large pot of lightly salted water to a boil. Add egg noodles and cook for 8 to 10 minutes or until al dente; drain.
- In a large skillet over medium heat, fry onion in oil until browned. Mix in tuna and mushroom soup. Stir in sour cream and heat through. Mix together the cooked egg noodles and sauce and serve.

Nutrition Information

- Calories: 470 calories
- Total Fat: 23.1 g
- Cholesterol: 78 mg
- Sodium: 551 mg
- Total Carbohydrate: 45.6 g
- Protein: 20.5 g

264. Tuna Noodle Asparagus Casserole

"This is a good way to get the kids to eat asparagus."

Serving: 4 | Prep: 10 m | Cook: 35 m | Ready in: 45 m

Ingredients

- 1 (6 ounce) package wide egg noodles
- 1 (12 ounce) can white tuna in water, drained
- 1 (2.25 ounce) can sliced black olives
- 1 (10.75 ounce) can low-fat cream of mushroom soup
- 2 cups shredded sharp Cheddar cheese
- 5 dashes hot pepper sauce (such as Tabasco®), or to taste
- ground black pepper to taste
- 1 (15 ounce) can asparagus spears, drained and cut into thirds

Direction

- Preheat oven to 350 degrees F (175 degrees C).
- Bring a large pot of lightly salted water to a boil. Cook egg noodles in the boiling water, stirring occasionally, until cooked through but firm to the bite, about 5 minutes; drain.
- Stir noodles, tuna, black olives, and cream of mushroom soup together in the bottom of a casserole dish. Add 2/3 cup Cheddar cheese, hot pepper sauce, and black pepper to the noodle mixture; mix. Gently fold asparagus into the noodle mixture. Sprinkle remaining Cheddar cheese over the dish.
- Bake in preheated oven until hot and bubbly, about 30 minutes.

Nutrition Information

- Calories: 566 calories
- Total Fat: 24.4 g
- Cholesterol: 123 mg
- Sodium: 1134 mg
- Total Carbohydrate: 41 g
- Protein: 44.8 g

265. Tuna Noodle Casserole from Scratch

"No canned soup mix in this recipe! Mushrooms, onions, celery, and peas all go into this comfort casserole."

Serving: 6 | Prep: 30 m | Cook: 45 m | Ready in: 1 h 15 m

Ingredients

- 1/2 cup butter, divided
- 1 (8 ounce) package uncooked medium egg noodles
- 1/2 medium onion, finely chopped
- 1 stalk celery, finely chopped
- 1 clove garlic, minced
- 8 ounces button mushrooms, sliced
- 1/4 cup all-purpose flour
- 2 cups milk
- salt and pepper to taste
- 2 (5 ounce) cans tuna, drained and flaked
- 1 cup frozen peas, thawed
- 3 tablespoons bread crumbs
- 2 tablespoons butter, melted
- 1 cup shredded Cheddar cheese

Direction

- Preheat oven to 375 degrees F (190 degrees C). Butter a medium baking dish with 1 tablespoon butter.
- Bring a large pot of lightly salted water to a boil. Add egg noodles, cook for 8 to 10 minutes, until al dente, and drain.
- Melt 1 tablespoon butter in a skillet over medium-low heat. Stir in the onion, celery, and garlic, and cook 5 minutes, until tender. Increase heat to medium-high, and mix in mushrooms. Continue to cook and stir 5 minutes, or until most of the liquid has evaporated.
- Melt 4 tablespoons butter in a medium saucepan, and whisk in flour until smooth. Gradually whisk in milk, and continue cooking 5 minutes, until sauce is smooth and slightly thickened. Season with salt and pepper. Stir in tuna, peas, mushroom mixture, and cooked noodles. Transfer to the baking dish. Melt remaining 2 tablespoons butter in a small bowl, mix with bread crumbs, and sprinkle over the casserole. Top with cheese.
- Bake 25 minutes in the preheated oven, or until bubbly and lightly browned.

Nutrition Information

- Calories: 546 calories
- Total Fat: 31.2 g
- Cholesterol: 121 mg
- Sodium: 786 mg
- Total Carbohydrate: 39.9 g
- Protein: 27.2 g

266. Tuna Noodle Casserole I

"This is a quick and easy casserole, and has been a favorite for many years."

Serving: 4 | Prep: 10 m | Cook: 45 m | Ready in: 55 m

Ingredients

- 3 tablespoons chopped onion
- 1 tablespoon vegetable oil
- 1 (10.75 ounce) can condensed tomato soup
- 1 teaspoon chili powder
- 1/2 teaspoon salt
- 1 teaspoon Worcestershire sauce
- 1 1/2 cups egg noodles
- 1 1/4 cups shredded sharp Cheddar cheese
- 1 (5 ounce) can tuna, drained

Direction

- Cook noodles in a pot of boiling water until done. Drain.
- In a large skillet, sauté onion in oil. Add undiluted soup, chili powder, salt, and Worcestershire sauce. Simmer 5 minutes. Mix in noodles, 1 cup cheese, and tuna. Spoon into a greased 1 quart casserole dish.
- Bake at 350 degrees F (175 degrees C) for 30 minutes. While still hot, sprinkle with remaining 1/4 cup cheese.

Nutrition Information

- Calories: 353 calories
- Total Fat: 19.9 g
- Cholesterol: 67 mg
- Sodium: 1020 mg
- Total Carbohydrate: 22.1 g
- Protein: 22.2 g

267. Tuna Noodle Casserole II

"A creamy classic, great to make for those busy nights when a time consuming recipe just isn't an option."

Serving: 5

Ingredients

- 1 (12 ounce) package egg noodles
- 1 (10.75 ounce) can condensed cream of mushroom soup
- 1/2 cup evaporated milk
- 1 (5 ounce) can tuna, drained
- 3 cups shredded American cheese
- 1/3 cup chopped onion
- 1/2 cup crushed potato chips
- 1 pinch paprika

Direction

- In a large pot with boiling salted water cook egg noodles until al dente. Drain.
- In a large bowl combine the cooked egg noodles, cream of mushroom soup, evaporated milk, tuna, grated American cheese, and chopped onion. Pour into a greased 1.5 quart casserole dish. Sprinkle the top with the crumbled potato chips and the paprika.
- Bake in a preheated 425 degree F (220 degree C) oven for 15 to 20 minutes.

Nutrition Information

- Calories: 683 calories
- Total Fat: 33.1 g
- Cholesterol: 143 mg
- Sodium: 1543 mg
- Total Carbohydrate: 60.6 g
- Protein: 33.7 g

268. Turkey Noodle Soup Mix

"A gift for the holiday season when there is usually a lot of leftover turkey meat!"

Serving: 10 | Prep: 15 m | Ready in: 15 m

Ingredients

- 1/4 cup red lentils
- 2 tablespoons dried minced onion
- 1 1/2 tablespoons chicken bouillon granules
- 1/2 teaspoon dried dill weed
- 1/8 teaspoon celery seed
- 1/8 teaspoon garlic powder
- 1 bay leaf
- 1 cup uncooked medium egg noodles

Direction

- In a small (1 pint), glass jar, layer from bottom to top, lentils, minced onion, bouillon, dill, celery seed, garlic powder, bay leaf and noodles. Seal jar.
- Attach a card with the following instructions: Bring 8 cups water to boil in a large saucepan over high heat. Stir in jar of soup mix. Cover, reduce heat and simmer 15 minutes. Remove and discard bay leaf. Stir in 1 (10 ounce) package frozen mixed vegetables and 2 cups cooked, diced turkey meat. Cook 5 minutes more, or until vegetables and turkey are heated through and tender.

Nutrition Information

- Calories: 33 calories
- Total Fat: 0.3 g
- Cholesterol: 3 mg
- Sodium: 16 mg
- Total Carbohydrate: 5.9 g
- Protein: 1.8 g

269. Turos Csusza Pasta with Cottage Cheese

"This recipe is great for nights when you get home and need something to wind down. 'Turos Csusza' is a Hungarian dish I learned from my Dad last year when I turned twelve. It consists of bacon, egg noodles, sour cream, and cottage cheese. 'Elvezet!'"

Serving: 8 | Prep: 10 m | Cook: 15 m | Ready in: 25 m

Ingredients

- 1 (16 ounce) package egg noodles
- 3 1/2 slices smoked bacon
- 2 cups sour cream
- 1 (12 ounce) container cottage cheese
- salt to taste

Direction

- Preheat oven to 350 degrees F (175 degrees C).
- Bring a large pot of lightly-salted water to a boil. Add pasta and cook until al dente, 8 to 10 minutes; drain well.
- Cook the bacon in a skillet over medium-high heat until crisp; drain, crumble, and set aside.
- Place the drained noodles in a large baking dish. Stir the sour cream into the noodles. Spoon the cottage cheese evenly over the top of the noodle mixture. Sprinkle the crumbled bacon over the top; season with salt.
- Bake in preheated oven until the cottage cheese softens, 3 to 5 minutes.

Nutrition Information

- Calories: 438 calories
- Total Fat: 22 g
- Cholesterol: 87 mg
- Sodium: 317 mg
- Total Carbohydrate: 43.6 g
- Protein: 16.5 g

270. UberBraten Kielbasa and Sauerkraut Casserole

"A true German/Polish dish that is simply 'Delish'! I sometimes use Swiss cheese in place of the Cheddar, which is a good switch as well! This is a casserole that is very inexpensive, simple and quick to make - and not to mention leftovers are the best the next day as well!!"

Serving: 6 | Prep: 20 m | Cook: 30 m | Ready in: 50 m

Ingredients

- 1 (12 ounce) package kluski (egg) noodles
- 1/3 cup butter
- 1/3 cup all-purpose flour
- 1/2 teaspoon dry mustard powder
- 1/4 teaspoon ground black pepper
- 3 cups milk
- 3/4 cup shredded Cheddar cheese
- 2 cups sauerkraut, drained
- 1 (16 ounce) package kielbasa sausage, cubed
- 1/2 cup dry bread crumbs
- 1/4 cup shredded Cheddar cheese

Direction

- Preheat oven to 375 degrees F (190 degrees C).
- Bring a large pot of lightly salted water to a boil. Cook kluski noodles in the boiling water, stirring occasionally until cooked through but firm to the bite, about 8 minutes. Drain and set aside.
- Melt butter in a large pot over medium heat. Whisk in flour, dry mustard, and black pepper; cook until smooth, about 2 minutes. Whisk in milk, a little at a time, and bring white sauce to a boil. Cook for 1 minute, whisking constantly, to make a smooth, thick sauce. Whisk 3/4 cup Cheddar cheese into sauce until melted.
- Stir kluski noodles, sauerkraut, and kielbasa sausage into the sauce and transfer to a 3-quart casserole dish. Mix bread crumbs with 1/4 cup Cheddar cheese in a bowl and sprinkle over the casserole.
- Bake in the preheated oven until casserole is heated through, about 20 minutes.

Nutrition Information

- Calories: 770 calories
- Total Fat: 45 g
- Cholesterol: 158 mg
- Sodium: 1252 mg
- Total Carbohydrate: 61.1 g
- Protein: 28.6 g

271. Ultimate Pasta

"This pasta is quick and easy to make! You can use any different kind of noodles you would like. Serve in bowls with some garlic bread."

Serving: 5 | Prep: 3 m | Cook: 12 m | Ready in: 15 m

Ingredients

- 1 (16 ounce) package egg noodles
- 1 (10.75 ounce) can condensed cream of mushroom soup
- 1 cup cubed processed cheese
- 2 tablespoons butter
- 1/4 cup milk
- 1 teaspoon garlic powder
- salt and pepper to taste

Direction

- Bring a large pot of lightly salted water to a boil. Add pasta and cook for 8 to 10 minutes or until al dente; drain.
- In large saucepan over medium heat, combine mushroom soup, processed cheese, butter, milk, garlic powder, salt and pepper. Stir until cheese is melted. Stir in noodles and heat through.

Nutrition Information

- Calories: 526 calories
- Total Fat: 22 g
- Cholesterol: 106 mg
- Sodium: 889 mg
- Total Carbohydrate: 64.2 g
- Protein: 18.2 g

272. Venison Stroganoff

"This is an easy and very good recipe that my family loves, cooked with venison."

Serving: 4 | Prep: 15 m | Cook: 30 m | Ready in: 45 m

Ingredients

- 1 pound venison, cut into cubes
- salt and pepper to taste
- garlic powder to taste
- 1 onion, chopped
- 2 (10.75 ounce) cans condensed cream of mushroom soup
- 1 (16 ounce) package uncooked egg noodles
- 1 (8 ounce) container sour cream

Direction

- Season venison with salt, pepper and garlic powder to taste. Sauté onion in a large skillet; when soft, add venison and brown. Drain when venison is no longer pink and add soup. Reduce heat to low and simmer.
- Meanwhile, bring a large pot of lightly salted water to a boil. Add noodles and cook for 8 to 10 minutes or until al dente; drain.
- When noodles are almost done cooking, stir sour cream into meat mixture. Pour meat mixture over hot cooked noodles and serve.

Nutrition Information

- Calories: 772 calories
- Total Fat: 29.4 g
- Cholesterol: 192 mg
- Sodium: 1072 mg
- Total Carbohydrate: 85.9 g
- Protein: 40.4 g

273. Yummy Pork Noodle Casserole

"This is my Mom's pork noodle casserole. The added sour cream gives it a little twist on the usual version. The added red pepper and corn give it color and flavor. You can add and subtract any vegetables in this versatile recipe. This is one of my favorite comfort food recipes."

Serving: 6 | Prep: 15 m | Cook: 45 m | Ready in: 1 h

Ingredients

- 2 cups egg noodles
- cooking spray
- 3 tablespoons butter
- 1/4 cup chopped onion
- 1/4 cup chopped celery
- 1/4 cup chopped carrots
- 1/4 cup chopped red bell pepper
- 2 (10.75 ounce) cans condensed cream of chicken soup
- 1/2 cup sour cream, or more to taste
- 2 cups shredded Cheddar cheese
- 1 (8 ounce) can whole kernel corn, drained
- 3 cups cubed cooked pork
- 1 teaspoon salt
- 1/4 teaspoon ground black pepper
- 1/2 cup dry bread crumbs (optional)

Direction

- Fill a large pot with lightly salted water and bring to a rolling boil over high heat. Once the water is boiling, stir in the egg noodles, and return to a boil. Cook the pasta uncovered, stirring occasionally, until the noodles have cooked through, but are still firm to the bite, about 5 minutes. Drain well in a colander set in the sink.
- Preheat an oven to 350 degrees F (175 degrees C). Spray a 9x13-inch baking pan with cooking spray.
- Melt the butter in a skillet over medium heat. Stir in the onion, celery, carrots, and red bell pepper; cook and stir until the onion has softened and turned translucent, about 5 minutes. Stir in the noodles, cream of chicken soup, sour cream, Cheddar cheese, corn, and cooked pork, then season with salt and black pepper. Transfer mixture into the prepared baking dish. Sprinkle bread crumbs on top.
- Bake in the preheated oven until bubbly, 30 to 35 minutes.

Nutrition Information

- Calories: 580 calories
- Total Fat: 32.9 g
- Cholesterol: 142 mg
- Sodium: 1575 mg
- Total Carbohydrate: 32.9 g
- Protein: 38.2 g

Chapter 3: Ramen Noodles

***

274. Asian Chicken Noodle Salad

"This easy to prepare noodle salad has plenty of seeds, nuts, greens, chicken, and vegetables."

Serving: 4 | Prep: 15 m | Cook: 10 m | Ready in: 25 m

Ingredients

- 1 (3 ounce) package ramen noodle pasta, crushed
- 2 tablespoons butter, melted
- 1/2 cup sunflower seeds
- 1/2 cup pine nuts
- 3 cups shredded bok choy
- 5 green onions, thinly sliced
- 1 cup diced, cooked chicken breast meat
- 1 (5 ounce) can water chestnuts, drained
- 12 pods snow peas
- 1/2 cup vegetable oil
- 1/4 cup rice wine vinegar
- 1 tablespoon soy sauce
- 1/4 cup white sugar
- 1 tablespoon lemon juice

Direction

- Preheat oven to 350 degrees F (175 degrees C). In a large bowl, mix the noodles, sunflower seeds, and pine nuts with melted butter until evenly coated. Spread the mixture in a thin layer on a baking sheet.
- Bake 7 to 10 minutes in the preheated oven, stirring occasionally, until evenly toasted. Remove from heat, and cool slightly.
- In a large bowl toss together the noodle mixture, bok choy, green onions, chicken, water chestnuts, and snow peas.
- Prepare the dressing by blending the oil, vinegar, soy sauce, sugar, and lemon juice. Pour over salad, and toss to evenly coat. Serve immediately, or refrigerate until chilled.

Nutrition Information

- Calories: 736 calories
- Total Fat: 55.8 g
- Cholesterol: 42 mg

- Sodium: 1055 mg
- Total Carbohydrate: 43.8 g
- Protein: 20.4 g

275. Asian Coleslaw Light

"This Asian coleslaw is lightened up a bit by using only 3 tablespoons of olive oil and a sugar alternative like Splenda to make this kid friendly, flavorful crunchy salad. Try it with white or balsamic vinegar, too."

Serving: 6 | Prep: 15 m | Ready in: 2 h 15 m

Ingredients

- 1 (3 ounce) package beef ramen noodles
- 2 cups boiling water
- 3 tablespoons olive oil
- 3 tablespoons apple cider vinegar
- 3 tablespoons granular no-calorie sucralose sweetener (e.g. Splenda ®)
- 1 (16 ounce) bag coleslaw mix
- 6 green onions, chopped
- 1/2 cup sunflower seeds

Direction

- Place ramen noodles in colander; break into quarters. Pour boiling water over noodles to soften slightly. Use a fork to separate noodles. Rinse quickly with cold water; drain.
- Make a dressing by whisking together the flavor packet from the ramen noodles, olive oil, vinegar, and sweetener in a bowl. Place the ramen noodles, coleslaw mix, green onions, and sunflower seeds in a large bowl; toss to combine. Drizzle dressing over the coleslaw mixture and continue to toss until entire mixture is coated with dressing. Chill for 2 hours before serving.

Nutrition Information

- Calories: 135 calories
- Total Fat: 9.2 g
- Cholesterol: 6 mg
- Sodium: 72 mg

- Total Carbohydrate: 11.8 g
- Protein: 1.5 g

276. Asian Salad

"This salad is appreciated by everyone because of its unique blend of flavors."

Serving: 10 | Prep: 20 m | Cook: 10 m | Ready in: 30 m

Ingredients

- 2 (3 ounce) packages ramen noodles, crushed
- 1 cup blanched slivered almonds
- 2 teaspoons sesame seeds
- 1/2 cup butter, melted
- 1 head napa cabbage, shredded
- 1 bunch green onions, chopped
- 3/4 cup vegetable oil
- 1/4 cup distilled white vinegar
- 1/2 cup white sugar
- 2 tablespoons soy sauce

Direction

- In a medium skillet over low heat brown ramen noodles, almonds, and sesame seeds with melted butter or margarine. Once browned, take off heat and cool.
- In a small saucepan bring vegetable oil, sugar, and vinegar to boil for 1 minute. Cool. Add soy sauce.
- In a large bowl, combine shredded napa cabbage and chopped green onions. Add the noodle and soy sauce mixture. Toss to coat. Serve.

Nutrition Information

- Calories: 374 calories
- Total Fat: 32.3 g
- Cholesterol: 24 mg
- Sodium: 321 mg
- Total Carbohydrate: 19.5 g
- Protein: 4.7 g

277. Broccoli Slaw and Ramen Salad

"Chill this ramen broccoli slaw for an hour in its simple, sweet, and sour vinaigrette and you have a satisfyingly crunchy and easy coleslaw."

Serving: 4 | Prep: 10 m | Ready in: 1 h 10 m

Ingredients

- 1 (3 ounce) package ramen noodles, crushed, with seasoning packet
- 3/4 cup apple cider vinegar
- 2 tablespoons white sugar
- 1 tablespoon olive oil
- 1/2 teaspoon salt
- 1/2 teaspoon ground black pepper
- 1 (12 ounce) package broccoli coleslaw mix
- 1/2 cup dried cranberries (optional)

Direction

- Whisk ramen noodle seasoning packet, vinegar, sugar, olive oil, salt, and pepper together in a bowl to make the salad dressing. Add ramen noodles and broccoli slaw; toss together. Let sit until flavors meld, 1 to 2 hours.

Nutrition Information

- Calories: 149 calories
- Total Fat: 4.4 g
- Cholesterol: < 1 mg
- Sodium: 416 mg
- Total Carbohydrate: 25.6 g
- Protein: 1.1 g

278. Cheesy Ramen Noodles

"This is an extremely simple and delicious spin on the typical ramen noodles that can be EASILY made in the college environment!"

Serving: 1 | Cook: 5 m | Ready in: 5 m

Ingredients

- 2 cups water
- 1 (3 ounce) package any flavor ramen noodles
- 1 slice American cheese

Direction

- Bring water to a boil in a saucepan. Add ramen noodles and cook 2 minutes until tender. Pour out water, then stir in seasoning packet and cheese to serve.

Nutrition Information

- Calories: 163 calories
- Total Fat: 11.3 g
- Cholesterol: 27 mg
- Sodium: 733 mg
- Total Carbohydrate: 7.9 g
- Protein: 7.5 g

279. Chicken in Lemongrass Coconut Broth

"I made this soup after trying it at a Thai noodle house in my area. I just kept playing around with ingredients until I got something similar. I have the seasonings adjusted to my liking, however there is an adjustment guide in the footnotes if you would like a slightly different flavor. This soup is also good with rice or pasta, but ramen seems to be the favorite. You can use any flavor of ramen noodles."

Serving: 8 | Prep: 20 m | Cook: 25 m | Ready in: 45 m

Ingredients

- 1 fresh lemongrass stalk, outer leaves removed
- 2 quarts chicken stock
- 1/2 cup minced fresh ginger, divided
- 4 fresh kaffir lime leaves

- 1 tablespoon minced garlic
- 1 tablespoon Sriracha chile sauce
- 1 1/2 pounds skinless, boneless chicken breast halves, cut into 1-inch strips
- 1/2 cup fresh cilantro, bundled
- 2 (14 ounce) cans coconut milk
- 3 tablespoons brown sugar
- 2 tablespoons lime juice
- 1 tablespoon fish sauce
- 6 (3 ounce) packages ramen noodles (exclude seasoning packets)
- 2 large carrots, shredded
- 1 cup chopped tomatoes
- 3 green onions, chopped
- 1/4 cup chopped fresh cilantro, or to taste

Direction

- Mince the lower 2/3 of lemongrass stalk. Bruise the remaining upper portion of lemongrass stalk by hitting it with the back of a knife.
- Pour chicken stock into a large pot; add minced lemongrass, bruised lemongrass stalk, 1/2 the ginger, lime leaves, garlic, and Sriracha sauce. Bring to a boil, reduce heat, and simmer. Add chicken to simmering broth; cook until chicken is no longer pink in the center, about 10 minutes. Remove lemongrass stalk and lime leaves using a slotted spoon; discard.
- Place cilantro bundle in the broth and simmer for 2 minutes. Add coconut milk, remaining ginger, brown sugar, lime juice, and fish sauce. Remove cilantro bundle using a slotted spoon; discard. Simmer broth, 5 to 10 minutes.
- Fill a large pot with water and bring to a rolling boil. Add ramen and cook until softened, about 3 minutes. Drain and portion noodles into serving bowls.
- Mix carrots, tomatoes, and green onions into broth. Ladle broth over noodles; garnish with cilantro.

Nutrition Information

- Calories: 551 calories
- Total Fat: 24.2 g
- Cholesterol: 45 mg
- Sodium: 1646 mg
- Total Carbohydrate: 56.5 g
- Protein: 29.8 g

280. Chinese Broccoli Slaw

"This recipe was passed around for years in my Grandmother's beauty salon. She took it to every church supper. It was on the table every Thanksgiving and Christmas."

Serving: 8 | Prep: 15 m | Cook: 10 m | Ready in: 40 m

Ingredients

- 1/4 cup butter
- 2 (3 ounce) packages Oriental-flavor ramen noodle soup, seasoning packet reserved
- 1/2 cup slivered almonds
- 1/4 cup sesame seeds
- 1 (16 ounce) package broccoli coleslaw mix
- 1/2 cup chopped green onion
- 1/2 cup salad oil
- 1/4 cup apple cider vinegar
- 1/2 cup white sugar
- 2 tablespoons soy sauce

Direction

- Preheat an oven to 350 degrees F (175 degrees C).
- Melt butter in a microwave-safe bowl in the microwave. Crush the ramen noodles into small pieces; stir the crushed noodles, almonds, and sesame seeds into the butter. Spread the mixture onto a baking sheet.
- Bake in the preheated oven until golden brown and crunchy, 8 to 10 minutes; allow to cool completely.
- Toss together the coleslaw mix and the green onion in a large bowl.
- Whisk together the salad oil, vinegar, sugar, soy sauce, and reserved seasoning packets in a separate bowl; stir the noodle mixture into the

dressing. Pour the dressing over the coleslaw mix and toss to coat.

Nutrition Information

- Calories: 399 calories
- Total Fat: 28.5 g
- Cholesterol: 15 mg
- Sodium: 711 mg
- Total Carbohydrate: 32.4 g
- Protein: 4.7 g

281. Chinese Cabbage Salad I

"A delicious salad with a variety of tastes and textures. Uses packaged salad mixes."

Serving: 12 | Prep: 15 m | Cook: 10 m | Ready in: 25 m

Ingredients

- 1 (3 ounce) package ramen noodles, crushed
- 10 ounces cashew pieces
- 1 (16 ounce) package shredded coleslaw mix
- 1 bunch green onions, chopped
- 1/2 cup white sugar
- 1/2 cup vegetable oil
- 1/4 cup cider vinegar
- 1 tablespoon soy sauce

Direction

- In a preheated 350 degree F oven (175 degree C), toast the crushed noodles and nuts until golden brown.
- In a large bowl, combine the coleslaw, green onions, toasted ramen noodles and cashews.
- To prepare the dressing, whisk together the sugar, oil, vinegar and soy sauce. Pour the dressing over the salad, toss and serve.

Nutrition Information

- Calories: 290 calories
- Total Fat: 21.3 g
- Cholesterol: 3 mg
- Sodium: 263 mg
- Total Carbohydrate: 22.8 g
- Protein: 4.6 g

282. Chinese Cabbage Salad II

"This is a wonderful and crunchy cabbage salad with great texture and color. You can vary the flavor a little by using beef flavored ramen, if you like."

Serving: 5 | Prep: 15 m | Cook: 10 m | Ready in: 45 m

Ingredients

- 3 tablespoons red wine vinegar
- 2 tablespoons white sugar
- 1/2 teaspoon salt
- 1/4 teaspoon ground black pepper
- 1 (3 ounce) package chicken flavored ramen noodles, crushed, seasoning packet reserved
- 1/2 cup vegetable oil
- 1 (16 ounce) package broccoli coleslaw mix
- 1/2 cup chopped green onions
- 4 ounces toasted slivered almonds
- 1/4 cup sesame seeds, toasted

Direction

- In a small saucepan, cook the vinegar and sugar over medium heat until dissolved. Remove from heat and stir in salt, pepper, ramen seasoning packet and oil. Set aside to cool.
- In a large bowl, combine the uncooked ramen noodles, broccoli coleslaw mix, and green onions. Pour dressing over salad; toss evenly to coat. Refrigerate until chilled.
- Sprinkle with almonds and sesame seeds before serving.

Nutrition Information

- Calories: 481 calories
- Total Fat: 37.4 g
- Cholesterol: 0 mg
- Sodium: 472 mg
- Total Carbohydrate: 28.9 g
- Protein: 9.6 g

283. Chinese Chicken Soup

"This chicken ramen soup is spiced with turmeric, chile paste and ginger, and flavored with soy sauce."

Serving: 8 | Prep: 10 m | Cook: 25 m | Ready in: 35 m

Ingredients

- 2 tablespoons sesame oil
- 1/2 teaspoon ground turmeric
- 2 teaspoons chopped fresh ginger root
- 2 tablespoons chile paste
- 1 pound chopped cooked chicken breast
- 1 quart chicken broth
- 2 teaspoons sugar
- 1/4 cup soy sauce
- 1 cup chopped celery
- 1 (3 ounce) package ramen noodles
- 1 cup shredded lettuce
- 1/2 cup chopped green onion

Direction

- In a large pot, heat oil over medium heat. Cook turmeric, ginger and chile paste in oil until fragrant, 1 to 2 minutes. Stir in chicken, broth, sugar, soy sauce and celery. Bring to a boil, then introduce noodles and cook 3 minutes. Stir in lettuce and remove from heat. Serve garnished with green onions.

Nutrition Information

- Calories: 165 calories
- Total Fat: 8.5 g
- Cholesterol: 43 mg
- Sodium: 568 mg
- Total Carbohydrate: 6 g
- Protein: 16.5 g

284. Chinese Fried Noodles

"This is a quick, easy, and delicious recipe that all will enjoy. Try adding cooked, cubed pork or chicken, bean sprouts, water chestnuts, sliced almonds, or any of your favorite vegetables for versatility."

Serving: 6 | Prep: 15 m | Cook: 25 m | Ready in: 40 m

Ingredients

- 2 (3 ounce) packages Oriental flavored ramen noodles
- 3 eggs, beaten
- vegetable oil
- 4 green onions, thinly sliced
- 1 small carrot, peeled and grated
- 1/2 cup green peas
- 1/4 cup red bell pepper, minced
- 2 tablespoons sesame oil
- soy sauce

Direction

- Boil ramen noodles for 3 minutes, or until softened, without flavor packets. Reserve flavor packets. Drain noodles, and set aside.
- Heat 1 tablespoon oil in a small skillet. Scramble eggs in a bowl. Cook and stir in hot oil until firm. Set aside.
- In a separate skillet, heat 1 teaspoon of oil over medium heat. Cook and stir green onions in oil for 2 to 3 minutes, or until softened. Transfer to a separate dish, and set aside. Heat another teaspoon of cooking oil in the same skillet. Cook and stir the carrots, peas, and bell peppers separately in the same manner, setting each aside when done.
- Combine 2 tablespoons sesame oil with 1 tablespoon of vegetable oil in a separate skillet or wok. Fry noodles in oil for 3 to 5 minutes over medium heat, turning regularly. Sprinkle soy sauce, sesame oil, and desired amount of reserved ramen seasoning packets over noodles, and toss to coat. Add vegetables, and continue cooking, turning frequently, for another 5 minutes.

Nutrition Information

- Calories: 161 calories
- Total Fat: 13 g
- Cholesterol: 69 mg
- Sodium: 294 mg
- Total Carbohydrate: 6.9 g
- Protein: 4.3 g

285. Chinese Noodle Salad

"I didn't like this the first few times I tried it but now I love it! It's got a tangy taste and goes well with Chinese food or sandwiches. Leftovers are softer but great as a snack the next day."

Serving: 8 | Prep: 5 m | Cook: 1 m | Ready in: 6 m

Ingredients

- 1/4 cup rice vinegar
- 1/4 cup sugar
- 1/4 cup vegetable oil
- 2 (3 ounce) packages ramen noodles with seasoning packet
- 1/2 head romaine lettuce, chopped
- 1 (10 ounce) can mandarin orange segments, drained
- 1/4 cup slivered almonds

Direction

- In a microwave-safe bowl, mix together vinegar, sugar, and oil. Microwave on high until sugar dissolves, about 1 minute. Mix well, and set aside to cool.
- Crush ramen noodles in the packages. Pour into salad dressing.
- In a salad bowl, toss romaine lettuce with oranges, almonds, and salad dressing.

Nutrition Information

- Calories: 216 calories
- Total Fat: 12.3 g
- Cholesterol: 0 mg
- Sodium: 413 mg
- Total Carbohydrate: 24.9 g
- Protein: 3 g

286. Chinese Pasta Salad

"A simple cabbage salad with crunchy ramen noodles."

Serving: 8 | Prep: 20 m | Ready in: 20 m

Ingredients

- 1 medium head cabbage, shredded
- 4 green onions, sliced
- 1/2 cup slivered almonds
- 1 (3 ounce) package ramen noodles with seasoning packet
- 1/2 cup chopped fresh cilantro
- 1/4 cup vegetable oil
- 1/2 cup rice wine vinegar

Direction

- In large bowl, combine cabbage, green onion and almonds. Crush ramen noodles and add to bowl with cilantro. Toss.
- In small bowl, combine oil, vinegar and contents of ramen noodle seasoning packet. Toss dressing with cabbage mixture. Serve.

Nutrition Information

- Calories: 188 calories
- Total Fat: 13.1 g
- Cholesterol: 0 mg
- Sodium: 228 mg
- Total Carbohydrate: 15.8 g
- Protein: 4.3 g

287. Cinnamon Snack Mix

"Toss together this cute, crunchy and delicious snack mix at your next slumber party! It's so yummy, you may need to make two batches."

Serving: 24 | Prep: 10 m | Cook: 10 m | Ready in: 20 m

Ingredients

- 5 cups honey graham cereal
- 3 cups cinnamon-flavored bear-shaped graham cookies
- 2 cups ramen noodles, crushed
- 3/4 cup sliced almonds
- 1 cup golden raisins
- 1/3 cup butter
- 1/3 cup honey
- 1 teaspoon orange juice

Direction

- Preheat oven to 375 degrees F (190 degrees C).
- In a large bowl, mix honey graham cereal, bear-shaped graham cookies, ramen noodles, almonds, and golden raisins.
- In a small saucepan over low heat, melt butter, and blend in honey and orange juice. Spread over the honey graham cereal mixture, and toss to coat.
- Spread mixture onto a large baking sheet. Bake 10 minutes in the preheated oven.

Nutrition Information

- Calories: 161 calories
- Total Fat: 6.3 g
- Cholesterol: 7 mg
- Sodium: 213 mg
- Total Carbohydrate: 25.4 g
- Protein: 2 g

288. Cloggers Delight Salad

"Crunchy ramen noodle salad with almonds in a vinaigrette. Substitute cashews for variety."

Serving: 10 | Prep: 15 m | Ready in: 15 m

Ingredients

- 1 (3 ounce) package ramen noodle pasta, crushed
- 8 ounces cabbage, shredded
- 4 ounces slivered almonds
- 1/4 cup sunflower seeds
- 2 green onions, sliced
- 1/2 cup vegetable oil
- 1/3 cup cider vinegar
- 1/4 cup white sugar

Direction

- In large bowl, combine noodles, shredded cabbage, almonds, sunflower seeds and green onion. In small bowl, combine oil, vinegar and sugar. Toss dressing with salad just before serving.

Nutrition Information

- Calories: 227 calories
- Total Fat: 18.2 g
- Cholesterol: 0 mg
- Sodium: 169 mg
- Total Carbohydrate: 14.3 g
- Protein: 3.4 g

289. Crunchy Ramen Coleslaw

"This is a great side dish or salad item. I like to use spicy ramen noodles, for a more zesty flavor! This recipe is even better the next day!"

Serving: 15 | Prep: 10 m | Ready in: 1 h 10 m

Ingredients

- 1 (16 ounce) package coleslaw mix with carrots
- 2 (3 ounce) packages ramen noodles (any flavor), crushed

- 1 cup slivered almonds
- 1 cup shelled sunflower seeds
- 1 bunch green onions, chopped
- 1/2 cup vinegar

Direction

- Put coleslaw mix in a large bowl; add crushed ramen noodles, almonds, sunflower seeds, and green onions. Mix well.
- Pour vinegar into a jar and add seasoning packets from ramen noodles; cover jar and shake until seasoning is mixed into vinegar. Pour dressing over coleslaw mixture; toss to coat. Refrigerate for flavors to blend, about 1 hour.

Nutrition Information

- Calories: 147 calories
- Total Fat: 10.6 g
- Cholesterol: 2 mg
- Sodium: 51 mg
- Total Carbohydrate: 9.5 g
- Protein: 4.7 g

290. Crunchy Romaine Salad

"A wonderful combination of flavors in this very easy to prepare salad. A ton of crunch comes from ramen noodles, pecans, and romaine lettuce."

Serving: 10 | Prep: 20 m | Cook: 5 m | Ready in: 30 m

Ingredients

- 1 cup white sugar
- 3/4 cup canola oil
- 1/2 cup red wine vinegar
- 1 tablespoon soy sauce
- salt and ground black pepper, to taste
- 1 (3 ounce) package ramen noodles
- 1/4 cup unsalted butter
- 1 cup chopped pecans
- 1 bunch broccoli, coarsely chopped
- 1 head romaine lettuce, torn into bite-size pieces
- 4 green onions, chopped

Direction

- Combine sugar, oil, vinegar, soy sauce, salt, and pepper in a jar with a tight-fitting lid; shake until well blended. Break ramen noodles into small pieces, discarding flavor packet.
- Melt butter in a skillet over medium heat; cook and stir noodles and pecans until browned, about 5 minutes. Drain on paper towels and allow to cool.
- Combine noodles, pecans, broccoli, romaine lettuce, and green onions in a bowl; toss gently. Dress with 1 cup, or more, of dressing; toss to coat.

Nutrition Information

- Calories: 393 calories
- Total Fat: 29.6 g
- Cholesterol: 12 mg
- Sodium: 195 mg
- Total Carbohydrate: 31.6 g
- Protein: 3.8 g

291. Crunchy Romaine Toss

"This is a great crunchy salad that goes well with spaghetti or steak. The homemade dressing makes it even better!"

Serving: 8 | Prep: 20 m | Cook: 5 m | Ready in: 45 m

Ingredients

- 1/4 cup unsalted butter
- 1 (3 ounce) package uncooked ramen noodles, crushed
- 1 cup chopped walnuts
- 1 cup vegetable oil
- 1 cup white sugar
- 1/2 cup red wine vinegar
- 3 teaspoons soy sauce
- salt and freshly ground black pepper to taste
- 2 heads romaine lettuce, chopped
- 1 bunch broccoli, coarsely chopped
- 4 green onions, chopped

Direction

- Melt butter in a large skillet over medium heat. Cook and stir ramen noodles and walnuts until toasted, about 5 minutes. Transfer mixture to a plate lined with paper towels and set aside until cooled.
- Whisk together vegetable oil, sugar, vinegar, soy sauce, salt, and pepper in a small bowl.
- Combine ramen noodle and walnut mixture with lettuce, broccoli, and green onions in a large serving bowl. Pour in the dressing and toss to coat.

Nutrition Information

- Calories: 557 calories
- Total Fat: 43.3 g
- Cholesterol: 15 mg
- Sodium: 247 mg
- Total Carbohydrate: 41 g
- Protein: 6.3 g

292. Donna Leighs Creamy Broccoli Slaw

"This is addictive. It's a combination of several recipes I've tried with my own tweaks. I've used different ramen noodle flavors. Feel free to experiment based on your tastes."

Serving: 6 | Prep: 20 m | Cook: 5 m | Ready in: 25 m

Ingredients

- 1 cup mayonnaise
- 1/4 cup apple cider vinegar
- 2 tablespoons white sugar
- 1/8 teaspoon celery seed
- 1 (3 ounce) package Oriental-flavored ramen noodles, broken into small pieces
- 1 tablespoon olive oil
- 1 tablespoon sesame oil
- 1/4 cup slivered almonds
- 1 (12 ounce) package broccoli coleslaw mix
- 1/2 cup chopped onion
- 1/4 cup unsalted sunflower seeds

Direction

- Mix mayonnaise, vinegar, sugar, celery seed, and ramen noodle seasoning packet in a bowl; chill in refrigerator.
- Heat olive oil and sesame oil in a skillet over medium heat; cook and stir ramen noodles and almonds until toasted, stirring frequently, 3 to 5 minutes. Remove from heat and cool.
- Combine ramen noodles, almonds, broccoli coleslaw mix, onion, sunflower seeds, and dressing in a bowl; stir to coat.

Nutrition Information

- Calories: 466 calories
- Total Fat: 41.4 g
- Cholesterol: 14 mg
- Sodium: 516 mg
- Total Carbohydrate: 20.9 g
- Protein: 4.2 g

293. Dorm Room Cheesy Tuna and Noodles

"Cheap, easy, cheesy tuna and noodles for college students on a shoe string budget. If you really wanna dress it up, you can add thinly sliced almonds or sunflower seeds for more flavor and texture. Of course this defeats the purpose of it being cheap and easy, but at least it's more enjoyable."

Serving: 2 | Prep: 2 m | Cook: 5 m | Ready in: 7 m

Ingredients

- 1 cup boiling water
- 1 (3 ounce) package any flavor ramen noodles
- 1 (3 ounce) can water-packed tuna, drained
- 2 slices American cheese

Direction

- Pour water into a microwave safe bowl, and cook in the microwave until very hot, about 2 minutes at high heat. Add ramen noodles, and microwave 2 minutes more to cook.

- Drain and discard water from noodles, then stir in seasoning packet, tuna, and American cheese. Place back into microwave, and cook until hot, 1 to 2 minutes more. Stir before serving.

Nutrition Information

- Calories: 334 calories
- Total Fat: 15.5 g
- Cholesterol: 39 mg
- Sodium: 1266 mg
- Total Carbohydrate: 27.8 g
- Protein: 20.3 g

294. Easy Broccoli Slaw Salad

"This is a cool, delicious, crunchy, savory and sweet broccoli slaw that will satisfy. Try this instead of coleslaw. Tastes just as good if not better the next day."

Serving: 8 | Prep: 10 m | Ready in: 2 h 10 m

Ingredients

- 2/3 cup olive oil
- 1/3 cup cider vinegar
- 2/3 cup white sugar
- 2 (3 ounce) packages chicken ramen noodles, broken
- 10 ounces broccoli coleslaw mix
- 3/4 cup sliced almonds
- 3/4 cup golden raisins (optional)
- 1/2 cup sliced green onions
- 1/2 cup chopped green bell pepper

Direction

- Whisk olive oil, vinegar, sugar, and ramen noodle seasoning packets together in a bowl.
- Combine broccoli coleslaw mix, broken ramen noodles, almonds, raisins, green onions, and green bell pepper together in a bowl; fold in dressing. Refrigerate at least 2 hours. Stir again before serving.

Nutrition Information

- Calories: 438 calories
- Total Fat: 26.5 g
- Cholesterol: 0 mg
- Sodium: 403 mg
- Total Carbohydrate: 47.4 g
- Protein: 4.9 g

295. Easy Chicken Skillet

"Quick and easy stir-fry chicken skillet with ramen noodles for when you don't really feel like cooking, but want something homemade."

Serving: 4 | Prep: 15 m | Cook: 15 m | Ready in: 30 m

Ingredients

- 1 tablespoon canola oil
- 3 skinless, boneless chicken breast halves - trimmed and cut into large pieces
- 1 1/2 cups water
- 2 (3 ounce) packages chicken-flavored ramen noodles, broken into pieces
- 2 cloves garlic, crushed
- 1 red bell pepper, chopped
- 1 cup frozen broccoli
- 4 green onions, chopped
- 1 tablespoon dried parsley
- 1 tablespoon soy sauce

Direction

- Heat canola oil in a large skillet over medium-high heat; cook and stir chicken until no longer pink in the center and juices run clear, about 5 minutes. Add water, ramen noodles, and 1 seasoning packet from ramen noodles; stir to combine.
- Stir garlic, red bell pepper, broccoli, green onions, parsley, and soy sauce into chicken-broth mixture; bring to a boil. Reduce heat and simmer until broccoli is cooked and noodles are cooked through but firm to the bite, about 10 minutes, stirring occasionally.

Nutrition Information

- Calories: 298 calories
- Total Fat: 5.3 g
- Cholesterol: 49 mg
- Sodium: 752 mg
- Total Carbohydrate: 33.7 g
- Protein: 28.3 g

296. Easy Chinese Chicken Salad

"This salad is always a hit. Everyone loves it! Can be refrigerated 2 to 3 hours before serving."

Serving: 6 | Prep: 15 m | Ready in: 15 m

Ingredients

- Salad:
- 1 rotisserie chicken, meat removed and shredded
- 1/2 medium head cabbage, chopped
- 4 green onions, sliced
- 1 (3 ounce) package ramen noodles (such as Nissin® Top Ramen)
- 3 tablespoons sesame seeds
- 3 tablespoons slivered almonds
- Dressing:
- 1/2 cup olive oil
- 3 tablespoons apple cider vinegar
- 2 tablespoons white sugar
- 1 teaspoon salt
- 1 teaspoon ground black pepper

Direction

- Toss chicken meat, cabbage, onions, ramen noodles, sesame seeds, and almonds together in a large bowl. Beat olive oil, vinegar, sugar, salt, and pepper together in a small bowl; drizzle over the salad and toss to coat.

Nutrition Information

- Calories: 361 calories
- Total Fat: 28.5 g
- Cholesterol: 37 mg
- Sodium: 486 mg
- Total Carbohydrate: 12.5 g
- Protein: 14.7 g

297. Easy King Saimin Hawaiian Ramen

"Try these ono (or delicious) saimin noodles, a staple of any Hawaiian diet. My version is a simple, cheap, late-night snack, but don't be afraid to put all kinds of yummy things in your bowl!"

Serving: 2 | Prep: 10 m | Cook: 20 m | Ready in: 30 m

Ingredients

- 2 eggs
- water
- 1 (10 ounce) package refrigerated fresh ramen noodles (such as Sun Noodle)
- 1 (.75 ounce) packet dashi granules (such as Hondashi® Soup Stock)
- 4 slices fully cooked luncheon meat (such as SPAM®), cut into bite-sized pieces
- 1 green onion, thinly sliced

Direction

- Bring 3 cups of water to a boil in a pot; add eggs and boil until yolks are barely set, about 6 minutes. Remove eggs from hot water, cool under cold running water, and peel.
- Bring 2 cups of water to a boil in the same pot. Add noodles and dashi. Cook, stirring occasionally, until noodles are tender yet firm to the bite, about 3 minutes.
- Divide soup and noodles between 2 bowls; add eggs, luncheon meat, and green onion.

Nutrition Information

- Calories: 881 calories
- Total Fat: 29.7 g
- Cholesterol: 246 mg
- Sodium: 2357 mg
- Total Carbohydrate: 111.5 g

- Protein: 42.4 g

298. Fast and Easy Tofu LoMein

"This easy-to make recipe is very inexpensive. I made it for my boyfriend's family and his mother is Filipino! They loved it! You can really mix in a lot of different ingredients to spice it up or make it your own. Try different Ramen noodle flavors."

Serving: 4 | Prep: 5 m | Cook: 25 m | Ready in: 30 m

Ingredients

- 1 (16 ounce) package extra firm tofu
- 2 tablespoons olive oil
- 2 (3 ounce) packages Oriental flavored ramen noodles
- 1 (16 ounce) package frozen stir-fry vegetables
- 1 1/2 cups water
- 1 tablespoon soy sauce, or to taste

Direction

- Press tofu between paper towels to remove some of the water; cut in to bite size cubes. Heat olive oil in large skillet over medium-high heat. Add tofu, and fry until golden brown, about 15 minutes. Stir occasionally to prevent burning.
- Meanwhile bring water to a boil in a medium saucepan. Add noodles from ramen packages, reserving the seasoning envelopes. Boil for about 2 minutes, just until the noodles break apart. Drain.
- Add the stir-fry vegetables to the pan with the tofu, and season with the ramen noodle seasoning packet. Cook, stirring occasionally until vegetables are tender, but not mushy. Add noodles, and stir to blend. Season with soy sauce to taste and serve.

Nutrition Information

- Calories: 383 calories
- Total Fat: 19.8 g
- Cholesterol: < 1 mg

- Sodium: 1333 mg
- Total Carbohydrate: 38.6 g
- Protein: 17.1 g

299. Fugi Salad

"A unique salad that will become a favorite of your family and friends."

Serving: 8 | Prep: 10 m | Cook: 10 m | Ready in: 20 m

Ingredients

- 2 tablespoons butter
- 3/4 cup blanched slivered almonds
- 1/2 cup sesame seeds
- 1 medium head cabbage, chopped
- 8 green onion, chopped
- 2 (3 ounce) packages ramen noodles
- 1/2 cup vegetable oil
- 1/2 cup white sugar
- 1/3 cup rice wine vinegar
- 1/4 teaspoon ground black pepper
- 2 teaspoons salt

Direction

- In a skillet over low heat, melt the butter or margarine; add the almonds and sesame seeds. Cook until lightly toasted.
- In a large bowl, combine the cabbage, onions, almonds, sesame seeds and broken uncooked ramen noodles.
- Wisk together the oil, sugar, vinegar, pepper and salt. Pour over salad, toss, and serve.

Nutrition Information

- Calories: 364 calories
- Total Fat: 27 g
- Cholesterol: 8 mg
- Sodium: 911 mg
- Total Carbohydrate: 28.3 g
- Protein: 5.8 g

300. Italian Bean Ramen

"Beans, veggies, and instant ramen--this is the easiest meal you never knew you wanted."

Serving: 6 | Prep: 20 m | Cook: 30 m | Ready in: 50 m

Ingredients

- 3 tablespoons olive oil
- 1 large onion, chopped
- 3/4 teaspoon salt
- 5 large cloves garlic, finely chopped
- 1 1/2 tablespoons chopped fresh rosemary
- 3 medium carrots, sliced
- 2 large celery stalks, diced
- 1 medium potato, diced
- 4 cups water
- 1 (15.5 ounce) can cannellini beans, drained and rinsed
- 1 (14.5 ounce) can diced tomatoes
- 2 (3 ounce) packages ramen noodles, coarsely broken in package (flavor packets discarded)
- 1/3 cup chopped fresh parsley
- 6 tablespoons grated Parmesan cheese

Direction

- Heat oil in a large, heavy pot over medium heat. Cook onion with salt, covered, stirring occasionally, until lightly browned, about 10 minutes. Add garlic and rosemary and cook, stirring, 1 minute. Add carrots, celery, potato, and water and bring to a boil. Reduce heat and simmer, covered, until carrots are tender, about 15 minutes.
- Puree 1/2 cup of beans with 1 cup of soup broth in a blender. Add to soup along with remaining cup beans and diced tomatoes, and bring to a boil. Add ramen noodles, then reduce heat and simmer, stirring occasionally, until just tender, about 3 minutes. Stir in parsley.
- Sprinkle 1 tablespoon Parmesan cheese over each serving of soup.

Nutrition Information

- Calories: 231 calories
- Total Fat: 9.5 g
- Cholesterol: 4 mg
- Sodium: 771 mg
- Total Carbohydrate: 28.7 g
- Protein: 7.5 g

301. LowCholesterol Egg Drop Noodle Soup

"A quick, satisfying bowl of egg drop soup for those watching their cholesterol. For a vegetarian version, use vegetable broth instead of chicken broth."

Serving: 1 | Prep: 15 m | Cook: 5 m | Ready in: 20 m

Ingredients

- 1 cup chicken broth
- 1/2 cup shredded lettuce
- 1/4 cup sliced mushrooms
- 1/4 cup sliced onion
- 1/2 (3 ounce) package instant ramen noodles (exclude seasoning packet)
- 3 tablespoons egg substitute (such as Egg Beaters®)
- 1 tablespoon soy sauce
- 1 teaspoon sesame oil

Direction

- Combine chicken broth, lettuce, mushrooms, and onion in a small saucepan; bring to a boil. Add ramen noodles to the boiling liquid and cook until softened, stirring occasionally, about 3 minutes.
- Drizzle egg substitute into the broth while stirring continually until the substitute solidified, about 30 seconds. Remove saucepan from heat; stir soy sauce and sesame oil into the soup.

Nutrition Information

- Calories: 137 calories

- Total Fat: 6.7 g
- Cholesterol: 5 mg
- Sodium: 2109 mg
- Total Carbohydrate: 11 g
- Protein: 8.4 g

302. Mad Hatter Salad

"A mixture of cole slaw, green onions and broccoli combined with a dry mixture and a delicious dressing to create a wonderful salad that everyone will want the recipe for. Great for family, church, or barbeque gatherings!"

Serving: 12 | Prep: 20 m | Cook: 15 m | Ready in: 35 m

Ingredients

- 1 (16 ounce) package coleslaw mix
- 8 green onions, chopped
- 1/2 cup butter or margarine
- 1 head fresh broccoli, cut into florets
- 2 (3 ounce) packages chicken flavored ramen noodles
- 1 cup slivered almonds
- 1 cup unsalted sunflower seeds
- 1/2 cup white sugar
- 1/4 cup apple cider vinegar
- 1/2 cup vegetable oil
- 1 teaspoon soy sauce

Direction

- In a large bowl, toss together the coleslaw mix, green onions and broccoli. Set aside.
- Melt the butter in a large skillet over medium heat. Crumble the ramen noodles into a bowl, and mix with the almonds and sunflower seeds. Sprinkle the seasoning packets over all. Add to the skillet; cook and stir until noodles and nuts are toasted, about 8 minutes.
- In a jar with a tight fitting lid, combine the sugar, vinegar, oil and soy sauce. Seal, and shake vigorously to blend.
- Just before serving, combine the slaw mixture with the nuts and noodles. Pour the dressing over all, and stir briefly to coat.

Nutrition Information

- Calories: 395 calories
- Total Fat: 28.8 g
- Cholesterol: 23 mg
- Sodium: 252 mg
- Total Carbohydrate: 28.9 g
- Protein: 8 g

303. Mie Goreng Indonesian Fried Noodles

"This tasty noodle dish is the same one my mom used to make for me when I was growing up. It's definitely comfort food. You can alter it with adding your favorite meats and veggies."

Serving: 6 | Prep: 20 m | Cook: 15 m | Ready in: 35 m

Ingredients

- 3 (3 ounce) packages ramen noodles (without flavor packets)
- 1 tablespoon vegetable oil
- 1 pound skinless, boneless chicken breast halves, cut into strips
- 1 teaspoon olive oil
- 1 teaspoon garlic salt
- 1 pinch ground black pepper, or to taste
- 1 tablespoon vegetable oil
- 1/2 cup chopped shallots
- 5 cloves garlic, chopped
- 1 cup shredded cabbage
- 1 cup shredded carrots
- 1 cup broccoli florets
- 1 cup sliced fresh mushrooms
- 1/4 cup soy sauce
- 1/4 cup sweet soy sauce (Indonesian kecap manis)
- 1/4 cup oyster sauce
- salt and pepper to taste

Direction

- Bring a pan of water to a boil, and cook the ramen until tender, about 3 minutes. Plunge

the noodles into cold water to stop the cooking, drain in a colander set in the sink, and drizzle the noodles with 1 tablespoon of vegetable oil. Set aside.
- Place the chicken strips in a bowl, and toss with olive oil, garlic salt, and black pepper. Heat 1 tablespoon of oil in a wok over high heat, and cook and stir the chicken until it is no longer pink, about 5 minutes. Stir in the shallots and garlic, and cook and stir until they start to turn brown. Add the cabbage, carrots, broccoli, and mushrooms, and cook and stir until the vegetables are tender, about 5 minutes.
- Stir in the ramen noodles, soy sauce, sweet soy sauce, and oyster sauce, mixing the noodles and sauces into the vegetables and chicken. Bring the mixture to a simmer, sprinkle with salt and pepper, and serve hot.

Nutrition Information

- Calories: 356 calories
- Total Fat: 14.3 g
- Cholesterol: 43 mg
- Sodium: 1824 mg
- Total Carbohydrate: 34 g
- Protein: 22.7 g

304. Million Dollar Chinese Cabbage Salad

"This recipe is always a hit...with kids too! I used to call it my 'Million Dollar Salad' because buying the sesame seeds was so expensive. Now I buy the sesame seeds in bulk at a health food store and it's much more affordable."

Serving: 10 | Prep: 15 m | Cook: 15 m | Ready in: 40 m

Ingredients

- 1/2 cup vegetable oil
- 1/2 cup white sugar
- 1/4 cup wine vinegar
- 1 tablespoon soy sauce
- 2 (3 ounce) packages ramen noodles (without flavor packets), lightly crushed
- 1/2 cup slivered almonds
- 1 cup sesame seeds
- 1 head napa cabbage, chopped
- 1 bunch green onions, chopped

Direction

- In a bowl, whisk together vegetable oil, sugar, wine vinegar, and soy sauce until the sugar has dissolved. Refrigerate the dressing while preparing the salad.
- Preheat oven to 350 degrees F (175 degrees C).
- Spread the broken ramen noodles, almonds, and sesame seeds onto a baking sheet.
- Bake the ramen noodle mixture until lightly browned, about 15 minutes, stirring often. Watch carefully to prevent burning. Allow mixture to cool.
- Just before serving, mix together the napa cabbage and green onions with toasted ramen mixture in a salad bowl until thoroughly combined; toss with the dressing.

Nutrition Information

- Calories: 338 calories
- Total Fat: 23.7 g
- Cholesterol: 0 mg
- Sodium: 177 mg
- Total Carbohydrate: 27.7 g
- Protein: 6.3 g

305. Napa Cabbage Noodle Salad

"A delicious salad with lots of crunch."

Serving: 7 | Prep: 10 m | Ready in: 1 h 10 m

Ingredients

- 1 large head napa cabbage, shredded
- 1/2 cup olive oil
- 1 (3 ounce) package ramen noodles, crushed
- 1/2 cup sesame seeds

- 3 ounces blanched slivered almonds
- 1 cup canola oil
- 2 teaspoons soy sauce
- 2/3 cup white sugar
- 2 tablespoons balsamic vinegar
- 6 tablespoons white wine vinegar

Direction

- Place the cabbage in a large bowl, cover, and place in the refrigerator to chill for 30 minutes. Heat the olive oil in a skillet over medium heat, and cook and stir the ramen noodles, sesame seeds, almonds until lightly browned; set aside to cool.
- Prepare the dressing by mixing the canola oil, soy sauce, sugar, balsamic and white vinegars in a blender until smooth.
- About 30 minutes before serving, toss the dressing and cabbage mixture together; chill. Just before serving, toss the noodle mixture with the cabbage mixture.

Nutrition Information

- Calories: 666 calories
- Total Fat: 59.4 g
- Cholesterol: < 1 mg
- Sodium: 149 mg
- Total Carbohydrate: 31.5 g
- Protein: 6.8 g

306. Napa Cabbage Salad

"This is a yummy, crunchy cabbage salad with toasted ramen noodles and almond slivers. The bowl is always licked clean at potlucks!"

Serving: 6 | Prep: 15 m | Cook: 15 m | Ready in: 30 m

Ingredients

- 1 head napa cabbage
- 1 bunch minced green onions
- 1/3 cup butter
- 1 (3 ounce) package ramen noodles, broken
- 2 tablespoons sesame seeds
- 1 cup slivered almonds
- 1/4 cup cider vinegar
- 3/4 cup vegetable oil
- 1/2 cup white sugar
- 2 tablespoons soy sauce

Direction

- Finely shred the head of cabbage; do not chop. Combine the green onions and cabbage in a large bowl, cover and refrigerate until ready to serve.
- Preheat oven to 350 degrees F (175 degrees C).
- Make the crunchies: Melt the butter in a pot. Mix the ramen noodles, sesame seeds and almonds into the pot with the melted butter. Spoon the mixture onto a baking sheet and bake the crunchies in the preheated 350 degrees F (175 degrees C) oven, turning often to make sure they do not burn. When they are browned remove them from the oven.
- Make the dressing: In a small saucepan, heat vinegar, oil, sugar, and soy sauce. Bring the mixture to a boil, let boil for 1 minute. Remove the pan from heat and let cool.
- Combine dressing, crunchies, and cabbage immediately before serving. Serve right away or the crunchies will get soggy.

Nutrition Information

- Calories: 631 calories
- Total Fat: 51.3 g
- Cholesterol: 27 mg
- Sodium: 653 mg
- Total Carbohydrate: 39.8 g
- Protein: 9.2 g

307. Oceans of Fun Bento

"Getting ready to take a family vacation to the beach? Kickstart the kiddos' enthusiasm by serving them an ocean-themed lunch. It's a good way to sneak in some spinach (seaweed) to boot. Get creative with the rest of the bento by using baked fish crackers, grapes for sea pebbles, seaweed chips, all things ocean related cookie cutters including fish, turtle, shark, star for starfish, lobster, etc. for other items to go in the box. Don't forget that special sweet treat. I used gummy octopus but Swedish fish and gummy worms would work well too."

Serving: 1 | Prep: 10 m | Cook: 15 m | Ready in: 28 m

Ingredients

- 1/2 hot dog
- 2 cups water
- 1 (3 ounce) package ramen noodles
- 6 cauliflower florets
- 1/4 cup chopped baby spinach

Direction

- Place hot dog half on a flat work surface. Cut a slit from the bottom to within 1 inch of the top. Turn the hot dog half 90 degrees to the uncut side and repeat. Cut each of 4 "legs" halfway down the middle to make 8 octopus "legs".
- Bring a small pot of water to a boil; add hot dog octopus. Cook until heated through, 2 to 3 minutes. Drain.
- Bring 2 cups water to a boil in the same pot. Add ramen noodles and cauliflower; cook until softened, 3 to 4 minutes. Stir in ramen seasoning until dissolved. Remove from heat; add spinach. Let stand until spinach wilts, about 3 minutes.
- Assemble bento box with ramen noodle mixture and octopus hot dog.

Nutrition Information

- Calories: 152 calories
- Total Fat: 9.2 g
- Cholesterol: 12 mg
- Sodium: 597 mg
- Total Carbohydrate: 12.8 g
- Protein: 5.5 g

308. Quick and Easy Ramen Soup

"Quick, easy, affordable, and comforting Asian soup for two. Transfer soup to a bowl and serve with a bowl of kimchi on the side. Soup tastes great when you add kimchi according to your taste."

Serving: 2 | Prep: 10 m | Cook: 27 m | Ready in: 37 m

Ingredients

- 1 pound boneless chicken breasts
- 4 cups water
- 2 (3 ounce) packages ramen noodles (without flavor packet)
- 1 1/2 cups frozen peas and carrots
- 2 egg yolks
- 1/4 cup chopped scallions, or to taste
- 1 tablespoon soy sauce
- 1 cup kimchi

Direction

- Bring a pot of water to a boil; cook chicken until no longer pink in the center, 15 to 20 minutes. An instant-read thermometer inserted into the center should read at least 165 degrees F (74 degrees C). Drain water and shred chicken using a knife and fork.
- Bring 4 cups water to a boil; add noodles and cook until tender, about 5 minutes. Add chicken, peas and carrots, and egg yolks; cook over high heat, stirring constantly, until soup is heated through, about 5 minutes. Add scallions and soy sauce; cook for 2 minutes more.
- Transfer soup to bowls and serve with kimchi on the side.

Nutrition Information

- Calories: 726 calories
- Total Fat: 23.7 g
- Cholesterol: 322 mg
- Sodium: 1538 mg
- Total Carbohydrate: 67.7 g
- Protein: 60.5 g

309. Quick Asian Beef Noodle Soup

"Very quick to make with inexpensive ingredients. Can be made low fat by substituting ground turkey and baked ramen noodles, and by omitting oil."

Serving: 4 | Prep: 10 m | Cook: 20 m | Ready in: 30 m

Ingredients

- 1 pound lean ground beef
- 1 onion, chopped
- 1 tablespoon minced garlic
- 1 teaspoon ground ginger
- 4 cups water
- 1 medium head bok choy, chopped
- 2 (3 ounce) packages beef flavored ramen noodles
- 2 teaspoons vegetable oil
- 2 tablespoons soy sauce

Direction

- Brown meat in a large skillet. Drain off fat, and rinse meat using a colander.
- Transfer meat to a large cooking pot. Stir in onion, garlic, and ginger. Add water, and bring soup to a boil. Stir in bok choy. Reduce heat, and simmer for about 3 minutes.
- Stir in noodles. Simmer 3 minutes longer, or until bok choy and onions are crisp tender and noodles are soft. Stir in seasoning packets, oil, and soy sauce.

Nutrition Information

- Calories: 511 calories
- Total Fat: 26.7 g
- Cholesterol: 85 mg
- Sodium: 1129 mg
- Total Carbohydrate: 36.6 g
- Protein: 30.6 g

310. Ramen Chicken Noodle Soup

"This tasteful chicken noodle soup with a zesty Asian flair features chicken broth, soy sauce, garlic, ginger and colorful vegetables, and it's ready in less than 30 minutes."

Serving: 4 | Prep: 5 m | Ready in: 25 m

Ingredients

- 3 1/2 cups Swanson® Chicken Broth or Swanson® Natural Goodness® Chicken Broth or Swanson® Certified Organic Chicken Broth
- 1 teaspoon soy sauce
- 1 teaspoon ground ginger
- 1 dash black pepper
- 1 medium carrot, sliced diagonally
- 1 stalk celery, sliced diagonally
- 1/2 red bell pepper, cut into 2-inch-long strips
- 2 green onions, sliced diagonally
- 1 clove garlic, minced
- 4 ounces broken-up uncooked ramen noodles
- 1 cup cooked, shredded boneless, skinless chicken breast meat

Direction

- Heat the broth, soy sauce, ginger, black pepper, carrot, celery, red pepper, green onions and garlic in a 2-quart saucepan over medium-high heat to a boil.
- Stir the noodles and chicken in the saucepan. Reduce the heat to medium and cook for 10 minutes or until the noodles are done.

Nutrition Information

- Calories: 111 calories
- Total Fat: 4 g
- Cholesterol: 31 mg
- Sodium: 1057 mg
- Total Carbohydrate: 7.4 g
- Protein: 11.6 g

311. Ramen Noodle Frittata

"Ramen noodles are baked into a frittata and topped with shredded cheese. My kids love this frittata for lunch! It's so easy to make!"

Serving: 4 | Prep: 5 m | Cook: 15 m | Ready in: 20 m

Ingredients

- 2 (3 ounce) packages chicken flavored ramen noodles
- 6 eggs
- 2 teaspoons butter
- 1/2 cup shredded Cheddar cheese

Direction

- Place noodles in a saucepan filled with boiling water, reserving the seasoning packet. Cook until tender, and drain. In a medium bowl, whisk together the eggs and seasoning packets from the noodles. Mix in noodles.
- Melt butter in a large skillet over medium heat. Add the noodle mixture, and cook over medium-low heat until firm, 5 to 7 minutes. Cut into fourths, and turn over to brown the other side for 1 to 2 minutes. Sprinkle cheese over the top, and serve.

Nutrition Information

- Calories: 339 calories
- Total Fat: 15.7 g
- Cholesterol: 302 mg
- Sodium: 681 mg
- Total Carbohydrate: 28.8 g
- Protein: 20.3 g

312. Ramen Noodle Soup

"This soup is just very very good....you can find ramen noodles at most supermarkets, or at Asian grocery stores."

Serving: 2 | Prep: 5 m | Cook: 10 m | Ready in: 15 m

Ingredients

- 3 1/2 cups vegetable broth
- 1 (3.5 ounce) package ramen noodles with dried vegetables
- 2 teaspoons soy sauce
- 1/2 teaspoon chili oil
- 1/2 teaspoon minced fresh ginger root
- 2 green onions, sliced

Direction

- In a medium saucepan combine broth and noodles. Cover and bring to a boil over high heat; stir to break up noodles. Reduce heat to medium and add soy sauce, chili oil and ginger. Simmer, uncovered, for 10 minutes. Stir in sesame oil and garnish with green onions.

Nutrition Information

- Calories: 291 calories
- Total Fat: 10.2 g
- Cholesterol: 0 mg
- Sodium: 1675 mg
- Total Carbohydrate: 42.4 g
- Protein: 6.9 g

313. Ramen Scrambled Eggs

"This recipe is great for a quick and easy breakfast! Add hot sauce at the end, if desired!"

Serving: 1 | Prep: 5 m | Cook: 10 m | Ready in: 15 m

Ingredients

- 1 (3 ounce) package ramen noodles (any flavor)
- 1 teaspoon chopped fresh parsley, or to taste
- 1 tablespoon vegetable oil
- 1/2 onion, chopped
- 2 eggs
- 1 teaspoon water, or as desired
- 1 pinch salt

Direction

- Bring a pot of water to a boil; add ramen noodles and cook for 3 minutes. Drain water and stir seasoning packet and parsley into noodles.
- Heat oil a non-stick skillet over medium heat; cook and stir onion until fragrant, about 2 minutes. Add noodles and stir for 2 minutes more.
- Whisk eggs, water, and salt together in a bowl; pour into same skillet as noodle mixture. Cook and stir eggs until set and cooked through, 2 to 4 minutes.

Nutrition Information

- Calories: 343 calories
- Total Fat: 26 g
- Cholesterol: 372 mg
- Sodium: 595 mg
- Total Carbohydrate: 13.5 g
- Protein: 14.5 g

314. Ramen Spinach Pasta Salad Supreme

"A delicious blend of flavors will keep this super salad on the top of your list! Quick, too!"

Serving: 20

Ingredients

- 2 (3 ounce) packages chicken flavored ramen noodles
- 8 cups torn spinach leaves
- 2 cups cooked and cubed chicken
- 1 cup seedless red grapes, halved
- 1 cup sliced red bell peppers
- 1/2 cup chopped cashews
- 1/2 cup Gorgonzola cheese, crumbled
- 4 cloves garlic, minced
- 1 lemon, juiced
- 1/3 cup olive oil
- 1/4 cup light mayonnaise
- 1 red bell pepper, sliced
- 20 grape clusters, for garnish

Direction

- Cook ramen noodles according to package directions, without adding the flavor packets. Drain noodles and cool. Cut noodles into large bite size pieces.
- In a large bowl combine the torn spinach leaves, cooked turkey or chicken, halved grapes, red pepper, cashews, Gorgonzola or blue cheese, and ramen noodles.
- In a small bowl mix flavor packets, garlic, and lemon juice and let stand at least 15 minutes. Add oil and mayonnaise and whisk until smooth.
- Pour dressing over salad and toss until thoroughly mixed. Garnish with red pepper rings and small grape clusters, if desired. Serve.

Nutrition Information

- Calories: 147 calories
- Total Fat: 8.6 g
- Cholesterol: 17 mg
- Sodium: 177 mg
- Total Carbohydrate: 11 g
- Protein: 7.2 g

315. Rubys Spicy Red Salad

"This is a crunchy vegi salad inspired by Trishie's Chinese-Style Salad Dressing."

Serving: 6 | Prep: 20 m | Ready in: 20 m

Ingredients

- 2 cups shredded red cabbage
- 1/2 red onion, thinly sliced
- 2 red bell peppers, diced
- 1 cup sliced sugar snap peas
- 2 green onions, thinly sliced
- 1 red jalapeno pepper, finely minced
- 5 radishes, diced

- 5 strawberries, diced
- 1 tablespoon crushed ramen noodles
- 1 tablespoon slivered almonds

Direction

- Combine the red cabbage, red onions, red peppers, sugar snap peas, green onions, jalapeno peppers, and radishes in a large bowl. Toss well. Sprinkle the strawberries, ramen noodles, and almonds on top of the salad.

Nutrition Information

- Calories: 55 calories
- Total Fat: 0.8 g
- Cholesterol: < 1 mg
- Sodium: 21 mg
- Total Carbohydrate: 10.2 g
- Protein: 2.1 g

316. SixMinute SingleServing Spaghetti

"Ideal for college dorm rooms, this recipe will satisfy a serious Italian food craving and takes just minutes to prepare using only a microwave. Can also be cooked on the stovetop. Add a variety of extra veggies for a healthier, more filling meal. Top with cheese and serve with crusty garlic bread, grilled chicken, or a fresh salad. And of course a big glass of wine!"

Serving: 1 | Prep: 5 m | Cook: 4 m | Ready in: 9 m

Ingredients

- 1 (3 ounce) package ramen noodles, without flavor packet
- 1 cup fresh baby spinach
- water to cover
- 1/4 cup pasta sauce
- 1 tablespoon sun-dried tomatoes packed in oil, drained and chopped
- 1 tablespoon extra-virgin olive oil, or to taste
- 2 tablespoons grated Parmesan cheese

Direction

- Break block of ramen into 4 equal pieces. Place in a medium microwave-safe bowl and top with spinach. Fill bowl with water until noodles are covered. Microwave on high until noodles are cooked and spinach is wilted, 3 1/2 minutes.
- Pour out excess water. Add pasta sauce, sun-dried tomatoes, and olive oil; mix until noodles are coated. Microwave again until sauce is warm, about 30 seconds. Top with Parmesan cheese.

Nutrition Information

- Calories: 601 calories
- Total Fat: 33.1 g
- Cholesterol: 10 mg
- Sodium: 838 mg
- Total Carbohydrate: 61.7 g
- Protein: 14.2 g

317. Slightly Healthier College Ramen Soup

"Have you ever eaten ramen for breakfast, lunch, and dinner during an exam period, time of stress, or out of laziness? If so, this recipe is for you. The addition of carrots, mushrooms, and egg make this a more filling ramen soup."

Serving: 1 | Prep: 5 m | Cook: 10 m | Ready in: 15 m

Ingredients

- 2 1/2 cups water
- 1 carrot, sliced
- 4 fresh mushrooms, sliced
- 1 (3 ounce) package ramen noodle pasta with flavor packet
- 1 egg, lightly beaten
- 1/4 cup milk (optional)

Direction

- In a medium saucepan bring the water to a boil over high heat. Stir in the carrot and mushrooms and boil for about 7 minutes. Add the noodles and the flavoring packet; stir to break up the noodles. Reduce heat to medium and simmer for 3 minutes. Slowly pour in the egg and stir for 30 seconds until the egg has cooked. Stir in the milk.

Nutrition Information

- Calories: 500 calories
- Total Fat: 19.2 g
- Cholesterol: 191 mg
- Sodium: 1796 mg
- Total Carbohydrate: 66 g
- Protein: 17.4 g

318. Slow Cooker Chicken Thai Ramen Noodles

"An easy way to fancy up everyday ramen noodles!"

Serving: 6 | Prep: 20 m | Cook: 4 h 15 m | Ready in: 4 h 35 m

Ingredients

- 3 cups water
- 1 tablespoon soy sauce
- 1 (13.5 ounce) can light coconut milk
- 1 tablespoon Thai garlic chile paste
- 1/2 cup peanut butter
- 1 onion, chopped
- 2 cloves garlic, minced
- 1 inch piece fresh ginger, grated
- 2 green bell peppers, diced
- 2 pounds skinless, boneless chicken thighs, diced
- 2 (3 ounce) packages ramen noodles
- 1/2 cup diced cucumber
- 2 green onions, chopped
- 1/2 cup chopped fresh cilantro
- 1/2 cup chopped fresh basil

Direction

- Combine water, soy sauce, coconut milk, chile paste, and peanut butter in slow cooker crock. Stir in onion, garlic, ginger, green pepper, and diced chicken. Cook on High until chicken is no longer pink, about 4 hours.
- Stir the ramen noodles into the crock; reserve seasoning packets. Cook on High until noodles are soft, 15 to 20 minutes. Season to taste with ramen seasoning packets. Garnish soup with cucumbers, green onions, cilantro, and basil before serving.

Nutrition Information

- Calories: 479 calories
- Total Fat: 32.5 g
- Cholesterol: 85 mg
- Sodium: 458 mg
- Total Carbohydrate: 16.3 g
- Protein: 31.3 g

319. South Sea Salad

"This is one of my favorite salad recipes passed on to me from my friend Pam D. A wonderful light and crunchy salad. Great with seared Ahi tuna."

Serving: 12 | Prep: 15 m | Cook: 5 m | Ready in: 20 m

Ingredients

- Salad:
- 1 large head romaine lettuce, chopped
- 1 large head bok choy, chopped
- 1/2 cup sliced almonds
- 1/2 cup sunflower seed kernels
- 2 (3 ounce) packages ramen noodles, crumbled (flavoring packets reserved for other use)
- 2 (15 ounce) cans mandarin oranges, drained
- Dressing:
- 2 tablespoons butter
- 1/2 cup olive oil
- 1/4 cup white sugar
- 1/4 cup vinegar

- 1 tablespoon soy sauce

Direction

- Mix romaine lettuce and bok choy in a large bowl; add almonds and sunflower seed kernels. Sprinkle crumbled ramen noodles over the lettuce mixture; add Mandarin oranges and toss.
- Melt butter in small skillet over medium heat; cook until browned, 2 to 3 minutes. Remove from heat.
- Beat olive oil, vinegar, sugar, and soy sauce together to dissolve the sugar until the mixture is smooth; whisk browned butter into the mixture.
- Drizzle dressing over the salad and toss to coat.

Nutrition Information

- Calories: 268 calories
- Total Fat: 18.3 g
- Cholesterol: 5 mg
- Sodium: 393 mg
- Total Carbohydrate: 23.8 g
- Protein: 4.6 g

320. Spicy Japanese Crab Noodle Salad

"This is a cold noodle salad with crab, bean sprouts, red bell pepper, and cucumber in a spicy chile dressing. If you want to make it more substantial, you can add some squid rings."

Serving: 2 | Prep: 25 m | Cook: 8 m | Ready in: 33 m

Ingredients

- Dressing:
- 1 tablespoon red wine vinegar
- 1 tablespoon soy sauce, or more to taste
- 1 tablespoon sugar
- 1 1/2 teaspoons mirin (Japanese rice wine)
- 1 1/2 teaspoons sesame oil
- 1 teaspoon Chinese chili bean sauce (doubanjiang), or more to taste
- 1 teaspoon balsamic vinegar
- salt to taste
- Salad:
- 4 ounces instant ramen noodles (without flavor packet)
- 4 ounces cooked octopus, cut into bite-sized pieces (optional)
- 1/2 cucumber, thinly sliced
- 1/2 red bell pepper, sliced into rings
- 2 ounces cooked crab meat, broken up
- 2 ounces bean sprouts
- 2 scallions, sliced
- 1 tablespoon toasted nori (seaweed), crumbled, or more to taste

Direction

- Mix red wine vinegar, soy sauce, sugar, mirin, sesame oil, chili bean sauce, and balsamic vinegar in a small bowl to make dressing. Season with salt.
- Bring a small pot of water to a boil. Cook instant noodles until tender, about 3 minutes. Drain and transfer to a large bowl.
- Mix octopus, cucumber, red bell pepper, crab meat, bean sprouts, and scallions with noodles. Add dressing and mix to combine. Divide among serving plates and top with crumbled nori.

Nutrition Information

- Calories: 465 calories
- Total Fat: 14.6 g
- Cholesterol: 74 mg
- Sodium: 1303 mg
- Total Carbohydrate: 52.2 g
- Protein: 31 g

321. Spicy Korean Chicken and Ramen Noodle Packets

"Change it up for dinner tonight with these delicious Spicy Korean Chicken and Ramen Noodle Packets that are bursting with flavor."

Serving: 4 | Prep: 20 m | Cook: 25 m | Ready in: 45 m

Ingredients

- 3 tablespoons gochujang (Korean chile paste)
- 3 tablespoons soy sauce
- 1/3 cup water
- 2 tablespoons sesame oil
- 1 1/2 teaspoons sugar
- 2 boneless, skinless chicken breasts, thinly sliced
- 1 cup (1-inch) slices green onions
- 1 cup thinly sliced red cabbage
- 2 cups thinly sliced button mushrooms
- 1 zucchini, thinly sliced
- 2 (3 ounce) packages ramen noodles, cooked al dente
- Reynolds Wrap® Aluminum Foil

Direction

- Preheat the oven to 425 degrees F.
- Mix together the gochujang, soy sauce, water, sesame oil and sugar in a large bowl until combined.
- Place the sliced chicken, green onions, cabbage, mushrooms, zucchini and cooked ramen noodles into the large bowl with the gochujang mixture and toss until coated.
- Place a 1 1/2 to 2 feet long sheet of Reynolds Wrap(R) Aluminum Foil on a table and place 1/4 of the ramen noodle mixture into the center of the foil. Fold up the ends and then the outside to create a foil packet.
- Repeat the process 3 more times and place the foil packets on a cookie sheet tray.
- Bake in the oven for 25 minutes or until chicken is cooked throughout.

Nutrition Information

- Calories: 193 calories
- Total Fat: 9.4 g
- Cholesterol: 29 mg
- Sodium: 1341 mg
- Total Carbohydrate: 13.3 g
- Protein: 14.8 g

322. Spicy Thai Steak and Vegetable Stir Fry

"Ramen noodles and colorful vegetables make steak and cabbage a simple stir fry that is on the table in no time. Serve it with chop sticks and they'll think you ordered take out!"

Serving: 4 | Prep: 20 m | Cook: 15 m | Ready in: 35 m

Ingredients

- 1 1/2 cups water
- 2 (3 ounce) packages beef flavored ramen noodles
- 1/2 cup beef broth
- 2 tablespoons Thai chili peanut sauce
- 1 tablespoon soy sauce
- 1/8 teaspoon ground ginger
- 1 tablespoon olive oil
- 3/4 pound beef top round steak, cut into 1/4-inch strips
- 1 tablespoon olive oil
- 1/2 carrot, cut into matchsticks
- 1 stalk celery, thinly sliced
- 3 green onions, thinly sliced
- 1/4 cup thinly sliced red bell pepper
- 2 cups shredded cabbage
- 1 cup bean sprouts
- 4 fresh mushrooms, thinly sliced
- salt and pepper to taste

Direction

- Bring the water to a rolling boil over high heat. Once the water is boiling, stir in the ramen noodles with only 1 seasoning packs, and return to a boil. Cook until the noodles are tender, stirring occasionally, about 3 minutes. Drain well in a colander set in the sink. Whisk

the beef broth, peanut sauce, soy sauce, and ground ginger together in a bowl; set aside.
- Heat 1 tablespoon olive oil in a large skillet. Stir in the steak; cook and stir until the steak is no longer pink, 3 to 5 minutes. Remove the meat from the pan and set aside. Heat the remaining 1 tablespoon olive oil in the same skillet. Stir in the carrot, celery, green onion, and bell pepper. Cook and stir until the vegetables begin to soften, about 2 minutes. Add cabbage, bean sprouts, and mushrooms. Stir in the sauce. Cover and cook until the vegetables are tender, about 3 minutes.
- Toss in the cooked ramen noodles and steak. Season with salt and pepper, and serve in bowls.

Nutrition Information

- Calories: 409 calories
- Total Fat: 17.5 g
- Cholesterol: 52 mg
- Sodium: 873 mg
- Total Carbohydrate: 34.9 g
- Protein: 28.1 g

323. StirFried Beef and Broccoli with Crisp Ramen Noodle Cake

"A classic Asian dish gets an instant-ramen makeover."

Serving: 4 | Prep: 20 m | Cook: 20 m | Ready in: 40 m

Ingredients

- Ramen Noodle Cake:
- 2 (3 ounce) packages ramen noodles (exclude seasoning packets)
- 2 tablespoons vegetable oil, divided
- Sauce:
- 3/4 cup water
- 3 tablespoons oyster sauce
- 1 tablespoon low-sodium soy sauce
- 1 tablespoon cornstarch
- 1 teaspoon white sugar
- 1/2 teaspoon toasted sesame oil (optional)

- Stir-Fry:
- 2 1/2 tablespoons vegetable oil, divided
- 1/2 pound broccoli florets
- 1/3 cup water
- 3 large cloves garlic, finely chopped
- 2 tablespoons minced fresh ginger
- 1 pound flat iron steak, thinly sliced across the grain
- 1/4 teaspoon salt

Direction

- Preheat oven to 350 degrees F (175 degrees C). Bring a saucepan of salted water to a boil. Break each ramen noodle block into 4 pieces and cook, stirring occasionally, until just tender, about 3 minutes. Drain noodles in a colander and rinse under cold water.
- Heat 1 tablespoon oil in a 12-inch nonstick skillet (with lid) over medium-high heat until shimmering. Spread noodles evenly to cover bottom of skillet. Cook noodles, pressing on them occasionally with a slotted spatula, until underside is golden brown, 3 to 6 minutes. Slide ramen cake onto a large plate, invert a second plate over top, then flip cake over (so cooked side is now on top). Add remaining tablespoon oil to skillet. Slide ramen cake back into skillet and cook over medium-high heat, pressing it occasionally, until underside is golden brown, 3 to 5 minutes. Slide ramen cake onto a baking sheet and keep warm in oven (do not clean skillet).
- While ramen cake cooks, whisk together water, oyster sauce, soy sauce, cornstarch, sugar, and sesame oil (if using).
- Heat 1 tablespoon oil in same skillet over medium-high heat until shimmering. Add broccoli and stir-fry 1 minute. Add water and cook, covered, over medium heat until crisp-tender, 2 to 3 minutes. Transfer broccoli to a bowl and wipe out skillet.
- Heat remaining 1 1/2 tablespoons oil in skillet over medium-high heat until shimmering. Stir-fry garlic and ginger 10 seconds. Add beef and salt and stir-fry until beef is browned, about 2 minutes.

- Stir sauce, then add to skillet and bring to a boil, stirring. Add broccoli and cook, stirring, until heated through, about 30 seconds. Remove from heat.
- Slide ramen cake onto a cutting board and cut into quarters. Top each ramen wedge with 1 cup beef-broccoli mixture.

Nutrition Information

- Calories: 377 calories
- Total Fat: 29.3 g
- Cholesterol: 52 mg
- Sodium: 563 mg
- Total Carbohydrate: 12.8 g
- Protein: 16.2 g

324. TaiwaneseStyle Beef Noodles

"Beef stew cooked with onions, carrots, and tomatoes in a slow cooker, paired with ramen and veggies. This is my mom's recipe for the famous Taiwanese beef noodle soup. I don't eat beef noodles anywhere else because I can't find anything like this anywhere!"

Serving: 8 | Prep: 35 m | Cook: 2 h 20 m | Ready in: 2 h 55 m

Ingredients

- 3 pounds beef heel muscle, cut into 3/4-inch cubes
- 2 beefsteak tomatoes, sliced
- 4 carrots, sliced
- 1 onion, sliced
- 4 slices fresh ginger, or to taste
- 1 1/2 teaspoons beef seasoning
- 3 cups water
- 1 cup soy sauce
- 1 cup beef broth
- 1 cup ketchup
- 1 cup Chinese rice wine
- 28 ounces raw ramen noodles
- 1 cup cold water
- 1/2 head Chinese white cabbage, or to taste, cut into chunks
- 1/2 cup diced garlic
- 1/2 cup sliced scallions

Direction

- Place beef cubes in a large pot of cold water; bring to a boil. Drain and pat dry.
- Arrange beefsteak tomatoes, carrots, onion, and fresh ginger in the bottom of a slow cooker. Lay beef cubes on top. Sprinkle beef seasoning over beef cubes.
- Mix 3 cups water, soy sauce, beef broth, ketchup, and rice wine together in a bowl. Pour into the slow cooker.
- Cook on High until beef is tender, 2 to 3 hours.
- Bring 2 quarts water to a boil in a large pot. Add ramen noodles; cook until softened, 2 to 3 minutes. Add 1 cup cold water; bring back to a boil. Transfer noodles to a large bowl with a slotted spoon. Cook cabbage in the boiling water until tender, 3 to 5 minutes. Drain.
- Stir beef mixture and cabbage into the bowl of noodles. Garnish with garlic and scallions.

Nutrition Information

- Calories: 718 calories
- Total Fat: 36.8 g
- Cholesterol: 148 mg
- Sodium: 2781 mg
- Total Carbohydrate: 35.9 g
- Protein: 52 g

325. The Mighty Chicken Stuff

"This is a dish I came up with due to boredom. It's fun, easy, and best of all the leftovers taste better than the original prepared dish!"

Serving: 8 | Prep: 20 m | Cook: 30 m | Ready in: 50 m

Ingredients

- 1 pound skinless, boneless chicken breast halves
- 3 (3 ounce) packages chicken flavored ramen noodles

- 1 (13 ounce) package Ranch-flavored tortilla chips
- 1 (10.75 ounce) can condensed cream of mushroom soup
- 2 cups sour cream
- 1 cup milk
- 1 (16 ounce) package frozen broccoli florets, thawed
- 4 cups shredded Cheddar cheese

Direction

- Preheat the oven to 325 degrees F (165 degrees C).
- Place chicken in a large saucepan with enough water to cover by at least 2 inches. Mix in the seasoning packets from the ramen noodles. Bring to a boil, and cook until chicken is no longer pink in the center. Remove chicken and set aside to cool. Add the ramen noodles to the boiling chicken water. Cook until tender, about 2 minutes. Drain. Chop chicken into bite sized pieces when it is cool enough to handle.
- In a medium bowl, stir together the cream of mushroom soup, sour cream and milk. Grease a 9x13 inch baking dish, and begin layering the ingredients as follows. 1/3 of the tortilla chips, 1/2 of the noodles, 1/2 of the chicken, 1/2 of the broccoli, 1/3 of the cheese, and 1/2 of the soup mixture. Repeat layers a second time, then top with remaining tortilla chips and cheese.
- Bake for 30 minutes in the preheated oven, until heated through and bubbly.

Nutrition Information

- Calories: 811 calories
- Total Fat: 46.9 g
- Cholesterol: 119 mg
- Sodium: 1298 mg
- Total Carbohydrate: 60.1 g
- Protein: 39 g

326. Turkey Sausage Noodles

"Ramen noodles tossed with a sauce of turkey sausage, peas and sour cream. This is a great and inexpensive recipe that really perks up the taste of good old ramen noodles!"

Serving: 4 | Prep: 10 m | Cook: 10 m | Ready in: 20 m

Ingredients

- 2 tablespoons olive oil
- 1/2 pound turkey sausage, cut into pieces
- 1 large onion, chopped
- 3 (3 ounce) packages chicken flavored ramen noodles
- 3 tablespoons all-purpose flour
- 2 cups water
- 1 cup frozen green peas
- 1/4 cup sour cream

Direction

- In a large skillet, warm oil over medium heat and sauté sausage and onion for 10 minutes. Meanwhile, bring a large pot of water to a boil.
- In a small bowl, whisk together 2 seasoning packets from ramen noodles, flour and water until smooth; add this sauce and peas to skillet.
- Bring mixture to a boil, cover and cook for 5 minutes or until heated through.
- Add noodles to large pot of boiling water and cook for 3 minutes; drain.
- Remove sausage mixture from heat and stir in sour cream; do not boil. Mix in noodles and serve.

Nutrition Information

- Calories: 439 calories
- Total Fat: 12.4 g
- Cholesterol: 43 mg
- Sodium: 772 mg
- Total Carbohydrate: 55.4 g
- Protein: 25.6 g

Chapter 4: Rice Noodles

***

327. A Pad Thai Worth Making

"The wonderful national noodle dish of Thailand, it is now served in many trendy restaurants. It can be adjusted to your taste, add ingredients that you like and make it as spicy or tart as you want to. It is also great as a basis for a stir fry of leftovers. This is a recipe for those who like it HOT, if you can't handle the heat, go easy on the chile sauce."

Serving: 3 | Prep: 15 m | Cook: 15 m | Ready in: 30 m

Ingredients

- 1 (8 ounce) package dried flat rice noodles
- 3 tablespoons fish sauce
- 1/4 cup fresh lime juice
- 1 tablespoon white sugar
- 2 tablespoons oyster sauce
- 1 1/2 tablespoons Asian chile pepper sauce, divided
- 1/4 cup chicken stock
- 1/4 cup vegetable oil
- 1 tablespoon chopped garlic
- 8 ounces medium shrimp - peeled and deveined
- 8 ounces skinless, boneless chicken breast halves - cut into 1 inch cubes
- 2 eggs, beaten
- 3 cups bean sprouts
- 6 green onions, chopped into 1 inch pieces
- 2 tablespoons chopped unsalted dry-roasted peanuts
- 1/4 cup chopped fresh cilantro
- 1 lime, cut into 8 wedges
- 2 cups bean sprouts

Direction

- Fill a large bowl with hot tap water and place the noodles in it to soak for 20 minutes.
- In a small bowl, stir together the fish sauce, lime juice, sugar, oyster sauce, 2 teaspoons of the chile sauce and chicken stock. Set aside.
- Heat a wok or large skillet over high heat and add vegetable oil. When the oil is hot, stir in garlic and cook for about 10 seconds. Add shrimp and chicken; cook, stirring constantly

until shrimp is opaque and chicken is cooked through, 5 to 7 minutes.
- Move everything in the wok out to the sides and pour the eggs in the center. Cook and stir the eggs until firm. Add the noodles to the wok and pour in the sauce. Cook, stirring constantly, until the noodles are tender. Add a bit more water if needed to finish cooking the noodles. Stir in 3 cups of bean sprouts and green onions. Remove from the heat and garnish with chopped peanuts. Taste for seasoning, adjusting the spice or lime juice if needed.
- Serve garnished with fresh cilantro and remaining bean sprouts and lime wedges on the side.

Nutrition Information

- Calories: 742 calories
- Total Fat: 27.8 g
- Cholesterol: 280 mg
- Sodium: 1591 mg
- Total Carbohydrate: 83.1 g
- Protein: 41.4 g

328. Asian Noodle Bowl

"Tender slices of broiled bison skirt steak are served atop steaming bowls of Asian-inspired noodle soup with veggies and your choice of toppings."

Serving: 4 | Prep: 25 m | Cook: 5 m | Ready in: 40 m

Ingredients

- 1 pound bison skirt steak or bison ribeye steak
- 2 tablespoons soy sauce
- 1 (14.5 ounce) can beef broth
- 2 cups water
- 6 ounces vermicelli rice noodles or angel hair pasta
- 3/4 cup purchased peanut sauce
- 2 cups bite-size broccoli florets
- 2 medium carrots, cut into thin bite-size strips
- 1/4 cup chopped peanuts
- 2 sliced green onions
- 2 tablespoons chopped fresh cilantro (optional)
- Asian chili sauce (Sriracha sauce) (optional)
- Soy sauce (optional)

Direction

- Preheat broiler. Place bison skirt steak on the unheated rack of a broiler pan. Brush both sides of bison skirt steak with the 2 tablespoons soy sauce. Broil 4 to 5 inches from the heat for 5 to 6 minutes or until an instant-read thermometer registers 145 degrees F, turning once. Cover with foil and let stand for 10 minutes.
- Meanwhile, bring broth and water to boiling over medium-high heat in a large saucepan. Add vermicelli noodles and cook, uncovered, for 3 minutes or until noodles are tender. Use kitchen scissors to snip the noodle strands into smaller pieces. Stir in peanut sauce, broccoli, and carrots. Remove from heat. Cover and let stand for 10 minutes.
- Thinly slice bison skirt steak against the grain into bite-size pieces. Divide noodle mixture among 4 bowls. Top with bison skirt steak pieces. Sprinkle with peanuts and green onions or cilantro. If desired, serve with Asian chili sauce and additional soy sauce.

329. Asian Vegan Tofu Noodles

"A vegan rice noodle base with marinated tofu and vegetables. I like to also serve it with vegan chili-mayo, but it tastes great without as well."

Serving: 2 | Prep: 25 m | Cook: 15 m | Ready in: 55 m

Ingredients

- 1/4 (16 ounce) package dried rice noodles
- 1/2 (12 ounce) package firm tofu, cubed
- 1/4 cup soy sauce
- 3 tablespoons coconut oil, divided
- 1 teaspoon teriyaki sauce

- 2 cloves garlic, minced, divided
- 1/4 teaspoon cayenne pepper, or to taste
- salt and ground black pepper to taste
- 1 red bell pepper, cubed
- 1/2 cup fresh green beans, cut into 1/2-inch pieces
- 1 teaspoon grated fresh ginger
- sesame seeds, or to taste
- 1/2 teaspoon vegetable seasoning, or to taste
- Sauce:
- 4 tablespoons vegan or eggless mayonnaise
- 1 tablespoon fresh lemon juice, or to taste
- 1 tablespoon Asian red chile sauce, such as Sriracha®, or to taste
- 1 teaspoon cider vinegar
- 1 splash soy sauce
- salt and freshly ground black pepper to taste

Direction

- Place noodles in a large bowl and cover with boiling water. Set aside until noodles are softened, about 15 minutes. Drain and rinse thoroughly.
- Combine tofu, soy sauce, 1 tablespoon coconut oil, teriyaki sauce, 1/2 of the garlic, cayenne pepper, salt, and pepper in a bowl and set aside while preparing the rest of the ingredients.
- Heat remaining 2 tablespoons coconut oil in a large skillet over low heat and cook the remaining garlic until fragrant, about 2 minutes. Add bell pepper and green beans and cook until softened, about 5 minutes. Remove tofu from marinade and add to vegetables. Sprinkle with sesame seeds and mix well. Season with vegetable seasoning, salt, and pepper. Stir-fry for 2 minutes. Cover and cook for 3 minutes. Add drained noodles and stir to combine.
- Combine vegan mayonnaise, lemon juice, red chile sauce, vinegar, soy sauce, salt and pepper in a bowl. Serve with the tofu noodles.

Nutrition Information

- Calories: 528 calories
- Total Fat: 27.2 g
- Cholesterol: 0 mg
- Sodium: 2534 mg
- Total Carbohydrate: 60.4 g
- Protein: 13.1 g

330. Authentic Pad Thai

"Inspired by the pad thai at Thai Tom, this recipe features a tamarind paste, vinegar, sugar, and fish sauce mixture over perfectly stir-fried eggs, chicken breast, and rice noodles, garnished with peanuts, chives, and fresh bean sprouts."

Serving: 6 | Prep: 15 m | Cook: 15 m | Ready in: 1 h

Ingredients

- 12 ounces dried rice noodles
- 1/2 cup white sugar
- 1/2 cup distilled white vinegar
- 1/4 cup fish sauce
- 2 tablespoons tamarind paste
- 1 tablespoon vegetable oil
- 2 boneless, skinless chicken breast halves, sliced into thin strips
- 1 tablespoon vegetable oil
- 1 1/2 teaspoons garlic, minced
- 4 eggs, beaten
- 1 1/2 tablespoons white sugar
- 1 1/2 teaspoons salt
- 1 cup coarsely ground peanuts
- 2 cups bean sprouts
- 1/2 cup chopped fresh chives
- 1 tablespoon paprika, or to taste
- 1 lime, cut into wedges

Direction

- Place rice noodles in a large bowl and cover with several inches of room temperature water; let soak for 30 to 60 minutes. Drain.
- Whisk sugar, vinegar, fish sauce, and tamarind paste in a saucepan over medium heat. Bring to a simmer, remove from heat.
- Heat 1 tablespoon vegetable oil in a skillet over medium-high heat. Add chicken; cook

and stir until chicken is cooked through, 5 to 7 minutes. Remove from heat.
- Heat 1 tablespoon oil and minced garlic in a large skillet or wok over medium-high heat. Stir in eggs; scramble until eggs are nearly cooked through, about 2 minutes. Add cooked chicken breast slices and rice noodles; stir to combine.
- Stir in tamarind mixture, 1 1/2 tablespoons sugar, and salt; cook until noodles are tender, 3 to 5 minutes. Stir in peanuts; cook until heated through, 1 to 2 minutes. Garnish with bean sprouts, chives, paprika, and lime wedges.

Nutrition Information

- Calories: 583 calories
- Total Fat: 21.3 g
- Cholesterol: 132 mg
- Sodium: 1479 mg
- Total Carbohydrate: 78.8 g
- Protein: 21.5 g

331. Authentic Pad Thai Noodles

"This is an authentic Thai recipe, with the proper ingredients (no ketchup or peanut butter). It is easy, quick, and absolutely delicious."

Serving: 4 | Prep: 30 m | Cook: 20 m | Ready in: 2 h

Ingredients

- 2/3 cup dried rice vermicelli
- 1/4 cup peanut oil
- 2/3 cup thinly sliced firm tofu
- 1 large egg, beaten
- 4 cloves garlic, finely chopped
- 1/4 cup vegetable broth
- 2 tablespoons fresh lime juice
- 2 tablespoons soy sauce
- 1 tablespoon white sugar
- 1 teaspoon salt
- 1/2 teaspoon dried red chili flakes
- 3 tablespoons chopped peanuts
- 1 pound bean sprouts, divided
- 3 green onions, whites cut thinly across and greens sliced into thin lengths - divided
- 3 tablespoons chopped peanuts
- 2 limes, cut into wedges for garnish

Direction

- Soak rice vermicelli noodles in a bowl filled with hot water until softened, 30 minutes to 1 hour. Drain and set aside.
- Heat peanut oil over medium heat in a large wok.
- Cook and stir tofu in the wok, turning the pieces until they are golden on all sides.
- Remove tofu with a slotted spoon and drain on plate lined with paper towels.
- Pour all but 1 tablespoon of used oil from the wok into a small bowl; it will be used again in a later step.
- Heat the remaining 1 tablespoon of oil in the wok over medium heat until it starts to sizzle.
- Pour in beaten egg and lightly toss in the hot oil to scramble the egg.
- Remove egg from the wok and set aside.
- Pour reserved peanut oil in the small bowl back into the wok.
- Toss garlic and drained noodles in wok until they are coated with oil.
- Stir in vegetable broth, lime juice, soy sauce, and sugar. Toss and gently push noodles around the pan to coat with sauce.
- Gently mix in tofu, scrambled egg, salt, chili flakes, and 3 tablespoons peanuts; toss to mix all ingredients.
- Mix in bean sprouts and green onions, reserving about 1 tablespoon of each for garnish. Cook and stir until bean sprouts have softened slightly, 1 to 2 minutes.
- Arrange noodles on a warm serving platter and garnish with 3 tablespoons peanuts and reserved bean sprouts and green onions. Place lime wedges around the edges of the platter.

Nutrition Information

- Calories: 397 calories
- Total Fat: 23.3 g

- Cholesterol: 41 mg
- Sodium: 1234 mg
- Total Carbohydrate: 39.5 g
- Protein: 13.2 g

332. Authentic Pho

"This authentic pho isn't quick, but it is delicious. The key is in the broth, which gets simmered for at least 6 hours."

Serving: 4 | Prep: 20 m | Cook: 8 h | Ready in: 9 h 20 m

Ingredients

- 4 pounds beef soup bones
- 1 onion, unpeeled and cut in half
- 5 slices fresh ginger
- 1 tablespoon salt
- 2 pods star anise
- 2 1/2 tablespoons fish sauce
- 4 quarts water
- 1 (8 ounce) package dried rice noodles
- 1 1/2 pounds beef top sirloin, thinly sliced
- 1/2 cup chopped cilantro
- 1 tablespoon chopped green onion
- 1 1/2 cups bean sprouts
- 1 bunch Thai basil
- 1 lime, cut into 4 wedges
- 1/4 cup hoisin sauce (optional)
- 1/4 cup chile-garlic sauce (such as Sriracha®) (optional)

Direction

- Preheat oven to 425 degrees F (220 degrees C).
- Watch Now
- Place beef bones on a baking sheet and roast in the preheated oven until browned, about 1 hour.
- Watch Now
- Place onion on a baking sheet and roast in the preheated oven until blackened and soft, about 45 minutes.
- Watch Now
- Place bones, onion, ginger, salt, star anise, and fish sauce in a large stockpot and cover with 4 quarts of water. Bring to a boil and reduce heat to low. Simmer on low for 6 to 10 hours. Strain the broth into a saucepan and set aside.
- Watch Now
- Place rice noodles in large bowl filled with room temperature water and allow to soak for 1 hour. Bring a large pot of water to a boil and after the noodles have soaked, place them in the boiling water for 1 minute. Bring stock to a simmer.
- Watch Now
- Divide noodles among 4 serving bowls; top with sirloin, cilantro, and green onion. Pour hot broth over the top. Stir and let sit until the beef is partially cooked and no longer pink, 1 to 2 minutes. Serve with bean sprouts, Thai basil, lime wedges, hoisin sauce, and chile-garlic sauce on the side.
- Watch Now

Nutrition Information

- Calories: 509 calories
- Total Fat: 11 g
- Cholesterol: 74 mg
- Sodium: 3519 mg
- Total Carbohydrate: 65.6 g
- Protein: 34.9 g

333. Authentic Vietnamese Spring Rolls Nem Ran Hay Cha Gio

"This is a recipe I learned while traveling through Vietnam. The ingredients are relatively simple and easy to find in any grocery store. I've cooked this a number of times since getting back and it's always been a hit. They taste great with dipping sauce."

Serving: 12 | Prep: 1 h | Cook: 5 m | Ready in: 1 h 25 m

Ingredients

- 2 ounces dried thin rice noodles
- 3/4 cup ground chicken
- 1/4 cup shrimp - washed, peeled, and cut into small pieces

- 2 large eggs, beaten
- 1 carrot, grated
- 4 wood fungus mushrooms, chopped
- 2 green onions, chopped
- 1/2 teaspoon white sugar
- 1/2 teaspoon salt
- 1/2 teaspoon ground black pepper
- 24 rice paper wrappers
- 2 cups vegetable oil for frying

Direction

- Soak rice noodles in cold water until soft, about 20 minutes. Drain well; cut into 2-inch long pieces.
- Combine the noodle pieces, chicken, shrimp, eggs, carrot, wood fungus mushrooms, and green onions in a large bowl. Sprinkle in sugar, salt, and black pepper; stir filling mixture well.
- Soak 1 rice paper wrapper in a shallow bowl of warm water to soften, about 15 seconds. Remove from water and place on a damp cloth laid out on a flat surface.
- Place 1 tablespoon of filling mixture into the center of the softened rice paper. Fold the bottom edge into the center, covering the filling. Fold in opposing edges and roll up tightly. Repeat with remaining rice paper wrappers, soaking and filling each one individually.
- Heat oil in a work or large skillet over medium heat.
- Fry the spring rolls in batches of 3 or 4 until crisp and golden brown on both sides, about 5 minutes. Drain on paper towels.

Nutrition Information

- Calories: 132 calories
- Total Fat: 5.2 g
- Cholesterol: 45 mg
- Sodium: 225 mg
- Total Carbohydrate: 14.4 g
- Protein: 6.5 g

334. Carries Pad Thai Salad

"This is my favorite Pad Thai creation. After I started making it at home, I could never go back. This is a full meal, suitable for vegetarians and meat-eaters alike. Please enjoy!"

Serving: 4 | Prep: 20 m | Cook: 8 m | Ready in: 38 m

Ingredients

- 1 (12 ounce) package dried rice noodles
- 1/2 cup white sugar
- 1/4 cup water
- 1/2 lime, juiced
- 2 tablespoons soy sauce
- 2 tablespoons fish sauce
- 1 teaspoon tamarind concentrate
- 1/4 cup peanut oil
- 1 clove garlic, minced
- 4 eggs
- 1 tablespoon paprika
- 1/4 teaspoon chili powder, or to taste (optional)
- 1 head lettuce, chopped, or as needed
- 2 tablespoons flaxseed oil
- 1/2 cup fresh bean sprouts, or to taste (optional)
- 1/2 cup chopped green onion
- 1/2 cup chopped fresh cilantro
- 1/2 cup chopped peanuts
- 1/2 lime, cut into wedges

Direction

- Place noodles in a bowl with enough hot water to cover; soak noodles until soft, about 10 minutes. Strain.
- Combine sugar, water, lime juice, soy sauce, fish sauce, and tamarind in a large saucepan over medium heat. Simmer gently, stirring occasionally, until sauce is slightly thickened, 3 to 5 minutes.
- Heat peanut oil in a skillet over medium heat. Add garlic; stir just until fragrant, 30 seconds to 1 minute. Add eggs; cook and stir until almost set, 2 to 3 minutes. Add strained noodles to egg mixture; stir in 1/2 of the

sauce. Continue to cook and stir noodle mixture until hot, adding additional sauce as desired, 2 to 3 minutes more. Sprinkle paprika and chili powder over the noodles.
- Layer lettuce on a serving dish or in individual bowls; drizzle with flaxseed oil. Place noodle mixture on lettuce; garnish with bean sprouts, green onion, cilantro, and peanuts. Serve with lime wedges.

Nutrition Information

- Calories: 807 calories
- Total Fat: 35.3 g
- Cholesterol: 186 mg
- Sodium: 1244 mg
- Total Carbohydrate: 109.1 g
- Protein: 16.6 g

335. Chinese Chicken Salad

"The greatest chicken salad, especially if your clan isn't crazy about the usual soy flavored dressing."

Serving: 6

Ingredients

- 3 1/2 boneless chicken breast halves, cooked and diced
- 1 head lettuce, torn into small pieces
- 4 green onions, sliced
- 4 stalks celery, sliced thin
- 1/2 cup walnuts, chopped
- 2 tablespoons sesame seeds, toasted
- 6 ounces Chinese noodles, heated briefly to crisp
- 6 tablespoons seasoned rice vinegar
- 4 tablespoons white sugar
- 1 teaspoon salt
- 1/2 cup peanut oil

Direction

- In a large salad bowl combine the chicken, lettuce, green onion, celery, nuts, seeds and noodles. Mix all together. Set aside.

- To Make Dressing: Put vinegar in a small bowl. Dissolve sugar and salt in vinegar before adding oil. Shake/Beat well.
- Add dressing to salad and toss to coat. Serve and enjoy!

Nutrition Information

- Calories: 517 calories
- Total Fat: 31.6 g
- Cholesterol: 48 mg
- Sodium: 757 mg
- Total Carbohydrate: 38.8 g
- Protein: 23.9 g

336. Classic Pad Thai

"This recipe is a perfect example of Thai cooking for beginners. Once mastered, you'll forget stopping for take-out and make this easy stir-fry a weeknight staple."

Serving: 4 | Prep: 15 m | Cook: 15 m | Ready in: 30 m

Ingredients

- 8 ounces medium width rice vermicelli noodles
- 3 tablespoons vegetable oil
- 1/4 pound ground chicken
- 1 teaspoon hot pepper sauce
- 1 red pepper, thinly sliced
- 1/2 pound peeled, deveined raw shrimp
- 3 cloves garlic, minced
- 2 teaspoons freshly grated gingerroot
- 1/2 cup vegetable or chicken broth
- 1/2 cup Heinz Tomato Ketchup
- 1/4 cup lime juice
- 3 tablespoons granulated sugar
- 3 tablespoons fish sauce
- 1 1/2 cups bean sprouts
- 3 green onions, thinly sliced
- 1/4 cup fresh coriander or parsley leaves
- chopped peanuts

Direction

- Cover noodles with boiling water and let stand for 5 minutes; drain well and reserve.
- Heat half the oil in a wok or deep skillet set over high heat. Crumble in chicken and add hot sauce; stir-fry for 3 to 5 minutes or until browned. Reserve on a platter.
- Add remaining oil and peppers to pan; stir-fry for 3 minutes. Add shrimp and stir-fry for 2 minutes. Stir in garlic, ginger, broth, ketchup, lime juice, sugar and fish sauce. Bring to a boil. Add noodles and reserved meat; toss mixture to combine. Heat through.
- Add sprouts and toss gently. Sprinkle with onions, coriander and peanuts.

Nutrition Information

- Calories: 553 calories
- Total Fat: 18.2 g
- Cholesterol: 104 mg
- Sodium: 1298 mg
- Total Carbohydrate: 70.2 g
- Protein: 30.3 g

337. Creole Crab Noodles

"Crab, and its old friends, the Holy Trinity, are a classic combo, and so it was no surprise they worked so well in an Asian-style rice noodle dish – an experiment gone right. Garnish with sliced green onion."

Serving: 2 | Prep: 20 m | Cook: 15 m | Ready in: 35 m

Ingredients

- For the Sauce:
- 3 cloves garlic, crushed
- 3 tablespoons ketchup
- 1/4 cup seasoned rice vinegar
- 1 tablespoon soy sauce
- 1 tablespoon fish sauce (optional)
- 1 tablespoon hot sauce, or to taste
- 1 teaspoon paprika
- 1/2 teaspoon cayenne pepper
- 1 teaspoon ground cumin
- 8 ounces rice noodles
- 2 tablespoons vegetable oil
- 1/3 cup diced celery
- 1/3 cup minced red and green jalapenos
- 1/3 cup diced green onions
- 1/2 pound crabmeat

Direction

- Whisk garlic, ketchup, rice vinegar, soy sauce, fish sauce, hot sauce, paprika, cayenne pepper, and cumin together in a bowl.
- Place rice noodles in a large bowl; cover with boiling water and stir with tongs. Let soak for 10 minutes.
- While noodles soak, heat vegetable oil in a pan over medium-high heat. Cook and stir celery, jalapenos, and green onions until tender and fragrant, about 10 minutes.
- Drain noodles and place in the pan; add the sauce and crabmeat. Cook and stir until noodles are coated evenly and everything is heated through, 2 to 3 minutes.

Nutrition Information

- Calories: 669 calories
- Total Fat: 16 g
- Cholesterol: 62 mg
- Sodium: 1982 mg
- Total Carbohydrate: 105.4 g
- Protein: 25.2 g

338. Dads Pad Thai

"This is the best Pad Thai recipe ever. My father's Pad Thai is better than most Thai restaurants! I like it because of all the fresh ingredients, it is not greasy. It's satisfying and healthy. There is no meat in this recipe."

Serving: 4 | Prep: 20 m | Cook: 5 m | Ready in: 25 m

Ingredients

- 3/4 pound bean sprouts
- 6 ounces pad thai rice noodles

- 4 eggs
- salt
- 3 tablespoons lime juice
- 3 tablespoons ketchup
- 1 tablespoon brown sugar
- 1/4 cup fish sauce
- 3 tablespoons peanut oil
- 1 tablespoon minced garlic
- 1 1/2 teaspoons red pepper flakes
- 2 cups grated carrots
- 2/3 cup chopped peanuts
- 1 cup green onions cut into 1-inch pieces

Direction

- Bring a pot of water to a boil. Blanch the bean sprouts in boiling water for approximately 30 seconds, remove, and drain well. When the water returns to a boil, add noodles. Cook for 3 to 5 minutes until tender but firm; drain and rinse under cold water
- Beat the eggs with a pinch of salt in a small bowl. Stir together the lime juice, ketchup, brown sugar, and fish sauce in a separate bowl; set aside.
- Heat the oil in a wok or large skillet over medium-high heat. Fry the garlic for a few seconds. Add the pepper flakes and carrot, and cook for one minute, then remove. Add the beaten egg, and gently scramble. When the eggs have set, pour in the carrots, sauce, bean sprouts, noodles, peanuts, and green onion; toss together.

Nutrition Information

- Calories: 553 calories
- Total Fat: 28 g
- Cholesterol: 186 mg
- Sodium: 1421 mg
- Total Carbohydrate: 62.4 g
- Protein: 18.4 g

339. Fried Seafood Laksa Noodles

"This is one of my favorite Asian recipes. It's fast and easy."

Serving: 4 | Prep: 30 m | Cook: 10 m | Ready in: 40 m

Ingredients

- 1 tablespoon vegetable oil
- 2 red onions, minced
- 3 green chile peppers, sliced
- 3 cloves garlic, minced
- 1 teaspoon crushed ginger
- 1 tablespoon light soy sauce
- 1 tablespoon ground white pepper, or to taste
- salt to taste
- 7 ounces fresh prawns
- 1 squid, cleaned and sliced into rings, or more to taste
- 4 ounces fresh spinach, finely chopped
- 1 carrot, sliced
- 18 ounces fresh rice noodles, rinsed and drained

Direction

- Heat vegetable oil in a wok or large skillet over medium-high heat. Add onions, green chile peppers, garlic, and ginger; cook and stir until golden, about 2 minutes. Stir in soy sauce, white pepper, and salt; cook for 1 minute.
- Stir prawns and squid into the wok; cook and stir until prawns turn pink, 2 to 3 minutes. Add spinach and carrot; cook until spinach is wilted, 2 to 3 minutes. Add noodles; toss to fully incorporate.

Nutrition Information

- Calories: 392 calories
- Total Fat: 4.5 g
- Cholesterol: 75 mg
- Sodium: 388 mg
- Total Carbohydrate: 71.8 g
- Protein: 15.3 g

340. Grilled Shrimp and Rice Noodle Salad

"A quick and refreshing dish with a Thai flair."

Serving: 4 | Prep: 45 m | Cook: 10 m | Ready in: 55 m

Ingredients

- 1 pound uncooked medium shrimp, peeled and deveined
- 1 tablespoon low-sodium soy sauce
- 1 teaspoon grated lime zest
- 1/2 (16 ounce) package dry rice stick noodles
- 1/4 cup lime juice
- 3 tablespoons low-sodium soy sauce
- 3 tablespoons honey
- 1 tablespoon sesame oil
- 1 teaspoon grated lime zest
- 1/2 teaspoon anchovy paste
- 1/4 teaspoon hot pepper sauce
- 1 1/2 cups diced fresh peaches
- 1 cup shredded napa cabbage
- 2 carrots, shredded
- 1/4 cup chopped fresh cilantro
- 2 tablespoons chopped fresh basil
- 2 cloves garlic, minced
- 16 cherry tomatoes
- 6 skewers

Direction

- Preheat grill for medium heat and lightly oil the grate.
- Combine shrimp, 1 tablespoon soy sauce, and lime zest in a bowl. Allow shrimp to marinate at room temperature while preparing remaining ingredients.
- Bring a large pot of water to a boil. Add rice stick noodles to boiling water and remove from heat. Cook until noodles have cooked through, but are still firm to the bite, 3 to 5 minutes. Rinse will cold water until chilled; drain well.
- Whisk lime juice, remaining 3 tablespoons soy sauce, honey, sesame oil, remaining 1 teaspoon lime zest, anchovy paste, and hot pepper sauce in a large bowl. Add peaches, cabbage, carrots, cilantro, basil, and garlic and toss to coat. Stir rice noodles into vegetable mixture until combined; set aside.
- Thread about 8 shrimp on 4 wooden skewer by piercing shrimp through the tail and the upper body. Pierce cherry tomatoes onto remaining 2 skewers.
- Place shrimp and tomato skewers on preheated grill. Cook tomatoes until they begin to split, about 3 minutes per side; transfer to a platter. Continue to cook shrimp until they are bright pink on the outside and is no longer transparent in the center, 2 to 3 minutes more. Remove tomatoes and shrimp from skewers.
- Transfer noodle salad to a large platter. Surround salad with tomatoes and shrimp; drizzle any remaining lime dressing over shrimp.

Nutrition Information

- Calories: 437 calories
- Total Fat: 4.8 g
- Cholesterol: 173 mg
- Sodium: 851 mg
- Total Carbohydrate: 73 g
- Protein: 25.1 g

341. Guay Diaw Lawd Pork Belly Chicken Wing and Noodle Stew

"This recipe creates a stunning dish with many layers and textures. Fortunately, it is very easy to make in just one pot! This recipe feeds about 5 people, but it can easily be increased for a party if needed. Serve with red pepper flakes, chile vinegar, and fried garlic alongside for guests to flavor the soup as they wish. Leftovers are easily reheated."

Serving: 5 | Prep: 40 m | Cook: 1 h | Ready in: 2 h

Ingredients

- 10 dried shiitake mushrooms
- 1/2 cup peeled and chopped cilantro root

- 1/4 cup coarsely chopped garlic
- 2 tablespoons black peppercorns
- 2 (32 ounce) cartons beef stock
- 9 ounces pork belly, cut into 3/4-inch pieces
- 1 pound chicken wings
- 9 ounces firm tofu, cut into 1/3-inch chunks
- 9 ounces pickled radish (jap chai), diced
- 2 tablespoons oyster sauce, or more to taste
- 2 tablespoons dark sweet soy sauce (pad se ew), or more to taste
- 1 dash fish sauce, or more to taste
- sea salt to taste
- 1 (16 ounce) package wide rice noodles
- 2 cups bean sprouts
- 1 cup green onions, sliced
- 1 cup chopped cilantro leaves

Direction

- Place shiitake mushrooms in a small bowl. Cover with hot water and let soak until tender, about 20 minutes. Drain. Squeeze out excess water and slice.
- Pound cilantro root, garlic, and black peppercorns into a coarse paste in a mortar and pestle. Transfer paste to a large pot.
- Pour beef stock into the pot. Add pork belly and chicken wings. Bring to a simmer; cook for 10 minutes. Add sliced shiitake mushrooms, tofu, and pickled radish. Simmer soup until chicken wings are cooked through, about 45 minutes. Stir in oyster sauce and soy sauce. Season with fish sauce and sea salt.
- Place a steamer basket into a large pot and fill with water to just below the bottom of the steamer. Bring water to a boil. Add noodles, cover, and steam until tender, about 5 minutes.
- Place some noodles in each serving bowl and ladle soup on top. Garnish with bean sprouts, green onions, and cilantro.

Nutrition Information

- Calories: 647 calories
- Total Fat: 15.7 g
- Cholesterol: 34 mg
- Sodium: 1612 mg
- Total Carbohydrate: 96.6 g
- Protein: 28.7 g

342. Joes Fusion Chicken Pad Thai

"My girlfriend and I were craving pad Thai! So we looked at a few recipes and made our version. It is not exactly traditional pad Thai, so -- lo and behold -- the name!"

Serving: 5 | Prep: 20 m | Cook: 30 m | Ready in: 50 m

Ingredients

- 1 pound boneless, skinless chicken breast halves, cut into bite-size pieces
- salt and ground black pepper to taste
- 3/4 cup white sugar
- 1 teaspoon ground cayenne pepper
- 3 tablespoons white wine vinegar
- 6 tablespoons fish sauce
- 1 tablespoon creamy peanut butter
- 1 tablespoon olive oil
- 5 cloves garlic, minced
- 4 large eggs, lightly beaten
- 1 (16 ounce) package pad Thai rice noodles
- 1/2 cup fresh bean sprouts
- 2 cups beef broth
- 1/2 cup chopped green onion

Direction

- Bring a large pot of water to a boil.
- Season chicken with salt and black pepper; set aside.
- Whisk sugar, cayenne pepper, white wine vinegar, fish sauce, and peanut butter together in a bowl.
- Coat the inside of a large skillet or wok with olive oil and place over high heat.
- Cook and stir chicken in the hot oil just until the meat is white outside but still pink inside, about 3 minutes.
- Remove chicken and set aside in a bowl.
- Lower the heat under the skillet to medium-low. Cook and stir garlic in the skillet until it becomes translucent, 1 to 2 minutes.
- Cook and stir eggs into garlic until loosely cooked, 2 to 3 minutes.

- Pour peanut sauce into the garlic and eggs, and stir to combine. Bring sauce to a simmer.
- Stir rice noodles into the boiling water. Cook until noodles are still slightly tough, about 5 minutes.
- Drain the noodles.
- Return chicken to the skillet with eggs and sauce. Simmer until chicken is no longer pink in the center and the juices run clear, stirring frequently, 5 to 8 more minutes.
- Stir bean sprouts, rice noodles and beef broth into the skillet. Bring to a simmer, and cook until noodles are tender and most of the broth has been absorbed, about 10 minutes.
- Sprinkle with green onions to serve.

Nutrition Information

- Calories: 585 calories
- Total Fat: 11.3 g
- Cholesterol: 200 mg
- Sodium: 1791 mg
- Total Carbohydrate: 89.7 g
- Protein: 29.4 g

343. Korean Egg Roll Triangles

"This is a recipe my mom taught me.... it's call yaki-mon-do in Korean. They are similar to Chinese egg rolls, fun to eat and easy to make. My friends all love them, and so does my husband. They are great for parties."

Serving: 6 | Prep: 45 m | Cook: 15 m | Ready in: 1 h

Ingredients

- 1/2 (8 ounce) package dry thin Asian rice noodles (rice vermicelli)
- 1/2 medium head cabbage, cored and shredded
- 1 (12 ounce) package firm tofu
- 2 small zucchini, shredded
- 4 green onions, finely chopped
- 4 cloves garlic, finely chopped
- 1 tablespoon ground black pepper
- 2 tablespoons Asian (toasted) sesame oil
- 2 eggs, slightly beaten
- 2 teaspoons salt
- 1 (12 ounce) package round wonton wrappers
- 1/2 cup vegetable oil for frying

Direction

- Bring a pot of water to a boil, drop in the rice noodles, and boil until the noodles are soft but not mushy, 3 to 5 minutes, stirring occasionally. Rinse with cold water, and drain in a colander set in the sink. Chop the noodles up into small pieces, and set aside.
- Wrap the shredded cabbage in a kitchen towel or a length of cheesecloth, and squeeze the excess moisture out. Place the cabbage, tofu, zucchini, green onions, garlic, black pepper, sesame oil, eggs, salt, and chopped rice noodles in a large bowl, and mix with your hands until evenly mixed and the tofu is broken up into very small chunks.
- Place a round wonton wrapper onto a work surface, and spoon 1 to 2 teaspoons of filling into the center of the wrapper. Dip your finger in water and moisten the edge of the wrapper about halfway around, then fold the wrapper over, enclosing the filling, and pinch the edges together to make a half-moon shape. Lay the completed rolls on a cookie sheet while you finish filling and folding the rest.
- Heat the vegetable oil in a heavy skillet, and working in batches, fry the rolls until golden brown, 2 to 3 minutes per side.

Nutrition Information

- Calories: 534 calories
- Total Fat: 28.4 g
- Cholesterol: 67 mg
- Sodium: 1177 mg
- Total Carbohydrate: 56.9 g
- Protein: 14.6 g

344. Nicolas Pad Thai

"The result of loving pad Thai and endless tweaks to the ingredients lead me to this amazing dish."

Serving: 4 | Prep: 15 m | Cook: 15 m | Ready in: 8 h 30 m

Ingredients

- 2 cups pad Thai rice noodles, soaked in water overnight and drained
- 1/2 cup vegetable broth
- 2 tablespoons vegetable oil
- 1 tablespoon brown sugar
- 1 tablespoon soy sauce
- 1 tablespoon rice wine vinegar
- 1 1/2 teaspoons peanut butter
- 1 teaspoon chopped fresh cilantro
- 1 teaspoon onion powder
- 1 teaspoon tamarind paste
- 1 teaspoon hot chile paste
- 3/4 teaspoon garlic powder
- 1/2 teaspoon sesame oil
- 1/2 teaspoon crushed red pepper flakes
- 1/4 teaspoon ground coriander
- 1/4 teaspoon ground ginger
- salt and ground black pepper to taste
- 3 tablespoons vegetable oil
- 1/3 cup chopped broccoli
- 1/3 cup chopped carrots
- 1/3 cup snow peas, trimmed
- 1/3 cup sliced water chestnuts, drained
- 1/3 cup baby corn, drained
- 1/3 cup sliced fresh mushrooms
- 1/3 cup sliced zucchini
- 1 tablespoon vegetable oil
- 1 tablespoon chopped peanuts for topping
- 1 tablespoon chopped cilantro
- 1 pinch paprika for garnish

Direction

- Soak uncooked noodles in 8 cups of water until soft, 8 hours or overnight.
- Drain rice noodles and set aside.
- Whisk together vegetable broth, 2 tablespoons vegetable oil, brown sugar, soy sauce, rice wine vinegar, peanut butter, 1 teaspoon fresh cilantro, onion powder, tamarind paste, hot chile paste, garlic powder, sesame oil, red pepper flakes, ground coriander, ground ginger, salt, and ground black pepper in a saucepan.
- Heat sauce over medium heat until it bubbles; reduce heat to low, and simmer sauce while you prepare the remaining ingredients.
- Heat 3 tablespoons of vegetable oil in a large wok over medium heat.
- Cook and stir broccoli, carrots, snow peas, water chestnuts, baby corn, mushrooms, and zucchini in the wok until tender, 8 to 10 minutes.
- Add the drained noodles and 1 tablespoon vegetable oil to vegetables. Cook and stir until noodles are heated through, 2 to 3 minutes.
- Remove the wok from heat and pour the sauce over vegetables and rice noodles.
- Toss to fully coat the vegetables and rice noodles with sauce.
- Garnish with peanuts, 2 tablespoons chopped cilantro, and paprika.

Nutrition Information

- Calories: 520 calories
- Total Fat: 24.2 g
- Cholesterol: 0 mg
- Sodium: 467 mg
- Total Carbohydrate: 70.9 g
- Protein: 5.1 g

345. One Pot ThaiStyle Rice Noodles

"Chicken, vegetables, and noodles prepared in a light tasting but full-flavored Asian-inspired sauce."

Serving: 4 | Prep: 20 m | Cook: 15 m | Ready in: 40 m

Ingredients

- 2 tablespoons cornstarch
- 1 1/2 tablespoons water
- 6 cups chicken broth

- 2 1/2 tablespoons soy sauce
- 1 tablespoon fish sauce
- 1 tablespoon rice vinegar
- 1 tablespoon chile-garlic sauce (such as Sriracha®), or more to taste
- 2 teaspoons vegetable oil
- 2 teaspoons minced fresh ginger root
- 2 cloves garlic, minced
- 1 teaspoon ground coriander
- 1 (16 ounce) package thick rice noodles
- 1 cup sliced zucchini
- 1 cup sliced red bell pepper
- 2 cooked chicken breasts, cut into 1-inch cubes
- 1/4 cup crushed peanuts (optional)
- 1/4 cup chopped fresh cilantro (optional)

Direction

- Stir cornstarch and water together in a small bowl until smooth. Pour chicken broth into a large pot and stir cornstarch mixture, soy sauce, fish sauce, rice vinegar, chile-garlic sauce, vegetable oil, ginger, garlic, and coriander into broth. Cover and bring to a boil.
- Place rice noodles in the boiling sauce, reduce heat to medium, and simmer until noodles are tender, 5 to 10 minutes. Stir zucchini, red bell pepper, and chicken into sauce. Bring back to a boil, cover, and simmer until vegetables are just become tender, about 5 more minutes.
- Remove from heat and let stand, covered, for 5 minutes to thicken. Serve garnished with crushed peanuts and cilantro.

Nutrition Information

- Calories: 587 calories
- Total Fat: 9.2 g
- Cholesterol: 30 mg
- Sodium: 2736 mg
- Total Carbohydrate: 104.9 g
- Protein: 17.4 g

346. Pasta with Vietnamese Pesto

"I like pasta with pesto because it is a one-bowl, one-pot deal. This is a really yummy pesto. If you can't find fresh lemon grass, use an equal amount of grated lemon zest instead."

Serving: 4 | Prep: 30 m | Cook: 5 m | Ready in: 35 m

Ingredients

- 1 pound dried rice noodles
- 1 1/2 cups chopped fresh cilantro
- 1/2 cup sweet Thai basil
- 2 cloves garlic, halved
- 1/2 teaspoon minced lemon grass bulb
- 1 jalapeno pepper, seeded and minced
- 1 tablespoon vegetarian fish sauce
- 4 tablespoons chopped, unsalted dry-roasted peanuts
- 7 tablespoons canola oil
- 1/2 lime, cut into wedges
- salt and pepper to taste

Direction

- Soak rice noodles in a large bowl of cold water for 30 minutes. Drain the noodles, and set them aside.
- Make the pesto: In a blender or food processor combine the chopped cilantro, basil, garlic cloves, lemongrass, jalapeno peppers, imitation fish sauce or salt, and 2 tablespoons of the peanuts. Whirl just until the herbs and peanuts are coarsely chopped. While the machine is running add the oil in a thin stream. Then add the remaining peanuts and run the machine in short spurts until the peanuts are coarsely chopped.
- Place soaked rice noodles into a large skillet with 1/2 cup water over medium-high heat. Stir until most of the water has been absorbed and the noodles are tender.
- Add almost all of the pesto, and stir well, adding a few tablespoons of water if the pesto is clumping.
- Taste the pasta and add more pesto, lime juice, imitation fish sauce, salt, or pepper if you like. Garnish the pasta with the remaining 2 tablespoons of peanuts, and serve right away.

Nutrition Information

- Calories: 694 calories
- Total Fat: 29.8 g
- Cholesterol: 0 mg
- Sodium: 217 mg
- Total Carbohydrate: 98.8 g
- Protein: 6.8 g

347. Pho Ga Soup

"Vietnamese chicken noodle soup. After ordering this soup at a local Vietnamese restaurant, I decided to try to make it at home. This is a very flexible recipe. Feel free to substitute some of your favorite vegetables or try different noodles. Enjoy!"

Serving: 6 | Prep: 15 m | Cook: 15 m | Ready in: 30 m

Ingredients

- 1 tablespoon vegetable oil
- 1 small yellow onion, chopped
- 1 (8 ounce) package baby bella mushrooms, chopped
- 4 cloves garlic, minced
- 8 cups water
- 1 (6.75 ounce) package rice stick noodles (such as Maifun®)
- 8 teaspoons chicken bouillon
- 2 cooked chicken breasts, shredded
- 4 green onions, chopped
- 1/3 cup chopped fresh cilantro
- 2 cups bean sprouts
- 1 lime, sliced into wedges
- 1 dash Sriracha hot sauce, or more to taste

Direction

- Heat vegetable oil in a large saucepan over medium-high heat; sauté onion, mushrooms, and garlic until tender, 5 to 10 minutes. Add water, rice noodles, and chicken bouillon to onion mixture; bring to a boil. Reduce heat to low.
- Mix shredded chicken, green onions, and cilantro into soup; simmer for 5 minutes more. Transfer soup to serving bowls and top with bean sprouts, a squeeze of lime juice, and Sriracha hot sauce.

Nutrition Information

- Calories: 231 calories
- Total Fat: 5.4 g
- Cholesterol: 28 mg
- Sodium: 149 mg
- Total Carbohydrate: 32 g
- Protein: 13.5 g

348. Pork and Shrimp Pancit

"A traditional Pancit taught to me by a Filipino friend while stationed overseas. Delicious and easy! Thanks, Ditas!"

Serving: 4 | Prep: 20 m | Cook: 20 m | Ready in: 40 m

Ingredients

- 1 (6.75 ounce) package rice noodles
- 5 tablespoons vegetable oil, divided
- 1 small onion, minced
- 2 cloves garlic, minced
- 1/2 teaspoon ground ginger
- 1 1/2 cups cooked small shrimp, diced
- 1 1/2 cups chopped cooked pork
- 4 cups shredded bok choy
- 3 tablespoons oyster sauce
- 1/4 cup chicken broth
- 1/4 teaspoon crushed red pepper flakes
- 1 green onion, minced

Direction

- Soak the rice noodles in warm water for 20 minutes; drain.
- Heat 3 tablespoons oil in a wok or large heavy skillet over medium-high heat. Sauté noodles for 1 minute. Transfer to serving dish, and keep warm. Add remaining 2 tablespoons oil to skillet, and sauté onion, garlic, ginger, shrimp and pork for 1 minute.
- Stir in bok choy, oyster sauce and chicken broth. Season with pepper flakes. Cover, and

cook for 1 minute, or until bok choy is wilted. Spoon over noodles, and garnish with minced green onion.

Nutrition Information

- Calories: 488 calories
- Total Fat: 20.8 g
- Cholesterol: 119 mg
- Sodium: 394 mg
- Total Carbohydrate: 44.4 g
- Protein: 29.1 g

349. Quick ChineseStyle Vermicelli Rice Noodles

"Quick and delicious Chinese-style rice noodles."

Serving: 4 | Prep: 15 m | Cook: 3 m | Ready in: 18 m

Ingredients

- 1 (8 ounce) package dried rice noodles
- 2 tablespoons vegetable oil
- 1 clove garlic, minced
- 1 tablespoon soy sauce
- 1/2 tablespoon chili sauce
- salt and pepper to taste
- 1 green onion, chopped

Direction

- Bring a large pot of water to a boil. Add rice noodles, and cook for 2 to 3 minutes or until al dente; do not overcook, or they will become mushy. Drain.
- Heat oil in a large skillet over medium heat. Sauté garlic until tender. Stir in noodles, and season with soy sauce, chili sauce, salt and pepper. Sprinkle top with chopped green onion.

Nutrition Information

- Calories: 271 calories
- Total Fat: 7.1 g
- Cholesterol: 0 mg

- Sodium: 357 mg
- Total Carbohydrate: 48 g
- Protein: 2.3 g

350. Saigon Noodle Salad

"This Vietnamese-style noodle salad is my 'too hot to cook' staple. It is bursting with flavor and makes great use of leftover grilled meat or shrimp."

Serving: 4 | Prep: 25 m | Ready in: 30 m

Ingredients

- Dressing:
- 1/4 cup water, or more to taste
- 3 tablespoons lime juice
- 3 tablespoons fish sauce
- 3 tablespoons brown sugar, or more to taste
- 1 clove garlic, minced
- 1 teaspoon minced fresh ginger root
- 1/2 teaspoon Sriracha chile sauce
- Salad:
- 1 (8 ounce) package (linguine-width) rice noodles
- 2 cups thinly sliced Napa (Chinese) cabbage
- 1 1/2 cups matchstick-cut carrots
- 8 ounces grilled shrimp
- 1 cup bean sprouts
- 1/2 English cucumber, halved lengthwise and cut into thin slices
- 2 green onions, thinly sliced
- 2 2/3 tablespoons chopped fresh mint
- 2 2/3 tablespoons chopped fresh cilantro
- 2 2/3 tablespoons chopped fresh basil
- 1/2 cup coarsely chopped peanuts

Direction

- Whisk water, lime juice, fish sauce, brown sugar, garlic, ginger, and Sriracha together in a bowl until the sugar is dissolved.
- Bring a large pot of water to a full boil; remove from heat and soak rice noodles in the hot water for 1 minute. Stir to separate the noodles and continue soaking until the noodles are

- tender, about 3 minutes more. Drain noodles and rinse with cold water until cooled. Shake noodles in colander to drain as much water as possible.
- Mix noodles, cabbage, carrots, shrimp, bean sprouts, cucumber slices, green onions, mint, cilantro, and basil together in a large bowl. Drizzle the dressing over the salad and toss to coat. Top with chopped peanuts.

Nutrition Information

- Calories: 450 calories
- Total Fat: 10.1 g
- Cholesterol: 109 mg
- Sodium: 1265 mg
- Total Carbohydrate: 71 g
- Protein: 20.4 g

351. Shrimp Pad Thai

"This is a Pad Thai recipe I got from a restaurant. The sauce is made with ketchup, fish sauce, sugar, lemon juice and vinegar, and it's sprinkled liberally with bean sprouts and chopped peanuts."

Serving: 4 | Prep: 30 m | Cook: 30 m | Ready in: 1 h

Ingredients

- 1 (8 ounce) package rice noodles
- 1 1/2 teaspoons vegetable oil
- 1 onion, diced
- 1 teaspoon minced garlic
- 12 medium fresh shrimp, peeled and deveined
- 1 tablespoon ketchup
- 1 tablespoon fish sauce
- 1 tablespoon white sugar
- 1 tablespoon lemon juice
- 1 tablespoon white wine vinegar
- 2 eggs, lightly beaten
- 1/4 pound bean sprouts
- 1/2 cup unsalted dry-roasted peanuts, chopped
- 1/4 pound bean sprouts
- 1 lemon, sliced
- 1/2 cup chopped peanuts
- 1/4 cup coarsely chopped cilantro

Direction

- In a medium bowl, soak the noodles in cold water for 15 min; drain. Cover noodles with hot water, and soak for 15 minutes; drain. Rinse with cold water, drain, and set aside.
- Heat oil in a wok or large heavy skillet over medium heat. Sauté onion and garlic until onion is soft and translucent, about 5 minutes. Add shrimp, and cook until pink. Stir in ketchup, fish sauce, sugar, lemon juice and vinegar. Pour in the beaten egg, and cook without stirring until egg is partially set. Add drained noodles, 1/4 pound bean sprouts, and 1/2 cup peanuts. Mix while cooking until noodles are tender.

Nutrition Information

- Calories: 541 calories
- Total Fat: 23.2 g
- Cholesterol: 120 mg
- Sodium: 488 mg
- Total Carbohydrate: 68.7 g
- Protein: 20.2 g

352. Singapore Noodle Curry Shrimp

"One skillet, and it's dinner!"

Serving: 6 | Prep: 15 m | Cook: 10 m | Ready in: 25 m

Ingredients

- 2/3 cup chicken broth
- 1 tablespoon oyster sauce
- 1 1/2 tablespoons soy sauce
- 1 1/2 teaspoons white sugar
- 3 tablespoons peanut oil
- 1 1/2 teaspoons curry powder
- 1 clove garlic, minced
- 1 teaspoon minced fresh ginger root

- 1 small red bell pepper, diced
- 1 small red onion, chopped
- 4 green onions, chopped into 1 inch pieces
- 1 (12 ounce) package frozen cooked cocktail shrimp
- 1 1/2 cups frozen baby peas
- 1/2 (8 ounce) package rice noodles, broken into 3 inch pieces and soaked

Direction

- Combine chicken broth, oyster sauce, soy sauce and sugar in a small bowl, and set aside.
- In a large skillet, heat the oil over medium-high heat. Add curry powder, garlic, and ginger; stir-fry for 10 seconds. Add peppers, onions, and scallions; stir-fry for 3 to 5 minutes. Stir in chicken stock mixture, and bring to a boil over high heat. Add shrimp and peas, and cook until hot. Add noodles, and cook until dish is heated thoroughly. Serve immediately.

Nutrition Information

- Calories: 231 calories
- Total Fat: 7.6 g
- Cholesterol: 110 mg
- Sodium: 491 mg
- Total Carbohydrate: 25 g
- Protein: 14.8 g

353. Spicy Peanut Shrimp Rice Noodles

"An unusual Thai-inspired combination that tastes great!"

Serving: 4 | Prep: 15 m | Cook: 30 m | Ready in: 1 h

Ingredients

- 1 tablespoon vegetable oil
- 3/4 white onion, chopped
- 4 cloves garlic
- 1/2 teaspoon red pepper flakes
- 1 pound frozen shrimp, thawed
- 2 (14.5 ounce) cans fire-roasted diced tomatoes
- 2 tablespoons creamy peanut butter
- 1 teaspoon red chile paste, or more to taste
- 1 (8 ounce) package wide rice noodles
- hot water to cover
- 1/4 cup chopped fresh cilantro, or to taste
- 1/4 cup Greek-style yogurt, or to taste
- 1/4 cup chopped peanuts, or to taste

Direction

- Heat vegetable oil in a large pan or skillet over medium heat; sauté onion, garlic, and red pepper flakes until garlic is slightly browned, 2 to 3 minutes. Add shrimp; cook and stir until shrimp begin to firm, about 5 minutes.
- Stir tomatoes, peanut butter, and red chile paste into shrimp mixture; bring to a boil. Reduce heat and simmer until sauce thickens, about 20 minutes.
- Place noodles in a large bowl and cover with hot water. Set aside until noodles are softened, about 15 minutes. Drain and rinse thoroughly.
- Divide noodles among serving plates; top with shrimp sauce. Garnish each serving with cilantro, yogurt, and peanuts.

Nutrition Information

- Calories: 514 calories
- Total Fat: 14.7 g
- Cholesterol: 175 mg
- Sodium: 990 mg
- Total Carbohydrate: 66.3 g
- Protein: 27.5 g

354. Spicy Shrimp Pad Thai

"I used other pad thai recipes from this website and added shrimp and my own little flavor and spice."

Serving: 4 | Prep: 30 m | Cook: 20 m | Ready in: 50 m

Ingredients

- 1 (8 ounce) package dried rice noodles
- 2 teaspoons peanut oil

- 1 small onion, diced
- 2 cloves garlic, minced
- 3 tablespoons rice wine vinegar
- 3 tablespoons ketchup
- 3 tablespoons fish sauce
- 3 tablespoons sweet chile sauce
- 2 tablespoons creamy peanut butter
- 1 tablespoon light soy sauce
- 1 tablespoon fresh lime juice
- 1 tablespoon white sugar
- 1 teaspoon red pepper flakes
- 1/2 teaspoon cayenne pepper
- 12 uncooked medium shrimp, peeled and deveined
- 2 eggs, lightly beaten
- 1 cup unsalted dry-roasted peanuts, chopped
- 1/2 pound bean sprouts
- 1/4 cup shredded carrots (optional)
- 1/2 lime, cut into wedges
- 1/4 cup chopped green onions
- 1/4 cup coarsely chopped cilantro

Direction

- Place noodles in a large bowl and cover with hot water. Set aside until noodles are softened, about 15 minutes. Drain and rinse thoroughly.
- Heat oil in a wok over medium heat. Cook and stir onion and garlic until onion is translucent, about 5 minutes.
- Combine rice wine vinegar, ketchup, fish sauce, chile sauce, peanut butter, soy sauce, lime juice, sugar, red pepper flakes, and cayenne pepper together in a bowl. Set aside.
- Add shrimp to the wok. Cook and stir until pink, about 4 minutes. Add the ketchup mixture and stir. Move all ingredients to one side to clear a small space in the pan. Pour in eggs and cook without stirring until partially set, about 3 minutes.
- Stir the drained noodles into the shrimp and egg mixture. Add 1/2 cup peanuts, 1/4 cup bean sprouts, and carrots. Cook and stir until noodles are heated through, about 2 minutes. Garnish with the remaining peanuts, bean sprouts, lime wedges, green onions, and cilantro.

Nutrition Information

- Calories: 619 calories
- Total Fat: 28 g
- Cholesterol: 120 mg
- Sodium: 1421 mg
- Total Carbohydrate: 75.6 g
- Protein: 22 g

355. Spicy Thai Shrimp Pasta

"This recipe is great for summer barbeques as a side dish for kabobs or Asian satay. May also be served warm. Optional: add a 1/2 cup of finely chopped peanuts."

Serving: 6 | Prep: 15 m | Cook: 5 m | Ready in: 8 h 20 m

Ingredients

- 1 (12 ounce) package rice vermicelli
- 1 large tomato, diced
- 4 green onions, diced
- 2 pounds cooked shrimp, peeled and deveined
- 1 1/2 cups prepared Thai peanut sauce

Direction

- Bring a large pot of water to a boil. Add rice vermicelli, and cook 3 to 5 minutes or until al dente; drain.
- In a medium bowl, toss together rice vermicelli, tomato, green onions, shrimp, and peanut sauce. Cover, and chill in the refrigerator 8 hours or overnight.

Nutrition Information

- Calories: 564 calories
- Total Fat: 19.3 g
- Cholesterol: 230 mg
- Sodium: 375 mg
- Total Carbohydrate: 52.4 g
- Protein: 46.3 g

356. Spring Rolls with Coconut Peanut Sauce

"Strips of carrot, bell pepper, cucumber and shredded red cabbage and more are rolled into rice noodle wrappers and served with a creamy peanut sauce."

Serving: 8

Ingredients

- Spring Rolls:
- 2 carrots, julienned
- 1 red bell pepper, julienned
- 1 English cucumber, peeled and julienned
- 1 cup shredded red cabbage
- 4 scallions, white parts thinly sliced lengthwise
- 2 avocados, halved and sliced
- 16 basil leaves
- 16 mint leaves
- 4 ounces dry rice noodles
- 16 sheets rice paper
- Peanut Sauce:
- 1/2 cup creamy peanut butter
- 1/2 cup Silk® Unsweetened Coconutmilk
- 2 tablespoons soy or tamari sauce
- 2 tablespoons fresh lime juice
- 1 clove garlic, minced
- 1/2 teaspoon toasted sesame oil
- 2 teaspoons hot sauce (such as Sriracha), or more to taste

Direction

- Chop all vegetables to 2-inch length and cook rice noodles according to instructions on pack.
- Working one at a time, soak a sheet of rice paper in a shallow dish of warm water until soft, about 10 seconds.
- Lay softened sheet gently on a flat surface, then mound vegetables, noodles and avocado or tofu in the center of sheet.
- Gently fold bottom and top of rice paper to cover filling and then roll up like a burrito. Repeat with remaining rice paper and fillings.
- To serve, mix peanut sauce ingredients in a small bowl and serve with spring rolls.

Nutrition Information

- Calories: 292 calories
- Total Fat: 16.4 g
- Cholesterol: 0 mg
- Sodium: 403 mg
- Total Carbohydrate: 32.2 g
- Protein: 7.6 g

357. Thai Curry Soup

"This delicious Thai-style soup has coconut milk, shrimp, mushrooms, and spinach. Chicken may be substituted for the shrimp; either way, I love this soup anytime!"

Serving: 4 | Prep: 15 m | Cook: 35 m | Ready in: 50 m

Ingredients

- 2 ounces rice noodles (pad thai noodles)
- 1 tablespoon olive oil
- 1 clove garlic, minced
- 1 1/2 tablespoons minced lemon grass
- 1 teaspoon ground ginger
- 2 teaspoons red curry paste
- 1 (32 ounce) carton chicken broth
- 2 tablespoons soy sauce
- 1 tablespoon white sugar
- 1 (13.5 ounce) can reduced-fat coconut milk
- 1/2 cup peeled and deveined medium shrimp
- 1/2 cup sliced mushrooms
- 1 (10 ounce) bag baby spinach leaves
- 2 tablespoons fresh lime juice
- 1/4 cup chopped cilantro
- 2 green onions, thinly sliced

Direction

- Bring a large pot of lightly salted water to a boil. Add rice noodles and cook until al dente, about 3 minutes. Drain and rinse well with cold water to stop the cooking; set aside.
- Heat oil in a large saucepan over medium heat. Stir in garlic, lemon grass, and ginger; cook and stir until aromatic, 30 to 60 seconds. Add the curry paste, and cook 30 seconds

more. Pour in about 1/2 cup of the chicken broth, and stir until the curry paste has dissolved, then pour in the remaining chicken stock along with the soy sauce and sugar. Bring to a boil, then reduce heat to medium-low, partially cover, and simmer 20 minutes.
- Stir in coconut milk, shrimp, mushrooms, spinach, lime juice, and cilantro. Increase heat to medium-high, and simmer until the shrimp turn pink and are no longer translucent, about 5 minutes.
- To serve, place some rice noodles into each serving bowl and ladle soup on top of them. Garnish each bowl with a sprinkle of sliced green onion.

Nutrition Information

- Calories: 247 calories
- Total Fat: 13.1 g
- Cholesterol: 30 mg
- Sodium: 1695 mg
- Total Carbohydrate: 23.8 g
- Protein: 8.2 g

358. Thai Rice Noodle Salad

"Just made it up 5 minutes ago and it's really good. It can be served warm or cold; toss again right before serving. Do not overcook the noodles."

Serving: 4 | Prep: 20 m | Ready in: 30 m

Ingredients

- 1 (8 ounce) package dried rice noodles
- 1 tablespoon olive oil
- 1/4 head romaine lettuce, chopped
- 1/4 red bell pepper, diced
- 1/4 cup chopped red onion
- 3 green onions, chopped
- 1/4 cucumber, diced
- 2 tablespoons chopped fresh basil, or to taste
- 2 tablespoons chopped fresh cilantro, or to taste
- 1 (1 inch) piece fresh ginger root, minced
- 1/4 jalapeno pepper, seeded and minced
- 2 cloves garlic, minced
- Sauce:
- 1/3 cup olive oil
- 1/4 cup rice vinegar
- 1/4 cup soy sauce
- 1/4 cup white sugar
- 1 lemon, juiced
- 1 lime, juiced
- 1 teaspoon salt
- 1/4 teaspoon ground turmeric
- 1/4 teaspoon paprika

Direction

- Fill a bowl with boiling water; add rice noodles. Cover bowl and let sit until noodles are softened, about 10 minutes. Drain. Add 1 tablespoon olive oil and toss to coat.
- Mix romaine lettuce, red bell pepper, red onion, green onions, cucumber, basil, cilantro, ginger root, jalapeno pepper, and garlic with rice noodles.
- Whisk 1/3 cup olive oil, rice vinegar, soy sauce, white sugar, lemon juice, lime juice, salt, turmeric, and paprika together in a bowl; pour over rice noodle mixture and toss to coat.

Nutrition Information

- Calories: 472 calories
- Total Fat: 21.9 g
- Cholesterol: 0 mg
- Sodium: 1592 mg
- Total Carbohydrate: 65.2 g
- Protein: 3.9 g

359. Turkey Lettuce Wraps with Shiitake Mushrooms

"This dish is very versatile. Try serving the filling on flour tortillas with hoisin sauce for a moo shoo type dish – or use it to top brown rice and veggies for rice bowls."

Serving: 4 | Prep: 40 m | Cook: 20 m | Ready in: 1 h

Ingredients

- 2 cups water
- 2 ounces mai fun (angel hair) rice noodles
- 1 teaspoon vegetable oil
- 4 shiitake mushrooms, sliced
- 2 teaspoons vegetable oil
- 1 (16 ounce) package ground turkey
- 6 green onions, chopped
- 1/4 cup chopped water chestnuts
- 4 teaspoons finely minced fresh ginger root
- 2 teaspoons minced garlic
- 3 tablespoons soy sauce
- 2 tablespoons brown sugar
- 1 tablespoon rice vinegar
- 1 teaspoon sesame oil
- 1 teaspoon finely grated orange zest
- 12 leaves green leaf lettuce
- Toppings
- 1/2 cup bean sprouts
- 1 carrot, grated
- 1/2 cup salted peanuts
- 1/2 cup chopped fresh cilantro
- 1/2 cup sweet chili sauce

Direction

- Bring 2 cups of water to a boil in a small saucepan. Turn off heat; stir in rice noodles. Cover, and allow noodles to soak until soft, 5 to 7 minutes. Rinse with cold water. Drain well.
- Heat 1 teaspoon of the oil in a large skillet over medium-high heat. Cook the mushrooms in the hot oil until they are browned and softened, about 2 minutes. Remove the mushrooms from the pan. Reserve.
- Heat the remaining 2 teaspoons of oil in the pan. Cook and stir the turkey in the oil until it is no longer pink, 5 to 7 minutes. Stir in the green onions, water chestnuts, ginger, and garlic; continue to cook for 1 minute. Mix in the reserved mushrooms, soy sauce, and brown sugar. Simmer briefly to combine the flavors. Take the pan off the heat; stir in the rice vinegar, sesame oil, and orange zest.
- To assemble lettuce wraps, place a bit of turkey filling on each lettuce leaf. Top each with cooked noodles, and a sprinkle of bean sprouts, carrots, peanuts, and cilantro. Serve with sweet chili sauce for dipping.

Nutrition Information

- Calories: 481 calories
- Total Fat: 22.4 g
- Cholesterol: 84 mg
- Sodium: 1284 mg
- Total Carbohydrate: 43.5 g
- Protein: 29.9 g

360. Vietnamese Beef Noodle Soup

"This is a simplified version of a Vietnamese beef noodle soup. The Vietnamese make the broth from scratch, and simmer it for hours."

Serving: 4 | Prep: 30 m | Cook: 15 m | Ready in: 45 m

Ingredients

- 4 ounces dried rice noodles
- 6 cups cold water
- 3 (10.5 ounce) cans condensed beef broth
- 1 teaspoon chopped fresh ginger root
- 1/2 teaspoon kosher salt
- 1 Thai chile, chopped
- 1/2 pound boneless top round steak, sliced very thin
- 1/4 pound fresh basil
- 4 tablespoons snipped fresh cilantro
- 1/4 pound mung bean sprouts
- 4 green onions, thinly sliced
- 4 wedges lime
- hot pepper sauce (optional)
- oyster sauce (optional)

Direction

- Soak noodles in cold water for 30 minutes. Drain. Bring water to a boil in large pot. Add noodles, and boil 3 to 5 minutes - don't overcook. Drain, and rinse with cold water. Set aside.
- Meanwhile, combine beef broth, ginger, salt, and Thai pepper in a saucepan. Bring to a boil, and simmer for 15 minutes.
- Place equal portions of noodles into 4 large soup bowls, and place raw beef on top. Ladle hot broth over noodles and beef. Garnish with lime wedges, basil leaves, cilantro, mung beans, and green onions, and serve with hot pepper sauce and oyster sauce.

Nutrition Information

- Calories: 258 calories
- Total Fat: 5.8 g
- Cholesterol: 43 mg
- Sodium: 2160 mg
- Total Carbohydrate: 30.9 g
- Protein: 20.9 g

361. Vietnamese Beef Pho

"This soup is served with a plate full of fresh garnishes as well as various sauces. This allows each person to season their serving to taste. The soup is somewhat unusual, because the meat is cooked in the bowl. The beef is sliced very thin, almost thin enough to see through. You might want to have the butcher slice it for you. The boiling hot broth is poured over the noodles and raw meat. The meat is quickly cooked in the hot broth in the time it takes to garnish the soup."

Serving: 6 | Prep: 10 m | Cook: 1 h 20 m | Ready in: 1 h 30 m

Ingredients

- 4 quarts beef broth
- 1 large onion, sliced into rings
- 6 slices fresh ginger root
- 1 lemon grass
- 1 cinnamon stick
- 1 teaspoon whole black peppercorns
- 1 pound sirloin tip, cut into thin slices
- 1/2 pound bean sprouts
- 1 cup fresh basil leaves
- 1 cup fresh mint leaves
- 1 cup loosely packed cilantro leaves
- 3 fresh jalapeno peppers, sliced into rings
- 2 limes, cut into wedges
- 2 (8 ounce) packages dried rice noodles
- 1/2 tablespoon hoisin sauce
- 1 dash hot pepper sauce
- 3 tablespoons fish sauce

Direction

- In a large soup pot, combine broth, onion, ginger, lemon grass, cinnamon, and peppercorns. Bring to a boil, reduce heat, and cover. Simmer for 1 hour.
- Arrange bean sprouts, mint, basil, and cilantro on a platter with chilies and lime.
- Soak the noodles in hot water to cover for 15 minutes or until soft. Drain. Place equal portions of noodles into 6 large soup bowls, and place raw beef on top. Ladle hot broth over noodles and beef. Pass platter with garnishes and sauces.

Nutrition Information

- Calories: 528 calories
- Total Fat: 13.6 g
- Cholesterol: 51 mg
- Sodium: 2844 mg
- Total Carbohydrate: 73.1 g
- Protein: 27.1 g

362. Vietnamese Salad Rolls

"A nice light appetizer. Delicate rice wrappers are filled with noodles, shrimp, carrots, lettuce and basil. Cooked chicken or beef may be substituted for shrimp."

Serving: 8 | Prep: 20 m | Cook: 5 m | Ready in: 25 m

Ingredients

- 1 (8 ounce) package rice vermicelli

- 8 ounces cooked, peeled shrimp, cut in half lengthwise
- 8 rice wrappers (6.5 inch diameter)
- 1 carrot, julienned
- 1 cup shredded lettuce
- 1/4 cup chopped fresh basil
- 1/2 cup hoisin sauce
- water as needed

Direction

- Bring a medium saucepan of water to boil. Remove from heat. Place rice vermicelli in boiling water, remove from heat, and let soak 3 to 5 minutes, until soft. Drain, and rinse with cold water.
- Fill a large bowl with hot water. Dip one rice wrapper in the hot water for 1 second to soften. Lay wrapper flat, and place desired amounts of noodles, shrimp, carrot, lettuce and basil in the center. Roll the edges of the wrapper slightly inward. Beginning at the bottom edge of wrapper, tightly wrap the ingredients. Repeat with remaining ingredients.
- In a small bowl, mix the hoisin sauce with water until desired consistency has been attained. Heat the mixture for a few seconds in the microwave.
- Serve the spring rolls with the warm dipping sauce.

Nutrition Information

- Calories: 187 calories
- Total Fat: 1.5 g
- Cholesterol: 57 mg
- Sodium: 344 mg
- Total Carbohydrate: 31.2 g
- Protein: 11.6 g

363. Vietnamese Spring Rolls

"I love these, they're really addictive and healthy!"

Serving: 4 | Prep: 10 m | Cook: 15 m | Ready in: 25 m

Ingredients

- 1/2 (6.75 ounce) package dried rice noodles
- 8 rice wrappers (8.5 inch diameter)
- 8 fresh mint leaves
- 8 cooked medium shrimp, sliced in half lengthwise
- 1 1/2 cups bean sprouts
- 3 tablespoons fish sauce, or to taste
- 1/2 cup cilantro leaves

Direction

- Place the rice noodles in a large bowl of hot water until cooked, about 15 minutes. Drain and rinse with cold water. Fill a large bowl with hot water, and soak the rice wrapper sheets one at a time until softened, but still rather firm; about 20 seconds. Place the sheets on a large dish cloth, separate from each other. Place a mint leaf into the center of each wrapper. Place two shrimp halves over the mint leaf, top with a small handful of the noodles, and 5 to 6 bean sprouts. Season to taste with fish sauce, and garnish with cilantro leaves.
- Roll them, burrito style, by folding the bottom of the wrapper over the filling in the center. Fold in the left and right sides, then roll the entire thing away from you tightly.

Nutrition Information

- Calories: 145 calories
- Total Fat: 0.4 g
- Cholesterol: 20 mg
- Sodium: 890 mg
- Total Carbohydrate: 29.7 g
- Protein: 5.2 g

364. Vietnamese Spring Rolls With Dipping Sauce

"These Vietnamese spring rolls are the perfect recipe for beating the heat. Poached shrimp, rice noodles, herbs, and lettuce are rolled into a thin rice wrapper. Serve with the sweet and sour dipping sauce."

Serving: 4 | Prep: 20 m | Cook: 5 m | Ready in: 1 h 25 m

Ingredients

- 1/4 cup white vinegar
- 1/4 cup fish sauce
- 2 tablespoons white sugar
- 2 tablespoons lime juice
- 1 clove garlic, minced
- 1/4 teaspoon red pepper flakes
- 2 ounces rice vermicelli
- 8 large shrimp, peeled and deveined
- 4 rice wrappers (8.5 inch diameter)
- 2 leaves lettuce, chopped
- 3 tablespoons finely chopped fresh mint leaves
- 3 tablespoons finely chopped cilantro
- 4 teaspoons finely chopped Thai basil

Direction

- Whisk vinegar, fish sauce, sugar, lime juice, garlic, and red pepper flakes together in a small bowl. Set the dipping sauce aside.
- Fill a large bowl with room temperature water. Add rice vermicelli and soak for 1 hour.
- Bring a large pot of water to a boil. Drop in shrimp and cook until curled and pink, about 1 minute. Remove the shrimp and drain. Slice each shrimp in half lengthwise. Transfer rice vermicelli noodles to the pot of boiling water and cook for 1 minute. Remove and drain in a colander. Immediately rinse the vermicelli with cold water, stirring to separate the noodles.
- To assemble the rolls, dip 1 rice wrapper in a large bowl of room temperature water for a few seconds to soften. Place wrapper on a work surface and top with 4 shrimp halves, 1/4 of the chopped lettuce, 1/2 ounce vermicelli, and 1/4 each of the mint, cilantro, and Thai basil. Fold right and left edges of the wrapper over the ends of the filling and roll up the spring roll. Repeat with remaining wrappers and ingredients. Cut each roll in half and serve with dipping sauce.

Nutrition Information

- Calories: 137 calories
- Total Fat: 0.7 g
- Cholesterol: 64 mg
- Sodium: 1170 mg
- Total Carbohydrate: 22.5 g
- Protein: 10.1 g

365. VietnameseStyle Shrimp Soup

"Quick and tastes like a authentic vietnamese soup :) Before throwing anything into the pot, make sure all your ingredients are prepped- this soup is really quick cooking!"

Serving: 6 | Prep: 15 m | Cook: 20 m | Ready in: 35 m

Ingredients

- 1 tablespoon vegetable oil
- 2 teaspoons minced fresh garlic
- 2 teaspoons minced fresh ginger root
- 1 (10 ounce) package frozen chopped spinach, thawed and drained
- salt and black pepper to taste
- 2 quarts chicken stock
- 1 cup shrimp stock
- 1 teaspoon hot pepper sauce (optional)
- 1 teaspoon hoisin sauce (optional)
- 20 peeled and deveined medium shrimp
- 1 (6.75 ounce) package long rice noodles (rice vermicelli)
- 2 green onions, chopped (optional)

Direction

- Heat the vegetable oil in a large pot over medium heat. Stir in the garlic and ginger; cook and stir 1 minute. Add the spinach and season with salt and pepper. Cover, and cook until the spinach is hot, about 3 minutes. Pour in the chicken stock, shrimp stock, hot pepper

sauce, and hoisin sauce. Recover, and bring to a simmer over medium-high heat.
- Once the soup reaches a simmer, stir in the shrimp and noodles. Cover, and cook 4 minutes, then stir in the green onions, and cook 5 minutes more. Season to taste with salt and pepper before serving.

Nutrition Information

- Calories: 212 calories
- Total Fat: 4.7 g
- Cholesterol: 52 mg
- Sodium: 1156 mg
- Total Carbohydrate: 28.6 g
- Protein: 14.4 g

Index

A

Almond, 11, 13, 17, 20–23, 27, 30, 32, 35–36, 81–82, 160, 162–171, 173–175, 180–182

Anise, *191*

Apple, 13, 77, 81–82, 133, 152, 160–162, 168, 170, 173

Apricot, *39, 77, 89–90*

Artichoke, *40*

Asparagus, *41, 54, 98–99, 135–136, 153*

Avocado, *31, 206*

B

Bacon, 23, 48, 50, 69, 92, 124–125, 144, 156

Baking, 15–17, 19–22, 35, 39, 41, 47, 56, 58–59, 61, 72–73, 77–82, 84–86, 89–90, 92, 98, 100–101, 103, 105–107, 110, 112–113, 115, 120–121, 123, 125, 129, 131, 133, 142, 146, 149–151, 154, 156, 158–159, 162, 166, 174–175, 184, 186, 191

Baking powder, *82*

Balsamic vinegar, *160, 175, 182*

Bamboo shoots, *25*

Basil, 14–15, 27, 79, 87, 111, 126–127, 132–134, 144, 181, 191, 196, 200, 202–203, 206–211

Bay leaf, *57, 66, 102, 155*

Beans, 12, 29, 43, 59, 66, 72, 78–79, 88, 109, 114, 130, 143, 150, 172, 189, 209

Beef, 16, 20–21, 25, 28, 33, 38, 42–46, 48–49, 51, 58–64, 68–70, 73–74, 78–81, 83–86, 88, 92–97, 102–106, 108–109, 113–115, 117, 120–122, 124–132, 135, 137–140, 144–147, 150, 160, 163, 177, 183–185, 188, 191, 197–198, 208–209

Beef stock, *43, 117, 137, 197*

Biscuits, *92*

Black pepper, 11, 14, 16–17, 23, 31, 33, 35, 38, 40–41, 43, 45, 49–51, 53, 55, 57–61, 63–71, 75–78, 85–87, 91–94, 96–99, 103, 107, 111–113, 115–117, 119, 122–125, 127–128, 130, 132–135, 137, 140–142, 145–149, 151, 153, 156, 158, 161, 163, 167, 170–171, 173–174, 177, 189, 192, 197–199, 211

Bread, 41, 43, 56, 62, 65, 68, 73, 76, 78, 87, 95, 100, 102, 106–108, 111, 119–120, 129–130, 136, 144, 147, 154, 156–158, 180

Broccoli, 33–34, 45–47, 53, 63, 98, 136, 143, 151, 161–163, 167–169, 173–174, 184–186, 188, 199

Broth, 14, 17, 21–22, 25, 27–28, 32, 36, 42, 45, 48, 53, 57, 59–60, 63–65, 69–70, 72, 76, 78, 83, 90–91, 94, 99, 103–104, 109–111, 117, 125–127, 132, 134–136, 139, 143–145, 161–162, 164, 169, 172, 177–178, 183–185, 188, 190–191, 193–194, 197–201, 203–204, 206–209

Brown rice, *208*

Brown sugar, 20, 25–26, 29, 33–34, 38, 92–93, 112, 120, 132, 152, 162, 195, 199, 202, 208

Butter, 11–12, 15, 18–20, 22–25, 28–30, 34, 38–44, 46, 49–50, 52, 55–60, 62–65, 67–68, 70, 72–79, 81, 84, 89–90, 95–98, 100–101, 103, 105, 109–114, 116, 119–126, 129–133,

135-136, 142, 145, 148-152, 154, 156-160, 162, 166-168, 171, 173, 175, 178, 181-182,

190, 197, 199, 204-206

C

Cabbage, 22, 25, 49-51, 64-65, 69, 76, 88, 103-104, 122-123, 143, 160, 163, 165-166,

170-171, 173-175, 179-180, 183-185, 196, 198, 202-203, 206

Cake, *77, 119, 184-185*

Cannellini beans, *172*

Capers, *40*

Caramel, *15*

Caraway seeds, *105*

Carrot, 11, 14, 21-22, 37, 41-42, 45-46, 54, 56-57, 64, 66, 83, 87-88, 90, 94, 99, 107-108,

111, 126, 128, 132, 134, 143, 151, 158, 162, 164, 166, 172-174, 176-177, 180-181,

183-185, 188, 192, 195-196, 199, 202-203, 205-206, 208-210

Cashew, *19, 35, 81, 163, 166, 179*

Cauliflower, *176*

Cayenne pepper, *57, 59, 88, 189, 194, 197, 205*

Celery, 11, 14, 16-17, 20-21, 30, 32-38, 41-42, 45-46, 56-58, 64, 66, 71, 73, 79, 81, 83, 85,

87-90, 96, 99, 108, 110-111, 118, 126, 128, 132, 134, 139, 143, 146, 151, 154-155, 158,

164, 168, 172, 177, 183-184, 193-194

Cheddar, 17, 26-27, 30, 32, 43, 47, 49, 58-59, 61, 71, 79-81, 83, 86-87, 90, 93, 96-97, 101,

106, 108-109, 111, 115, 126, 129, 136, 149-150, 152-154, 156, 158, 178, 186

Cheese, 17, 26-27, 30, 32, 38-39, 41, 43-44, 47-49, 51-

56, 58-59, 61-65, 68, 71-73, 76-77,

79-81, 83-90, 93-94, 96-99, 101-103, 105-106, 108-113, 115-124, 126, 129-131, 133-136,

138, 142, 146-150, 152-158, 161, 168-169, 172, 178-180, 186

Cherry, *121, 196*

Cherry tomatoes, *196*

Chestnut, *11, 17, 25, 76, 159, 164, 199, 208*

Chicken, 11, 14-17, 21-22, 24, 26-27, 29-30, 32-38, 41-42, 47-48, 52-58, 61-68, 72, 75, 78,

81-83, 86-87, 90-92, 98-100, 103, 108, 111, 113, 116-117, 125-128, 132-134, 136,

138-143, 151, 155, 158-159, 161-164, 169-170, 172-174, 176-181, 183, 185-194, 196-201,

203-204, 206-207, 209, 211

Chicken breast, 11, 14, 17, 21, 26-27, 29-30, 33-35, 47, 52-58, 64-65, 67-68, 78, 83, 91, 99,

116, 126-128, 133, 136, 139-140, 142-143, 159, 162, 164, 169, 173, 176-177, 183, 185,

187, 189-190, 193, 197, 200-201

Chicken leg, *37*

Chicken liver, *55*

Chicken soup, 21, 24, 26, 30, 32, 37-38, 55-56, 62, 65, 67, 72, 81, 86-87, 117, 125, 128, 138,

158, 164

Chicken stock, *33-34, 66, 82, 92, 99, 111, 161-162, 187, 204, 211*

Chicken thigh, *181*

Chicken wing, *196-197*

Chinese cabbage, *163, 174*

Chipotle, *111*

Chips, 13, 18-24, 27-28, 30-31, 47, 52, 80, 114, 155, 176, 186

214

Chives, *78, 116, 189–190*

Chocolate, *12, 18–20, 22–24, 27, 30–31*

Chopped tomatoes, *26, 83, 162*

Cider, *13, 22, 140–141, 160–163, 166, 168–170, 173, 175, 189*

Cinnamon, *39, 61, 72, 77, 81–82, 101, 105, 109–110, 121, 131, 133, 149, 152, 166, 209*

Cloves, *14, 25, 29, 33, 40, 43–46, 59–60, 63, 75, 78, 88, 93–94, 99, 109, 114, 118–119, 131, 135, 137, 140, 142, 150–151, 169, 172–173, 179, 181, 184, 189–190, 193–198, 200–201, 204–205, 207*

Cocktail, *204*

Coconut, *26–27, 30, 32, 161–162, 181, 188–189, 206–207*

Coconut milk, *162, 181, 206–207*

Coconut oil, *188–189*

Coleslaw, *22, 130, 160–163, 166–169, 173*

Coriander, *11, 193–194, 199–200*

Corned beef, *62, 129–131*

Cottage cheese, *44, 47, 61, 72, 77, 90, 97–98, 101, 103, 105, 112–113, 123–124, 142, 149, 152, 156*

Crab, *182, 194*

Crackers, *55–56, 67, 131, 176*

Cranberry, *105, 161*

Cream, *16–17, 20–21, 24, 26–27, 30, 32, 35, 38–39, 42, 45–49, 51–53, 55–56, 59–60, 62–71, 73–74, 80–81, 83–84, 86–89, 92, 95–98, 101–107, 109–118, 121–125, 128–129, 135, 137–142, 144–145, 149–150, 152–153, 155–158, 186*

Cream cheese, *39, 48–49, 62, 80, 84, 97–98, 103, 106, 109–112, 115, 121–122, 138, 152*

Crumble, *23, 38, 51, 63–64, 79, 114, 121–122, 156, 173, 194*

Cucumber, *31, 181–182, 202–203, 206–207*

Cumin, *59, 194*

Curd, *72*

Curry, *42, 203–204, 206–207*

Curry paste, *206–207*

Curry powder, *42, 203–204*

Custard, *109, 119*

D

Date, *89*

Dijon mustard, *60*

Dill, *60, 104, 155*

Dry sherry, *43, 55, 58*

Dumplings, *109, 124*

E

Egg, *23–24, 33, 37–109, 111–117, 119–158, 164, 170, 172, 176, 178–181, 187–190, 192, 195, 197–198, 203, 205*

Egg white, *82, 91, 128, 152*

Egg yolk, *82, 98, 176*

Evaporated milk, *17, 24, 57–58, 121–122, 155*

F

Fat, *10–186, 188–212*

Fennel, *94*

Feta, *119*

Fish, *26, 66, 162, 176, 187, 189, 191–195, 197, 200, 202–203, 205, 209–211*

Fish sauce, *162, 187, 189, 191–195, 197, 200, 202–203, 205, 209–211*

Five-spice powder, *14*

Flank, *25, 45–46*

Flour, *20, 29, 41, 45–46, 48, 52, 59–60, 63–65, 67–70, 74, 78, 80, 82, 91, 104, 111, 130, 135–136, 139, 145–147, 154, 156, 186, 208*

French bread, *43, 136*

Fresh coriander, *193*

Fruit, *77*

G

Garam masala, *52*

Garlic, *14–16, 21–22, 25, 28–29, 31, 33–34, 37, 40, 42–46, 49–50, 53–54, 59–60, 63–64, 66, 68–70, 75, 78–80, 84, 88, 93–94, 97, 99–103, 105–111, 113–115, 117–122, 125, 127–128, 131–133, 135–137, 140–143, 145, 147, 150–151, 154–155, 157, 162, 169, 172–174, 177, 179–181, 184–185, 187, 189–208, 211*

Garlic bread, *102, 106, 120, 147, 157, 180*

Ginger, *22, 28, 34, 40, 54, 98, 161–162, 164, 177–178, 181, 183–185, 189, 191, 194–195, 199–204, 206–209, 211*

Gorgonzola, *179*

Grain, *11, 25–26, 32, 59–60, 94, 135, 184, 188*

Grapes, *176, 179*

Gravy, *38, 72, 95, 104, 107, 116, 132, 138, 147*

Green beans, *43, 72, 109, 130, 189*

Ground ginger, *177, 183–184, 199, 201, 206*

H

Ham, *41, 64–65, 71, 85, 118*

Heart, *40*

Herbs, *94, 109, 111, 200, 211*

Hoisin sauce, *26, 33, 191, 208–212*

Honey, *13, 33, 166, 196*

I

Ice cream, *24*

Iceberg lettuce, *23, 35*

J

Jam, *25*

Jelly, *12, 29, 91*

K

Ketchup, *59–60, 68–69, 92–93, 141, 185, 190, 193–195, 203, 205*

Kidney, *78–79, 88, 150*

Kidney beans, *78–79, 88, 150*

Kohlrabi, *97*

L

Lamb, *109, 131*

Leek, *99, 109*

Leftover turkey, *134, 155*

Lemon, *10, 31, 39-42, 46, 78, 98-99, 102, 105, 113-114, 119, 131, 135-136, 159, 179, 189, 200, 203, 206-207, 209*

Lemon juice, *10, 31, 39-40, 46, 78, 99, 102, 113-114, 119, 131, 135-136, 159, 179, 189, 203, 207*

Lemongrass, *161-162, 200*

Lentils, *155*

Lettuce, *11, 14-15, 17, 23, 31, 35, 164-165, 167-168, 172, 181-182, 192-193, 207-211*

Lime, *31, 150-151, 161-162, 187-196, 200-202, 205-209, 211*

Lime juice, *31, 162, 187-188, 190, 192-196, 200-202, 205-207, 211*

Lime leaves, *161-162*

Linguine, *14, 202*

Lobster, *176*

Long-grain rice, *32*

M

Macaroni, *57, 87, 119*

Mandarin, *11, 165, 181-182*

Mango, *31*

Maple syrup, *22*

Margarine, 20, 39, 48, 57-58, 63, 77, 80, 97, 103, 122, 149-150, 160, 171, 173

Marjoram, *57, 132*

Marshmallow, *12, 15, 20, 23-24, 28-29, 31*

Mayonnaise, *88-89, 129, 131, 168, 179, 189*

Meat, 11, 13, 16, 29, 35, 37, 42-43, 48, 52-54, 56-59, 62, 64, 66, 68-70, 72, 79, 85, 91-94, 96, 100, 102-103, 105-106, 108-109, 111, 115-116, 121, 127, 131-132, 136-140, 142-148, 155, 157, 159, 170, 173, 177, 182, 184, 192, 194, 197, 202, 209

Milk, 17, 23-24, 30, 39, 41, 52-53, 56-58, 62-63, 65-68, 71, 74, 80-82, 84-85, 87, 92, 107, 109-110, 117, 119, 121-122, 128-130, 136, 138, 149-150, 152, 154-157, 162, 180-181, 186, 206-207

Milk chocolate, *23*

Mince, *162*

Mint, 31, 202-203, 206, 209-211

Mirin, *182*

Mozzarella, *44, 49, 84, 99, 115-116, 120-122, 148-149*

Mung beans, *209*

Mushroom, 16-17, 24-25, 27, 32-36, 42, 45-47, 51-52, 54-63, 67-68, 70-71, 73-74, 80-81, 83-87, 89, 92, 94-99, 101-102, 107, 110-111, 113-114, 120-124, 128-129, 133, 135-139, 143-145, 147, 153-155, 157, 172-174, 180-181, 183-184, 186, 192, 196-197, 199, 201, 206-208

Mustard, 25, 60, 63, 76, 88-89, 92-93, 102-104, 129-130, 149, 156

Mustard powder, *25, 103, 156*

Mustard seeds, *76*

N

Noodle soup, 41, 56–57, 64, 83, 111, 126, 132, 134, 143, 151, 155, 162, 172, 177–178, 185,
    188, 201, 208

Noodles, *10–212*

Nori, *182*

Nut, 10, 28, 159, 163, 173, 193

    Nutmeg, *63, 152*

O

Octopus, *176, 182*

Oil, 10–17, 21–23, 25–29, 31, 33–37, 40, 44–46, 51–55, 57, 61, 66, 68, 70–72, 74–76, 78–79,
    83, 85, 88, 91, 93–95, 98–100, 102, 104, 109–111, 115–116, 118–119, 124, 128, 133,
    135–137, 139–143, 146–148, 150–151, 153–154, 159–175, 177–184, 186–190, 192–208, 211

Olive, 10, 13, 16, 22, 26–27, 31, 33, 36, 40, 44, 55, 68, 71, 75, 78, 88, 95, 98–99, 102, 104,
    109–111, 114–115, 118–121, 135–136, 141–142, 148, 150–151, 153, 160–161, 168–175,
    179–184, 186, 197, 206–207

Olive oil, 10, 13, 16, 22, 26–27, 31, 33, 36, 40, 44, 55, 68, 71, 75, 78, 88, 95, 98–99, 102,
    109–111, 115, 118–119, 135–136, 141–142, 148, 150–151, 160–161, 168–175, 179–184, 186,
    197, 206–207

Onion, 10–11, 13–17, 20–23, 25–28, 30, 32–38, 41–52, 54–66, 68–70, 73, 75–76, 78–81,
    83–111, 113–115, 117–118, 121–133, 135–137, 139–140, 142–148, 151, 153–155, 157–160,
    162–175, 177–181, 183–188, 190–195, 197–199, 201–209, 211–212

Orange, 11, 25, 29, 105, 165–166, 181–182, 208

    Orange juice, *29, 105, 166*

Oregano, 44, 59, 94, 108–109, 126–127, 132, 144

Oyster, 14, 21–22, 33–34, 91–92, 173–174, 184, 187, 197, 201, 203–204, 208–209

Oyster mushrooms, *33*

Oyster sauce, 14, 21–22, 33–34, 91–92, 173–174, 184, 187, 197, 201, 203–204, 208–209

P

Pappardelle, *118*

Paprika, 14–15, 51, 55–56, 58–60, 92–93, 98, 100, 102–105, 107–108, 124–125, 140, 155,
    189–190, 192–194, 199, 207

Parmesan, 41, 43–44, 54, 65, 71, 73, 85, 87–88, 93, 99, 110, 115–119, 133–136, 142, 148–150,
    172, 180

Parsley, 27, 44, 51, 57, 60, 63–64, 84, 90–91, 93–96, 98–101, 110–111, 113–115, 117–118,
    132–133, 140, 143, 148, 151, 169, 172, 178–179, 193

Parsnip, *90*

Pasta, 36, 38, 44, 47, 51, 55, 59, 61, 66, 72–74, 79, 82–83, 87, 93–94, 96–98, 100–103,
    106–107, 111–113, 115, 117–120, 122–123, 125, 131, 133, 136, 138, 140, 142, 146–147,
    149–153, 156–159, 161, 165–166, 179–180, 188, 200, 205

Peach, *196*

Peanut butter, 11, 15, 19–20, 22–23, 28, 30, 34, 181, 190, 197, 199, 204–206

    Peanut oil, *45–46, 53, 190, 192–193, 195, 203–204*

Peanuts, 12, 18–21, 23, 27, 30–31, 187–190, 192–195, 199–200, 202–205, 208

Peas, 21–22, 26, 34, 36, 43–44, 47, 56, 67, 71, 83, 92, 95–96, 98, 107, 110–111, 116, 141, 145,

    148, 150-152, 154, 159, 164, 176, 179–180, 186, 199, 204

Pecan, *120, 167*

Peel, *13, 170*

Pepper, 11, 14, 16–17, 22–23, 25–27, 30–33, 35–38, 40–41, 43–46, 49–61, 63–71, 73, 75–79,

    83–88, 90–94, 96–104, 107–119, 121–128, 130, 132–137, 139–143, 145–151, 153–154,

    156-158, 161, 163-164, 167-171, 173-174, 177, 179-184, 187, 189, 192-202, 204-209,

    211–212

Peppercorn, *41–42, 66, 90–91, 197, 209*

Pepperoni, *120–121*

Pesto, *118, 200*

Pine nut, *10, 159*

Pineapple, *26–27, 30, 32, 77, 105, 121*

Pizza, *93–94, 120*

Poppy seeds, *17, 35*

Pork, 14–15, 64, 75, 79, 95, 122–125, 158, 164, 196–197, 201

Pork belly, *196–197*

Pork chop, *95, 124–125*

Potato, *47, 52–53, 80, 143, 155, 172*

Poultry, *66, 132*

Prawn, *195*

Preserves, *77, 89–90*

Pulse, *130*

R

Radish, *179–180, 197*

Raisins, *12, 23, 31, 39, 77, 81–82, 101, 109–110, 132, 166, 169*

Red cabbage, *179–180, 183, 206*

Red lentil, *155*

Red onion, *22, 44, 83, 122, 179–180, 195, 204, 207*

Red wine, *33, 53, 59, 107, 109, 132, 146, 163, 167, 182*

Red wine vinegar, *33, 53, 132, 163, 167, 182*

Rice, 10–11, 14–15, 20–21, 25–27, 30, 32, 34, 54, 76, 91–92, 124, 140, 147, 159, 161, 165,

    171, 182, 185, 187–211

Rice noodles, *10, 14, 187–192, 194–204, 206–211*

Rice vinegar, *11, 165, 193–194, 200, 207–208*

Rice wine, 14, 26, 34, 91–92, 159, 165, 171, 182, 185, 199, 205

Ricotta, *119*

Roast beef, *138*

Roast chicken, *61*

Rosemary, *98–99, 108–109, 117, 132, 143, 172*

Rye bread, *129–130*

S

Sage, *79, 123, 150–151*

Salad, 10–11, 13, 17, 22–23, 26, 31, 35–36, 41, 43, 95, 102, 106, 119–120, 129, 136, 159–163,

    165–167, 169–171, 173–175, 179–182, 192–193, 196, 202–203, 207, 209

Salmon, *26, 150–151*

Salsa, *83, 85, 150*

Salt, 11, 16–17, 22–23, 25–26, 29, 31, 35, 37–38, 43–45, 49–61, 63–76, 78–80, 82, 84–94,
96–100, 102–104, 106–124, 126–128, 130–131, 133–137, 139–141, 143, 146–147, 149–151,
154, 156–158, 161, 163, 167–168, 170–174, 178–179, 182–184, 189–193, 195, 197–200, 202,
207–209, 211–212

Sashimi, *31*

Sauces, *174, 209*

Sausage, *72, 76, 79, 88, 114–115, 122–123, 133, 146, 156, 186*

Savory, *33, 61, 89, 95, 111, 136, 152, 169*

Sea salt, *108, 123–124, 197*

Seafood, *100, 148, 195*

Seasoning, 14, 35, 49, 58, 66, 84–85, 94–95, 98–99, 101, 107, 114–115, 117, 124, 131–134,
139, 147, 150, 161–165, 167–169, 171–173, 176–179, 181, 183–186, 188–189

Seaweed, *176, 182*

Seeds, 13, 17, 23, 35, 76, 105, 159–160, 162–163, 166–168, 170–171, 173–175, 189, 193

Sesame oil, 11, 14, 21–22, 25–26, 28, 33–34, 52–53, 91, 164, 168, 172, 178, 182–184, 196,
198–199, 206, 208

Sesame seeds, *13, 23, 35, 160, 162–163, 170–171, 174–175, 189, 193*

Shallot, *57, 173–174*

Sherry, *43, 55, 58, 111*

Shiitake mushroom, *42, 196–197, 208*

Sirloin, *42–43, 51, 95, 191, 209*

Soup, 16–17, 21, 24, 26–27, 30, 32, 35, 37–38, 40–41, 43, 47, 51–53, 55–57, 62–68, 71–74, 76,
78–83, 86–92, 95–96, 98–100, 102, 107–108, 111–113, 117–118, 121–123, 125–129, 132,
134, 137–139, 142–145, 151, 153–155, 157–158, 161–162, 164, 170, 172, 176–178, 180–181,
185–186, 188, 191, 196–197, 201, 206–209, 211–212

Soy sauce, 10–11, 13–15, 20–22, 26, 28–30, 32–34, 36, 40, 45–46, 53–54, 57, 76, 91–92,
99–100, 159–160, 162–164, 167–169, 171–178, 181–185, 188–190, 192, 194–197, 199–200,
202–203, 205–208

Spaghetti, *49, 77, 115, 118–121, 126, 146, 167, 180*

Spinach, 40, 44, 49, 75, 92, 99–100, 108, 118–119, 141–143, 176, 179–180, 195, 206–207, 211

Spring onion, *91*

Squash, *87, 148*

Squid, *182, 195*

Star anise, *191*

Steak, 25, 31, 33, 43–46, 48, 51, 60, 75, 95, 122, 135, 138–139, 144, 146–148, 167, 183–184,
188, 208

Stew, 59, 62, 68, 74, 92–93, 102, 105, 109, 114, 124–125, 132, 137–138, 140, 145, 185, 196

Stock, 33–34, 40, 42–43, 57, 66, 75, 82, 87, 90, 92, 99–100, 111, 117, 127, 137, 161–162, 170,
187, 191, 197, 204, 207, 211

Strawberry, *180*

Stuffing, *125–126*

Sucralose, *160*

Sugar, 10–11, 13–15, 17, 20–23, 25–26, 29, 33–36, 38–39, 61, 72, 75, 77, 80–82, 84, 89–90,

92-93, 97-98, 101, 104-106, 109-110, 112-113, 119-121, 132-133, 141, 149, 152, 159-171,

173-175, 179-184, 187, 189-190, 192-195, 197, 199, 202-208, 211

Sunflower seed, *159-160, 166-168, 173, 181-182*

Syrup, *10, 22*

T

Tabasco, *153*

Taco, *58, 85, 114, 150*

Tahini, *52-53, 119*

Tamari, *22, 206*

Tamarind, *189-190, 192, 199*

Tarragon, *52, 143*

Tea, *90*

Teriyaki, *25, 45-46, 188-189*

Teriyaki sauce, *25, 45-46, 188-189*

Thai basil, *191, 200, 211*

Thyme, 43, 45, 48, 53, 66, 88-89, 98-99, 110-111, 115, 117, 132, 143, 150-151

Toffee, *19*

Tofu, 132, 151, 171, 188-190, 197-198, 206

Tomato, 16, 26-27, 32, 38, 43-44, 48, 51, 54-55, 58-59, 61, 75, 78-80, 83-86, 88-89, 93-94,

96-97, 99, 102-103, 105-106, 108-109, 114-115, 124-125, 127, 131, 133, 140, 144,

147-148, 150, 154, 162, 172, 180, 185, 193, 196, 204-205

Tortellini, *87*

Turkey, 52, 73, 84, 98, 106-107, 111-112, 115,

134, 144, 148, 155, 177, 179, 186, 208

Turmeric, *164, 207*

V

Vanilla extract, *39, 77, 89-90, 105, 112, 119, 121, 149, 152*

Vegetable oil, 11, 14, 17, 21-23, 29, 34-35, 37, 51, 54, 57, 61, 66, 76, 79, 83, 85, 91, 93,

98-100, 104, 124, 128, 133, 137, 139-141, 143, 146-148, 151, 153-154, 159-160, 163-168,

171, 173-175, 177-178, 184, 187, 189, 192-195, 198-204, 208, 211

Vegetable stock, *40*

Vegetables, 14, 21, 25, 28, 32, 34, 36, 49, 53, 71, 75-76, 79, 87, 90-91, 94, 99, 119, 127,

143-144, 151, 155, 158-159, 164, 171, 174, 177-178, 183-184, 188-189, 199-201, 206

Venison, *157*

Vermouth, *44-45*

Vinegar, 11, 13-14, 17, 22-23, 26, 33-36, 53, 69, 92-93, 102, 132, 140-141, 159-163,

165-171, 173-175, 181-182, 189, 193-194, 196-197, 199-200, 203, 205, 207-208, 211

W

Walnut, *23, 118, 167-168, 193*

Water chestnut, *11, 17, 25, 76, 159, 164, 199, 208*

Whipping cream, *66, 103, 140-141*

White bread, *56*

White cabbage, *185*

White chocolate, *12*

White pepper, *54, 91–92, 195*

White sugar, 10–11, 13–14, 17, 21, 23, 34–36, 39, 72, 77, 80–81, 89, 97, 101, 105–106,

112–113, 119, 121, 133, 141, 149, 159–163, 166–171, 173–175, 181, 184, 187, 189–190,

192–193, 197, 203, 205–207, 211

White wine, *23, 59–60, 68, 175, 197, 203*

White wine vinegar, *23, 175, 197, 203*

Wild rice, *11*

Wine, 14, 23, 26, 33–34, 40, 46, 48, 53, 59–60, 68, 91–92, 107, 109, 113–114, 132, 135, 146,

159, 163, 165, 167, 171, 174–175, 180, 182, 185, 197, 199, 203, 205

Worcestershire sauce, *16, 43–45, 62, 68, 79, 84, 92–94, 97, 102, 110–111, 128, 149–150, 154*

Wraps, *11, 208*

Y

Yeast, *148*

Z

Zest, 29, 78, 99, 105, 107, 196, 200, 208

Conclusion

Thank you again for downloading this book!

I hope you enjoyed reading about my book!

If you enjoyed this book, please take the time to share your thoughts and post a review on **Amazon**. It'd be greatly appreciated!

Write me an honest review about the book – I truly value your opinion and thoughts and I will incorporate them into my next book, which is already underway.

Thank you!

If you have any questions, **feel free to contact at:** *chefjacklemmon@gmail.com*

Jack Lemmon
www.TheCookingMAP.com/Jack-Lemmon

Printed in Great Britain
by Amazon